THE WRITING OF CANADIAN HISTORY

Aspects of English-Canadian Historical Writing since 1900
Second Edition

In this classic study of Canadian historiography, Carl Berger considers the impact of subtle and unpredictable influences on a number of outstanding Canadian historians and thus on the development of scholarship in, and our understanding of, the history of Canada.

Berger's interest is focused on the creative edge of historical writing, on those authors who have broken out of traditional patterns of interpretation, and on the social and intellectual climate in which each developed his ideas. Beginning with George M. Wrong and Adam Shortt, Berger goes on to consider the work of Frank Underhill, Harold Innis, Arthur Lower, Donald Creighton, and William Morton. He explores the new directions in which these scholars have taken us, and reflects on the factors of each one's intellectual environment that have shaped his thinking.

Since publication of the first edition a decade ago, this volume has won a Governor-General's award and has been acclaimed as the classic study in Canadian historiography. This new edition offers an additional chapter to include the work of contemporary scholars and to bring the book up to date. In it Berger explores the plethora of approaches to the study of history that have sprung up in recent years: labour history, women's history, local history, social history, and intellectual history, to name a few. Berger identifies their establishment both as the reflection of a new, wide-open era in Canadian historical scholarship and also as part of a continuing tradition of vitality and innovation in the field.

Himself one of Canada's most distinguished historians, Berger is eminently qualified to present an overview of the body of Canadian historical writing. In this volume he does more: he offers a new understanding of the nation's intellectual life and the chain of influences that have directed it.

CARL BERGER is professor of history at the University of Toronto. He is the author of several books, among them *The Sense of Power: Studies in the Ideas of Canadian Imperialism*, and *Science, God, and Nature in Victorian Canada*.

D1363804

THE
WRITING OF
CANADIAN
HISTORY

Aspects of English-Canadian Historical Writing since 1900

Second Edition

CARL BERGER

UNIVERSITY OF TORONTO PRESS

Toronto   Buffalo   London

© University of Toronto Press 1986
Toronto   Buffalo   London
Printed in Canada
Reprinted 1988

ISBN 0-8020-2546-3 (cloth)
ISBN 0-8020-6568-6 (paper)

The first edition of this work was published in 1976 by
Oxford University Press Canada.

Canadian Cataloguing in Publication Data
Berger, Carl, 1939–
The writing of Canadian history

Includes bibliographical references and index.
ISBN 0-8020-2546-3 (bound) ISBN 0-8020-6568-6 (pbk.)

1. Historians – Canada. 2. Canada – Historiography.
I. Title.

FC149.B47 1987   971'.007'2   C86-094722-X
F1024.B47 1987

Publication of this work has been assisted by the
Canada Council and the Ontario Arts Council under
their block grant programs.

FOR MY PARENTS

CONTENTS

Preface to the First Edition ix

Preface to the Second Edition xi

Acknowledgements xiii

1. The Founders of Critical History:
   George M. Wrong and Adam Shortt 1

2. The Rise of Liberty 32

3. Frank Underhill: History as Political Criticism 54

4. Harold Innis: The Search for Limits 85

5. Arthur Lower and a National Community 112

6. A North American Nation 137

7. Reorientation 160

8. Reorientation and Tradition 187

9. Donald Creighton and the Artistry of History 208

10. William Morton: The Delicate Balance of Region
    and Nation 238

11. Tradition and the 'New' History 259

Bibliographical Note 321

Notes 324

Index 353

PREFACE
to the first edition

This study is an examination of aspects of English-Canadian historical thought and literature since the turn of the century. It deals with the central teachings of the major figures—George Wrong, Adam Shortt, Chester Martin, Harold Innis, Arthur Lower, Frank Underhill, Donald Creighton and William Morton—and also, in a less detailed fashion, with a more numerous group of other professional scholars who shaped the way Canadians understood their past. The main emphasis is on the creative edge of historical writing and on those authors who broke the traditional patterns of interpretation. I am less concerned with the historical literature that ratifies accepted views and fills in the details than with original conceptions that bore on the larger and central themes in Canadian history.

Written history represents a self-conscious effort to establish the meaning of experience for the present and is subtly and unpredictably coloured by the milieu in which the historian lives. The concerns and preconceptions of his own world constantly interject themselves into the complex dialogue between the living and the dead. History, therefore, is not an olympian record of past activity; it reveals a good deal about the intellectual climate in which it was composed. My primary purpose is to explain the attitudes historians brought to the study of the past and to relate historical literature more closely to its context, suggesting allusively the affinities between history and other contemporaneous expressions in Canadian intellectual life. As the English historiographer Herbert Butterfield once remarked, there are hidden and unsuspected factors behind any national tradition of historical writing, and these need to be raised as far as possible to the level of consciousness so that they can be neutralized and brought under control.

The history of history, or historiography, is the historical method turned in upon itself. The approach demands that the historian attempt to extricate himself to some extent from the body of literature from which he has learned about the past, and to see it with the same detachment he would bring to an analysis of the transactions of a remote age. Like all essays in self-knowledge, such efforts can only be partially successful for they are constrained by the very forces under examination. A depiction of historical writing in its intellectual setting is bound to leave an exaggerated impression of relativism, but such a work as this one simply could not be written without a faith in the ability of the historical imagination to penetrate a segment of the thought of the past and to understand it, however tentatively and incompletely, on its own terms.

The following analysis is deliberately selective. It is not intended as a comprehensive inventory and bibliography of the literature or as a biographical dictionary of historians. It omits any systematic consideration of French-Canadian writing. The two language traditions have, in historical thought as well as in other non-political spheres, occasionally touched and intersected, but in general they have been preoccupied with the backgrounds of two rather different 'nations'. While it may well be that a rigorous comparative examination might reveal unsuspected parallels, such a comparison must rest on preliminary appraisals of the individual traditions. Some of the reasons for the separation of French and English patterns in historical writing, however, are pursued in the body of this study. Finally, all the figures considered in any depth were born before the First World War. For reasons of space I have touched only lightly on their Victorian predecessors, and on the various schools of regional or local historians that flourished in the period. For reasons of perspective I have not accorded leading contemporary historians who were born in the inter-war years the amount of attention their contributions to the genre warrant.

For the sake of uniformity the past tense has been used throughout, even when dealing with authors whose work is as yet unfinished.

PREFACE
to the second edition

This edition has dispensed with the short conclusion from the original and contains an additional chapter on the vast exfoliation of historical literature over the last twenty years. My main aim in this chapter has been to identify and explain the major trends in contemporary historical writing in English about Canada and suggest the range, complexity, and kaleidoscopic nature of the literature. The treatment is necessarily selective and to a degree personal: I have discussed those books that are both representative examples of the historian's craft as well as documents that illustrate important changes in approaches, tastes, and thought.

No more than in the first edition is this new chapter intended to be a comprehensive inventory. There are many surveys of publications on particular topics and the most important of these are mentioned in the footnotes. I have updated the 'Bibliographical Note' to take into account studies on the tradition of Canadian historical writing that have appeared since this book was published in 1976.

C.B.
June 1986

PREFACE
to the second edition

ACKNOWLEDGEMENTS

I am grateful for the help and encouragement of numerous individuals and institutions. To J.M.S. Careless, S.D. Clark, D.G. Creighton, A.R.M. Lower, W.L. Morton, C.P. Stacey, and the late F.H. Underhill I owe a special debt for their memories, for their frank conversations about their own work and that of their contemporaries, and for their responses to some of my own partially formed ideas.

I would also like to thank Blair Neatby who permitted me to read the Underhill Papers at the Public Archives of Canada; Charles Armour of the Dalhousie University Library, who kindly sent me copies of D.C. Harvey's letters from the Archibald MacMechan Papers; Stan Hanson of the University of Saskatchewan Archives, Murray Memorial Library, Saskatoon; Ian Wilson and Anne MacDermaid at the Douglas Library, Queen's University; and the helpful staffs at the Public Archives of Canada, University of Toronto Rare Book Room and Archives, the Public Archives of Nova Scotia, and the Butler Library, Columbia University.

The entire manuscript was carefully read by Ramsay Cook and Michael Bliss, who took seriously my request for detailed criticism as well as general comments. William Toye of the Oxford University Press (Canada) rendered invaluable and fastidious editorial advice and guidance. Errors of fact, judgement, and style, however, cannot be blamed on them.

The research was facilitated over a long period by a C.D. Howe Memorial Fellowship, a Killam Research Fellowship, and a Humanities and Social Sciences grant-in-aid from the University of Toronto. This book has been published with the help of a grant from the Humanities Research Council of Canada, using funds provided by the Canada Council.

I am particularly grateful to my wife Marjorie, who typed the manuscript from a handwritten text that could only be deciphered with extraordinary patience and put up with a great deal while the project lurched its way to completion.

1 | THE FOUNDERS OF CRITICAL HISTORY: GEORGE M. WRONG AND ADAM SHORTT

During the nineteenth century clergymen, lawyers, and journalists who re-garded themselves as men of letters rather than narrow professionals wrote a great deal of history for a variety of reasons: to amuse themselves, to commemorate and memorialize the eminent, to strengthen patriotism, or to draw morals from the past. These amateurs promoted the acquisition and ordering of historical documents; some of them were even responsive to the new tendencies in historical scholarship that emanated from Ger-many, Britain, and the United States. The substantial beginnings of the critical study of the Canadian past, however, were laid in the years after 1894, when George Wrong was appointed to the Chair of History in the University of Toronto and Adam Shortt began his lectures on the early economic and social history of Canada at Queen's University. In quite dif-ferent ways both men represented forces that underlay a decisive change in the nature of historical study.

I

The earliest histories of parts of British North America were little more than prefaces to compilations of statistics, geographical information, and descriptions of resources, intended to promote settlement and investment and to correct misrepresentations about soil and climate. For example, Thomas Chandler Haliburton's *An Historical and Statistical Account of Nova Scotia*, published by Joseph Howe in 1829, was designed to make the colony better known in England as a prospective imperial partner.[1] It was not until the middle years of the century that general surveys appeared. One of the first, *The History of Canada from Its First Discovery to the*

Present Time (1855), by John Mercier McMullen—a recent immigrant from northern Ireland who became a Brockville journalist, bookseller, and printer—typified the main concerns of Victorian amateur historians. Its themes were the history of material progress and improvement and the political record of an extension of British parliamentary institutions and the rise of colonial self-government. Following Lord Durham's opinions, McMullen also set a pattern for the future with his contempt for the indolence and stagnation of the Old Régime, his doubts about the capacities of French Canadians to exercise constitutional freedoms, and his conviction that all progressive impulses derived from the industrious, energetic, and orderly Britons.

The decades after Confederation witnessed a substantial increase in the number of works published, the growth of a romantic, retrospective attitude to the past, and a multiplication of local historical societies. A large proportion of Victorian historical writing consisted of genealogical research and biographies; studies of provinces, towns, counties, and some ethnic groups; and multi-volume histories of regions. The localist character of the history of the period was perhaps due as much to the persistent loyalties to local communities as to the technical difficulties in integrating the history of a country that had so recently been politically unified.[2]

Still, the awakening of a larger sense of nationality imparted a determination to trace the life of the 'New Dominion' to its roots and to establish the patterns by which the past gave birth to the present. The young men of the Canada First movement in the early 1870s were acutely conscious of the need to familiarize Canadians with the exploits of their forefathers in order to strengthen self-confidence in the 'new nationality'. History writing was generally regarded as an especially instructive branch of literature: when the Royal Society of Canada was founded in 1881, history was grouped with English literature in Section II. Like other forms of literary expression that mirrored the distinctive experiences of Canadians, history was looked upon as an indispensable index of a maturing nationality. English-Canadian nationalists desired for themselves what François-Xavier Garneau had already provided for French Canada with his four-volume *Histoire du Canada* (1845-52), which had been written in response to Lord Durham's contention that French Canadians possessed neither a past nor a culture worthy of preservation.

The English-Canadian counterpart to the theme of the survival of French Canada was an obsession with responsible government. The floridly written histories of the journalist John Charles Dent justified the reform party. His major works, *The Last Forty Years: Canada Since the Union of 1841* (1881) and *The Story of the Rebellion* (1885), excoriated the 'Family Compact', censured the radical reformers, and rehabilitated the moderates. William Kingsford, a prosaic but industrious engineer, turned out a ten-volume *History of Canada* between 1887 and 1898 that related, with a plethora of arcane detail, the history of the Old Régime and of British rule since the Conquest, making much of the reconciliation of local self-government and imperial authority.[3] The constitutional historian John G. Bourinot explained the appearance of these studies and other works on the law and custom of the constitution—such as Alpheus Todd's *On Parliamentary Government in England* (1867)—by noting that such a subject 'naturally engages the attention of active intellects in a country at a time when its institutions have to be moulded, and it is necessary to collect precedents and principles from the storehouse of the past for the assistance of the present.'[4] In their occasional appraisals of Canadian intellectual progress, Victorian commentators like Bourinot were preoccupied with the obstacles to literary and historical pursuits and with the absence of outstanding original achievements. Invariably they dwelt on a common list of impediments: the smallness of the population divided into two linguistic groups, the absorption with pioneering and material growth, and the colonial condition that implied a reliance on imported reading matter, an imitative spirit, and a lack of faith in native ability. Always they mentioned that Canada as yet possessed no wealthy leisured class that in other societies served as the custodian and creator of literary culture. Yet equally often it was assumed that a national literature would almost automatically follow as a consequence of material maturity and the flowering of a national spirit.[5]

To these adverse circumstances that were held to discourage intellectual creativity generally was added another that impinged on history writing more particularly. This was the feeling that Canada, with its brief past, possessed no historical halo, no memorials to antiquity, and no impressive monuments such as those that reminded people of older countries of great transactions and legends. On a visit to Europe in 1881 William Withrow, editor of the *Methodist Magazine* and author of a school text on Canadian history, was struck by the contrast between a new country that had few historical associations and an old one, dotted with ruins, ancient churches, abbeys, and castles. 'In the hoary minsters and crumbling fanes,' he wrote, 'in the many places consecrated by heroism or by song—by the martyr's or the patriot's blood, or by the poet's lyre—one beholds a crystalized history which thrills the soul with a presence and power before unimagined.'[6] Bourinot, recalling that Gibbon was inspired to write the history of the Roman Empire while standing on the ruins of the Capitol, doubted that such a work could have been conceived in the forests of Canada.[7]

In spite of the absence of such tangible stimulants to the historical imagination, however, certain picturesque episodes in the Canadian past caught the attention of the writers of historical romances. William Kirby recreated the last days of the Old Régime in *The Golden Dog* (1877); Charles G.D. Roberts, whose *History of Canada* (1897) came second in a competition for a school text sponsored by the Dominion Educational Association, set two novels, *The Forge in the Forest* (1896) and *A Sister to Evangeline* (1898), in the era of the Acadian deportations; and Charles Mair drew upon the War of 1812 in *Tecumseh, A Drama* (1886).

But the desire for a dramatic, picturesque, romantic history received its most welcome expression in Francis Parkman's large-scale account of the struggle between France and Britain for the mastery of North America, which had a colourful pictorial style, a dramatic narrative, and a mythic theme. Some English Canadians not only admired his literary artistry but found his interests and prejudices agreeable also. For his seven-book series, which began with *The Conspiracy of Pontiac* (1851) and concluded with *A Half Century of Conflict* (1892), the American historian collected manuscript materials in France and England as well as Canada and made a point of visiting the scenes that figured prominently in his story. The victim of prolonged illnesses, he was fascinated by the wilderness; he tended to emphasize struggle as a condition of existence and greatly admired the spartan virtues of the soldier. He concentrated on the activities of outstanding individuals—La Salle, Frontenac, Montcalm, Wolfe—who represented peoples and principles rather than anonymous social or economic forces. He saw the whole history of America, from the earliest colonial settlements to the Peace of Paris in 1763, as a titanic engagement between Protestant individualism and Catholic authoritarianism. Parkman subscribed to the commonplace racial stereotypes of the period in which he wrote, identifying the Anglo-Saxon with a forceful masculinity and a particular capacity for self-government; he regarded the British Conquest as a happy calamity, a deliverance from an autocratic régime. He was critical of the Catholic Church and of the supernatural. 'It seems to me', he told Bourinot in 1887, 'that the chief obstacle to the development of the French-Canadian people lies in the excessive power of the hierarchy, which tends to repress growth both intellectual and material.'[8] In spite of his anti-clericalism, however, Parkman valued certain chivalric qualities in New France that he found lacking in the vulgar democracy and business domination of the United States in his own time.[9] New France for him also possessed all the romantic grandeur of a lost cause.

A more substantial impediment to historical writers than the feeling that Canada lacked a past of sufficient antiquity concerned the preservation of documents and memorabilia. The Literary and Historical Society of Quebec, founded in 1824, collected and published documents on the period of discovery and the military history of New France, and solicited family papers through newspaper advertisements. After 1857 the government of Nova Scotia took steps to preserve, arrange, and selectively reprint material on the early history of the colony. But Canadian writers still felt themselves at a disadvantage compared with their counterparts in Great Britain, where the Public Record Office received the records of all departments of state and where the Royal Commission on Historical Manuscripts, created in 1869, searched out papers held by private individuals and institutions. American state and local historical societies also had ambitious collecting and publishing programs: the Historical Society of New York, for example, received state aid to employ an agent in France to copy documents pertaining to the early history of Quebec. Supported by Parkman, the members of the Literary and Historical Society of Quebec petitioned the Dominion government to create a repository for historical material and in 1872 Parliament voted four thousand dollars for the establishment of an archives under the jurisdiction of the Department of Agriculture.[10] Douglas Brymner, one-time editor of *The Presbyterian* and associate-editor of the *Montreal Daily Herald*, was named archivist.

Brymner began his new career with three empty rooms in the West Block on Parliament Hill, a vague mandate, and a stroke of good luck. He successfully interceded with the British War Office to have four hundred thousand items of military records accumulated since the Conquest transferred to Ottawa.[11] Brymner made a preliminary reconnaissance of public records held by provincial governments and reported that these were not only disorganized but were also at the mercy of rats, fires, and mildew. He canvassed hundreds of prominent families in Ontario, with rather disappointing results. Reflecting on the social vagaries that affected his work, he wrote: 'In Great Britain many valuable collections have been preserved carefully among the muniments of the old families, and from these historians have drawn largely . . . . But here, owing to the shifting character of the population, to the changes in fortune met in communities like ours, the prospect of keeping together such collections beyond a very limited time is exceedingly faint. The papers come to be regarded as lumber; many of them in all probability have already been burned and others sold as waste paper.'[12]

In 1873 Brymner made the first of a number of journeys to Britain, both to acquaint himself with procedures and techniques of organizing and to locate manuscripts bearing on Canada that were in public repositories. He personally examined some of the holdings of the Tower of London, the Public Record Office, the War Office, the Hudson's Bay Company, and the British Museum; and his assistant, Abbé Verrault, made excursions to French archives and the Imperial library at St Petersburg. Brymner made abstracts of relevant items or, in the case of abundant collections, indicated those to be copied later. It was monotonous labour and he was not one to make light of privations or difficult circumstances. 'The bad weather', he informed an assistant, who apparently expressed some interest in travel and entertainment abroad, 'is setting in and winter in London is an indescribable horror, with dark, miserable, foggy days, gas lighted all day long .... The houses and public offices are most insufficiently heated and full of draughts. I believe they would kill you in a month. I have suffered a good deal from that curse, so that you need not believe that this absence is a holiday.'[13]

Brymner recognized that his own model for the Archives—the Registry Office of Scotland, where all the legal, historical, commercial, and statistical information on the Scottish people was kept—was impossible in Canada where divided jurisdictions complicated matters. Annual grants were made to enable him to acquire copies of documents held overseas and to support the arranging and cataloguing of the records of the old Province of Canada. It was later alleged that Brymner's copyists had transcribed a large amount of correspondence relating to the local history of Florida, and a censorious successor said that Brymner was indifferent to economic history because he scorned cataloguing the papers of the Canada Land Company.[14] But when he died in 1902 the Archives possessed 3,155 volumes of original manuscripts or copies, chiefly from the French and Conquest periods and from the correspondence of the Colonial Office. The published calendars Brymner compiled single-handedly numbered 10,755 pages.[15]

Paralleling the steady accumulation of archival holdings and the multiplication of books about the Canadian past was a new note that crept into discussions about the practices and procedures of historical scholarship. As early as 1864 John Langton, the auditor-general of Canada, drew the attention of the Literary and Historical Society of Quebec to the revolution that had lately taken place in the more scientific study of ancient history. Another observer in 1878 remarked on the 'immense change in the world of ideas caused by the general adoption ... of the evolution hypothesis', and proceeded to consider thinkers who had discovered in history laws comparable to those in the natural and physical worlds.[16] Darwinian evolution had far-reaching effects on the study of history. A direct analogy was drawn between processes of organic evolution and historical development, and history came to be regarded as the revelation of patterns and uniformities, not merely the record of countless unconnected episodes. Evolution underlined continuity and the very gradual development of institutions. 'It is in History as it is in Geology,' explained William Ashley, the new Professor of Political Economy and Constitutional History at the University of Toronto in 1889. 'Thirty or forty years ago geological changes were explained as the results of great cataclysms, great catastrophies, which suddenly destroyed one condition of things and created another. Now most geologists are inclined to regard such changes as exceedingly gradual and protracted. In somewhat the same way, history is coming to be regarded not as made up of a number of decisive strokes by a series of great men ... or of a number of great charters or constitutions, but as a slow growth and development.'[17]

Even when historians did not accept the search for all-embracing laws as their main aim—few of them, in fact, did—they were inspired by the procedure of the scientist: the painstaking accumulation and substantiation of facts in a calm, detached spirit. Scientific history owed a great deal to the example of German philologists and the teachings of Leopold von Ranke, who enjoined historians to recreate the past 'as it really was'. The ideal of Rankean history gained an unchallenged ascendancy among historical scholars in the United States in the last two decades of the century, and it strengthened both their claims for a separate professional status and their declaration of independence from the literary amateurs. Americans who had studied in Germany, or were inspired by the German example of the scientific pursuit of history in the 'seminary' or seminar, minimized Ranke's idealism and the role he had assigned to intuition in the reconstruction of the past. For them the German historian exemplified all that was objective, impersonal, and self-effacing.[18] Scientific history came to mean a rigid factualism and critical documentary analysis. H.P. Biggar, who attended a history seminar at the University of Berlin, reported in 1895: 'We would take up some annals of the Middle ages and discuss their value. Were they written by one man or two? When? From what point of view? We were thus taught the principles of internal textual criticism and in general how to deal with original sources.'[19] The exponents of scientific history were distrustful of elegantly written narrative works and believed that the profusion of sources that had been made available enabled them to correct the errors of their predecessors and to discount prejudices. Lord Acton, who planned the *Cambridge Modern History* (1902-10), told his contributors that all information was within reach and that through the collaboration of specialists all problems were capable of solution.[20]

The chief representatives of these new tendencies in historical study in the English-speaking world were Bishop William Stubbs and Edward Freeman at Oxford, Herbert Baxter Adams at Johns Hopkins University, and John Burgess at Columbia. (Historical study gradually became closely identified with universities and possessed its own specialized journals, like the *English Historical Review* (1884), and series of monographs, like the *John Hopkins University Studies in Historical and Political Science*.) Where Stubbs confined himself to the deciphering of medieval texts and to editing books of documents, Freeman advanced a general explanation for the evolution of the forms of representative government from the primitive German tribal assemblies to early Britain and then to the United States that hinged on the transmission of the 'germs' of liberty by certain favoured races. This concern with institutional evolution typified the practice of scientific history, for it provided 'an impersonal, external framework for historical events'.[21]

Some Canadian amateur scholars were thoroughly familiar with these developments. Bourinot, for example, applied Freeman's and Adams' science of politics to Canada and frequently lectured in American universities on comparative politics.[22] In contrast to Americans, relatively few Canadians studied in Germany, and among those who did, scientists and theologians outnumbered students of history. The canons of the new critical history—the emphasis on documentation, detachment, specialization, and a scientific frame of mind—made their way into Canada gradually. George Wrong embraced them with reservations; Adam Shortt went much further.

II

Born in 1860 on a farm at Grovesend, Elgin County, Canada West, the son of an unsuccessful farmer, Wrong received his early education in the grammar school in the village of Vienna. He lived with relatives in Toledo, Ohio, and then worked in a bookstore in Toronto, where he converted to evangelical Anglicanism. In 1879 he enrolled in theology at the low-church Wycliffe College and a year later entered the arts course at University College. After his graduation and ordination Wrong taught ecclesiastical history and apologetics at Wycliffe. Though he never held a parish, he delivered occasional sermons and from the mid-1880s onwards was involved in church-sponsored charity and social work. He was on the founding committee of the Toronto Mission Union, an interdenominational effort to spread knowledge of Christianity among the poor through scripture lessons; he presided over a Bible class for workingmen; and he actively supported the Ontario Society for the Reformation of Inebriates. At various times he raised funds for such social Christian projects as the rescue of homeless children, a settlement house, and the Grenfell mission in Labrador.[23]

When in 1892 Wrong heard of the death of Sir Daniel Wilson, the professor of English literature and history at University College, he fell down on his knees to ask God's guidance and searched his heart to decide whether to present himself as a candidate for the chair. Despite his youth, his lack of formal training in history, the fact that he had only one substantial publication (a short study of the crusade of 1383), Wrong was named lecturer in history and in 1894 was promoted to the chair of history. There had of course been university teachers of history before this—the Rev. John Forrest at Dalhousie since 1881 and George Ferguson at Queen's since 1870—but the appointment of Wrong, and that of Charles Colby at McGill in 1895, marked the acceptance of history as a separate subject. Wilson had lectured in ethnology (which even in

Wrong's day was still attached to history), archaeology, history, and English. From 1894 to his retirement in 1927 Wrong devoted his best efforts to securing the recognition of history as a distinct discipline, creating a separate department, and establishing the critical apparatus of the new historical scholarship.

A strategic step in Wrong's ascent from a rather lowly background to a position of some prominence in Toronto society was his marriage in 1886 to Sophia, the daughter of Edward Blake, the leader of the Liberal party and Chancellor of the University. Indeed, his promotion in 1894 gave rise to accusations of favouritism and led to a students' strike, but a government commission inquiry found no basis for charges of undue influence. The fortunate marriage provided an entrée into the upper reaches of society and Wrong assiduously cultivated his connections with Laurier, Lord Bryce, the British Ambassador to the United States, Governor-General Grey, and President Taft, with whom he played golf near the Blake summer home at Murray Bay on the lower St Lawrence. Wrong was on familiar terms too with Toronto businessmen like Sir Edmund Walker, art collector and President of the Bank of Commerce, and Sir Joseph Flavelle, a prominent industrialist and financier. Few were left unaware of these and other associations, for Wrong developed a notorious penchant for name-dropping, and it was very seldom that he did not allude to his acquaintances in a public address—to a recent conversation with Bryce, a confidence from Laurier, or in one instance to a discussion with an anonymous personage, referred to only as the best-informed observer on international relations in the English-speaking world.

Wrong placed great stress on form—in comportment and manners, in writing style, in dress. He was punctilious in his own sartorial standards and Maurice Hutton, the classics professor, once joked that Wrong was frequently mistaken for a successful stockbroker. He admired the social training, character building, and finish provided by private schools like Havergal College for girls and Bishop Ridley College for boys, which he helped found. Vincent Massey, one of the many students invited to the Wrong household on Walmer Road, recalled an atmosphere that he found altogether enchanting. It was the picture, he wrote, 'of the old-fashioned drawing room, with the Scottish maid Lizzie putting the oil lamp on the table ... ; Mrs. Wrong reading a volume of Trollope ... ; Mr. Wrong probably lying in front of the fire, occasionally using his snuff-box, and making remarks that his wife may have regarded as somewhat too frivolous; the children sitting about the room reading .... '[24] Another student, seeing things from a different angle, found dinner at the Wrong's, with two servants in attendance, excessively constraining and formal.[25]

Wrong's educational ideals harked back to the Oxford he had glimpsed during a few months of summer study. He liked the conversations that

brought Aristotle and Lloyd George together, and, as he patiently explained to one former student who found the opulence of life at Balliol
College disturbing, luxury would do a Canadian youth no harm. 'I doubt',
he said, 'whether the soul is after all much injured by the luxury of good
pictures, carved furniture, comfortable easy chairs and beautiful rooms.
Some of these things are more dependent upon taste than upon money
and a large number of people in Canada could have them if they only had
the good taste to desire them.'[26] It was for these reasons that Wrong sent
his most promising students to Balliol for further education and immersion into an intensely interesting political and social milieu, and he wel-
comed Flavelle's decision to finance fellowships—Canadian versions of the
Rhodes Scholarships—to enable them to go there.

In moulding the Toronto history department, Wrong relied on Oxford
for both personnel and teaching techniques. 'Seven or eight years ago I
was alone in the Department of History,' he told George Parkin, the administrator of the Rhodes Trust, in 1911: 'now we number seven; five of
my staff are graduates of Oxford. We are rapidly adopting the Oxford tutorial method. Slight stress is placed upon lectures and every week we
meet all the Honour men in small . . . classes where essays are read, and
criticism and discussion follow. It is a great privilege to be so closely in
touch with the young life of the country. I am afraid we are still a crude
people.'[27] In the early years he staffed his department with young
Englishmen—Keith Feiling, Kenneth Bell, and R. Hodder-Williams—and
Canadians who had studied at Oxford, like Edward Kylie. Though there
were some murmurings at his reliance on the old country for personnel, at
a time when fifty-four out of seventy-two members of the teaching staff in
the Faculty of Arts at Toronto were graduates of that university,[28] after the
war Wrong found it practically impossible to recruit men from England
with the salaries that Toronto offered. 'I think', he confessed in 1921, 'we
shall have to look more and more to our own men, preferably men who
have been away for a year or two; but I am coming to look upon England
as an exhausted mine as far as our needs are concerned.'[29]

Like other university intellectuals of his and the previous generation,
Wrong almost ritualistically condemned Canadian public life as disfigured
by excessive political partisanship, materialism, rawness, and a lack of intellectual leadership. 'We are hardly yet developing in this country', he
said during the war, 'that type of great citizen which has been developed
by many generations of public life in England, the educated man,
independent in fortune, independent in position, with nothing to gain personally from serving the state, who yet, from his early manhood to his dying day, gives his best thought and effort to serve in the political sphere.'
The political organism would not run itself; it required political education
that in turn depended on attracting the best elements of the community to

public affairs and positions of influence.[30] It was the obligation of the university intellectual to bring his wisdom to a discussion of contemporary issues, to communicate the results of his thought to the general public, and to train the young for national leadership.

The Historical Club, which Wrong established in 1904, was one contribution to this aim. Its elected membership was open to any senior male student in any faculty and the papers read and discussed were seldom obscurely historical but dealt with current issues: American politics, railway nationalization, or municipal reform. It met in the best homes of the city—frequently Walker's or Flavelle's—and, according to Wrong's intentions at least, was designed to bring together the experienced and more enlightened members of one élite with the potential intellectual leaders of the future.

Wrong's notion of intellectual leadership and the Anglophile character of his personal tastes were expressions of his commitment to the Canadian imperialist faith. He habitually spoke of Canadians as preeminently a British people. By this he meant not only that a substantial proportion of Canada's population possessed ethnic and sentimental attractions to the old country, but also that in its political institutions, the continuities of tradition, and respect for the law, Canada was a British country. Wrong was greatly attracted to the sense of Christian mission and the ideal of worldwide service that permeated the imperial impulse. 'Britain controls today', he declared in 1909, 'the destinies of some 350,000,000 alien people, unable as yet to govern themselves, and easy victims to rapine and injustice, unless a strong arm guards them. She is giving them a rule that has its faults, no doubt, but such, I make bold to affirm, as no conquering state ever before gave to a dependent people.'[31] One of his fondest hopes was that, through the imperial tie, Canadians would soon participate in discharging similar obligations throughout the Empire.

Wrong, like the imperial federationists George M. Grant and Colonel George Denison before him, maintained an imperial creed that rested on an emotional loyalty to the Empire and also on a consciousness that Canada possessed a 'national type' and a life of its own. It was characteristic of Wrong that he explained the differences between Canada and Great Britain in terms of social distinctions. England was an organic and highly structured society. In the Dominion, however, society was fluid and amorphous. 'In Canada social distinctions and birth count far less, the individual far much more. There is no unity in Canadian society; there is no well entrenched social caste favoured for its continuance by laws . . . . Positions are made rapidly. There is no gradation of rank well recognized by public opinion, and itself the outcome of a long social growth.'[32] To an English visitor—and indeed at times to Wrong himself—the new country seemed crude and lacking in social discipline. 'The man who has seen the society about him created in his own generation', Wrong wrote, 'will have a view of social relations different from that of a man born into a highly organized society, with ancient buildings, traditions, and gradations of rank.'[33] According to him, this was one of the many reasons why Canadians were restless with their subordinate position in the imperial system.

Wrong shared this impatience with Canada's ambiguous status. The Dominion enjoyed complete internal self-government but was dependent on Britain for protection and exerted no influence on the councils of the Empire. Its sovereignty was limited. The Canadian Parliament sat annually by an Act of the British Parliament; the country had no power even to change the site of its capital city; and a government overseas possessed the right to disallow Canadian legislation. Wrong did not draw from these facts the conclusion that seemed so logical to the legalistically minded John Ewart, who advocated the removal of all symbols of colonial status. Wrong did not value theoretical rights very highly and he believed that on all fundamental matters Canadians had always received what they wanted and would always have their way.

The task ahead was therefore to promote a functional partnership with Britain rather than to concentrate negatively on the removal of residual symbols. For a time Wrong thought that this partnership might be realized through some form of organic political union. In 1909 he helped found the Canadian branch of the Round Table movement, which was devoted to the study and discussion of imperial questions. Like most Canadian imperialists, however, he had reservations about such designs for union as the one outlined by Lionel Curtis, the founder of the Round Table, in *The Problem of the Commonwealth* (1916). Wrong rejected the idea of a Parliament for the entire Empire that would exercise supreme authority over foreign policy and defence and possess power to tax for those purposes. He had the historian's distrust of logical plans that appeared out of keeping with the pragmatic and evolutionary nature of constitutional relations in the Empire in the past, and he felt that the assertion and acceptance of Canada's equality with Britain should precede any kind of ultimate formal union—if, indeed, there was to be any formal union in the future.[34] The split in the Round Table movement in 1916 was at least partly due to the failure of Curtis to appreciate the nationalistic basis of the Canadian imperialism of men like Wrong.[35] The whole thrust of his imperialism stressed Canadian equality. 'I am extremely anxious', he had told Sir Robert Borden in 1912, in one of his many letters of advice on naval policy, 'to have any stigma removed from Canada that she is a ward and not a partner.'[36] When Wrong heard in 1918 about the Inquiry, a committee of scholars that was to accompany the American delegation to the Paris Peace Conference, the idea of a Canadian counterpart involving himself appealed to his nationalism as well as his self-interest. After his proposal was rejected on the grounds that English officialdom would provide all the information the Canadian representatives required, Wrong indignantly responded that it was humiliating that Canada had no voice at all in shaping official views. 'Canada goes to the Peace Conference with no opinion of her own on these matters. That is to say she goes as a colony and not as a nation.'[37] It is doubtful if the politicians and their official advisers ever took Wrong as seriously as he took himself. In any case his outbursts indicated both the strength of his nationalism and the interest in self-advancement that underlay his conception of intellectual service. It also exemplified the fusion of nationalist and imperial commitments that underlay his historical writing.

III

Wrong's understanding of the nature of history was coloured by his notion of intellectual leadership, his keen consciousness of social rank, and above all by his religious training. He was in some ways an ambiguous transitional figure in the process by which history freed itself from its amateur associations in the nineteenth century and became a university-based discipline, with a critical apparatus and a professional outlook of its own. Wrong had attended a seminar in Berlin during the summer of 1890 and was in close contact with American historians. He was aware of the deficiencies of historical writing in Canada in the 1890s—its excesses of partisanship, the repetition of unexamined myths, and factual inaccuracies. His most significant contribution to the new critical history was the establishment of the *Review of Historical Publications Relating to Canada* in 1896. Inspired by the *English Historical Review*, which was twelve years old, Wrong's journal made its appearance in 1897, a year after the founding of the *American Historical Review*. It was devoted to the careful scrutiny and evaluation of books and articles on Canadian history, current affairs, and especially imperial relations. Through responsible criticism it sought to instil a certain sobriety of statement, a healthy caution, and a respect for exactitude,[38] enlisting the efforts of such amateur scholars as Bourinot and William Wood, as well as university historians. By 1906 Wrong was able to pay contributors about a dollar a page.[39] Those familiar with the less rigorous standards of the book reviews in Canadian newspapers must have been shocked by a few of the more acerbic judgements made in the *Review*. A compilation of documents on Confederation, for example, was dismissed with the statement that out of its three hundred pages only a dozen contained anything new.[40] An unsigned appraisal of volume nine of Kingsford's *History* faulted his dependence on unreliable early writers, mentioned that in the 634 pages there were only 70 references to documents at the Public Archives, and condemned the absence of any perspective. 'A considerable biographical sketch is given of an obscure artist who chanced to make a portrait of Sir George Prevost. We have the story of Lady Sarah Lennox's elopement, of the preservation of the bridge at Jena, of the Duke of Wellington's duel with Lord Winchelsea, and even that of Wynyard's ghost . . . . '[41] In 1920 the *Review* became a quarterly, with articles on Canadian history as well as critical assessments of publications in the field. Under the editorship of W.S. Wallace the *Canadian Historical Review* functioned as the chief vehicle for the historical profession in English Canada.

Another of Wrong's ventures was the creation of the Champlain Society in 1905. Modelled on similar societies in Britain and the United States, and promoted by Sir Edmund Walker, Colby of McGill, and Dr James Bain of the Toronto Public Library, it was devoted to the reprinting of documents and rare out-of-print works in Canadian history.[42] With an initial membership of 250, the society by the early twenties had issued some fifteen volumes that were models of beautiful book-making as well as scholarly editing and included Lescarbot's history of New France, a collection of documents on seigneurial tenure, and the narratives of Hearne, Thompson, and Champlain.

Wrong laid great stress on communicating the results of historical research to the general reading public and students in the schools. Together with H.H. Langton he edited the thirty-two-volume Chronicles of Canada series, which was brought out by the aggressive publisher, Robert Glasgow, between 1914 and 1916. A conscientious member of the Ontario Educational Association, he also wrote a number of texts in British and Canadian history that were widely used in schools throughout the country.

Through the *Review*, the Champlain Society, and the creation of the department at Toronto, Wrong laid the basis for a more critical, professional study of history, but he did not give his complete allegiance to the principles of the new scientific school. When, in his inaugural address of 1895, he justified the status of history as an independent discipline, he did not invoke the idea of history as a science. The reason history had not been taught as a distinct discipline, he contended, was that, unlike mathematics, Greek or biology, it possessed no specialized vocabulary, and its meaning seemed accessible to anyone who could read. Yet it was a difficult field of study that required insight and imagination. For Wrong the most indispensable quality of the historian was not the capacity to ransack archives and recover new facts; it was an attitude of mind—insight, a 'chastened imagination', 'sympathetic understanding', and a knowledge and experience of human nature that had not changed over all recorded history. When Wrong referred to the spirit of scientific detachment he usually meant an effort to be fair, to comprehend all sides of a dispute, and to neutralize emotions surrounding controversies.[43]

Wrong himself did little archival research and his publications were more noteworthy for a pleasing style and a determination to be just than for original interpretations or fresh material. For him the instructive role of history was akin to that of religion: to heal, to conciliate, and to brood over the mysteries of life. It may be, he wrote in his finest work, *A Canadian Manor and its Seigneurs* (1908), that the chief service of the chequered and half-forgotten past when it speaks is to show how vain and transient is all we think and plan—'what shadows we are and what shadows we pursue'.[44] Wrong would have nodded assent to G.M. Trevelyan's later view that the appeal of history was in the last analysis poetic. 'The dead were and are not. Their place knows them no more and is ours to-day. Yet they were once as real as we, and we shall tomorrow be shadows like them.'[45]

Wrong almost never referred to Ranke, who had become a kind of patron saint to the American professional historians, but was drawn instead to the Cambridge scholar Lord Acton. It was not Acton's well-known views regarding the need for specialization and collaboration in historical research that interested him but rather his belief in the need of the historian to be impartial and to draw moral judgements. Wrong also believed that the student of the past should try to control his own feelings and write so that no one reading his work could guess his political or religious affiliations. The notion of history as a moral teacher, moreover, struck responsive chords in his religious consciousness. History had to deal with profound questions of human experience and moral law. 'The world we live in is, after all, a moral world,' Wrong wrote in 1913. 'The moral law is a law of nature, and he who ceaselessly violates it can no more succeed than can the man who is trying to make water run uphill.'[46] Alluding to Acton's prescription that the great achievement of history was to develop, perfect, and arm conscience, Wrong emphasized that the historian had a duty to pass moral judgements. 'The historian is the guardian of truth, truth not merely as to specific fact, but truth as expressing constructive standards of conduct.'[47] To Wrong the spiritual sources of conduct were as much facts to be assessed as anything else in human experience. Individuals in the past should not be judged exclusively by standards of their own times, for to so judge them would necessarily concede the relativity of morality. Nor should they be indignantly censured or routinely praised without a deliberate imaginative effort to comprehend the world in which they lived. The idea of history as moral judgement rested on the assumption that there existed an unchanging and timeless moral order, and implied that history itself was an agent of that morality.

History, then, was more than past politics, and the historian had to wrestle with problems that could never be solved by archival research. Wrong possessed a real appreciation for the frailty and perversity of human nature and he came to hold a tempered, slightly disillusioned view of historical progress. 'The doctrine of evolution', he told the Canadian Club of Ottawa in 1916, 'showed that Nature herself is the scene of unending conflicts and that progress, if there is such a thing as progress, is due to the results of this struggle. I suppose that all of us, in our callow days of dreaming, have thought that perhaps some day the scene of human society might be so perfected as to take on the characteristics of a beautiful garden.' He admitted that he had once believed that, but not any longer. Life was a perpetual struggle, and the 'best we can hope for is to lessen the evils of to-day and to have some little share in increasing the sum of human happiness . . . . The scene of our daily life is necessarily one of continued struggle; the instruments used are not very delicate, on the whole . . .'[48] The entire march of history, he believed, was a growth by the same slow method that nature used in all her greater processes. Social conditions may have been improved, manners softened, the populace more enlightened, but human nature remained constant. When Wrong asserted that a study of the past would make men wiser, he believed that it would teach them to live in the world as it was, not as some doctrinaires sought to remake it.

Wrong's respect for the limitations of humanity, his concern with imponderables, and his desire to have history address itself to such speculative questions as why a nation's culture changed, or whether there was such a thing as progress, made him sceptical of the self-sufficiency of the new historical methodology. He wrote in 1927, the year of his retirement, that man himself was the greatest obstacle to exact and final history. 'We may' he added, 'be well assured that until man has become a superman there will not be a science of history, for only a being more than man can read all the influences which mould his conduct.'[49]

As Wrong grew older he became more critical of the excessive specialization of academic history, especially as it was practised in the United States. His own ideals had been inspired by the 'older masters' of nineteenth-century Britain and the United States, men of independent means and a general culture who devoted their lives to multi-volume narratives of whole eras. They possessed an acquaintance of the world of affairs, and addressed their works to a literate reading public. They had unfortunately been superceded, he charged in the twenties, by a generation of academic professionals whose purpose seemed to be the amassing of facts and who wrote in a drab style, producing monographs on small subjects for other members of a guild.[50] Wrong did his best to keep his own traditional standards alive, and it was partly through his example and his teaching that the idea of 'scientific history' was never as enthusiastically embraced at Toronto as in some American universities.

In maintaining these reservations about the scientific character of history, Wrong was typical of other historians of his generation who never lost their respect for the art of telling a story with literary grace. Charles Colby, who identified the spirit of science with guarding against expressing one's own personal feelings, never endorsed the notion of finality and comprehensiveness in written history. 'In a broad sense', he said in 1905, 'all historical writing is provisional, since each age refuses to be content with the historiography left it by its predecessors .... I believe that every generation needs histories written for itself, however surely they may be doomed to eventual oblivion.'[51] Against the excessive claims of the scientific school, W.S. Wallace and J.L. Morrison of Queen's could place the legacy of Parkman and a British tradition of historical writing that stretched from Lord Macaulay to Lord Morley and G.M. Trevelyan.[52]

Wrong's major publications concentrated on two themes that were fundamental to Canadian history and were also prominent political issues in his time. The first (which will be examined in Chapter 2) was imperial history and Canada's evolving position in the Empire-Commonwealth. The second—the subject of A Canadian Manor and its Seigneurs (1908), The Fall of Canada: A Chapter in the History of the Seven Year's War (1914), and the two-volume Rise and Fall of New France (1928)—was the historical relation of the French and English in Canada.

Wrong gained his first-hand impressions of Quebec from many holidays spent at Murray Bay, a summer colony about eighty miles downriver from Quebec City, and from talks with priests and guides thereabouts. He learned the history of French Canada from the books of Francis Parkman and also from friends like J. Edmond Roy, Assistant Archivist at Ottawa, and the Church historian, Abbé A.H. Gosselin, whose parish histories he read with profit. In the attic of an old manor house at Murray Bay he discovered the records of the Scottish soldier who had been granted the seigneury just after the Conquest, and he told the story of the family against a background in which nature seemed to mock the activities of men. 'This majestic river, the mountains clothed in perennial green, the blue and purple tints so delicate and transient as the light changes,' he wrote, 'have occupied this scene for thousands of centuries.'[53] It seemed difficult to imagine that the area had a significant human history. For Wrong, as for many English-Canadian writers before and since, all that was admirable and permanent in Quebec society lay in the small rural villages like St Augustin, not in the provincial capital or the burgeoning industrial cities.[54]

Wrong wrote within a tradition of English-Canadian literature on Quebec that endeavoured to reconcile differences and promote a better understanding through sympathetic interpretations of its history and culture. This desire was at bottom a response to the widening gulf between the two peoples, accentuated by the cultural conflicts of the late nineteenth century, the rise of imperialism in English Canada, the Boer War, Bourassa's nationaliste movement, and the Ontario schools issue. Books like Byron Nicholson's The French-Canadian: A Sketch of His More Prominent Characteristics (1902), or the re-enactment of heroic events of the past during the Quebec Tercentenary Celebrations in 1908,[55] were means to dispel prejudices and illustrate the admirable aspects of Quebec society and its people. The impulse was intensified by the First World War and the conscription crisis. The phrase *bonne entente* was appropriated by a movement of Toronto businessmen and professionals and a few French-speaking sympathizers, who sought to encourage an 'entente cordiale' between the two peoples through interprovincial visits of élite figures. 'The French speakers', Sir Edmund Walker wrote in his journal of one meeting, 'seemed to be wondering if now the Ontario people would grant bilingual rights while the English speakers were wondering if the French Canadians would enlist and play their part in the war.'[56] But the phrase *bonne entente* denoted a more general attitude, a conviction that racial conflicts were due to misunderstanding, a lack of knowledge, and a failure of sympathy.

University teachers like Wrong, C.B. Sissons, and O.D. Skelton who joined the Unity League of Ontario and tried to explain, and up to a point defend, the French-Canadian position on the school issue, or Percival F. Morley, an analyst in the Ontario Department of Health who wrote *Bridging the Chasm: A Study of the Ontario-Quebec Question* (1919), censured both the defensive mentality of French Canadians and the race pride and temper of ascendancy of English Canada. Some not only worked to dispel ignorance in English Canada about French Canada but succeeded in projecting a collective portrait of Quebec society that highlighted its traditional, retrogressive features. The rich colour and conservative spirit of that province was regarded as a check on the dull uniformity of North America and a certain guarantee that Canada remained different from the United States. The anti-commercial ethic of the ordinary French Canadian was seen as a counterpoise to the excessively materialistic tone of English Canada. Both Sir Andrew Macphail, editor of *The University Magazine*, and the Toronto lawyer William Hume Blake envisaged Quebec as a solid anchor of a sane conservatism that was more resistant to the millenial enthusiasms, especially prohibition, than other parts of the country.[57] Both translated Louis Hémon's novel of life in the backwoods, *Marie Chapdelaine* (1913), into English. Wrong's son Hume told an English correspondent in 1925 that this book 'had a tremendous vogue here a couple of years ago, and there is a great deal of truth in it. It is not welcome to many French, I think on the grounds that it is considered to exaggerate their simplicity. I believe that a memorial to Hémon at Peribonka (he uses real places and real people) was destroyed by an irate populace not long ago!'[58]

George Wrong's histories of French Canada were addressed to furthering the aims of the *bonne entente* tradition. From his earliest contacts with Quebec he admired the stability and permanence of its social order and its religious flavour. Church spires dominated his picture of the province, just as they towered over the Laurentian villages. 'In human society', he wrote, 'there is no institution more perfectly organized than the Roman Catholic Church and in Quebec her traditions have a vitality and vigour lost perhaps in communities more initiated.' Wrong's admiration for the clerical leadership of the society was unbounded and he rebuked those who talked loosely of a priest-ridden province. The ecclesiastical buildings, he explained, may seem imposing and numerous, but 'we need to remember how large are the parishes and how few in number relatively are the churches; it is probable that in English-Canada there are half a dozen churches or more to every one in the Province of Quebec.' The faithful there accepted the authority of the Church as binding on their consciences in much the same way as the Prostestant accepted the Bible. The priest was not the authoritarian figure that exercised the Prostestant imagination. More often than not a son of the people, he worked by persuasion and consent. As for the educational system, it seemed altogether admirable to Wrong that it inculcated religious values and manners, which were given precedence over such conventional subjects as were exclusively taught in the public schools of the Anglo-Saxon world.[59]

Just as the village church symbolized the spiritual nature of the whole society, so too the ordinary French-Canadian farmer was taken to be representative of the entire people. The *habitants*, in Wrong's account, were tenacious in adhering to tradition and yet assertively independent. Contented with time-honoured ways of doing things, isolated from the turmoil of the urban, industrial world, they retained a certain old-world politeness and deference. 'They are sober and industrious; their family life is pure; they are prudent and frugal in their habits.' However, Wrong admitted another side to this idyllic portrait: inefficient agricultural practices, superstitions, and tragic lives in the remote areas. 'One sees pale women, overworked. . . . there are deformed cripples who might have been made whole by skill applied in time . . . . Many children are born but too many die. Still, most of the people live in comfort and they enjoy life — enjoy it probably much more than would an Anglo-Saxon community of the same type.'[60]

For Wrong, French Canada became a foil against which the moral critic could contrast a profoundly religious and stable society with the more disturbing features of his own rapidly changing and secular province. His strong identifications with the permanence and peacefulness of those villages he visited arose from his holidays and escape from the cares of Toronto. His admiration for the clergy of Quebec was in some respects an indirect reflection upon a career he had chosen earlier and abandoned, and an expression of the kind of leadership to which he aspired.

Wrong's favourable response to Quebec in his own time informed and shaped his descriptions of her past. His studies of New France were heavily indebted to Parkman and it was significant that he faulted the American historian for a lack of understanding and sympathy rather than for technical errors. 'One may almost say that Parkman never makes a mistake, certainly not a glaring one . . . . His narrative may show bias, but never does it betray slovenliness or inexactitude.' What marred Parkman's histories, in Wrong's opinion, was his failure to appreciate the real genius of the French Canadians. 'He thought them a king-ridden, priest-ridden folk, ignorant, lacking virility, and ineffective as colonizers.'[61] Wrong's histories were qualifications of Parkman's; they did not advance substantially new ways of seeing the Old Régime. Wrong showed that New France deservedly collapsed, but not from a lack of vigour. Indeed, the French had a special genius for colonization and adapting to the New World. New France fell because of tyranny and corruption. 'While a less developed people', Wrong explained, 'may be ruled for their own good by some external authority, it may be doubted whether any colony of Europeans has ever succeeded which did not contain within itself the chief directing energy and authority. . . . liberty is necessary for a strong colony. In the growth of a single tree a thousand influences of sun and air are involved and its roots feel their way in every direction; so it is with the life of a colony; only those on the spot can adjust the nice forces which make for natural growth. But this freedom the France of Louis XIV was never willing to give.'[62] Far more than Parkman, Wrong stressed the cohesion of eighteenth-century society on the banks of the St Lawrence and the warmth of human relations. In fact he projected back into the past his idealized image of the people and countryside around Murray Bay. And he made much also of the reconciliation that quickly followed the Conquest.

As for the continuing relations between the two peoples in his own day, Wrong thought the 'race question' far less intractable than it seemed on the surface. What separated French and English was not race—there was, he said, no mysterious power in race, and in any case both groups came from the same north-European stock—but rather differing cultures, educations, and traditions.[63] Social intercourse, an imagination to put oneself in another's place, and a tolerant familiarity with each of the two cultures would go far to discredit and destroy the extremist views on both sides. Wrong was quite emphatic on the point that in Quebec and in federal-government affairs, French was on a perfect equality with English, but that French linguistic rights should not be extended to the west.[64] Yet he also spoke of the possibility of having 'a nationality within a nation',[65] as was the case of Scotland within Britain. Indeed, the presence of the French culture not only made Canada a unique amalgam but it provided English Canadians with a gateway to one of the inexhaustible strands of European civilization. Wrong's undoubtedly sincere and warm affection for French

Canada as he saw it was in his mind not incompatible with his imperialism, or an acknowledgement that the French-Canadian element was a numerically declining minority.

Contradictory and even patronizing as Wrong's characterization of French Canada and its history might appear in retrospect, this aspect of his work was nonetheless an exemplification of his belief that history, like Christian teaching, healed and conciliated.

IV

Adam Shortt came to Canadian history through moral philosophy and political economy. A year older than Wrong, he grew up on a remote farm near the village of Kilworth and on the outskirts of Walkerton in southwestern Ontario. He received little formal education and taught himself in the library of the Walkerton Mechanics' Institute. He entered Queen's University in 1879 with the intention of training for the Presbyterian ministry, took philosophy from John Watson, and wrote an essay that his teacher judged 'the most complete critical statement of the Psychology of Mr. Herbert Spencer to be anywhere found'.[66] Between 1883 and 1886 Shortt studied at Edinburgh and Glasgow—philosophy with John Caird and physics with Lord Kelvin, as well as botany and chemistry. He returned to Queen's in 1886 as tutor in philosophy, instructor in botany, and demonstrator in chemistry. In his second year he also lectured in political economy, which had been on the curriculum of the Philosophy Department since 1878 and had been taught largely out of the texts of Adam Smith and the neo-classicists. Appointed to the Sir John A. Macdonald Chair of Political Science in 1891, Shortt increasingly incorporated books by the critics of classical economics into his courses, and turned towards an investigation of the financial history of early Canada. In 1894 he was holding classes on the economic and social history of the Old Régime,[67] and in the ten years after 1896 he published thirty-two articles on the origins of Canadian currency, banking, and exchange in the *Journal of the Canadian Bankers' Association.*[68]

The most striking feature of Shortt's outlook was his empiricism. While his background in 'mental and moral philosophy' sharpened his ability to examine and analyse abstract ideas, his scientific education abroad strengthened his fascination with the concrete facts of material life. Though in some ways he maintained the traditional Scottish association of economics and philosophy, he disdained theorizing and eschewed moralizing. G.M. Grant, the Principal of Queen's, who had witnessed Shortt's transition from a candidate for the ministry to a prospective science teacher and then to an economic historian, said of him in 1895 that he was 'as clamorous for "facts" as Mr. Gradgrind.'[69]

Shortt was the first native-born economist to adopt a historical approach to the Canadian economy, and his decision to cultivate that field coincided with the beginning of a period of intense economic development that involved the settlement of the prairies, the industrialization of central Canada, the growth of urban centres, and massive railway construction. For twenty years after the founding of *Queen's Quarterly* in 1893, Shortt regularly contributed articles on current events. This was a time when wage bargaining, tariffs, railways rates, banking and finance, the organization of municipal government, and inflation pressed to the forefront of public attention. After the turn of the century Shortt was called upon more and more for advice by governments, Canadian Clubs, reform groups, newspapers, and in at least one case by a clergyman who solicited his assistance in dealing with a single-tax crank in his congregation.[70] He served as a member of the Railway Taxation Commission of the Province of Ontario in 1904, and in 1907 and 1908 chaired eleven boards of conciliation set up under the Industrial Disputes Investigation Act. From 1908 to 1917 he was one of the two members of the Civil Service Commission of Canada, a position he regarded as providing an opportunity for creating a thoroughly professional and non-political class of goverment officers.

Though the immediate stimulus to Shortt's work in economic history may have been provided by Canadian developments, he also owed much to a group of German economists and their British and American followers. In the middle of the nineteenth century Wilhelm Rocher, Bruno Hildebrand, and Karl Knies had launched an attack on the doctrines of English classical economic theory and especially the notion of immutable economic laws. They contended that the economic order had to be understood in relation to time and place, and through a historical inductive approach rather than by deductions from universal principles. Their successors, like Gustav Schmoller, were even more concerned with the ethical and humanitarian dimensions of economic life and were more appreciative of the potentialities of the state as the guardian of the national welfare. Cliff Leslie, J.K. Ingram, and Arnold Toynbee in England took up the historical investigation of economic phenomenon, and American students brought back the teachings of the German economists to the United States. Some, including Richard T. Ely, repudiated *laissez-faire* and competitive individualism and became supporters of progressive reform. The impact of the German historical school on scholars generally was threefold: it intensified scepticism about generalizations regarding economic behaviour, put a new stress on the evolutionary character of institutions, and underlined the need for detailed historical research that would provide guidance for the formulation of policy.[71]

The tenets of the historical economists were brought directly to Canada by William J. Ashley, the Oxford-trained Professor of Political Economy and Constitutional History in the University of Toronto from 1888 to 1892. His inaugural lecture on political science (or political economy—the terms were used interchangeably), dedicated to Schmoller, contained a sympathetic exposition of German political economy and concluded with a declaration of his belief that the state had duties beyond the mere protection of life and property.[72] The two ideas underlying the new political economy, he explained, were that economics, history, administration, public finance, and political institutions should all be studied in the same objective spirit that the natural scientist brought to the observation of organisms and specimens, and that political science must be addressed to practical applications. The accumulation of facts and statistics, he added realistically, required no high intellectual powers but simply industry, honesty and 'chiefly intelligent drudgery'.[73]

The ideas of these historical economists partly provided the rationale for Shortt's work. He too recognized that economic life varied enormously over different parts of the world and that it was unjust to the classical writers to apply their principles universally. Nor did he confine political economy merely to the investigation of the production, exchange, and distribution of wealth. 'All political and social problems', he wrote in 1893, 'have an ethical basis, just as all physiological questions have a chemical basis.' The production of wealth involved the use of human beings, and 'we have constantly to ask to what extent this is justified.' The very democratization of society, moreover, implied that the economist must conduct his studies with reference to the best interests of a collectivity, not only of individuals. In spite of his awareness of the moral and ethical dimensions of the subject, however, Shortt insisted upon the limits of political economy as a prescriptive discipline. Its objective, he wrote, was 'not to supply definite and final solutions for all social questions. Its method was to discover the fundamental and secondary ideas and principles that guide society and to apply them 'in dealing with special concrete questions, where we have to take particular note of individual facts and details as well as of general principles.'[74]

Shortt had an ingrained scepticism about proposals for social reform. Though he married a leading feminist, Elizabeth Smith, who was also one of Canada's first female graduates in medicine, Shortt was able to state in 1909 that 'Eventually women will be allowed the privileges of voting, but I cannot see that any good result will follow.'[75] In 1897 he dismissed working-class socialism as 'the most individualistic self-interest' imaginable, and treated 'the socialists of the chair' as idle dreamers, 'theorists, agitators and extremists'. Shortt believed that defects in societies were due more to human imperfections than to structural weaknesses, and that the ideal socialist state could only be attained by 'eliminating all the powerful mainsprings of human nature'. Entirely typical of this approach to theories of change was his view that the question of whether the state should attempt to run particular enterprises on business lines was not at all an issue of 'state-socialism' but one that had to be settled on pragmatic grounds.[76]

Though Shortt favoured certain forms of profit sharing in industry, and was later to become critical of the reckless alienation of resources to 'outsiders', and announced himself in favour of the largest possible extension of the public ownership of public utilities provided they were not operated by politicians,[77] he believed in the generally beneficent and progressive arrangements of modern capitalism. He accepted combinations and consolidations in the business world as inevitable. The 'whole growth of economic organization, the subsequent development of the millionaire, and the final effort to avoid the ruinous waste of independent competition, are simply stages in the economic triumph of man over nature. This victory secures the supply of an increasing number of wants with a decreasing proportion of human effort.' For him the great magnate was not only the end product of the 'operation of natural selection'; like the scientist, the artist, or the statesman, he was motivated by a desire to create.[78]

There was no danger in great aggregations of economic power, trusts, or labour unions, Shortt believed, provided that the public interest was guarded by impartial boards of experts. He assumed that the scientifically trained political economist was not only the source of information, but also a neutral umpire standing above and adjudicating the clashes of special interests. Corporations should be allowed to grow in the interests of efficiency, but they had to be regulated by boards modelled on the lines of the Railway Commission.[79] Like the German and American economists, Shortt stressed the need to educate both state servants and the literate public; and he too advanced the claims of economic history as an instrument of policy making. 'This is an age of experts', he told a Winnipeg audience in 1912, 'and an age of minority rule. Efficiency of government cannot be given unless the person placed in office has information and the faculty of using his judgement.'[80] This was the need that the Canadian Political Science Association, founded in 1913, was to answer. 'One does not attempt fine work through the instrumentality of a mob,' Shortt wrote in explaining the organization's purposes. 'It is through a select, active minority that the most effective and progressive ideas as to political and social welfare must be introduced.'[81] The association, which had seven hundred members[82] but died at the outset of the war, was intended to bring together experts, individuals from the educated élite, and political leaders in order to create a forum where Canadians could address themselves to the solution of Canadian problems from a scientific point of view.

Shortt's faith in the progressive character of modern capitalism considerably affected his understanding of international relations. Unlike Ashley, who became a supporter of Chamberlain's tariff reform crusade, or even

Wrong, who placed great hopes for a time in the Round Table, Shortt made his reputation—with *Imperial Preferential Trade from a Canadian Point of View* (1904)—as one of the leading critics of economic imperialism. Always suspicious of sentiment, especially sentiment that could so easily be manipulated for economic ends, he rejected Chamberlain's 'gospel of rural contentment for the colonies' because preferential trade would blight Canada's assured industrial future. However, he never challenged the idea of the underlying community of culture of British peoples. This is why his pamphlet was admired not only by Henri Bourassa but also by William L. Grant, an advocate of imperial unity who believed that an economic conception of the Empire would vulgarize the imperial association.[83] Indeed, in 1907 Shortt agreed that Canada would assume powers in international affairs through the same irresistible logic that had led to internal self-government, and that this would 'consolidate' its connections with Britain and the Empire.[84]

Shortt had an immense faith in free trade and self-interest in binding the world communities together and ensuring world peace. The 'vast commercial & financial interests of the civilized nations really hold the balance of power,' he wrote during the war scare of 1895, 'and may be relied upon to oppose war & put the brakes on jingoistic governments.' As late as 1927, when he represented Canada at the International Economic Conference at Geneva, Shortt asserted that German and French cartels and trusts were more effective guarantees of European peace than the League of Nations.[85]

Shortt's economic thinking reinforced both a pre-existing bias in Canada against theory and a certain satisfaction with capitalism that was characteristic of early academic political economy. There was no established tradition of criticism of either the economy or society in the newly created departments of political economy in Canada, and no real parallel to that group of American economists, German trained and inspired by the social gospel, who provided some of the intellectual equipment of the early progressive movement. James Mavor, who succeeded Ashley at Toronto, though a radical in Scotland in his younger days, found much to denounce in government economic activity and discovered in even the Hydro-Electric Commission of Ontario, set up by a coalition of small businessmen and a Conservative government, proof of the evils of state ownership. Oscar Douglas Skelton, who took over from Shortt at Queen's in 1908, distinguished himself in 1911 by publishing a prize-winning critique of socialist doctrines. Stephen Leacock, who was appointed lecturer in political economy at McGill in 1900, was in some respects an exception, for his humorous stories satirized the rich, and his *Unsolved Riddle of Social Justice* (1920) endorsed a program of reform, including old-age pensions. But even Leacock's critique of injustice was conducted within the framework of capitalist values and an old-fashioned opposition to socialism. Significantly, one of the few appeals for an ethical political economy of reform was made in 1892 by J.G. Hume, a one-time student of Ely's and a philosopher, not an economist.[86] Within the established circles, the political economy of liberalism held pride of place.

Shortt's understanding of the nature and task of history was bound up with his social philosophy and his convictions regarding the purpose of trained experts as mediating figures. It was also a reflection of his personality. An inveterate collector of old letters, books, autographs, and other memorabilia, he expressed his thirst for facts and his passion for exactitude even in letters to his wife, wherein he discoursed in detail on the meals he had eaten and the rooms he rented while on his trips abroad. His more specialized publications—papers on currency and the founders of Canadian banking, on municipal government in Ontario, and on comparative treatments of the effects of wars and of the railway-building eras in Canadian history—never issued in any truly strategic generalizations about the past. His major contribution was rather one of urging a broadening of the scope and subject matter of history to include the social and economic life of the people, and the accumulation, organization, and publication of documentary evidence. It was in this latter capacity, and in his collaborative work with Arthur Doughty, Dominion Archivist from 1904 to 1935, that he left his lasting imprint on Canadian historical scholarship.

They were a complementary couple, Shortt and Doughty—the one with the scientific caution of the economic historian; the other with a romantic interest in war, exploration, and the Old Régime, a flair for public relations, and a phenomenal gift for collecting. Doughty, who had been educated at public schools and at New Inn Hall, Oxford, and had come to Canada at the age of twenty-six in 1886, had worked as a newspaper drama critic in Montreal and had held various positions in the civil service of Quebec. He was a man of taste who loved beautiful things, and among his numerous accomplishments was the composition of the libretto of a comic opera, the illuminating of books, and jointly editing six volumes of documents on the siege of Quebec. Under his directorship, the activities of the Archives were enormously expanded. In 1905, H.P. Biggar, who possessed an unrivalled knowledge of English, French, Spanish and Portuguese sources on the period of discovery and exploration, was appointed Chief Archivist of Canada in Europe with headquarters at the Public Record Office in London. He was charged with supervising copyists working there and in Paris. Thanks to the efforts of Lord Minto, a new archives building—a variation of the currently popular Scottish-castle mode—was opened in 1906. By 1912 the Archives had become a separate department under the jurisdiction of the Secretary of State and by 1925 it contained over 40,000 volumes of manuscripts, 45,000 books relating to Canada, and 25,000 historical prints, engravings, and drawings.[87] In that year a new wing was added to the building.

Doughty had all the virtues and some of the faults of a born collector: an acquisitiveness that bordered on the predatory, a gift for gaining the confidence of those who possessed the things he wanted, and an uncanny ability to talk them into parting with them. Governor General Grey once joked to Doughty that he had told the Duke of Devonshire 'about you. Told him to keep an eye on his miniatures while you are on the Premises.'[88] Where Brymner had dutifully pursued his researches in uncomfortable circumstances, Doughty gained access to the country houses of the aristocracy. In 1923 he established a Canadian History Society in the British Isles that comprised the principal male descendants of figures who held high office in the military and colonial services in Canada. The purpose of this society—and of a counterpart established in France a year later—was to draw the attention of old families to the needs of the Archives, and it was through the society that Doughty acquired the papers of General Murray, Lord Durham, and the Elgin-Grey correspondence. Doughty was indispensable, wrote J.C. Webster: 'He has the entrée to palaces, government offices, and private houses, both in England and France, which few can ever expect to have. This privilege is not merely official. It has come mainly from the influence of Doughty's personality. Most of his successes have come from the affection and interest which he has aroused in the minds and hearts of those with whom he has come in contact.'[89]

Doughty's efforts sometimes suffered from a lack of discrimination. In his day the Archives came into the possession not only of the more conventional historical sources—manuscripts, books, pamphlets, and maps—but of a variety of mementoes and museum pieces: Brock's uniform with the bullet hole in the chest; Wolfe's campaign chair; war trophies, guns, and trench signs from the 1914-18 conflict; and even a box of doll's furniture from the Queen's collection.[90] Doughty came to personify the institution to the public and customarily spoke of it as a personal creation. This did not endear him to some of his employees, who resented his taking the credit for work that was not his own.[91]

In his more expansive pronouncements Doughty attributed to the Archives purposes that transcended in significance the popularization of history or the preservation of documents that were useful in the transactions of affairs of state. Every scrap of paper recovered from the past, he believed, was an instrument of justice—not only because the original, authentic sources would either vindicate or qualify individual reputations but because they would dispel accretions of prejudice and glosses of opinion that had been interposed between the real past and the present. Doughty also entertained the hope that the holdings of the Archives would attract the attention of a better class of writers to the literary possibilities of Canadian historical subjects. Finally, an adequate history based on the original documents would remove mistaken impressions that divided French and English Canadians and sustain a common patriotism.

'History', Doughty affirmed, following the French-Canadian historian Cas-grain, 'is not only the guiding light, the pillar, history is not only the foun-dation stone of Patriotism, history carries with it the title deeds of nationalism.'[92]

Shortt's formal association with Doughty began in 1907 when the gov-ernment appointed a Historical Manuscripts Commission to advise the Minister of Agriculture, who was then responsible for the Archives, on acquisitions and to work in conjunction with the Dominion Archivist in planning a program of publishing selected manuscripts. Shortt, Wrong, and Colby were appointed to the Commission, along with two French-Canadian historians, Abbé August Gosselin and J. Edmond Roy.[93] One of the first volumes to appear was *Documents Relating to the Constitutional History of Canada, 1759-1791* (1907) compiled by Shortt and Doughty.

The following year saw the publication of Shortt's study of Lord Syden-ham, Governor-General of Canada from 1839 to 1841. Based on sources Doughty had acquired, the book was by far the best and the most durable volume in the Makers of Canada series, a twenty-volume project. In this businessman/pro-consul, Shortt found a kindred spirit, a man who laid the basis for a departmentalized administrative apparatus that Shortt, as Civil Service Commissioner, attempted to perfect. Sydenham's was a per-sonal rule, a denial of responsible government, yet his administrative re-forms provided the indispensable basis for self-government. 'That his fun-damental principles might live,' Shortt wrote, 'his practical application of them must perish, in their passing through a series of reincarnations.'[94]

The major monument to the collaborative efforts of Shortt and Doughty was *Canada and its Provinces*, which appeared in twenty-three volumes between 1913 and 1917. Planned since 1909, it enlisted over a hundred paid contributors and dealt with 153 topics and subjects. The enterprise was a joint product of professional historians (Wrong, W.S. Wallace, and Chester Martin); journalists (John Dafoe of the *Manitoba Free Press* and John Lewis of the Toronto *Globe*); amateur historians (Andrew Macphail, who wrote on the Maritimes, and Charles W. Gordon, who wrote on the Presbyterian Church); and technical experts (M.J. Patton of the Conserva-tion Commission, B.E. Fernow of the University of Toronto's Faculty of Forestry, and Edward Sapir, an ethnologist with the Geological Survey). The volumes covered not only history but contemporary problems and de-velopments, especially economic matters, and were a convincing testament to the need for specialization as preached by Acton, who, Shortt admitted, 'I regard as having the truest conception of history among modern writers.'[95]

When in 1917 Shortt resigned from the Civil Service Commission after a spirited clash with politicians, Sir Robert Borden appointed him chairman of a new body, the Board of Historical Publications. In this position Shortt planned an ambitious series of documentary publications on original immigration and settlements, on constitutional development in Nova Scotia, and on currency, banking, and domestic and foreign exchange. In 1919, the year of the Winnipeg General Strike, when war-inspired reformism was at high tide, Shortt wrote that a broad and impartial presentation of history would 'save us from many wild phases of economic and social doctrine.' In his view history was the only satisfactory court of appeal between those who sought to abolish the present economic and social order and those who wanted to preserve it.[96] There was no doubt where Shortt's own sympathies lay.

At the Board of Historical Publications Shortt's practice as a historian came more and more to resemble the archivist's ideal: the acquisition, ordering, and accurate reproduction of sources. His *Documents on Currency, Finance and Exchange of Canada under the French Regime* appeared in 1929 and, two years after his death in 1931, his *Documents Relating to the Currency, Exchange and Finance in Nova Scotia . . . . 1675-1758* was published. In 1926 he acquired for the Public Archives the records of the Baring Brothers, a British financial house that had been of immense significance in North American economic development in the nineteenth century. 'I am', he confessed of his coup, 'like the Irishman who, when asked how he was getting along, replied that he was never in a happier condition—he was tearing down a Protestant church and being paid for it.'[97]

Shortt spent his later years indexing and cataloguing these and other sources on Canadian economic history as the preliminary to a comprehensive interpretation that he would not live to write. Apart from his two published volumes on finance, he did not even complete the documentary series. Impeded by his scientific quest for all the relevant facts and by his recognition that the magnitude of the sources made his efforts premature, Shortt in the end was left with his coloured pencils, his indexes, and voluminous notes written in a unique shorthand that no one else could understand and that would never be used. The unkind judgement of an ex-student on Shortt's teaching applied also to his research work: 'To my mind,' wrote W.B. Munro, 'Shortt was never cut out to be a historian. He got swamped with details and was inclined to pour out great masses of not well digested historical material upon the hapless denizens of his classroom.'[98]

Shortt's forte, like Doughty's, was an unrivalled knowledge of original documents. Theirs was the fate of all pioneers who equip the expedition and point it in a general direction but leave it for others to discover the unknown territory in broad perspective. During the 1920s a new generation of Canadian historians made the Archives a vital scholarly centre. Attracted to Ottawa by the sources over which Doughty presided like the proprietor of a fabulous delicatessen, university teachers from across the country found in this 'mecca' a real *esprit de corps*. The main reading room, open at first until midnight every day of the year, became during the summer months not only a place for research but also a clearing house for the discussion of work in progress, mutual criticism, and education in the techniques of critical, documentary history. Young students invariably consulted Doughty or Shortt about the materials available. When Harold Innis began his research in Canadian economic history, he sought Shortt's advice, for, as he told the old man, 'you know more about this subject than anyone else alive.' Even Wrong, faced with the task of supervising graduate research in Toronto, solicited Shortt's opinion about manuscripts available in the archives in his own city.[99] Queen's University, which had become the only notable centre in the field of Canadian economic history, also took the lead in formalizing the educative function of the Archives. Largely on the initiative of J.L. Morrison and Duncan McArthur of that university, a School of Research in Canadian history was inaugurated in 1922. Held at the Archives during eight weeks in the summers, the program included lectures, seminars in the scrutiny and evaluation of evidence, and supervised research.

'It is very interesting', the Alberta historian, A.L. Burt, told his wife in 1926, 'to see the actual renaissance of Canadian history in the course of preparation.' The list of scholars who frequented the Archives in the twenties reads like a roll-call of the men who were to reshape Canadian historical writing. It included Burt himself, unravelling the complicated motivations behind the passing of the Quebec Act; Daniel C. Harvey, working on the early history of Prince Edward Island; Arthur S. Morton from Saskatoon, pursuing with an indefatigable curiosity items that would reveal the exact location of western fur-trading posts and canoe routes; Lester Pearson investigating for a short time the records of Loyalist settlement; George Glazebrook researching the biography of Sir Charles Bagot; and J.B. Brebner exploring British policy towards the Acadians. There were also students—like Harold Innis, Arthur Lower, George Wilson, George Brown, and Menzies Whitelaw—preparing senior theses for American graduate schools. And there was General Ernest Cruikshank, then in his seventies, who had been compiling the records of military campaigns in the Niagara region in the War of 1812 for forty years. Burt did not exaggerate when he wrote that 'all the professional historians in Canada are turning their eyes on the Archives during the summer months & a revolution is bound to come about as a result . . . . '[100]

V

There must be few academic disciplines that had as their founders two such radically different people as Wrong and Shortt. Wrong found in Acton's teaching the justification of history as a moral teacher, Shortt the rationale for the scientific and specialized quest for facts. The one stressed intuition and a chastened imagination as the necessary qualities of the historian's mind—the very mental habits that the empiricist distrusted. Wrong looked to the Balliol tutorial as the model for humane education, Shortt to the German-inspired American seminar as the seed-bed of scientific history.

Wrong was an ambiguous figure in the transition of historical study in Canada. He began the *Review* and other agencies associated with the new 'scientific' history, but he never accepted the nostrums of historical science to the same extent as Shortt did. The renaissance of Canadian history in the twenties and thirties would have been inconceivable without the preliminary work of Doughty and Shortt. Wrong was not in this respect indispensable. But among his students and the staff he recruited for the department he founded were men who completely transformed Canadian historiography by the time of his death in 1948: W.P.M. Kennedy, Chester Martin, Frank H. Underhill, A.R.M. Lower, John Bartlet Brebner, and Donald G. Creighton. In Wrong's case it was true that students reacted to their master by deflection as well as by imitation. They joked about his ignorance of 'the sources', his social snobbery, and his dilettantism. But strangely some of them in time came to resemble Wrong more than they cared to admit and perpetuated his engagement in public affairs and his esteem for form.

Wrong's own affinities were with the generation of university figures — like Maurice Hutton, Stephen Leacock, and Andrew Macphail — who saw themselves as men of general culture and members of an educated élite that included enlightened businessmen, clergymen, and politicians. They detested narrow specialization and recoiled against expertise that was purchased at the cost of dividing up humanistic studies. Shortt, on the other hand, with his stress on the scientifically trained expert and on scientific political economy, represented the beginnings of another tradition that was to be carried forward in economic history and in the tradition of state service of Queen's University.

2 | THE RISE OF LIBERTY

One of the most venerable themes in Canadian historical literature has been the steady growth of self-government. It preoccupied amateur writers and politicians alike in the Victorian age, and in the decade after the First World War it was regarded by a group of historians as the single most significant development in the entire Canadian past. Conscious that the long process by which Canada gained self-government had come to a climax with the acquisition of Dominion status during the First World War, Wrong, Chester Martin, W.P.M. Kennedy, W.S. Wallace and others determined to chronicle the patterns of Canadian constitutional development. In so doing they attributed to the principle of responsible government an importance that far transcended Canadian circumstance. 'The real significance of Canadian history', wrote one of them, 'lies in the fact that, in the evolution of that new and unprecedented phenomenon, the British Commonwealth of Nations, Canada has played a leading part. It was in Canada that responsible government ... was first worked out in the colonial sphere; and it was here that the forces of colonial nationalism first found free play within the circle of the Empire. The American Revolution disrupted the Old British Empire; the Canadian Revolution—if one may apply that term to the long, gradual, and peaceful process whereby Canada had achieved self-government—has, far from disrupting the New British Empire of to-day, probably strengthened the ties which bind it together.'[1]

Historians of Canada's rise from colonial subordination to a position of constitutional equality with Great Britain were in general agreement about the essential outlines of the past. They were concerned above all with the conflicts in the early nineteenth century between the elected assemblies and the nominated councils. The issue was joined when reform groups demanded control over the purse and local affairs and it culminated in the rebellions of 1837 and the mission of Lord Durham. Durham's *Report* was invariably extolled as one of the most farsighted policy statements in imperial history because its author saw that Canadian self-government and nationality could be reconciled with the maintenance of the imperial tie.[2] While Durham recognized the need for the Governor's advisors to have the confidence of the majority in the assembly, he also recommended that control over matters relating to land, immigration, currency and foreign relations remain exclusively under imperial jurisdiction. The historians of self-government, however, reserved most of their attention for the governorships of Sydenham, Bagot, Metcalfe, and Elgin. The resolution of the struggle for responsible government was climaxed by the formation of the Baldwin-Lafontaine ministry in 1848 and by Lord Elgin's signing of the Rebellion Losses Bill the next year.

Responsible government became a working principle of colonial politics in 1849, but it proved impossible to limit the matters over which the colonies exercised control. Canada asserted the right to make its own tariffs in 1859; the office of Governor-General was gradually transformed from that of an imperial official to a symbolic head of state; the power of the British Parliament to disallow Canadian legislation fell into disuse; and Canadian control over its own military and naval policy was acknowledged. The most dramatic advances towards autonomy were made during the First World War, when Canada was represented in the Imperial War Cabinet and Resolution IX of the Imperial War Conference of 1917 declared the Dominion to be an autonomous nation. Canada signed the peace treaties in its own right and was admitted to the League of Nations. The report of the Imperial Conference of 1926 described Canada as one of the 'autonomous Communities within the British Empire, equal in status, in no way subordinate one to another in any respect of their domestic or external affairs, though united by a common allegiance to the Crown, and fully associated as members of the British Commonwealth of Nations.' By 1931, when the Statute of Westminster formalized this doctrine of Dominion status, the theme of the evolution of self-government in Canada had been more fully investigated and documented than any other single aspect of its history.

The historical literature of this period, which treated the Canadian experience as the enlargement of freedom, assumed a teleological cast. It presented an advance that was a desirable consummation of past developments and prepared the country for a special role in the world. The whole process of Canada's constitutional evolution, however, was open-ended and ambiguous. It satisfied the hopes of imperialists like Wrong and Martin, who looked forward to the expansion of Canadian self-government within a co-operative imperial partnership; it also buttressed the views of those like John Ewart and O.D. Skelton who desired that Canada should assume full sovereignty in isolation from the Empire. In this sense the constitutional history of Canada written in the 1920s perpetuated an old quarrel between Canadians over the alignment of their country in international affairs.

I

The development of self-government in Canada was invariably described as slow, continuous, and analogous to the processes of organic evolution. While this feature was highlighted in nearly all the literature on the theme, it was perhaps best exemplified in *Empire and Commonwealth: Studies in Governance and Self-Government* (1929) by Chester Martin. Its value, however, lay less in Martin's conception of the subject than in the wealth of documentation and the feeling for the complexity and mystery of political history that he brought to his writing.

Martin was a representative member of the second generation of professionally trained historians who began to exploit the holdings of the Archives in the twenties, and he shared the imperial sympathies of most others who wrote on responsible government. Born in King's County, N.S., in 1882, he attended the University of New Brunswick and was awarded the first Rhodes Scholarship given in North America in 1904. He studied at Balliol, where the influence of Bishop Stubbs was still strong, and worked for two years on the staff of the Public Archives, an experience that whetted his appetite for research in original sources. He established the Department of History at the University of Manitoba in 1909 and taught there until 1929, when he went to Toronto as Wrong's successor.[3]

Martin was exceptionally sensitive to the unpredictability of history and to the ultimate impenetrability of human motives: he was fond of the dictum that history was the record of the contingent and the unforeseen. A somewhat aloof and detached person, he strove to be impartial and fair—often finding, as he quaintly put it, that the tragedy of history lay in right pitted against right. There was a definite propriety about his characterization of men and his reading of their purposes. He recognized, for example, that the politics of responsible government had been tied to demands for patronage and place, but he made little of this. He knew of Joseph Howe's more earthy antics but thought that the biographer should pass over such behaviour with a 'seemly reticence'. Suspicious of any deterministic or theoretical approach to the past, Martin was critical of attempts to present the attainment of self-government as the outcome of conflicts between 'nationalism', 'imperialism', or 'colonialism'.

Like most of his Canadian contemporaries, Martin was obligated to imperial historians in England and the United States. British interest in the history of the Empire had been stimulated by the imperial revival at the turn of the century and led to the establishment of the Institute for Imperial Studies at the University of London in 1912. Hugh Egerton and Reginald Coupland at Oxford, A.P. Newton at London, and Sir Charles P. Lucas, an official in the Dominions Department of the Colonial Office, were all favourably disposed to imperial unity and critical of efforts to treat the history of any component part of the Empire as a self-contained unit. William Grant (the son of G.M. Grant), who occupied the Beit chair of colonial history at Oxford from 1904 until 1910, when he returned to Queen's, insisted that Canadian history could be taught only in conjunction with the histories of Britain, France, and the United States.[4] In the realm of American colonial history a group of historians in the United States laid the groundwork for a radical reinterpretation in the first decade of the century. Herbert L. Osgood, George Louis Beer, and later Charles M. Andrews rejected the notion that the American Revolution was the inexorable and logical consequence of colonial history. More sympathetic to Britain than their nationalist predecessors, and determined to set early American history in the framework of the Empire as a whole, they struck a balanced assessment of the advantages and drawbacks of the early imperial system. Though critical of British leadership for its inability to comprehend conditions in the Thirteen Colonies, these Americans came to see the violent rupture of 1776 as the result of an unreasonable resistance to legitimate demands for political equality. To them the chief causes of the Revolution were constitutional, and, to a lesser extent, social. The breakup of the Empire, ran the implication, was neither inevitable nor unavoidable. This general conclusion carried important implications for students of Canadian history.[5]

Martin began his account of the 'transition from governance to self-government in North America' where the American historians had left off and with their general observations prominent in his mind. Like them, he believed that had the British been willing to loosen imperial control after the Seven Years' War, the struggles between elected assemblies and imperial officialdom would never have led to rebellion. The reflections that occurred to a Canadian on looking back on the American Revolution, he wrote, were apt to differ from those of an Englishman who viewed it with a certain fatalism, or of an American who saw it as the beginning of national greatness. A Canadian saw the break-up of the first British Empire in the light of his own country's experience in achieving responsible government, which was the historical solution to the 'American question'. There was therefore nothing inevitable about the Revolution, for in those colonies that remained outside the Republic and later formed the Dominion of Canada the same conflicts between elected assemblies and governors and appointed councils were to be repeated and resolved in a quite different way. This would have happened, Martin was later to insist, even if the British provinces had been towed out into the middle of the Pacific Ocean after the American Revolution.[6]

This belief—that the American Revolution was not inescapable and that understanding on the part of the British might have saved the first Empire in the New World—was the basis upon which Martin examined Canadian constitutional evolution. He insisted that the history of the second British Empire in its first fifty years was scarcely distinguishable from that of the first, and in his account of self-government in the Canadas and Nova Scotia he sought to answer the question of why the outcome had been different. 'The second Empire', Martin explained, 'was saved at last by wiser counsels and better men. It was not saved without a conflict, but the conflict was parliamentary not military, and the victors were to be found on both sides of the Atlantic.' The most remarkable aspect of Martin's analysis of the background to the winning of responsible government was his complete neglect of the rebellions in Upper and Lower Canada and of such radical figures as Mackenzie and Papineau. The rebellions appeared to him as unfortunate aberrations in an otherwise steady evolutionary pattern: the heroes of his history were the moderate reformers—Howe, Baldwin, and Lafontaine—and Lord Elgin, whom he called 'the most prophetic figure of the Commonwealth'. Responsible government was won by men who spurned theories and placed their confidence in the accommodations of politics and experience. The success of the reformers in Nova Scotia was aided by the spirit of moderation and a sense of magnanimity, but even in the Canadas, where the constitutional conflicts were embittered by racial antagonisms, men of moderation who worked for short-range goals won out in the end. Throughout his account Martin noted that responsible government depended on bi-racial co-operation and that it was won by party. It was attained 'not by spectacular feats of advocacy . . . but by the inexorable discipline of political parties upon the floors of the provincial assemblies.' *Empire and Commonwealth* was a celebration of the British parliamentary tradition and of principled men who employed empirical methods and a day-to-day opportunism, who had their minds fixed on immediate issues, and who disdained to design the future.[7]

Martin's book was also a commemoration of gradual change and political stability. 'Responsible government was now implanted in Canadian soil,' he wrote of the transactions of 1849, 'and its future was to depend upon its own organic growth.' As it was impossible to define the precise scope and limits of responsible government, Canadians—regardless of political persuasion—extended their control over additional powers. They took the pragmatic Baldwin-Lafontaine approach, undisturbed by constitutional anomalies and uninterested in venting political ideologies.

They understood the wisdom that the 'formulae of jurists have been powerless to circumscribe the accommodations of statesmen.' The long development from the appearance of the 'American question' to responsible government and the acquisition of Dominion status 'had all the steady growth and adaptability of the slow processes of nature.'[8] And in this unforeseen, cumulative, and uninterrupted sequence Martin located the key to political stability. 'It has seldom been necessary', he wrote in another connection ' . . . to appeal to political theories, to natural rights or the rights of man. Our statutes, concerned as they are with dry details of administrative law, reach no lofty height of declaration or political philosophy like the Declaration of Independence or the Declaration of the Rights of Man.' But 'the lowly paths of practice, while affording little vision of the distant scene, do afford a very good view indeed sometimes of the next step. The instability of a political theory as the basis of a state may be increased by its very loftiness.'[9] The evolution of self-government, and the parliamentary tradition with which it was identified, was like the growth of an oak: steady, slow, natural.

Out of a welter of circumstances, conflicting wills, and a multiplicity of motives and purposes had emerged a portentous development of enormous significance to Canada and the Empire. To Martin there was an unfathomable mystery and inscrutability about the phenomenon of responsible government. When he wrote of colonial politics he paraphrased or quoted the words the colonial politicans used, but when he came to describe the significance of responsible government he employed the language of late-Victorian idealism. Like Wrong and some other historians of the theme, Martin believed that the basis of the new Commonwealth was 'moral unity', a 'communion of the spirit'. Responsible government meant more than the negative breakdown of imperial control. It made possible the positive growth of mutual confidence and the recognition of powerful ties, not only those of blood and shared institutions but also of ideals of freedom and justice. Some time before, in 1916, Martin had referred obliquely to Herbert Spencer's principles of change from an indefinite homogeneity to a definite heterogeneity and asked whether in this precept one might find 'a kind of philosophical basis for the success of diversity in the British Empire'. 'It is', Martin wrote, 'the diversity of freedom which produces the unity of ideal.'[10] Martin's 'prophets' of the Commonwealth, Burke and Elgin, had understood this; the politicians who lost the first British Empire had not. Martin's *Empire and Commonwealth* was an extended demonstration of the wisdom of Burke's speech on the conciliation of the colonies. It was also one of the last echoes of high-Victorian philosophical idealism.

In Martin's work the patterns of constitutional evolution transcended regional and racial divisions. He paid much attention to the attainment of responsible government in Nova Scotia in 1848 and believed that the union of the Maritime colonies before general British North American federation would have ensured a more equal balance between provinces. Some of his earliest writings were on Manitoba politics and on Lord Selkirk as an empire-builder. He wrote at a time of great resentment in the West against national policies, and he drew a direct parallel between the prairie provinces in the twenties and the Canadian colonies a century before. He claimed that, with the transfer of the Northwest Territories from the Hudson's Bay Company to Canada in 1869, Canada itself was transformed 'from a Confederation of equal provinces into a miniature Empire, with a vast domain of subordinate colonial territory under its control. The spirit in which Canada then proceeded to deal with this new subordinate territory affords a curious parallel to British colonial policy at that time . . . . ' Thanks to the resistance of Riel, Manitoba entered Confederation as a province, but the remainder of the territories were to be directly governed and administered by Ottawa. The steps by which the territories passed from primitive colonial status under a Governor in Council to responsible government in 1897, and then to provincial status in 1905, were similar to the stages 'through which the central provinces had passed in the old colonial system from the *Quebec Act* to Confederation.'[11] In the 1920s, however, Manitoba, Saskatchewan, and Alberta were in a sense still colonies rather than provinces of the Dominion because the public lands were administered by the Government of Canada for the purposes of the Dominion. Martin was sympathetic to the claims of the western provinces for control of natural resources and in 1920 he published *'The Natural Resources Question': The Historic Basis of Provincial Claims*, a study commissioned by the Manitoba government, in which he documented the provincial case. When in 1930 public lands and other resources were turned over to the provinces, it seemed that Confederation had finally been completed. The three prairie provinces were now in a position of equality with the other provinces, and there seemed to be an almost providential coincidence—as in other events examined by Martin—between the symbolic end of Canada's imperial control of the west and the Statute of Westminster, which formally recognized the equality of the Dominions.

II

The set of assumptions about 'nationality', 'sovereignty', and self-government that underlay Martin's work were shaped by the pre-war imperial tradition and internationalist thought in the twenties. Canadian imperialists believed that the extension of Canadian self-government was entirely consistent with the preservation of imperial unity. They thought of Canada as a distinctive entity united to the larger Britannic community by ethnic ties, historical traditions, and common institutions and interests. From within the framework of the imperial tradition, Canada's contribution to the First World War, and its simultaneous acquisition of 'autonomy' and international recognition, seemed like the fulfilment of all its history. While Canada had entered the conflict as a colony, Wrong was convinced that in the later stages of the war it participated as a principal power, not a subordinate helper.[12] Like John Dafoe and Sir Robert Borden, the wartime Prime Minister, he believed that Canada, Britain, and (after 1917) the United States were fighting as partners to maintain moral values, the rule of law, and the principles of representative government. Wartime co-operation confirmed the reality and strength of the moral and spiritual unity of the Empire, and, indeed, of the English-speaking peoples. There remained, of course, the problem of building on this community of interest a co-operative foreign policy. But so striking was the bedrock of unity revealed in the war that formal constitutional reconstructions seemed to pale into insignificance. 'If only constitution mongerers will leave us alone', said William Grant in 1923, 'and let ties of common sympathy develop suitable machinery for co-operation, our descendants will one day look on rejoicing while the last disciple of M. Bourassa is hanged in the entrails of the last disciple of Mr. Lionel Curtis. Partnership necessarily implies neither dependence nor independence, but inter-dependence.'[13]

Internationalist convictions about Canada's foreign relations that were present in a rudimentary form in imperialist thought were immensely strengthened in the decade following the war. Canadians who had been associated with the Round Table groups became supporters of the League of Nations and their names were prominent on the membership rolls of the League of Nations Society in Canada. Founded in 1921, devoted to general public education in international affairs, and possessing a membership of over 5,000 in 1924,[14] the Society was in some respects a successor to a long line of imperial organizations. Among its most dedicated members it counted Sir Robert Borden; Newton W. Rowell, corporation lawyer and former leader of the Ontario Liberal party; and historians like Grant, Wrong, Martin, F.H. Soward of the University of British Columbia, and A.L. Burt of the University of Alberta. All of them would have agreed with Rowell's assertion that 'Two of the outstanding lessons of modern history are that the Nation-State is no longer an adequate form of political organization to meet the needs of human society, and that force is no longer a sane or practical method of permanently settling disputes between nations.'[15] And all of them drew a compelling parallel between Canadian historical experience and the needs of the modern world. Responsible government within the Commonwealth, a Canadian invention, was the key to reconciling nationhood and continuing membership in a supra-national organization. The great need of the League of Nations was to harmonize national sovereignty and international responsibilities. The Commonwealth was already a 'microcosm' of the League in this respect. For the Canadian internationalists Canada's historic part in transforming the Empire and its membership in the League of Nations were more than matters of status. These complementary roles were the grand and fitting outcome of its whole development.

Canada's experience implied, moreover, that it could not resign the responsibilities its new status entailed. Sir Robert Borden cautioned Canadians to remember 'that each nation stands at the threshold of every other, that all frontiers touch one another throughout the world, that there can be no hermit nation and no hermit continent.' 'If the League of the Commonwealth may not endure,' he asked, 'how is it possible that the League of Nations can survive . . . ? The League of the Commonwealth may serve as an exemplar to the League of Nations.'[16] Chester Martin concurred. He believed that the growth of self-conscious nationhood in the Dominions, their association in the Commonwealth, and their broader association in the League of Nations were cumulative, not competitive, processes. 'A deliberate policy of disassociation or isolation would be a departure from historic traditions . . . .'[17]

The most detailed explanation for the theory of sovereignty that buttressed this prescription was made by W.P.M. Kennedy, a constitutional and legal historian at the University of Toronto. Of Irish birth, educated at Trinity College, Dublin, and at Paris, Berlin, and Vienna, the mercurial and unpredictable Kennedy brought to the study of the Canadian constitution a training in religious and ecclesiastical history and a suspicion of extreme doctrines of national self-determination. He was sceptical of postwar efforts to redraw the map of Europe so as to reflect the claims to political nationhood of all groups possessing sufficient cohesiveness to be regarded as nationalities. Doubting not only the practicality of applying such a doctrine to a continent having an estimated sixty-eight nationalities, Kennedy in addition charged that modern nationalism and the striving for absolute sovereignty was a retrogressive and dangerous force.

Just as the liberal ideals of national self-determination identified with President Wilson descended from John Stuart Mill, Kennedy and the other critics of nationalism resurrected the ideas of Mill's critic, Lord Acton. Acton rejected the belief that all national groups necessarily had a right to complete self-determination on the broad ground that individual liberty and tolerance were more securely maintained in multi-national states like Austria-Hungary and the British Empire than in ethnically homogeneous political units. Kennedy took his chief contention directly from Acton when he wrote in 1921 that to 'identify the nation and the state is to make nationalism the basis of the state; and, when this is done, nationalism takes the place of those universal principles of justice and humanity on which the ideal state should be founded.' There was room within a state for more than one variety of national feeling, and in fact 'a state which is nationally homogeneous is perhaps in a less fortunate position than a state which contains two or more homogeneous national elements. The nation which coincides with the state is too liable to become intolerant, . . . ; but the state in which there is a variety of national feeling is forced to learn in the school of experience lessons which will prove useful in world issues.' A multinational state, moreover, 'will have the advantage of healthy rivalries among its component national types, and may be the means of creating a higher national feeling—a super-nationalism . . . in which toleration will be the essential feature—that high type of nationalism which is found in the "common spirit" of the British Empire . . . '[18] Robert Borden added: 'That every race should clothe itself in the garment of self-determination is in theory wholly unwise and in practice wholly unworkable . . . human progress is not advanced by the segregation of races, or by any influence which tends to perpetuate racial antagonisms. Lord Acton had pointed out that the true ideal lies in the union of different races in one state, to the service of which each brings its own peculiar qualities.'[19]

Kennedy's rejection of the Wilsonian ideal of national self-determination was further extended to a condemnation of theories of absolute sovereignty. His influential survey, *The Constitution of Canada: An Introduction to its Development and Law* (1922), which was consulted when the constitution of the Irish Free State was being drafted and provided a generation of Canadian students with a convenient text of their country's history, was an 'evolutionary account' of the rise of self-government that stressed the bankruptcy of the Austinian conception of absolute and indivisible sovereignty. Kennedy believed that the legal notion of absolute sovereignty was illusory and pernicious and that it was of major interest that Canada had groped its way towards an understanding of a relative autonomy that was more appropriate in the modern world. Responsible government had destroyed the belief that the sovereignty of the Crown could not be divided, or, in Lord John Russell's terms, that a governor had to be responsible either to the local assembly or to the British Parliament. Canada in Kennedy's day had attained a real and vital independence, but its actual status was limited both by the conditions of international life and by certain residual constraints from its colonial past. Kennedy recognized that Canada had a distinct social, economic, and political group life that determined its recognition as a state. It also possessed ties of interest, sentiment, and values with the Empire. Kennedy believed that on this basis the British Empire would remain a unity and the aspirations of its member nations for autonomy would find complete expression. 'In fact', he wrote, 'it is the insistence of the older doctrine of sovereignty, one exclusive and indivisible, which is the great stumbling block in the way of the evolution of the greater unities which political exigencies, as distinct from political dogma, require to-day.' Canada had pioneered in an experiment in sovereignty that was of immediate value to the League of Nations. The League would become an effective force 'only if the conception of the exclusive state, discredited by the facts of interdependence, is abandoned also in the practice of statesmanship. In the last resort absolute power is a mystic doctrine which has relevance neither to men nor to states. Instead of absolute sovereignty, . . . we must be content with the reality of relative autonomy, which alone provides . . . the condition of effective liberty and sane relationships.'[20]

Kennedy's contentions were addressed directly to the program of John Ewart. An Ottawa lawyer, Ewart was the author of over sixty pamphlets, which appeared between 1908 and 1932, and of an unpublished thirteen-volume constitutional history of Canada. He also envisaged Canadian history as a progressive growth from colonial status to full self-government, but he argued that Canada must declare its complete equality with Great Britain and remain linked to her only by a common monarch. He desired a forthright declaration of independence and equality that would once and forever sweep away all residual anomalies and thereby focus the dispersed loyalties of the Canadian peoples. To Chester Martin, Ewart misunderstood the pragmatic, non-theoretical nature of Canada's constitutional growth; to Kennedy he was a victim of an outmoded absolutist theory of sovereignty.[21] Even worse, both Ewart's pamphlets and his *Roots and Causes of the Wars (1914-1918)* (1925) were clearly isolationist. Ewart, on the other hand, saw the internationalism of his critics as spurious, nothing but the old ethnocentric imperialism in disguise.[22]

The co-existence of the two main ethnic groups within Canada, as well as the country's relationship with other states, was regarded by supporters of the League of Nations as a working model of internationalism. In a survey of the growth of Canadian national feeling, W.S. Wallace, the first editor of the *Canadian Historical Review*, recognized that the sense of nationality rested on a geographical separateness, the rejection of the American Revolution, and the legacies of the War of 1812, and that it had expressed itself in the struggle for responsible government and autonomy. His chief contention, however, was that there were two nationalisms in Canada, 'an English Canadian and a French Canadian one', and he endorsed Cartier's ideal of a political nationality in which distinctions of race would be accepted and recognized rather than treated as obstacles and ground down. Canadian national feeling could never be monolithic and homogeneous for it contained two subordinate forms of nationality. These two groups not only existed within a single state but shared a wider loyalty to a 'common fatherland, a common history'.[23] Canada's nationality was therefore a species of supra-nationalism, a small version of both the Commonwealth, and, hopefully, the League.

Wallace, Kennedy, and Martin were alert to the implications for Canada of the liberal doctrine of national self-determination carried to its logical conclusions. Once such a doctrine was conceded there was no basis on which to resist either the complete and total separation of Canada from the Commonwealth or the secession of Quebec from Canada itself. Writing at a time when the wartime division over the conscription issue had hardly healed, and when French-Canadian nationalists like Abbé Groulx were invoking a separate Laurentian state, the chroniclers of the rise of self-government in Canada made much of the fact that French-Canadian leadership had played an indispensable part, not only in the attainment of responsible government but in its subsequent advances. Despite their differences, French and English Canadians shared a common history in this effort and achievement.

Projecting these concerns even further back into Canadian history, they saw the years immediately following the Conquest as especially instructive. For it was in the 1760s and 1770s that the distinct group life of French Canada was recognized and acknowledged. A.L. Burt—a former Rhodes Scholar, the author of a sympathetic study of plans proposed for closer imperial union, and another Round Tabler who became an energetic exponent of the League of Nations after the war—conceived the idea of a scholarly examination of the origins of Canada's dual nationality in 1923. *The Old Province of Quebec*, which appeared ten years later, dealt in large part with the chief problem that the Conquest had presented for the first time in imperial history: the issue of incorporating a non-British people into the British Empire. With meticulous scholarship Burt reconstructed the period of military rule that laid the basis of trust and understanding between the two peoples and explored the background to the Quebec Act of 1774. These years, he wrote, constituted 'a watershed in the history of the British Empire, for the French in Canada were the first considerable body of an alien race to taste that liberty which is larger than English liberty and is the secret of the modern British commonwealth of nations.' The recognition and preservation of the basic institutions of French-Canadian life may have been connected with attempts to contain the expansion of the thirteen colonies, but a principle had been established all the same. The Quebec Act 'embodied a new sovereign principle of the British Empire: the liberty of non-English peoples to be themselves.'[24] The recognition of the political equality of a Catholic population, furthermore, took place in Canada many years before Catholic emancipation in Britain. History as the rise of liberty was also the history of freedom of conscience.

French-Canadian nationality was contained within the Canadian state, just as the 'supra-nationalism' of Canada itself was contained within the framework of the Commonwealth. The limitations on each were not imposed from the outside but arose in both cases from shared experiences and a dedication to preserve existing freedoms.

III

For reasons that are readily understandable there was a tendency for Canadian historians to exaggerate the progressiveness of Canada's contribution to responsible government and either to downplay or to criticize the record of British statesmanship. In his *British Supremacy and Canadian Self-Government, 1839-1854* (1919) the British historian J.L. Morrison repeatedly drew attention to the crudities of colonial culture and made no special claims for the prescience of Canadian politicians. Chester Martin treated responsible government as a joint product of individuals and forces on both sides of the Atlantic. But both Borden and Wrong were emphatic about claiming a pre-eminent place for Canada in the development of the Empire and tended to disparage British leadership and public opinion.

In a series of lectures delivered at the University of Toronto in 1921, Borden surveyed Canadian self-government and argued that Canada had not merely followed British practice but had in fact been far in advance of it. He especially disapproved of the Colonial Secretaries—like Lords Russell and Stanley in the 1830s and 1840s—who believed local responsible government inadmissible and sought to maintain the position of the Colonial Office as the controlling influence in Canada. They were, he contended, 'insular in spirit' and appealed to a Commons that was 'an audience of imperfect comprehension and limited vision.' A 'bureaucracy not familiar at first hand with conditions in the Colony and often unsympathetic with the aspirations of its inhabitants', he said of the Colonial Office at that time, 'could hardly avoid narrow views and mischievous policies.' Borden charged English statesmen of the past with a 'lack of vision' for not appreciating that it was only through responsible government and autonomy that the Empire would be preserved, and he wondered whether this outlook had ever really disappeared.

Declarations to the effect that Canada was an autonomous Dominion, he asserted, would lead nowhere if the self-governing Dominions were not given adequate voice and influence over the Empire's foreign policy. The situation in 1921, however, was similar to that existing in the 1830s:

> In the Foreign Office men of the highest distinction and ability have found their careers; from that Office have gone forth Ambassadors and Ministers to posts of great responsibility; it had behind it the splendid traditions of many centuries during which there was no over-

sea nation to claim unaccustomed rights. It was not unnatural that in such an atmosphere the spirit of Lord Stanley should linger . . . . While it is true that the Dominions were represented at Paris, that they took their place at the Peace Conference, and that they became signatories of the Peace Treaty, I have yet to learn that since the conclusion of peace their right to 'an adequate voice in foreign policy and in foreign relations' has been recognized in any effective or practical way.[25]

When C.P. Lucas chided Borden for depicting 'the development of Canada from a dependency to a nation as something which was wrung by clear-sighted, freedom-loving Canadians from purblind politicians in a repressive Mother Country', the former Prime Minister made a few concessions but reiterated that British politicians generally had not understood that the Empire could be held together only if its colonists were accorded all the rights of British subjects. They were misled by the illusion that self-government would be followed by separation: it was Canadians who had changed the Empire.[26] Little wonder that John Dafoe, who had many discussions about foreign policy with Borden in Paris and London, was left bewildered about whether 'he's a Grit in disguise or I'm a Tory.'[27]

While Borden's views were informed by his experience in wartime collaboration and conflict and expressed his disappointment with the failures of genuine consultative diplomacy, George Wrong arrived at a similar unfavourable reading of British attitudes out of a restlessness with the indefiniteness of Canada's status in the early twenties. The Chanak affair of 1922, when Canadian military support was requested to aid the Empire on the Dardanelles, proved to Wrong that whatever Canadians might think of their country's newly acquired status, its actual status and the prospects for a co-operative imperial foreign policy ultimately depended on whether the British fully accepted the implications of what Canadians believed had been done during the war. It was perhaps understandable that a people who had for generations managed an Empire should continue to speak of allowing Canada to do this and that, to persist in talking of the Empire in a possessive way, and to treat the residents of the Dominions as colonials. Such an attitude may be explicable, Wrong believed, but it was completely out of keeping with the outlooks of the emergent national states in the Empire. The corrective to such misconceptions, he wrote in 1925 with considerable impatience, 'is that the people of England should learn to imagine what they would think if Canada spoke of England's position in the Empire as they spoke of Canada's. Failure to exercise such imagination was a primary cause of the American Revolution.'[28] He later added that the only way to disabuse the English of outdated prejudices was for Canada to make a forthright declaration of equality as Ewart had advocated. This might begin, he suggested, by changing its title from Dominion to the

Kingdom of Canada 'and in that imply full equality of status with Great Britain.'[29] The Parliament of Canada had over Canada the same authority that the Parliament of Great Britain had over the people of Great Britain and this included, of course, the power to amend its own constitution, the end of imperial disallowance of legislation, and the reception of representatives of foreign countries. 'When Canada speaks of equality and of making her own treaties,' he explained, 'imagination is needed to realise what this involves . . . . We shall not hear of Great Britain permitting Canada to do something any more than we hear of Canada permitting Great Britain to do anything. If there is equality, it is as just to speak of Canada's declaration of war committing Great Britain as it is to hear of Great Britain's declaration committing Canada.'[30] If the full impact of equality was truly assimilated, then it would not seem far-fetched to see that in a war Canada might remain neutral, that its ports would be open to ships of Britain's enemies, and that Canadians in Britain would become foreigners. Canada was not a European state and should not be expected to assume the military obligations of one; its liabilities for defence had necessarily to be confined to the protection of its own interests. There was simply no other way to have the real psychological meaning of Canada's equality with Britain recognized than to go this far—and it was far indeed for someone who thought within the perimeters of Canadian imperialism.

One of Wrong's last extended pronouncements on the imperial question was his *Canada and the American Revolution: The Disruption of the First British Empire*, which was published in 1935. It was anachronistic and derivative as a piece of historical scholarship, but its central argument was consistent with his thinking about Canada's place in the Empire throughout the twenties. He drew explicit parallels between the American colonies on the eve of the Revolution and the position of Canada in the post-war period. Wrong did not blame the American colonists for resorting to rebellion, for he understood from his own feelings about Canada's position some of the impatience they felt in the 1770s. 'The American Revolution', he wrote, 'was not due to a single problem of taxation, nor to restrictions on trade, nor to grievances that involved real hardship, but to something behind each particular dispute. The era of colonial beginnings was over; foundations had been well and truly laid; and now the teeming life of a new world that had become self-reliant required complete freedom to shape its own destiny.' This desire for equality was frustrated by British leadership. The basic cause of the Revolution and the break-up of the first empire was the incapacity of the British to accept the American colonists as equals or, more precisely, as social equals. 'Society in London would hardly understand colonial conditions in which leaders who had hewn down trees and built their houses with their own hands claimed social equality with the highest.' The products of a rigid caste system that 'had long dominated and lived on the labour of the masses', the English aristocracy could not but see the colonies as 'outer planets deriving what light they had from the central sun'. Their failure was a failure of imaginative understanding that precluded them from fully grasping and completely accepting the equality of people in the colonies. They resorted to coercion; the colonists to revolution. 'A better way was found later in the second British Empire', Wrong pronounced, 'with the result that communities overseas many times more populous than the thirteen English colonies are now both completely free and also remain linked with the motherland . . . . '[31]

To Wrong, as to Martin, Canada's development confirmed that the Revolution was not inevitable. 'The position of Canada to-day shows that the ruin of the first British Empire was not necessary. Canada's ten million people . . . form a nation as complete in its liberties as all the people of Great Britain and the United States. While anomalies still exist in the great British commonwealth, containing half a dozen nations, the tie of allegiance to the crown and of mutual confidence holds them together . . . . Clearly time might have brought in the first empire what it has brought to Canada.' In breaking with the past the United States had paid a heavy price, both in its 'gravely defective' and rigid constitutional system and in the tradition of isolation that prevented it from playing a more positive role in the world.[32]

Wrong's was a double-edged case. He expressed a commonplace view that Canadian history confirmed that national equality was attainable within the Empire without a violent rupture of tradition. But he also emphasized repeatedly that it was the inability or unwillingness of the British to grasp and accept the full equality of colonials that had finally driven the Americans to revolt. Wrong was finally convinced that the sense of superiority and insularity of British opinion prevented the genuine acceptance of the new status of Canada. As he told Adam Shortt in 1923, the average Briton's attitude to the 'colonies' had not changed very much since the 1770s.[33] This was why Wrong, like Dafoe and others, insisted that the equality of Britain and Canada had to be announced in such forthright terms that there could no longer be any possibility of misunderstanding.

IV

Few historians were privileged both to interpret the past and to apply its lessons directly to the formulation of contemporary policy. O.D. Skelton's exposition of the patterns and implications of the development of Canadian self-government underlay his definition of the aims of Canadian foreign policy while he was Under-Secretary of State for External Affairs from 1925 until his death in 1941. The conclusions he drew from the familiar theme differed radically from the convictions of Borden, Wrong, and Martin, and these arose in part from his rather different set of allegiances.

Skelton was born in Orangeville, Ont., in 1878, and grew up in a family that was Presbyterian and Conservative. He was educated at Queen's University, where he concentrated on English literature, Latin, and Greek, and at the University of Chicago, which he entered as a graduate student in 1900 to study classics. He withdrew after one term, however. He went to England, sold stereopticon photographs there, and wrote examinations for the Home, Indian and Colonial Service. He stood well down on the list of competitors and was finally rejected because of poor eyesight. From 1901 to 1905 he was assistant editor of a literary journal, *The Booklover's Magazine*, that was published in Philadelphia. When the magazine passed into new ownership, Skelton was left without a job. After applying unsuccessfully for fellowships at Columbia and Harvard, he returned to Chicago to study political science.

At Chicago Skelton was attracted to R.F. Hoxie, a pioneer student of labour and socialism, and took courses from Thorstein Veblen ('he never seems to have made an unqualified statement in his life')[34] and the political scientist Charles Merriam. Theoretical economics and the sociology of Albion Small, however, left him cold. Skelton was more interested in contemporary social and economic issues. 'Strikes, trusts, taxes, socialism, tariffs, [and] banking', he told Adam Shortt, 'bulk a good deal larger in the public mind than the authenticity of John's gospel or the wherefore of the shyness of Hegel.'[35] He returned to Queen's in 1907 and a year later succeeded Shortt as Sir John A. Macdonald Professor of Political and Economic Science.

Skelton's commitment to the political economy of liberalism was in direct line with Shortt's convictions and was most clearly stated in the published version of his doctoral dissertation, *Socialism: A Critical Appraisal* (1911). The English-guild socialist G.D.H. Cole judged the book to be one of the most penetrating critiques of the faith ever written, and Lenin was said to have thought so highly of it that a copy was placed in his tomb in Moscow. Skelton's rejection of socialism was the negative side of his belief in the primacy of self-interest and individual initiative, of private property and open competition, as the sources of economic and social progress. He stressed the multiplicity of motives behind human actions—including, in addition to the simple materialist desire for wealth, Veblen's instinct for workmanship and a desire for achievement. And, like Shortt, he thought that the state should regulate economic life, mediate between contending groups, and supplement the weak points of free enterprise by taking measures to protect powerless members of the community. A singular truth the socialists refused to accept, Skelton wrote, was that 'the greatest and most constructive good of the community is frequently merely a by-product of individual striving for name and fortune and a winning hand.'[36] Skelton's faith in liberalism and individualism, and his scepticism about the capacity of any single group to grasp, let alone manage, the complex fabric of society, lay at the bottom of his numerous commentaries on contemporary problems in the pages of *Queen's Quarterly*. These convictions also informed his biography of the nineteenth-century businessman and politician Alexander Tilloch Galt, and his essay on Canadian economic history since 1867 in *Canada and its Provinces*. Skelton had been drawn into the orbit of the Liberal party in 1911 when he helped Mackenzie King prepare a case for reciprocity; shortly afterwards he was encouraged to write an official biography of Laurier. His two-volume *Life and Letters of Sir Wilfrid Laurier*, which appeared in 1921, was suffused with Skelton's respect for a man who he believed had been unfairly treated and misrepresented. Skelton not only explained Laurier's attitude to conscription sympathetically but charged that the Military Service Act of 1917 was meant to win an election more than the war. This was a line of argument immediately challenged by John Dafoe, one of the architects of the cause of the Union Government and a man who, according to Skelton, possessed a 'seemingly incurable prejudice against the French Canadians'.[37] It was probably Skelton's view of conscription that Wallace alluded to when he said that parts of the biography were 'positively poisonous'.[38]

Though Skelton acknowledged that Canadian national feeling in the later nineteenth century flowed in the channels of imperialism, he portrayed the British imperialism of Joseph Chamberlain as a calculating and relentless force, operating conspiratorially, and aimed at the subversion of Canadian self-government. Skelton shared none of the enthusiasm for empire. As early as 1902 he had told Shortt that

> Everytime I pick up a Canadian paper now and read the enthusiastically Britisher speeches or editorials or Board of Trade debates I wonder where I'm at and fainthearted fears trouble me that perhaps after all the ideal I've always cherished, Canadian independence, is fated to be only an ideal. However it's some consolation that it can't be any more impracticable than the policy of those who believe they can afford to neglect the U.S. as a factor in Canada's future, pile up tariff barriers & deepen national prejudices in a vain attempt to deflect the current of destiny, and who believe there can be any real or lasting common unity of interest between Canada and Australia or Timbuctoo, or whatever other part of the map a Jingostic spree may chance to paint red.[39]

He projected his own feelings into the Laurier biography, and his treatment of imperialism was coloured by a great distrust of British motives.

Skelton's animus towards imperialism and his admiration for Laurier's steadfast refusal to give way to the blandishments of the centralizers were also coloured by his democratic instincts. A shy and diffident person, Skelton abhorred ceremony and pomposity and had the democrat's suspicion of both the lofty ones of the earth and concentrations of power. Like Goldwin Smith, he thought of Europe as the sphere of privilege and feudal remnants and of North America as an egalitarian society and an experiment in democratic government. Though he was critical of the excesses of party politics in Canada, Skelton had an abiding faith in popular government and was incapable of the despairing editorializing of an Andrew Macphail or even the occasional pessimism of a George Wrong. Thus he repeated approvingly Laurier's complaints about the social pressures of country houses and duchesses on innocent Canadians in England.[40]

Skelton's Laurier was a Gladstonian liberal, devoted to preserving national unity, stemming imperialist schemes, and little interested in those economic and social problems that were intensified during his administration. The American historian Charles Beard, who was oblivious to the passions that Laurier's stands evoked for Canadians, thought the biography a 'plain, prosaic account of a plain, prosaic man', though he correctly wondered whether there were unsuspected depths to Laurier that were neglected in the book.[41]

Skelton also set himself apart from those historians more positively disposed to the continuing imperial relationship by his general emphasis on the economic bases of constitutional and imperial history. In some respects he shared Shortt's concern that the subject matter of history be expanded; he had, after all, been trained in political economy. In another sense, however, his insistence on the close connection between constitutional evolution and commercial policy was a measure both of his realism and of his intention to deflate the moralistic rhetoric of the nineteenth-century imperialists and their successors in the twenties. While men like Kennedy and Martin were hardly indifferent to the economic background of politics, it was never at the forefront of their analyses. More than any other Canadian writer on responsible government and autonomy up to that time, Skelton emphasized the relationship between constitutional change and shifts in economic policy and underlined the place of commercial policy in the extension of Canada's control over its own affairs. While this tendency was pronounced in his biographies of Galt and Laurier, it was most lucidly summarized in a short history of Canada written for an American readership, The Canadian Dominion: A Chronicle of Our Northern Neighbor (1919).

'The British Empire', Skelton wrote, 'had its beginnings in the initiative of private businessmen, not in any conscious state policy. Yet as the Empire grew the teachings of doctrinaires and the example of other colonial powers had developed a definite policy whereby the plantations overseas were to be made to serve the needs of the nation at home. The end of the empire was commercial profit; the means, the political subordination of the colonies; the debit entry, the cost of the military and naval and diplomatic services borne by the mother country.'[42] The cause of responsible government did not win its way merely by its own convincing logic, or by the prophetic character of its proponents. It was conceded as a reflex action once the preferential trading system ceased to serve British national interests. Once the colonies of British North America were no longer looked upon as economically indispensable, there was simply no point in maintaining complete political control or in paying for their defence.

Skelton regarded the period since Confederation not only as one in which Canada made progress in the direction of self-government, mainly in matters of trade and tariffs, but also as an era when its commercial and economic connections with the United States became more intimate and intricate. Then as now, he wrote, 'foreign relations meant first and foremost relations with her great neighbor to the south.'[43]

In a rather uncharacteristic concluding passage Skelton summed up the fulfilment of the evolution of Canadian self-government. He described the policy of imperial co-operation 'whereby each great colony became independent of outside control but voluntarily acted in concert with the mother country and the sister states on matters of common concern' as an effort to 'reconcile liberty and unity, nationhood and empire'. Canada believed that it had done its utmost to ensure the triumph of right in the war.

> Not less did she believe that she had a contribution to make toward that new ordering of the world after the war which alone could compensate her for the blood and treasures she had spent. It would be her mission to bind together in friendship and common aspirations the two larger English-speaking states, with one of which she was linked by history and with the other by geography. To the world in general Canada had to offer that achievement of difference in unity, that reconciliation of liberty with peace and order, which the British Empire was struggling to attain along the paths in which the Dominion had been the chief pioneer.[44]

This was as close as he ever came to affirming the main conclusions of most of the constitutional historians.

In his 1922 address on Canada and foreign policy to the Canadian Clubs of Toronto and Ottawa,[45] Skelton grappled with the problem of how Canada's newly won powers over external relations were to be employed. He rejected the idea that it was possible to formulate a common imperial policy through consultation on the model of wartime co-operation. He argued that foreign policy was an inseparable extension of domestic affairs

and that the foreign policy of most countries was concerned with economic and commercial matters. Where Canada was concerned, its most
significant external connections were commercial relations with the United
States; in this sphere its control over the making of treaties was most complete. History revealed a steady and inexorable tendency towards 'the control of foreign policy by Canada through the Canadian Parliament and the
Canadian Government', and Skelton saw no halting place in this process.
Though he disclaimed endorsing a position of isolation in terms of the Empire or the League, the clear implication in his analysis was to undermine
the other alternatives. Skelton not only depicted any effort to establish a
joint control over imperial foreign policy as a British design, thereby rele-
gating to oblivion the Canadian imperialist tradition, but pronounced all
such proposals as reversing 'the line on which the development of the British Empire and the development of Canadian self-government has
progressed'. As in the biography of Laurier, Skelton implicitly dismissed as
illegitimate the desire of Canadian imperialists for a consultative co-operative imperial foreign policy.[46]

Mackenzie King listened attentively to Skelton's address and duly noted
in his diary that the speaker had the right point of view and would make
an excellent man in the Department of External Affairs. Perhaps he also
recalled Skelton's laudatory review of King's *Industry and Humanity* in
1919, when he judged the book 'easily the most important contribution yet
made by any Canadian writer to the question of the organization of industry and particularly of the relations of capital and labor.'[47] In any case King
invited Skelton to help the Canadian government prepare for the Imperial
Conference of 1923, and two years later he became Under-Secretary of
State for External Affairs, a position which, when it had been first created,
Skelton had described as 'a mighty desirable billet for somebody'.[48] The
rest of Skelton's story belongs to the history of Canadian external policy.

V

There are few better examples in Canadian historical· literature of the
tendency to write history in order to shape the present and the future than
the works of the chroniclers of the rise of self-government. Canadian history as the progress of liberty became the central myth in both the political
discourse and the historiography of the twenties because of the implications it was held to contain for the immediate political problems of imperial relations. The evolution of freedom was central to the writing of Canadian history because of its very ambiguities and because it was amenable
to such divergent conclusions. Ewart and Skelton on the one side and Borden, Wrong, and Martin on the other agreed that Canada's future orienta-

tion would work itself out in terms of the preservation and extension of responsible government.

History as the record of self-government also underlined the pragmatic and evolutionary course of Canada's growth. The preservation of continuities, the respect for tradition, and the slow building of precedents upon established precedents moulded Canadian political culture and the country's national character. A progressive political tradition that ensured stability was described as a 'British' inheritance and carried social implications. When Wrong and Martin highlighted slow and organic change, conservation, and steadiness, they were reacting against the more impatient ideological claimants of their day—Ewart in constitutional matters and the labour radicals and middle-class reformers whose expectations for a new era were inspired by the heady millenialism of the war for democracy.

Just as nature worked in minute ways to fashion enormous changes, so too it seemed that, out of a confusion of circumstances, there had emerged in Canadian history a cumulative pattern of immense importance. The development of the constitution of Canada may have been singularly pragmatic and non-ideological, but those who contemplated its end product invested the whole process with a powerful idealism. While their histories dealt with a succession of statutes and official political transactions, they confirmed that the real underlying force in imperial unity lay in the moral and spiritual sphere. The most important ingredient of the new Commonwealth — Martin's 'communion of the spirit' — thus lay beyond conventional historical analysis and itself remained a matter of faith.

FRANK UNDERHILL: HISTORY AS POLITICAL CRITICISM

The desire for a national culture that would reflect the character of Canada in imaginative literature, art, and history became a master impulse in the intellectual life of the twenties, far stronger and more pervasive than similar stirrings in the later nineteenth century. The confident determination that Canadian cultural development must match the country's material growth and constitutional status manifested itself in a variety of ways: in the literary nationalism of the newly formed Canadian Authors' Association; in the founding of journals of discussion and the arts, such as the *Canadian Forum* (1920); and in the formation of nation-wide organizations such as the Canadian Historical Association (1922), the expansion of the Association of Canadian Clubs, and the revival of the Canadian Political Science Association.

For some young intellectuals the quest for authentically Canadian modes of expression necessarily involved a critical attitude to the past, and a sharper perception of the discrepancy between current requirements and inherited forms. In nearly every department of intellectual endeavour a youthful minority challenged the standards and sometimes disparaged the achievements of their elders. Frank Scott, a McGill professor of law and a poet, and other contributors to the short-lived *Canadian Mercury* (1928-9), proclaimed the need to emancipate Canadian literature from its lamentable state of 'amiable mediocrity'. The artist A.Y. Jackson denounced the tastes of those Montreal collectors who preferred imported pictures of cows, old women peeling potatoes, and windmills to faithful and unsentimental renderings of the landscape of their own country. Critics compiled a list of sins besetting Canadian society: imitativeness; romanticism; Victorianism, which was equated with prudery and sanctimoniousness; and puritanism, the synonym for a heartless business civilization and the repression of the natural appetites. On the more positive level they were inspired by the landscapes of the Group of Seven. These painters came to be regarded as the leading edge of a nationalistic Canadian expression because they had (or so it was thought) successfully broken with the dead hand of tradition, discarded Old World techniques, experienced the north country directly, and boldly conveyed its shapes and colours. The intellectual temper of the young was optimistic, impatient of the derivativeness of Canadian culture, and suffused with a determination to express the country in concepts appropriate to itself and in terms of its natural, material environment.

Frank Underhill was the chief representative among historians of the iconoclastic and debunking spirit of the twenties. His mind played upon the antithesis between the inherited and conventional ways of explaining the Canadian political tradition and the actualities of economic motives and environmental forces. Always at his best as a critic, he expressed in the later twenties a young generation's impatience with the idealism and romanticism of the past. His speciality was the crisp and highly polished short essay directed against the fatuities and pomposities of his present; moral indignation ignited his facility for coining ringing epigrams in the style of his two heroes, Bernard Shaw and H.L. Mencken. Underhill was not a historian in the conventional mould, and his judgement of another of his favourite writers may apply equally to him. Goldwin Smith, he wrote, 'left behind him no great work which recreates and reinterprets for us a past period of history.'[1] Underhill was really a political journalist, a popularizer of others' ideas, whose main concerns from the later twenties throughout the thirties were political ideas: the adjustment of traditional liberalism to modern society, the advocacy of democratic socialism, and an isolationist foreign policy. But because he related these ideas to Canadian political culture generally, he raised profoundly significant questions about history. His attitude to the past itself was negative. He did not so much attempt to recreate it; rather, assuming the role of an impatient interrogator, he asked why history had produced so unsatisfactory a state of things in the present.

Underhill's contributions to Canadian historical thought before 1940 centred on three themes: an attack on the assumptions of the constitutionalist historians for their lack of realism in dealing with politics; an attempt to employ conceptions derived from the American historiography of Charles A. Beard and to a lesser extent Frederick Jackson Turner in order to explain the origins of Canadian political parties in terms of the conflict of interest groups; and an analysis of the weaknesses of the radical tradition in Canada. His preoccupation with the history of Canadian reform and liberalism was related to his active support of democratic socialism: his historical essays gave the Co-operative Commonwealth Federation a sense of its own position—an ancestry—in the Canadian past. The patterns of Underhill's writings reflect the ways in which the cultural criticism of the twenties was channelled into political radicalism in the Depression decade.

I

The most arresting feature of Underhill's background was its Victorian conventionality and lower middle-class propriety. He was born in 1889 in the village of Stouffville, near Toronto. His grandfather, a cobbler, had come to Canada from Plymouth, Eng., in 1867. His father followed the same trade and eventually became a small-scale boot-and-shoe manufacturer, village councillor, and reeve. The family was Liberal in politics and staunchly Presbyterian in religion. 'I was just born with this native feeling that if you don't keep a tight hold on yourself you'll never accomplish anything,' he recollected many years later. 'Well, that's . . . the essence of puritanism. Not merely in the matter of sex but in . . . everything, you must keep under self-imposed discipline.'[2] Like many others of his generation, Underhill was to lose interest in the formalities of religion and vigorously denounce the 'puritan' strains in Canadian life; but he never completely escaped its influence. Perhaps his deep-seated suspicion of displays of emotion had its origins in the same 'puritanism'. His family, he also recalled, were not the richest in the village but they mixed with the 'best people'. There were boys up main street that his mother never wanted him to play with: unlike most of his contemporaries at school, he never worked during the summers but spent his days reading.

Underhill attended the University of Toronto from 1907 to 1911 and studied classics, English, and history. His enthusiasm for classics was strong, as the student Year Book suggested when it summed him up in a couplet:

> *Concluding all were desperate sots and fools*
> *That durst depart from Aristotle's rules.*[3]

The honours classics course was the ornament of University College and had been transformed by Maurice Hutton from a concentration on the mechanics of language to a broad study of the literature, history, and philosophy of Greece and Rome. It left its mark not only in Underhill's occasional use of classical allusions and his succinct, lucid writing style, but also in his interest in political ideas and those enduring questions of political philosophy that had been first confronted in the ancient world. One of his favourite teachers, W.S. Milner, Professor of Ancient History, had justified the study of classics on the general grounds that such an education was the essential training for an intellectual élite that would bring to the commercial North American democracy a consciousness of the higher values of life. The aim of the educational system, Milner explained, 'is the creation of national like-mindedness—in short, public opinion . . . . The public opinion which really preserves the stite is a combination of character and knowledge, and created by leadership, and this leadership the higher education of the state must supply if it is to justify itself.'⁴ Underhill's other teachers, W.J. Alexander in English and G.M. Wrong in history, subscribed to the same essentially aristocratic prescription. They saw themselves as university figures who had a far higher avocation than the reproduction of research scholars. They were the instructors of the potential leaders of the nation, men (never women) who, in the society they took as their model, maintained the quarterlies and reviews, filled the public service, found their way into cabinets, and represented the close association between the university and public life. Underhill assimilated this view of the role of the educated élite in democratic society and never abandoned it. Apart from classical literature, his most exciting reading in his undergraduate years was in political philosophy—Hobbes, Locke, Burke, and Mill—and in the critics of Victorian society like Matthew Arnold.

Underhill was one of G.M. Wrong's favourites and a member of the Historical Club. His first publication, a paper on the commission form of government for cities, was first given at this club.⁵ Through Wrong, Underhill came into contact with the British imperialist Lionel Curtis and the Toronto Round Table group, and in 1911 he was awarded a Flavelle Fellowship for study at Oxford. He was a protégé of figures in the Canadian Round Table and proceeded to Oxford in the company of Wrong's son Murray and Vincent Massey.

To go to Oxford was to make the pilgrimage to the source of his teachers' conception of the role of the intellectual in society and to experience a political culture that was, compared with Canada's, incredibly rich and complex. Underhill's initial impressions of Balliol College, however, were hardly enthusiastic. Perhaps it was his Presbyterianism that made him uneasy with the 'shameful luxury' in which the students lived and the insulated comfortableness of their lives. 'The zeal for discovery of truth isn't nearly so important as the ability to make epigrammatic remarks about that elusive substance,' he told Wrong. ' . . . It is appalling to see the matter-of-fact way in which the great majority here frankly accept conditions as they are, and still worse to see them setting out to use those conditions to make a place and name for themselves . . . . '⁶ Underhill did not participate as fully in the social life of the college as his sponsors had hoped. 'I came from the lower-middle class,' he said in retrospect, 'and you always knew that, and you always resented the fact, I suppose subconsciously, that you came from the lower-middle classes and you'd never be quite as civilized as these Englishmen you were mixing with.'[7]

Underhill was exposed to a wide range of the social criticism and rebelliousness of late Edwardian England. He read the Webbs and H.G. Wells, and heard the supreme egoist Shaw explain why he was a superior dramatist to Shakespeare. He gravitated towards the Balliol Fabian Society in which his chief tutor, A.D. Lindsay, and G.D.H. Cole, were leading lights, and he was caught up in the excitement of the debate over the way the traditional ends of liberalism could be attained through collectivism. Underhill joined the imperially oriented Ralegh Club that had been founded by the supporters of the Round Table.

Underhill left Oxford in 1914 to take up a teaching post at the University of Saskatchewan in Saskatoon. The next year he volunteered for service in the Canadian army as a private. Sent to England, he spent an intolerable period of inactive camp life at Shorncliffe. In 1917 Lionel Curtis secured his transfer to an English regiment, the First Hertfordshires, and a commission. He trained as a Lewis Gun officer and was wounded in France. At the end of the war he transferred to the Canadian army and taught history to the veterans at Ripon, Yorkshire, under the auspices of the Khaki College, a pioneer effort in soldier education that was conceived by President Henry M. Tory of the University of Alberta and supported by the YMCA.[8]

Underhill's war experience sharpened his sense of Canadian nationalism and convinced him that if only the same determination and organizing capacity the Canadians had demonstrated in battle could be channelled into the country's domestic politics, the future would indeed be bright. In the only sustained piece of historical scholarship he ever completed, he analysed the activities of the Canadian troops in a book published under the auspices of the Royal Colonial Society in 1923. His descriptions of the battles were in the bald, factual language of the military historian, but behind the unadorned prose lay a strong pride in the national achievement. In writing of the Somme and Passchendaele, names that were later to become synonymous with the stupidities and brutal wastefulness of war, Underhill discounted criticisms of the military leadership and stressed positive accomplishments. The Canadian Corps, he asserted in conclusion, 'is the greatest national achievement of the Canadian people since the Dominion came into being; and its story is to be cherished not only as proof of Canadian military capacity but as the noblest example yet given of the ability of Canadians, working in concert with a single inspiration, to accomplish great ends .... The four years' career of her fighting troops in France forms the real testimony to Canada's entrance into nationhood, the visible demonstration that there has grown up on her soil a people not English nor Scottish nor American but Canadian—a Canadian nation.'[9] He supported conscription in 1917 and helped organize the Canadian Officers Training Corps at the University of Saskatchewan in the early twenties. However disenchanted he might have been with the discrepancy between the rhetoric of idealism and the invocation to selfless national service when contrasted with the grim realities of the front, Underhill had no misgivings about Canada's participation in the war.

He returned to Saskatchewan in 1919 at a time when farmers' grievances against the Union government and the national economic policies were breaking all the restraints and inhibitions on independent political action. He was caught up in the passion of western protest and shared, up to a point, the optimistic sense of the malleability of institutions, a faith that came naturally in a new society that had been created within almost a single generation. The co-operative movement and the wheat pools appeared as harbingers of a genuinely qualitative change in social and economic relations, instances in the Canadian West of step-by-step *ad hoc* improvements on the gradual ascent to a Fabian vision of a collectivist society.

Underhill may have admired the ferment of radical farmer politics and the forthright and informed journalism of J.W. Dafoe of the *Manitoba Free Press*, and the socially conscious politics of J.S. Woodsworth may have crystallized his hopefulness about reform in Canada, but he had reservations about life in the West. Like his contemporary, Arthur Lower, another easterner who romanticized the West after he had left it, Underhill found the Prairies, as he told his Oxford tutor, 'not a very comfortable place to live in, or at any rate I don't find the great open spaces particularly alluring to an academic person like myself.'[10] 'The trouble with the West,' he explained to a friend, Carleton Stanley, 'is that it is peopled by money making individualists who have never thought about any of the problems of man in society until the recent hard times have compelled some thinking. And naturally most of the thinking has been superficial and in politics they jump at the most obvious half baked solutions of North American democracy. However, they are learning but the universities are doing very little to assist their learning.'[11] Underhill's notions of university life had been formed at Toronto and confirmed at Oxford: he was a traditionalist in the Saskatoon setting. He introduced a history club modelled on Wrong's and was involved in the activities of the local League of Nations Society. He told his students to subscribe to the best papers and periodicals—*The Times, New Statesman, Round Table* and the *Manitoba Free Press* ('probably the only paper in Canada appearing daily that is worth reading')—in order to be well informed and cultivated in the art of conversation.[12] 'English Politics', he told a class, 'are interesting because the right people write books on Public life. People on this continent haven't intelligence enough to write books.'[13] For all the debunking and unkind remarks in his private correspondence at this time about Toronto and its opinion makers, Underhill longed to return to the East.

He taught the usual range of courses in history during his early years at Saskatchewan, but his chief preoccupation after the mid-twenties was in the field of political science rather than history. In 1925 he was made Professor of Political Science—as well as Lecturer in History—and prepared courses on comparative government, political theory, and international relations. More and more he found the literature of the American progressive movement and American writing on politics more attractive than Canadian history. He became and remained an avid reader of the *New Republic*, and found Walter Lippmann's books, *Preface to Politics* (1914) and especially *The Phantom Public* (1925), with their studied scepticism about the possibility of democracy, 'the most penetrating studies of politics on this continent.'[14] Yet his interest in Canadian history, or rather the Canadian political tradition, remained strong. When he took a half-year sabbatical in 1926 he went to Toronto to begin research on the Toronto *Globe* of the 1860s and its editor, George Brown. 'It has been most interesting,' he told A.S. Morton, 'and I am picking up all sorts of sidelights on the Confederation period which I have never seen in the books .... One keeps coming across curious parallels also between Upper Canada of Brown and the Western Canada of our own day.'[15] Such parallels, however, did not seem all that encouraging. 'I am becoming more and more impressed', he told another correspondent in 1926, 'with the futility of radicalism or any other philosophy of politics. The strong will always rule and the weak will always be exploited, and the only difference from generation to generation is in the possessors of power. The purpose of philosophy is to make us feel more comfortable, not to make us see more clearly.'[16] Perhaps it was the ineffectuality and gradual disintegration of the Progressive party that lay behind this pessimism.

Later in the spring of 1926 he moved to Ottawa to work in the Parliamentary Library. The House of Commons was in the throes of the customs scandal and Underhill spent as much time in the visitors' gallery and the offices of members of the Ginger Group, particularly Woodsworth's, as he had done researching the files of the *Globe* of sixty years before. His first professional paper, a study of the Clear Grits and Upper Canadian radicalism that drew direct parallels with contemporary progressivism, was read to the Canadian Historical Association by his friend, the classicist Charles Cochrane, the next spring. Underhill was in Saskatchewan preparing for his move to the University of Toronto history department, where he was to teach until 1955. Shortly after his arrival in Toronto, Barker Fairley asked him to review books for the *Canadian Forum* and he joined the editorial board of that journal. The divergent attractions in his intellectual life—his insatiable interest in both contemporary politics and the past, which found satisfaction in his conversations with J.S. Woodsworth and in his work in the Parliamentary Library, in the demands of journalism, and in the more reflective sustained labours of the historian—had by now firmly set.

II

In his 'O Canada' column in the *Canadian Forum*, which ran from March 1929 to 1932, in numerous book reviews, and in scholarly articles published between 1927 and 1935, Underhill sought to undermine the idealistic approach of the constitutional historians and direct attention to a more realistic, economic interpretation of politics. He was of course not their only critic. When the grand summation of the constitutionalists, the sixth volume of the *Cambridge History of the British Empire*, appeared in 1930, they were chastized for various sins of omission and commission. Their approach, it was charged, represented an imperialistic and Anglo-Canadian point of view, neglected the influence of the United States on Canadian development, and underplayed the significance of French Canada.[17] Underhill's animadversions went much further, however. He selectively borrowed from American historical writing certain major ideas that he then employed to repudiate the very framework the constitutionalists had established.

The progressive history, or 'new history', of Frederick Jackson Turner, Charles A. Beard, James Harvey Robinson, and Vernon Parrington developed in the United States in the generation after 1890 and was the counterpart in historical writing of the progressive movement in American politics.[18] These historians all espoused the conviction that in an age of reform, history itself had to be reformed. It was necessary to subordinate the past to the needs of the present, to concentrate on the nature and origins of contemporary problems, and to broaden the scope of history to include social, economic, and intellectual tendencies and the milieu of the 'common man'. The most striking feature of Turner's essay of 1893 on the significance of the frontier in American history, of Beard's *An Economic Interpretation of the Constitution of the United States* (1913)—of which Underhill wrote that it 'burst on my mind like a flash of lightning'[19] when he read it just after the war—and of Parrington's *Main Currents in American Thought* (1927, 1930) was the stress placed on conflicts among economic interests in American history. Beard, for example, held that the mainspring behind the creation of the Constitution of 1787 was the conflict between those who possessed different kinds of property: the Federalists—who held depreciated securities, demanded repayment at par, and generally desired a strong central government that could withstand agrarian-debtor radicalism—*versus* the anti-Federalists, who favoured paper-money inflation. Not only was the constitution the work of a small minority who derived economic advantages from their success, but its ratification was achieved through undemocratic means.

The distinguishing feature of progressive history was the concentration on the persistent and enduring struggle between the mass of the people and powerful economic classes—over the ratification of the Constitution, in the rivalry between Jeffersonian and later Jacksonian democrats and the Federalists, in the triumph of business in the Civil War, and in the progressive movement of the late-nineteenth and early twentieth centuries. It was a view of history that was environmentalist, preoccupied with domestic conflict, and determined to get behind the surface appearance of things to the real sources of events. Progressive history was cynical about ideas, theories, and ideologies: reality was a congeries of external and material factors that ideas and beliefs merely reflected.[20] Ideas, or at least certain ideas, were sometimes regarded as distortions of reality; the duty of the historian was to reveal their origins and biases in order to free men from their paralysing influences.[21] In its materialistic view of reality progressive history expressed the spirit of an era in which political discourse was monopolized by the rebate and the bribe, corruption in municipal government, and party subservience to big business.

Also implicit in progressive history was the view of historical knowledge as relative to time and circumstance. The ideal of objective history was impatiently dismissed as an impossible anachronism dating back to von Ranke. Relativity was carried to its logical conclusion by Beard, who argued that written history was an act of faith, and that the historian should frankly declare his belief in certain social truths and write history accordingly.[22] Underhill responded enthusiastically to Beard's argument and to Carl Becker's article of 1932, 'Everyman His Own Historian'. 'The truth', Underhill wrote in that year, 'is that all great historians from Thucydides to the present have been men who lived intensely in their own age and who brought their own intense sense of values to the interpretation of the material on which they worked . : . . The historian must ever endeavour to be conscious and critical of his own system of values, but he cannot escape from it or from the dominant ideas of his own age. The patterns which he finds in the events of the past are the image of the patterns which are already in his own mind.'[23] Underhill became a merciless critic of those Canadian scholars who still adhered to what he considered the myth of objectivity and non-participation in politics.

Underhill learned a good deal from the American progressive historians, but there was another more native source for his view of politics as the struggle between classes and material interests. His years in the West had exposed him to incessant radical-farmer criticism of the two-party system and the tariff. The Canadian Progressive party was mainly a revolt against the domination of the economy by the industrial and financial powers of

Montreal and Toronto. One of the most familiar refrains in agrarian rhetoric was the complaint that the hegemony of these interests was maintained through their undue influence within the Liberal and Conservative parties. The protective tariff of 1878 occupied the same prominence in the Canadian progressive mind as did the 'great crime' of 1876—the demonitization of silver—in American populism. It symbolized the dominance of the 'vested interests' over the productive classes in society. The history of Canada since 1878, wrote William Irvine in his comprehensive indictment of Canadian society, *The Farmers in Politics* (1920), has been the history of class rule. The same political analysis, with different degrees of sophistication, was familiar to any reader of that Bible of agrarian discontent, the *Grain Growers' Guide*; Edward Porritt's *The Revolt in Canada Against the New Feudalism* (1911); Gustavus Myers' uncompleted muckraking study, *History of Canadian Wealth* (1914); and E.A. Partridge's visionary plan for a western utopia, *A War on Poverty* (1926). The blunt and caricatured economic interpretation of Canadian politics popularized in all these publications was basic to the charge that the protective system was the work of minority interests that had subverted democracy.

Drawing upon American progressive history as well as agrarian social criticism in Canada, Underhill indicted the ingenuous view of politics held by the constitutional historians. It seemed to him that W.P.M. Kennedy and Chester Martin had placed inordinate emphasis on the continuity and non-revolutionary character of Canadian history, thereby extracting the passion and adventure from that history and tending to create a conservative bias. In their deficiencies these historians reflected what Underhill believed to be a widespread failure of Canadians generally to be realistic about politics. They were blinkered by a tradition that insisted on the superiority of British compared with Republican institutions, assumed that Canadian life was inherently more stable and ordered than that of the United States, and maintained the belief that the relationship between French and English Canadians had been characterized by toleration, compromise, and conciliation. These conventions had originated in the past and were sustained by a 'belated colonialism'. 'We in Canada', Underhill wrote, 'are suffering from a literary theory of our constitution. It prevents us from realizing how British institutions when transplanted to America actually work, and it is high time we shook ourselves free from it. Perhaps a good preliminary step toward this end would be to place Burke and Bagehot upon a Canadian Index.'[24] He contrasted some books on American history that advanced economic and sectional interpretations with 'the naive romanticism with which our histories still take politicians at their face value and still talk about principles as if Burke's definition of party were still the last word on the subject.'[25] Perhaps the most formidable block to a more realistic assessment of Canadian politics was the traditional suspicion of the United States and the resulting unwillingness to acknowledge that, as Underhill put it, in so many ways 'the United States is simply Canada writ large.'[26]

Underhill equated the vaunted serenity and stability in Canadian life to an anaemic lack of vitality, and attributed this placidity to the fact that the Dominion lagged about a generation behind the United States in the state of its industrialization. He had even less patience with efforts to glorify the tradition of bi-racial co-operation in the attainment of responsible government and Canadian politics generally. 'The two races', he wrote, 'have never coalesced, have never understood one another or tried to understand one another.'[27] French Canadians had always participated in Canadian politics as a 'racial party'. Ever since responsible government, they always sat in the government, with the exception of the period 1911 to 1921. 'They had by that time become so accustomed to the sweets of office that their short period in opposition was regarded by them as an intolerable injustice, a breach of the Confederation pact, a denial of the rights guaranteed to them by the Quebec Act. Everyone can still recall the wailings and howlings which filled the air in Quebec during that distressful decade. And no more striking proof of their supreme political ability could be given than the almost uniform success with which the French, by posing as suffering martyrs, have managed to get their own way in Canada.'[28]

As an essayist Underhill assumed an air of imparting revelations, puncturing pomposities, and informing readers that things are not what they appear to be. He exaggerated, even caricatured, some of the major conclusions that the constitutional historians had reached, but he also expressed a growing sense of dissatisfaction felt by others with the everlasting raking about in the dry bones of constitutional history and the neglect of economic and social history. The treatment of politics had been reverential and idealistic, and for younger scholars like Fred Landon and even older ones like William Grant, Underhill's iconoclasm was liberating.[29]

This emancipating critique of Canadian historical writing was the negative preliminary to the interpretation of the Canadian political tradition along Beardian lines.[30] Underhill began where Beard had started, with James Madison's Tenth Federalist paper in which that architect of the American constitution wrote that the most enduring source of factions, or political groups, was the unequal distribution of different kinds of property. The strategic date in Underhill's analysis was the year 1854, which witnessed the disintegration of the coalition that had won responsible government and the beginnings of the Liberal-Conservative party of John A. Macdonald and George Etienne Cartier. The Macdonald-Cartier party was a loosely organized and conglomerate collection of shifting groups and interests, but Underhill maintained that it was based on four essential elements: the French-Canadian Roman Catholics led by Cartier; Montreal big business allied with some English-Canadian support from the Eastern

Townships and headed by Alexander Galt; the moderate reformers of Upper Canada who followed Baldwin and Hincks; and Macdonald's Orange loyalists and Tories. What kept these groups together was not ideological affinities or shared values but interests, especially economic interests.

The driving force behind the Macdonald-Cartier party was the determination of the business interests to exploit the resources of the northern half of the continent and to ensure the commercial dominance of Montreal over the St Lawrence valley and the interior. The close association of government with transportation development, especially the Grand Trunk Railway, was notorious. Cartier, who was the solicitor of that railway and its defender in politics, was able to command the French-Canadian vote in return for special favours for the Catholic province: the incorporation of religious orders, the extension of separate schools in Upper Canada, and the maintenance of clerical control of education in Lower Canada. The English-speaking voters of the townships, the French Canadians, and Montreal business all had an interest in the flow of trade from the West through the St Lawrence route.

The opposition to this alliance came from the Clear Grits of Upper Canada, a group that Underhill described as representative of the agrarian frontier democracy of the Ontario peninsula. This faction, which found its intellectual centre in Toronto and its organ of opinion in George Brown's *Globe*, was Canada's counterpart of Jacksonian democracy and Lincoln Republicanism. It was also an ancestor of the Progressive party of the 1920s. These agrarian interests combined with the commercial and financial groups of Toronto to resist all schemes that were intended to promote Montreal's domination in transport, credit, and wholesale distribution. The Clear Grits initiated the campaign for the annexation of the Northwest, thereby combining the frontier desire for cheap land with metropolitan drives for securing the trade of the Prairies. Underhill came to the conclusion that the party struggles of the 1850s and early 1860s, which paralysed the government of the union and led by necessity to Confederation, were based on sectional and economic interests, not mainly cultural, ethnic or religious issues.

Confederation itself represented the welding of the scattered portions of British North America into a political union within which the business interests could expand, consolidate their power, and realize their ambitions. According to Underhill, the main function of Macdonald's government, just as it had been the policy of Alexander Hamilton in the United States, was to serve the interests of big business. Through the building of the transcontinental railway, tariff protection, and the maintenance of a strong central government, Macdonald successfully tied the business interests to his party and to the state.

Underhill was convinced that one of the chief reasons for the vitality of political life in the 1870s and 1880s was that party divisions represented real divisions of economic interests. The Liberal party of Mackenzie, the offspring of the Clear Grits, maintained the Grits' opposition to the intimate connections between government and business and their essentially agrarian biases. In the American terminology that Underhill invariably employed, it was Jeffersonian, an expression of 'pioneer agrarian democracy' and 'simple democratic instincts'. Between Mackenzie and Laurier, however, the character of the party changed; the Hamiltonian policies were embraced; and against the Conservatives' alliance with the CPR and the Bank of Montreal was forged the Liberal Party's alliance on the railway builders, Mackenzie and Mann, and the Bank of Commerce. By the beginning of the century no clear divisions of interests between the parties existed. Both were 'dominated by the business interests of the great Eastern industrial and financial centres, and the essential philosophy of each was to foster national development by handing over the resources of the country to be exploited by triumphant business.' Class and sectional conflicts were now reconciled and accommodated within the parties, but this merely enabled business, the most well-organized interest, to dominate both.

In this state of affairs it was evident that certain groups could not find satisfaction in either party. The election of 1911 revealed substantial discontent; the returns of 1921 confirmed what Underhill saw as a revival of the agrarian radicalism of the Grits and the anti-business bias of the Mackenzie Liberals. His own essential complaint about the party system was not so different from that of the western progressives. Its fundamental defect, he wrote, was 'that it does not provide an effective means by which economic interests other than those of organized business can exercise a reasonable influence in the determination of national policy.' Similarly, his conception of class owed nothing to Marx—whom he had begun to read and did not finish—but much to the traditional liberal and progressive complaint that certain groups were being prevented by monopolistic forces from enjoying the fruits of their labour.

The most notable feature of Underhill's interpretation of the party system was the extent to which his zeal for applying—or imposing—the prevailing categories of American historiography to Canadian circumstances was unqualified by any deep immersion in the sources. Except for the *Globe* and the Confederation Debates, Underhill relied on well-known works in Canadian history, such as Skelton's biography of Galt, or the mordant anti-party commentary of Goldwin Smith, who defined Canadian statecraft as 'government appropriations'. Yet there was nothing tentative about his essays. Having perhaps already arrived at the conclusion that, in respect to party history at least, the United States was Canada writ large, he was content to let his very generalized views stand as though they were fully explored statements.

There is a curious inconsistency, moreover, in Underhill's discussion of 'interests' and 'ideas' in the political tradition. He originally set out to discredit the idealist explanations for political divisions, and his entire analysis of the history of Canadian political parties accorded priority to economic and sectional interests, though he conceded that religion, for example, had played a role, usually in obscuring the real issues at stake. 'Man does not live by bread alone,' he wrote in 1935. 'He also requires slogans, catchwords, rationalizations of his activities.'[31] Slogans, catchwords, and rationalizations are terms not often used by historians who assume even a limited autonomy for the role of ideas and perceptions in behaviour. Yet when Underhill wrote of the reformers, and especially when he examined the thought of individual intellectuals he admired, like Goldwin Smith and John Ewart, he did not consider the possibility that their ideas were merely the reflections of extraneous non-ideological factors, or of idiosyncratic personalities. Underhill, like the American historians from whom he borrowed so heavily, 'was more apt to emphasize the environmental analysis and functional development of thought for which he had little sympathy, and he was more likely to minimize any environmental interpretations when discussing ideas he particularly admired.'[32] It often seemed that in Underhill's history, intellectuals and reformers possessed ideas, but businessmen and the masses had only interests and raw appetites.

Underhill described 'business' in a highly abstract fashion, making almost no allowances for significant divisions within the business community and treating it invariably as an ogrish, evil force. But he also expressed admiration, at least in the late 1920s, for the large-scale organizations of Canadian capitalism. 'The success of enterprises like the T. Eaton Co., the Massey-Harris Co., the Bank of Montreal, and other such concerns organized and managed by Canadians', he wrote in 1927, 'has done more to strengthen our national feeling than all the speeches and posturing of our politicians since we first elected representative assemblies.'[33] Yet while he was to write at length of the corrupting influences of business in politics and to reject the values for which it stood, he bore no animus against the businessmen he had first met at Wrong's Historical Club or the more thoughtful representatives of that class he knew in the thirties. One suspects that Underhill, whose phrases were always more radical than his real intentions, was carried away by the language of radicalism and the requirements of the progressive history.

III

Underhill was acutely conscious of the relationship between his interpretation of Canadian political history and the revival of reform in the early thirties. His view of history imparted to the newly established social demo-cratic party, the CCF, a sense of its place in the Canadian political tradition and of its roots in the past. By portraying the political tradition as a series of conflicts of economic interest-groups, he sharpened the historical per-spective of a party that sought to combine farmer, labour, and socialist ele-ments against business domination of the economy and politics.

Underhill was one of the founders of the League for Social Reconstruc-tion, which was set up in 1932 to provide a nucleus around which the intellectual critics of capitalism could gather.[34] The LSR drew its main sup-port from academics at McGill and the University of Toronto and its mem-bership included Frank Scott; Eugene Forsey, a lecturer in economics and political science at McGill; King Gordon, the son of the social gospeller and best-selling novelist Charles W. Gordon, and Professor of Christian Ethics at United Theological College in Montreal; Graham Spry, who had organ-ized the Canadian Clubs; and the economists Harry Cassidy and J.F. Par-kinson and the classicist Eric Havelock, all of Toronto. It was modelled on the English Fabian Society, and its members envisaged their role in politics as providing research into specific social and economic problems and drawing up an agenda of concrete proposals for reform. In 1933 Underhill and his friends drafted the Regina Manifesto of the CCF party and during the rest of the decade occupied positions of influence in its councils.

The immediate stimulus to the organization of the League was the onset of the Depression. Underhill recalled that the League was founded as a re-sult of a discussion he had with Scott while attending the Institute of Polit-ics at Williamstown, Mass., in 1931. But there was also a significant degree of continuity between the political radicalism of the early thirties and the cultural criticism and nationalism of the twenties. In fact one of the first suggestions for the creation of a Canadian Fabian Society was made in Scott's *Canadian Mercury* in March 1929 in an appeal for some kind of na-tional organization that would draw together those young people who had read Wilson Macdonald's 'Ode to Confederation' and Grove's *A Search for America*, who had followed the speeches of Agnes Macphail and J.S. Woodsworth, had heard of Canada First and John S. Ewart, but who found it all a bit confusing because they were offered no co-ordinated centre.[35] Woodsworth asked Underhill whether he had seen this article and sug-gested that perhaps the time had come to 'take the lead in organizing some society which in Canada would do the work that was done by the Fabian Society in Great Britain.'[36]

Though the LSR was organized three years later, it represented a trans-ference, as well as an intense politicization, of some of the main themes of the twenties, especially the enmity towards the blotched and wasteful standards of the business civilization. It is true, of course, that it took the collapse of the *Canadian Mercury* to open Scott's eyes to the realities of the social system he had taken for granted, an illuminating comment in itself on his academic radicalism.[37] But there is a continuity between his debunking efforts of the late twenties and the radical satire of his poem, 'The Social Register of Canada'. Eugene Forsey, writing in the spring of 1929, repeated an observation that had been made many times in the *Canadian Forum* regarding the extent to which Canada had already experimented with collectivist measures and institutions, and advocated a comprehensive system of social protection and insurance.[38] In some respects Forsey, Scott, and Underhill were predisposed to radicalism before the Great Crash.

According to the LSR manifesto, the Canadian Fabians looked forward to the establishment in Canada of a social order in which the basic principle regulating production, distribution, and service would be the common good rather than the profit motive. It advocated the public ownership of public utilities in transportation, communications, electric power, and other industries approaching positions of monopoly; the nationalization of banking and other financial institutions; the further development of co-operatives, especially in agriculture; extensive welfare measures; steeply graduated income and estate taxes; and a foreign policy that would be devoted to freer international trade and disarmament.

In its manifesto and in *Social Planning for Canada* (1935), the most elaborate critique of capitalism published in Canada up to that time, the LSR endorsed the substitution of a planned and socialized economy in place of the inefficient and wasteful system that deprived certain classes and groups of the benefits of a liberal democratic society. Truly reflecting the inspiration of its English model, the LSR displayed an immense faith in bureaucratic planning, social engineering, and rationality. A National Planning Commission, staffed by economists and engineers, was to supervise and regulate the economy in conjunction with a broad mandate from Parliament and democratic participation at the local level. The case for planning reflected the belief that, after a century and a half of expansion, the economy had reached its limits of growth and would drift into a purposeless maturity if deliberate efforts were not undertaken to ensure stability and regulation.[39]

The democratic socialism of the LSR was ameliorative, gradualist, and dedicated to peaceful change through the parliamentary system. Its vision of the future co-operative commonwealth rested on the traditional social-gospel rejection of the competition ethic and the profit motive. Scott, Forsey, and Gordon were also members of the Fellowship for a Christian Social Order, and Scott in particular had been inspired by the Christian socialism that shone through R.H. Tawney's *On Equality* and *The Acquisitive Society*. The general ends of the LSR were quite compatible with the goals of liberalism. 'True freedom—opportunities for unfettered personal development—can only be enjoyed by people whose work and incomes are secure against arbitrary disaster and afford them a reasonable chance of a decent living and leisure . . . ', ran the declaration of faith. 'The control which is needed to secure economic efficiency is therefore the essential prelude to a truer personal liberty than we have as yet achieved.'[40] From another perspective one observer caught the spirit of the movement when he referred to the CCF and its professorial advisors 'as a rather genteel sprig clipped from the suburban hedge of English Fabianism', and impishly added that there were 'no Lenins lurking on our university staffs . . . .'[41]

Underhill's reflections on the purposes and philosophy of the LSR were rooted in his previous fascination with the problems of liberalism and collectivism. At Oxford he had been drawn to L.T. Hobhouse's *Liberalism* (1911) and other attempts to restate the ends of traditional liberalism in a collective society; he admired Herbert Croly's *The Promise of American Life* (1909), a key document of American progressivism, for its argument that individual liberty treasured by the Jeffersonians could only be preserved through the supervisory, interventionist Hamiltonian state. One of the most disappointing features of liberalism in Canada was that its development seemed to have been interrupted and that it had, after the mid-nineteenth century, ceased to draw direct inspiration from Britain and Europe. Laurier, Underhill believed, had been a Whig who never had any sensitivity to the development of collectivist ideas that elsewhere replaced the nostrums of *laissez-faire*. 'He remained a mere constitutional liberal to the end and never acquired the interest in social questions and the tendency to expand the functions of the state which marked the English liberalism of his generation.'[42] With Mackenzie King, Canadian liberalism still appeared totally devoted to its historic mission of breaking down the barriers to freedom rather than with creative collectivist measures which, in an industrial society, were necessary to protect it. Underhill invariably associated British socialism with an updated liberalism. 'English socialism', he contended, 'has always emphasized that it is only another method of seeking the same ends which the individualistic generation that preceded it had in view. Its end is the emancipation of individuality, the free development of personality.'[43]

Why had Canadian liberalism failed to march in step with the evolution of English liberalism? One answer was that, until the Depression, an expansive economy had never led to any searching criticism of the business view of government. Underhill also attributed the weaknesses of Canadian liberalism to a certain 'Boeotian placidity' and lack of concern about the fundamentals of political philosophy characteristic of Canada all through its history. 'The weakness of our Canadian society', he wrote in 1934, 'is that we have no radical tradition in our past . . . . It can never be too strongly repeated that radicalism to be effective, requires social background and tradition.'[44] Behind the British Labour party there stretched a tradition of radical speculation and social criticism running back to the Levellers of the seventeenth century, the outraged sages of the nineteenth century, Thomas Carlyle and Matthew Arnold, the Benthamites and Tory radicals, socialists John Ruskin and William Morris, and the Fabians. Back of Croly and the American progressives lay an equally distinguished ancestry of protest against big business by the Jeffersonians, Jacksonians, and a multitude of writers whose manifestos and criticisms were chronicled by Vernon Parrington. In Britain and the United States the reform traditions had a paternity, a memory, and a myth. In comparison Canadian history revealed only sporadic outbursts of pioneer farmers. 'We have never gone through a generation or a decade', Underhill explained, 'when we were compelled to discuss the fundamentals of our institutions.'[45] The constitutional historians had praised the non-revolutionary and non-ideological character of Canadian development for its stability. The price paid for inheriting our institutions, Underhill believed, was that Canadians never questioned them. Organic political evolution had produced a dull, uninquiring acceptance of things as they were. Preoccupation with the need to reconcile religious and racial divisions deflected attention from class and economic realities.[46] The result was that Canadian radicals had to import their 'philosophical equipment' from John Dewey, Charles Beard, Walter Lippman, and, of course Bentham and the Fabians. Still, Underhill was optimistic about certain indigenous foundations on which a more co-operative social order could be constructed. In the later twenties he had attacked some of the traditional images Canadians had entertained about American society, not so much because he wanted to obliterate completely the importance of the boundary but because he thought national differences could only be meaningfully expressed in social and economic terms. 'If we are to look for anything distinctively Canadian ... ,' he noted in 1929, 'it must be found in the way in which we have handled the social and economic questions which arise in the process of exploiting the resources of our half of the continent.' The main difference between Canada and the United States was that Canadians had never given themselves over completely to capitalistic individualism. 'In such enterprizes as the Ontario Hydro, the Canadian National Railways, and the provincial telephone systems of the West, we have experimented in another method of providing public services than that of trusting to the private capitalist in search of profit .... The best defence of a distinct Canadian nationality is to make sure that these great strategic public services should be owned and controlled by the people themselves.'[47] The task of the CCF was to build on this tradition.

IV

Central to Underhill's definition of the purposes of the LSR was his abiding belief in the university intellectual as a committed activist. His notion of intellectual leadership had its roots in the teaching of Wrong and Milner, and one of the features of English life he most admired was the easy personal intercourse between the practical statesman and the university don. Whenever he wrote of intellectual leadership, moreover, he invariably drew his illustrations from nineteenth-century British critics, the Fabians, and the American progressives. Both the Fabians and the progressives shared the conviction that education should help men and women formulate social goals. They tended generally to be contemptuous of businessmen and patronizing to the working classes. Seeing themselves as benefactors of the lower orders, they brought to the cause of reform not only a critical spirit but also a sense of *noblesse oblige*.[48] Underhill's ideal was the intellectual as both social critic and reformer. It seemed to him that an educated man who was not vociferously at odds with the conventions of his society was a contradiction in terms.

Underhill's examination of the weaknesses of the radical tradition and his explanation of the role of the LSR invariably dwelt on the need for experts and intellectual leadership. The Progressive party had failed to resolve a fatal disagreement within its ranks between the advocates of group government, who wanted to abolish parties and have Parliament represent definite occupational interests, and more traditional liberals who saw the movement as a reformist party drawing support from diverse groups and classes. Underhill had rejected the notion of group government as unworkable,[49] and he described the progressive faith in popular democracy as an antiquated conception in a complex industrial age. It seemed to him that agrarian protest based on farmers' economic grievances was an insufficient basis for a sustained reform party because agrarian outrage lacked a definite and coherent ideology with which it could resist the fate of third parties in North American politics. It was also weakened by the traditional agrarian suspicion of 'partyism' and by an attitude of utopianism about the resolution of conflicts of power and class. Underhill was convinced that agrarian and labour protest could become effective and potent only if they possessed a body of doctrine and intellectual leadership from the urban centres.

Underhill's insistence on the need for intellectual leadership also rested on his measured pessimism about what he called the old, naive theory of democracy and the rationality of the electorate. He was much influenced in this direction by Walter Lippmann's books on public opinion, which raised the question of what Freudian psychology and its revelations about the irrationality of man and the place of stereotypes in behaviour implied for democratic theory; and he was equally taken with Lippmann's teaching that democracy required informed and disinterested expert leadership that would break the bonds of ignorance and guide public opinion. 'American experience', Underhill commented in 1933, 'has shown that the greater the burden of making decisions and casting votes which is put upon the elector, the more ineffectively he will perform his functions. He is capable of making broad decisions upon general issues if the issues are presented clearly to him. The idea that he has a mysterious fund of virtue and insight from which, like an oracle, the correct answers to all questions can be elicited must be given up in our disillusioned age.'[50] The program of the LSR was designed to remedy this failure of democracy. The role of the proposed National Planning Commission of experts was to implement in detail mandates received by politicians in general elections. The art of governing consisted in forming a bridge between public opinion, which itself could be shaped, and those who possessed expertise and knowledge.

Underhill tended to associate two quite distinct elements whenever he spoke of intellectual leadership. Often he identified the intellectual leader with the great protestors and moral critics of the nineteenth century who supposedly had functioned as general philosophers to the community. In defending the traditional classical program at the University of Toronto as late as 1929, and in venting his disgust with the proliferation of commercial and technical courses, Underhill harked back to an ideal that defined the ends of education as the encouragement of the inquisitive, speculative turn of mind and the capacity for philosophical reflection rather than as a mastery of practical skills.[51] On the other hand he frequently underlined the need for the 'trained scientific intellect'—the experts, economic planners, and advisers who would institute in detail the general wishes of the community. Underhill himself, of course, was more of a gadfly than a trained scientific intellectual, and for all his exhortations about expert leadership his real home temperamentally was with the exhorters rather than with the technicians and economists.[52]

The relationship of the academic intellectual to politics and society was already a hackneyed subject and was not unconnected with social pretensions. Late-nineteenth century Canadians like George M. Grant and, later, Stephen Leacock and Sir Andrew Macphail, had been conscious of the ambiguous position of the educated man in democratic society. They also abominated the odious politics of spoils and the seeming impossibility of Canadian political life to measure up to what they perceived as the standards of Great Britain. They too harked back to the example of the Victorian sages, the Carlyles and Arnolds. 'We are a class set apart,' wrote Macphail. 'We have elevated ourselves into the exploiting, the parasitic class;. . . But we can justify our existence by telling the truth even about ourselves . . . . It will not do any longer to stand by and declare that we are holy men who would be defiled by coming in contact with the world, preferring to sit in a well and gazing at the stars.'[53] Macphail's own uncompromising fulminations against the destruction of an independent and self-sufficient agricultural society typified one expression of the intellectual's estrangement.

The other response was best represented by the political economist Adam Shortt. He envisaged the social scientist as occupying a neutral position above the competing interests in society and bringing to an examination of economic problems the detachment of the scientist. The social scientist was an expert who could best make his contribution to society through service on government commissions and regulatory bodies, not in general invective and moralistic preaching. In the new industrial state the economists were to take their place alongside those other experts, the geological surveyors and agricultural scientists, that the Dominion had found necessary long before. The development of the social sciences in the first two decades of the century produced a group of economists whose outlook was utilitarian and research orientated and who—like Duncan MacGibbon, who wrote *The Canadian Grain Trade* (1932) and who served on the Board of Grain Commissioners, or Robert Coats of the Department of Labour—worked in a milieu totally foreign to that of the traditional protesters like Macphail. However different the functions of the 'moralist' and 'expert' may have been, both figures represented ways in which the university-trained intellectual could assert an influential role in society.

The problem of the relationship between the intellectual and his fellow citizen was perhaps most acutely felt by those, like Underhill, whose education had been classical and traditionalist. The lack of social recognition was a recurrent but underplayed accompaniment of their lamentations about the absence of intellectual leadership and the decline of the position of the professor. 'Forty or fifty years ago,' one of Underhill's friends complained in 1923, 'a Canadian university professor was one of the well-to-do men of the community. He could enter any social circle he chose. Not only in the lecture-room but also in the community at large he moulded public opinion. To-day he has the social position of a Roman client, and is the butt of newspapers. A generation ago in the smaller Canadian towns the parson and the school-master, along with the lawyer and the judge, were the intellectual aristocracy. To-day, except in a Catholic or Lutheran village, there is not a school boy who would raise his cap to the cloth;. . . The magnate of the place, whose views are canvassed on politics or the town library, is usually the owner of a shirt factory, or an automobile agent.'[54] An excessively nostalgic estimation of the influence of the earlier academic, perhaps, but these remarks illuminated the feelings of those, like Underhill, who had imbibed the teaching of Milner and Wrong on intellectual leadership and found themselves in a society that offered little scope. Academic observers were to attribute this change to the growth in the size of the Canadian community, to the intensification of materialism, the dilution of religion, and the growth of specialized knowledge.[55] Possibly it was also due to the professionalization of the disciplines and the decline of the gentleman academic, typified by Wrong, with his faith in his own opinion-moulding role and his easy access to businessmen and politicians.

Underhill insisted on intellectual leadership in national affairs; the LSR not only advanced a program of reform but also constituted a vehicle for activity that would narrow the gap between the intellectual and society. If its aims were attained, then that gap would close completely, for the 'intellectual' and the 'expert' would be one of the leaders and councillors of the nation.

There was a direct connection between Underhill's preoccupation with intellectual leadership and his attraction to certain intellectuals in the Canadian past. The figures who caught his attention were men of ideas: Goldwin Smith, John Ewart, and that most cerebral of politicians, Edward Blake, leader of the Liberal party between 1879 and 1887. When Underhill wrote of the party system, he accorded priority to divisions of economic interest and the convictions of the mid-nineteenth century Grit radicals; when he examined intellectuals he stressed the accuracy and penetration of Smith's judgements in politics and the prophetic character of Ewart's essays on imperial relations.[56] He was attracted to Blake because it seemed to him that Blake and Laurier had come closest in Canada to being two intellectuals in politics, and also because Blake was leader of the Liberal party at a strategic juncture, midway between the *laissez-faire* Grittism of Alexander Mackenzie and the transformation of the party into an instrument of business interests under Laurier in the 1890s.

Underhill contended that in the 1870s and 1880s Liberals and Conservatives were clearly separated by different 'principles of action'. Macdonald 'lined up behind his party the transportation and commercial interests with the ambitions to repeat for their own profit and power in the northern half of the continent the tremendous economic expansion which they had seen taking place to the south.' The Liberals were thrust into the role of critics of the CPR and the alliance with business. Blake was a failure on this score because most Canadians, according to Underhill, accepted that the private capitalist would develop the country for the good of all. Blake's main positive contribution — 'the quintessence of Canadian Liberalism' — was in insisting on the Canadian control of Canadian affairs. He attempted to terminate appeals to the Privy Council, and in 1876 he and Mackenzie succeeded in altering the instructions to the governor-general so that this official would no longer function as an independent imperial authority. Blake consistently supported the Dominion's right to conclude commercial treaties with foreign countries, and, in contrast to the Conservatives' emphasis on separateness from the United States, insisted on Canada's independence from Great Britain and its need for the American market. By 1939 it appeared to Underhill that Blake's main contribution was to enhance Canadian autonomy. This conviction was prompted by Underhill's own growing isolationism.[57]

V

In the thirties Underhill became obsessed with the possibility of another war in Europe and with the problems arising from Canadian relations with the League of Nations and the Commonwealth. The intensification of the crises in international affairs after the Japanese invasion of Manchuria in 1931-2, and the Italian attack on Ethiopia in 1935, invigorated efforts by academics and journalists to clarify the issues at stake in face of the indifference of the Canadian public and the reluctance of all but a very few political figures to break what seemed a 'conspiracy of silence' on the subject. Through study groups and conferences, branch meetings of the Canadian Institute of International Affairs, lectures sponsored by such organizations as the Canadian Institute on Economics and Politics, and above all through the university quarterlies, a relatively small group of academics, journalists, and a few politicians sought to arouse a more general interest in the implications of international developments. Underhill was a regular participant in this debate, and his endorsement of 'isolationism' was an expression in a different sphere of the same values that underlay his historical essays. He insisted that Canadians attempt to see their foreign relations in categories appropriate to their position and that their analysis be realistic, hard-boiled, and based on the economic interpretation of international conflict.

During the twenties Underhill made no abrupt departure from the prevalent view that Canada's national status was quite compatible with its membership in the Commonwealth. Indeed, in an article on the *Globe's* attitudes to the Empire in the decade before Confederation, an offshoot of his research on mid-Victorian liberalism, he concluded that 'its fundamental faith that the two seeming opposites, Canadian autonomy and imperial unity, were the most reconcilable things in the world, has been justified by events.'[58] In his student days he had close associations with the Round Table movement, though like most Canadian members he had been opposed to any kind of formal federation. All his life he had a profound admiration for certain features of British political culture and university life. 'The real glory of Britain', he wrote in 1929, ' . . . is not a particular form of parliamentary government but the spirit of political liberalism, the belief in fair play, the conviction that things turn out best when differences are adjusted by free discussion.'[59] Though he had analysed the Canadian party tradition in North American terms, and borrowed heavily from the American progressive tradition, the sources of his hopes about the LSR and the realignment of Canadian political parties were the Fabian Society and the British

Labour Party. While he never returned to Britain or Europe after 1919, Underhill followed as closely as was possible at a distance the major developments of the British left. In the twenties he did not quarrel with the idea of the underlying spiritual and moral unity of the Empire that the constitutional historians had made so central to their work, even though his critical spirit could not resist comparing the periodic Commonwealth Conferences to self-congratulatory Rotarian conventions and lampooning the effulgent rhapsodizing on this theme. He was angered by those, like R.B. Bennett at the Ottawa Conference of 1932, who sought to pervert these values for economic benefits, power, and self-interest.

The truth was that, like most nationalists of the twenties, Underhill took the winning of 'status' for granted and devoted his attention to a more adequate understanding of the internal Canadian reality in terms of environmental circumstance. What changed this was the threat after 1930 that Canada might be involved in a general European conflict with the same unthinking and automatic enthusiasm that had characterized her entry into the First World War. Underhill was concerned with the immaturity of Canadian attitudes to foreign policy and with the failure to distinguish between interests and sentimental and moralistic considerations. 'The real colonialism of Canada', he charged in 1932, 'consisted in the complete passivity with which, after sacrificing sixty thousand men, we accepted other people's ideas — whether they were good or bad ideas does not matter — about world organization.'[60] Canada had entered the League of Nations because membership marked her recognition by other states, not because of any adherence to Wilsonian internationalism. Commitments were made without intensive examination of implications or even debate. Underhill found a discrepancy between Canada's complex economic involvements with other countries and the moralistic exhortations of the League of Nations supporters similar to that which he had earlier found between Canada's typically North American interest-group parties and high-minded descriptions of them in terms of principles.

Over and over again he reiterated that foreign policy had to be defined in relation to economic self-interest and power. 'Until we grasp the fact that war is an inherent institution in our present capitalist civilization and that it can only be eliminated by a world-wide reconstruction of our social and economic institutions', he argued in 1935, 'we shall always be liable to storms of irrelevant emotion; and we shall be unable to resist when we are invited to fight for democracy or freedom or parliamentary institutions or international law or collective sanctions.'[61] In language that was itself loaded with emotion, he sought to deflate and discredit the emotional appeals of the British connection and internationalism. The League of Nations—'a society of retired burglars defending the principle of property'[62]—represented the victors who had imposed an unjust settlement in Europe in 1919; the British Empire represented certain class interests in areas that had no significance for Canada. 'The essential drive of British imperialism', he charged, 'is always the same: it is to get the Dominions to lend their resources, human and material, to the support of British policy . . . to get our assistance in making the world safe for British capitalism.'[63]

Some of Underhill's choicest debunking rhetoric was reserved for the supporters of the League, especially those elder statesmen 'who have never recovered from the intoxication of those glorious days in 1919 when Canadians were buzzing about the hotels of Paris helping to remake the boundaries of Europe.'[64] Or: 'The elderly sadists of the last war are emerging from their obscurity to join the war-dance again, their eyes glistening and their mouths watering as they think of the young men whom they will send to slaughter.'[65] Or: ' . . . we must let them know in unmistakable terms that the poppies blooming in Flanders Fields have no more attraction for us.'[66]

Back of Underhill's castigations and his disclosures of the carnal and inglorious motives of nations and leagues of nations lay the widespread contemporary disillusionment with the outcome of the First World War. He was familiar with the works of the revisionist historians like C.B. Fay and H.E. Barnes, who had implicated France and Russia in causing the war and who destroyed the myth of the German plot, and also with the findings of the Nye committee of the United States Senate, which sustained the accusation that America had been drawn into the First World War because of the pressures of financial interests and the 'merchants of death'. Underhill's indictment of British imperialism owed much to John Hobson's classic statement, *Imperialism* (1902), and it was in part inspired by Charles Beard's *The Open Door at Home* (1935), an appeal for an isolationist policy abroad and social planning within. It also ran back to the indigenous anti-imperialist tradition of Goldwin Smith, Henri Bourassa, and John Ewart. For Underhill the economic interpretation of foreign policy was a weapon for discrediting slogans—'liberty', 'collective security', 'moral commitments', 'parliamentary government'—that were dangerous because of their appeal to a people who were steeped in puritanism and incapable of resisting uplifting crusades.

Underhill's censorious, and sometimes sneering, speeches and essays on foreign policy may have appealed to his fellow isolationists—though Frank Scott made a far more reasoned and sustained case for the same policy of neutrality in *Canada Today: A Study of Her National Interests and National Policy* (1938)—and perhaps to a generation of students who despised the military, had read or heard of Hemingway and Remarque, Barbusse and Sassoon, and were adamant that they would not be betrayed as their fathers had once been.[67] One student who had gone to a meeting of the Victoria College CCF Club in 1936 told a friend of Underhill's encounter with an earnest female questioner: ' "Professor Underhill, in the next war, if there's general conscription and they tell you you've got to fight or they'll take you out and shoot you, what should a good socialist do?" Underhill . . . was very sarcastic.'[68]

VI

Underhill's sarcastic articles on Canadian foreign policy precipitated a crisis over academic freedom at the University of Toronto in 1940-1. The episode brought to a head a number of tendencies in the relationship between the radical intellectual and conservative university administrators and politicians that had developed during the thirties. The temper of the decade was fearful and repressive and there were frequent denunciations of the 'atheists' and 'communists' teaching in universities. In 1931 the Toronto Police Commission tried to prevent a meeting of the Fellowship of Reconciliation, a peace organization, by passing a resolution forbidding the use of any public hall in the city for the discussion of any subject that might foment or be the occasion for a disturbance. When sixty-eight members of the teaching staff of the University of Toronto—including Underhill, Innis, Creighton, Cassidy, Fairley, and Martin—signed a petition denouncing this infringement on freedom of assembly and free speech, the Board of Governors disassociated the university from this stand. Local papers immediately identified the signatories of the statement with Bolshevism and noted solicitously that thoughtful parents would hesitate to send their offspring to such an institution. When Sir Edward Beatty, president of the CPR, was given an honorary degree at the University of Western Ontario in 1935, he used the occasion to denounce the teaching of socialism by academics, especially younger economists.

It was a difficult period for professors who were intimately associated with the LSR and CCF. In 1933 the Board of Governors of United Theological College refused to renew the appointment of King Gordon on the grounds of economy, even though the General Council of the United Church recommended that he be retained. When he was dismissed in 1934, some thought the real reasons were his radical views. When W.H. Alexander, head of the Classics Department at the University of Alberta, was nominated to contest the West Edmonton seat for the CCF, the Board of Governors prohibited all members of the faculty from running for a seat in the House of Commons. Demands for the disciplining of Carlyle King of the University of Saskatchewan followed an address he gave to a service club in 1938 urging that Canada not become involved in another war to defend British possessions. The editor of the student paper in the same institution was dismissed by the student council for writing in a Remembrance Day issue that the soldiers had been led like sheep to the slaughter in the First World War. An example of the more extreme vigilante attitude was the action of the Librarian of the University of Toronto, Stewart Wallace, who dropped the library's subscription to the *New Republic* in 1937 because it contained an article on the monarchy, written by a British socialist, that he found inconsistent with his oath of allegiance.

It was inevitable that in such an atmosphere the freedom of the academic should become an issue. The most generally accepted definition of academic freedom in Underhill's university had been given by President Sir Robert Falconer in 1922: it was the freedom for a professor to pursue his investigations and to teach without interference from state authorities. However, Falconer expressed the ingrained caution of the experienced administrator—remembering the not-so-distant days when political interference in the internal affairs of the university was common—when he stressed the limits on the participation of academics in other and, in his mind, essentially unrelated activities. The preservation of academic freedom within the university necessitated the curtailment of the rights of a professor as a citizen. Since the institution depended on the government for financial support, it was essential that no faculty member be guilty of political partisanship. The welfare of the university depended on the goodwill of the entire community, and an academic who made inflammatory political statements endangered the very institutional basis of genuine academic freedom.[69] In 1931 Falconer disapproved of Underhill's 'political journalism' on these grounds. When Underhill objected that professors in the United States and Britain frequently participated in political debate, Falconer countered that the practice in independent British universities and privately endowed American ones could not be taken as models of what could be done at Toronto.[70] He evaded, however, Underhill's point that political journalism was not a new activity, for George Wrong had written for the *Globe* and Chester Martin for the *Manitoba Free Press*. Perhaps the real objection to Underhill's journalism was his extravagant and irritating manner of attack. Wrong for one admitted to him in 1933 that it was true that those who assailed things as they were had a more difficult time than those who pliantly accepted the established order, and he said that Underhill had a perfect right to his opinions. But Wrong added that academic freedom was the freedom to search for truth and that its essential purpose was to protect the university from the very political spirit Underhill sought to perpetuate within it. Characteristically he found Underhill's manner of expression more deplorable than what he was actually saying.[71]

In making his case for the academic's involvement in politics, Underhill was implicitly extending the application of academic freedom beyond what was acceptable to traditionalists like Falconer and Wrong. The logical corollary of his insistence on intellectual leadership and radical social action was to challenge the *status quo* that Falconer and Wrong took for granted. From Underhill's point of view the freedom to search for truth within the confines of the university was a hollow freedom indeed when it assumed a political quietism and even a reluctance to defend openly the principle of freedom of speech.

Underhill was involved in a number of skirmishes over his statements in radio addresses and articles. In the spring of 1937 he published an isolationist article in *Maclean's Magazine,* and in a radio broadcast he remarked on the influence of mining millionaires on the editorial policy of the *Globe and Mail,* noting the implied threat to freedom of the press. The objects of his criticism were two men who had made their fortunes in the mining business: William H. Wright, the owner of the paper, and George McCullagh, its publisher. The tempestuous McCullagh was a friend of the Premier of Ontario, Mitchell Hepburn, and had been appointed to the Board of Governors of the University of Toronto. His appointment in fact mirrored a change in the composition of that body that was hastened in the Hepburn years. In 1908-9 the Board of Governors was made up of fourteen educationalists and four businessmen; by 1946 it consisted of fourteen financiers and four educationalists. In inspirational radio addresses and through his own Leadership League, McCullagh advocated a total Canadian commitment to support Britain, a National Government, a reduction in both government expenditures and the civil service, and a rededication to the old-fashioned virtues of Horatio Alger. After an editorial in the *Globe and Mail* urged that Underhill be denied the facilities of the Canadian Broadcasting Corporation and intimated that he should be investigated by the Board of Governors, Underhill promised H.J. Cody, Falconer's successor, that he would try to avoid undesirable publicity by being careful about the way in which he expressed himself in public.[72]

In April 1939 Hepburn and the Leader of the Opposition, George Drew, attacked George Grube, a member of the LSR—referred to by Hepburn as 'that Foreigner Grube'—for declaring at a CCF meeting that the Canadian defence budget was a waste of public funds in the interests of British imperialism. Underhill was also denounced for his statements that the poppies in Flanders fields no longer held any attraction for Canadians and that we should thumb our noses when asked to participate in another European war.[73] Underhill's remarks had been made years before but had been recently quoted in a survey of Canadian foreign policy, *Canada Looks Abroad* (1938) by R.A. MacKay and E.B. Rogers, as an example of isolationist opinion. Hepburn promised provincial action. While Grube was not subject to disciplinary action by the Board of Governors because of the independence of Trinity College, where he taught, Underhill was asked to explain his statements and to say whether they were published accurately and with his knowledge. An attack on him in the legislature took place during the debate on the education budget. The implications were obvious. After Underhill was interviewed by Cody and representatives of the Board, and strong representations were made by a number of senior academics—including Malcolm Wallace, the Principal of University College, and Innis and Martin, who warned Cody that if he gave way his career would be over as far as the staff was concerned—the case was dropped. Underhill submitted a statement of his military-service record, satisfactorily explained the origins of the offending sentences, and regretted using phrases that could be taken by some people as expressions of contempt for the Canadian soldiers who died in the war. He also promised that in the future he would behave as reasonable men would expect a professor to behave, but he could not guarantee that his public comments would not again be taken out of context and used against him. Underhill was a watched man: six months later he was questioned again about opinions expressed at a university banquet on the necessity to preserve freedom of speech in wartime.

Underhill's final and most serious clash with the university authorities arose from a speech he delivered at the YMCA Institute of Politics and Economics on 23 August 1940 at Lake Couchiching. He spoke without a complete text, but the substance of what he had to say had been prepared as an article for the *Forum* just before, and ten days after the speech he committed to paper what he remembered. The gist of his argument was that the Ogdensburg agreement, which set up a permanent joint board for North American defence, signalized a new era in Canadian relations with the United States and Great Britain. Canada had gone to war to demonstrate its identity of interests with Britain, but the fall of France and the altered balance of power in Europe meant that its new loyalty was to its own defence in North America in alliance with the American republic. No matter what the outcome of the Second World War, Underhill contended, British power would decline and Canadian security would more and more depend upon co-operation on the continent.[74] The Canadian Press summary of this speech reported Underhill as saying that:

> We now have two loyalties—one to Britain and the other to North America. I venture to say it is the second, North America, that is going to be supreme now. The relative significance of Britain is going to sink, no matter what happens.

This version of his speech was reported in the Toronto press, and again demands were made for his dismissal.

Whether Underhill spiced his address with extravagant invective cannot be proven, though it is not beyond the bounds of possibility. Those who had been irritated by his remarks before the outbreak of war probably associated his very name with suggestions for thumbing a nose at Britain and shooting the British flag full of holes to let the air of liberty in. Arthur Meighen predictably wrote to the Minister of Justice urging that Underhill be interned for the negative effect his words would have on recruiting.[75] No stenographic report of Underhill's address was made, and the Chairman of the Board of Governors of the university, Dr D. Bruce Macdonald, stated that no action would be taken and that Underhill had submitted incontrovertible evidence that he was pro-British and wanted Britain to win the war. Underhill's case had been strengthened by student testimonials to his teaching and by professorial representation on behalf of academic freedom. He promised Cody that he would make no public speeches for a year. The case, it appeared, was settled.

Suddenly, in January 1941, the Board of Governors asked Underhill to resign because his connection with the university was causing it adverse publicity and harm. It is unclear who initiated this demand. Members of the Board allegedly intimated that Hepburn was behind it and that the issue was connected with the education budget. Hepburn denied this, and his acting Minister of Education declared that he had made a private call to Cody urging the university to drop the matter. Underhill himself was convinced that Hepburn's appointees on the Board, McCullagh's henchmen, were the real villains. At any rate Underhill denied that public opinion was against him or that he had ever made a gentleman's agreement several years before not to speak in public. He was not charged with a specific transgression but with being a troublemaker. 'For the past thirteen years,' Cody explained, 'Mr. Underhill's personality and methods of publically expressing himself outside the University had been brought before my predecessor and myself and before the Board of Governors. The Board is once more engaged in discussing Mr. Underhill's personality, not on his Couchiching speech, but on his general record.'[76] Privately Underhill began to explore the prospects of a position in an American university or in the Ottawa bureaucracy.

His chief defenders, apart from a delegation of professors, were two members of the Board of Governors who constituted themselves a committee to interview other members: J.M. Macdonnell of the National Trust Company and J.S. McLean of Canada Packers, who had hosted the Historical Club. In 1935 Underhill had sent copies of the LSR's *Social Planning in Canada* to both of them. 'I'm certain that what saved me', Underhill told the Columbia University historian John Bartlet Brebner after the uproar in the autumn, 'was the fear that there would be trouble from the staff, plus the combination of Canada Packers and National Trust Co.—who happen to be much more important in the business world than the concerns with which most of the Governors are connected.'[77]

The contention that appeared to carry most weight in January 1941, as in the autumn of 1940, was not the abstract right to academic freedom but the implications of Underhill's dismissal on public opinion in the United States. Canada was at war; the United States was involved in an intense debate over continued isolation or involvement. It was feared that the Underhill affair, a small matter in itself, might be used by isolationists in the Republic to blacken the British cause. The situation was exceptionally delicate. 'Already', Brebner told Innis, 'American periodicals have made a certain amount of capital out of Canadian restraints on public expression, and anti-British groups have pointed to Canada in support of their allegations that the British can be as dictatorial as anyone.'[78] The same plea for restraint was made by Hugh Keenleyside, an official in the Department of External Affairs, whose assistance Underhill had sought. Keenleyside told Cody that any action against Underhill should be postponed until the international crisis had passed. Mackenzie King, to whom Underhill had sent copies of his Blake essays, O.D. Skelton, and other figures in the Department of External Affairs followed the case closely. Underhill himself was convinced that their concern, if not their actual intervention, was crucial. 'The argument which told most', he said, 'was that it would look very bad in the United States if a Toronto professor should be fired for being pro-American just at this critical moment.'[79] Though the Board of Governors again turned their attention to Underhill briefly in June 1941, attempts to force his resignation or dismissal ended and were not renewed.

Underhill emerged from this experience a shaken and rather chastened man. His personal crisis was in a way the reflection in an individual life of the general crisis of the war and the challenge to traditional liberal values that he had all too often taken for granted. His intellect was anti-romantic and distrustful of sentiment and emotion: he had dedicated himself to exposing the hiatus between the publicly accepted and inherited concepts with which men think and the realities these conceptions tended to obscure, whether they were in politics, history, or foreign policy. What linked his criticism of Canadian historical writing, his interpretation of the history of the party system, his democratic socialism, and his isolationism was the desire to see things as they really were and to ground analysis in economic facts. He was more impressive as a negative critic than as a constructive thinker or a creative writer of large-scale projects. Often, as was the case with his articles on foreign policy, he was driven to extravagant ridicule by the very momentum of his rhetoric. He seemed at such times to be a facile rather than an original critic, simply chastizing his readers with the latest revelations from the New Republic or the New Statesman. He verged, in fact, towards a point where the traditional liberal institutions and freedoms seemed merely outmoded clichés to be sneered at. During the Second World War he drew back and profoundly changed his mind.

4 | HAROLD INNIS:
THE SEARCH FOR LIMITS

To turn from Underhill to Innis is to take leave of the more negative and iconoclastic temper of the twenties and thirties and move toward that period's creative centre. A political economist, Harold Innis began where Adam Shortt had left off—with the conviction that the contemporary Canadian economy could only be adequately understood in relation to its unique historical antecedents. In conjunction with others, Innis then advanced one of the most original contributions to Canadian social science, the idea that the exploitation of a succession of staple commodities explained the nature of Canadian development and the singular patterns of its institutions and culture.

I

The characteristic features of Innis's outlook—his scepticism, his strong commitment to Canada and to traditional liberal individualism, and his almost obsessive dedication to scholarship—had their roots in his family background and his experience in the First World War. Born on a farm near Otterville, Oxford Co., Ont., in 1894, Innis was educated in a one-room country school, Otterville High School, and Woodstock Collegiate Institute. He developed an intense curiosity about the routine and details of farm activity, machinery, and the habits of animals, and an uncanny ability to recognize small differences in commonplace things. According to his wife, he kept in touch with the farm all his life: with the changing seasons he would often remark on what his family would then be doing. He had, she said, 'a deep preference for country people as against city people'.[1] A friend who knew him well believed that the farm gave Innis a certain simplicity, a down-to-earth common sense, an ability to communicate with a wide variety of people, and the capacity for hard, continuous work.[2]

Innis grew up in a devout family and in an unquestioning Baptist faith. 'They were Baptists', a neighbour said of the family and the grandfather, 'hard-shelled Baptists we used to call them . . . "Old Innis" we used to call him . . . . He expressed great doubt if anyone who was not baptised as the Baptists baptise would have much chance of getting to heaven.'[3] Innis led a sheltered life in a home of few cultural adornments: his mother liked *The Family Herald* and named her son after that paper. With money he earned teaching school in 1911-12 Innis subscribed to the Toronto *Globe* and learned new words from Laurier's speeches on the naval issue. It came as a shock to him in his second term at McMaster University in Toronto to find fellow students 'who tend towards materialism or who believe there is no God . . . .'[4]

In the spring of 1916, when he was considering enlistment in the army, he told his sister that the artillery was safer than the infantry and that if he did not volunteer for the former he might later be conscripted into the latter; he mentioned also that those who had not served in the military would have no chance after the war. But Innis, like so many other young men of his generation, volunteered out of a deep sense of religious duty. 'I think you will agree with me', he explained to his sister after saying that Germany had to be beaten if right were to prevail, 'that I am taking the only step I possibly could and have any faith in Christianity. If I had no faith in Christianity I don't think I would go, but it is as He said, you must desert everything [,] take up the cross and follow me . . . . He that saveth his life shall lose it and he that loseth his life for my sake shall have it.'[5] Christian principles were at stake and it was simply every able-bodied man's duty to fight.[6]

Innis joined the field artillery as a private, took part in the attack on Vimy Ridge in April 1917, and was wounded in July. In contrast to the religious idealism that had in part moved him to volunteer, the harsh realities of army life were bound to encourage a sobering scepticism. 'It is', he reported, 'simply a case of walking in mud, sleeping in mud, and eating mud if your grub happens to touch anything . . . . At present I am looking after a sick mule.'[7] Innis loathed the rigid discipline, routine, and capricious bureaucracy of modern army life. While recovering at a hospital in England he explored the possibility of doing an M.A. thesis on the psychology of the Canadian soldier. 'The hated subservience to officers,' he wrote of the soldier, and here he generalized his own revolt against regimentation, 'the detested persistence of obedience to orders, the monotony of the bugle, have all alike tended to crush the spirit of independence and individuality which have become so dear to him, since he has been bereft of them.'[8] Not a little of that anti-bureaucratic strain in Innis's thought was a reaction of an independent farm boy to the organization of the army.

Innis returned from the war with a strong affection for Canada and a real feeling of comradeship with the men who had served at the front. There is no doubt that the war strengthened his nationalism. In justifying the necessity for conscription, he had told his family in 1917 that 'Canada is fighting for herself as much as for Britain, America is fighting for herself. Should the allies fail, Canada's position would be pitiful.'[9] He remembered the resentment many Canadian soldiers experienced when they were publicly thanked in England for coming to help the mother country: 'We ... felt that we were concerned with fighting for Canada and for Canada alone.' And he recalled too that the treatment of Canadians and others by officers and non-commissioned officers sent out from Great Britain 'must have been an important factor in hastening the demands for autonomy throughout the Commonwealth.'[10] Innis had gone into the war believing that the Canadians were fighting for the principles of Christian civilization, and though he returned somewhat chastened of this idealism—and, like most veterans, remained cynical about the ritualistic oratory of November 11—he never lost the feeling of obligation to preserve those liberal values for which he believed the men of 1914-18 had fought. Much later, in the midst of another world war, he described himself as a psychological as well as a physical casualty of the conflict; he identified his hatred of regimentation and coercion and his defence of individualism with his obligation to defend the heritage for which his comrades had died. Innis was to become cynical about many things, and he was to elude the pressures his family put upon him to enter the ministry, but he never lost his sense of brotherhood with the veterans.

II

Innis became interested in economics during his convalescence in England and he wrote a prize-winning essay on 'The Press' under the auspices of the Khaki College. He enrolled in the University of Chicago in 1918 in order to deepen his knowledge of political economy, as a preparation, so he then thought, for a career in law. There was a tradition at McMaster that the best students were encouraged to do their postgraduate training at Chicago, and a young lecturer, William Donald, who had just published a study of the Canadian iron and steel industry that had been a thesis written for that university, may well have influenced Innis in this direction. At Chicago Innis studied with Frank Knight, who taught economic theory and statistics with such scepticism that 'one could never again become lost in admiration of statistical compilations ... '; J.M. Clark, from whom he learned of 'overhead costs', which assumed a central importance in Innis's studies in Canadian economic history; C.S. Duncan, who emphasized in his lectures on marketing the connections 'between the physical characteristics of a commodity and the marketing structure built up in relation to it'; and Chester Wright, who taught courses on trusts and American economic history and who supervised Innis's doctoral thesis on the Canadian Pacific Railway.[11]

The influence of Thorstein Veblen, who had been forced to leave Chicago some time before because his domestic economy was even more radical than his political economy, was still fresh with the graduate students at that university. Innis read his books, admired Veblen's 'tremendous irony', and shared both the liberating effects of his criticisms of static classical and neo-classical economics and his concern with the effects of industrialism and the dynamics of growth and decay. He responded to Veblen's 'anxiety to detect trends and escape their influence', and though he showed no signs of accepting Veblen's complicated theory of instincts, Innis was alerted to look for the impact of technology on habits, values, and structures.[12]

Innis's thesis was published as A History of the Canadian Pacific Railway in 1923, three years after he was appointed to the Department of Political Economy in the University of Toronto. It was a relatively straightforward examination, from 'an evolutionary and scientific point of view', of the negotiation of the contract, freight and passenger traffic, rates, profitability, and capitalization down to 1921. The framework of Canadian history in which he analysed the function of the railway was traditional. In his discussion of Confederation, Innis stressed that the regions that were joined together—the Maritimes, the St Lawrence basin, the Red River Settlement, and the Pacific coast—had developed independently and autonomously. The construction of the railway, he wrote, 'was the result of the direction of energy to the conquest of geographical barriers'.[13] As such it represented the triumph of human ingenuity and will over physical obstacles.

For all its 'scientific' flavour and non-commital character, the study concluded with a moralistic reiteration of western grievances against the CPR. Innis had taught in a rural Alberta school during the summer of 1915 and had come to understand the ingrained prairie opinion of the railway. He completed his book at a time when the Progressive party was subjecting all national policies to penetrating scrutiny. Innis dwelt on the covetousness of the people of Ontario, a characteristic that had developed in 'the trading and governing classes to the point of selfishness and acquisitiveness'. The determination to build the CPR and attract the trade of the West arose 'largely from the acquisitiveness characteristic of Eastern Canada', and this was achieved 'to some extent at least at the expense of Western Canada'.

In spite of the current protest, however, Innis believed that this selfish dominance of eastern Canada would continue. 'Western Canada', he wrote, 'has paid for the development of Canadian nationality, and it would appear that it must continue to pay. The acquisitiveness of eastern Canada shows little sign of abatement.'[14]

In some respects Innis's first book foreshadowed his later concerns: the broad interest in the conditions that facilitated the spread of western civilization across northern America, the significance of drainage basins and river systems, and the function of staple exports in shaping the economies of the separate regions. But there was in it no appreciation of the geographical coherence of the country, which was to be one of his major contributions to Canadian historical studies. If, as J.B. Brebner later claimed, it proved to be the cornerstone of a new structure in Canadian intellectual life,[15] the work itself gave no precise indication of the superstructure that would be erected upon it. In fact Innis's subsequent research grew out of an awareness of its limitations. Innis confessed in an autobiographical retrospect that he had a feeling it was inadequate, and he resolved that 'I must, therefore, satisfy an uneasy conscience by continuing along lines which would offset its defects.'[16] The place of the CPR study in his intellectual growth was not only that of a base on which he built but also a foil against which his efforts to excel were directed.

During the 1920s Innis threw himself into the study of Canadian economic history with single-minded determination. He resolved to make a thorough inventory of the archival sources and a bibliography of the published materials. He was instrumental in setting up the periodical *Contributions to Canadian Economics* in 1928 and, in co-operation with Arthur Lower, he edited two large volumes of documents on Canadian economic history before 1885. In preparing his courses for the commerce students on economic geography, the export trade, and contemporary marketing, Innis became aware of the difficulties of using maps that were based on political rather than topographical criteria and of the deficiencies in his knowledge of the various industries. One of the most arresting aspects of his growing mastery of his subject was the extent to which it depended on extensive travelling, not only within Canada but in Europe as well.

In the summer of 1924 Innis and a friend—John Long, a Toronto high-school teacher—canoed two thousand miles down the Mackenzie River and returned on the Hudson's Bay Company steamer, the *Laird River*.[17] In 1926 he visited the Yukon and the Klondike and the next summer travelled through northern Ontario, Quebec, and the Maritimes. He went down into the Hollinger Mines at Timmins and spent days in the grain elevators at Port Arthur. In 1929 he went west and then up the newly completed Hudson's Bay Railway to the port of Churchill; in 1930 he was in

Newfoundland investigating the outports and the techniques of the fisheries. By the early 1940s the only places in the country Innis had not visited were the western Arctic and the east side of Hudson's Bay. His curiosity about the actual technology and mechanics of the extractive industries was insatiable, and wherever he went he formed lasting acquaintances with fur traders, fishing-boat captains, geologists, prospectors, and mining engineers. He admired men of experience and practical knowledge—men like Alexander Macphail, one of the chief organizers and managers of the wheat pools, whose diary he would edit;[18] or Alexander Johnston, one-time member of Parliament and Deputy Minister of Marine and Fisheries from the Province of Nova Scotia from 1910 to 1932, to whom he would dedicate his massive study of the cod fisheries.

Arthur Lower—who traded stories with Innis about trips into the North, who knew of his tall friend's clumsiness in a canoe and had seen him put a fish-hook in his thumb—wondered how he ever managed these travels. But Innis gloried in the strenuous relief from sedentary academic routine. 'I walked at least ten miles through mills yesterday,' he reported to his mother, 'but it is what I need. I shall get into shape with this exercise and I am feeling fine though tired.'[19] His observations on the places he saw were cryptic and characteristically sceptical. He defined a typical frontier town—Hearst, Ont.— as 'a town with a bear tied to a post'.[20] On his way back from Churchill, Innis stayed at The Pas, a supply centre for northern Manitoba mining development, where the only form of entertainment was 'a movie [based on a book] by Zane Grey probably on mining in Wyoming or some other state.' As someone said, ' "our edges are being ground down." '[21] From these travels Innis gained not only an unrivaled familiarity with the geography of Canada and a mastery of the technology of industries, but also a unique perspective on the impact of industrialism in the North. One of the reasons he became so dissatisfied with the inherited conceptions of the patterns of economic growth was because he witnessed at first hand the peculiar features of development on Canada's resource frontier.

Innis's quest for personal contact with British and European scholarship was as intense as his determination to see the staple industries of Canada first hand. James Mavor and C.R. Fay, well-connected British-born colleagues in his department, provided him with letters of introduction to outstanding workers in those fields. On a trip to Europe in 1922 Innis saw Graham Wallas; was invited for talks with Sidney and Beatrice Webb, who advised him on where to get Labour Party and Fabian Society publications; and met André Siegfried, the French scholar who followed Canadian developments closely and before the war had written one of the most penetrating books on the country, *The Race Question in Canada*. In the spring of 1928 Innis attended the International Geographical Congress at Cambridge and met economists and geographers at Oxford, Cambridge, and Manchester. 'I did the usual things,' he informed his wife, who, as usual, stayed behind, 'visiting people and smoking their cigarettes and drinking their wine.'[22] In Berlin he saw Louis Hamilton, a German scholar who had once taught at the University of Saskatchewan and who provided him with entrées to the geography departments at Bonn, Stuttgart, Frankfurt, Freiburg, Geneva, and Prague. Five years later he was back in Cambridge for another conference and met such major figures as Clapham, Keynes, Harrod, and Trevelyan.[23]

These travels to university centres in the old world and to the Canadian frontier highlighted the discrepancy Innis perceived between a political economy based on European experience and the distinctive requirements of an economic history of new countries. 'Perhaps the most serious obstacle to effective work in Canadian economics and economic history', he wrote in 1929, 'is the lack of a philosophy of economic history applicable to new countries . . . . Much of the work has been defective through the attempt to fit the phenomena of new countries into the economic theories of old countries . . . .' Just as economic history was a necessary corrective to economic theory, so too the economic history of new countries that had developed in relation to older economies would serve as a balance to theories of growth based on those older societies. The problem of all economic histories of Canada was that the studies that had been done were either heavily factual and lacking in broad interpretation, as was the case with the work of Adam Shortt, or they were based on stages of growth models derived from the English industrial revolution. New countries, Innis insisted, develop in relation to old countries: 'Canada has never been self-sufficient, and her existence has depended primarily on trade with other countries.'[24] The nexus was the staple commodity in demand in Europe and relatively easily exploited in Canada. Innis's call for an economic history more appropriate to Canadian experience was, in terms of cultural history, a direct parallel to the insistence of the painters of the Group of Seven for a more authentic, indigenous art freed from the bondage of European paradigms.

In searching his way towards a more adequate theory of economic growth, Innis was indebted to the work of at least two other scholars. The first was William A. Mackintosh of Queen's University. Like Innis, Mackintosh had taught in a one-room prairie school and had personal knowledge of the conditions that had given rise to agrarian radicalism in politics and to farmers' co-operative enterprises. A student of O.D. Skelton and a graduate of Harvard, he was familiar with the ideas of Frederick Jackson Turner and G.S. Callender, an American economic historian who was one of the first to isolate the strategic function of staple exports in the economic life of new areas. Callender's text, *Selections from the Economic*

History of the United States (1909), advanced the proposition that 'the most important feature of the economic life in a colony or newly settled community is its commercial relation with the rest of the world.' In a lecture to the School of Historical Research at the Archives in Ottawa in 1922, Mackintosh proposed a more systematic examination of Canadian economic history along these lines.[25] 'In the settlement of new countries', he wrote in his study of agricultural co-operation in western Canada two years later, 'one problem takes precedence over all others—the problem of discovering a staple product with a ready market. The world makes a path to the door of those regions fortunate enough to possess such a product, and all commodities of other countries are obtainable in exchange . . . . So well do young communities understand this fact, that it is almost possible to write the history of the settlement of North America in terms of the search for new vendible products . . . . '[26] Innis was familiar with Mackintosh's argument and in later conversation even exaggerated his indebtedness to it;[27] but at the time he felt that Mackintosh had dealt too exclusively with the later stages of Canadian history and had attributed to the wheat economy a national solidarity that had its origins much earlier. In any case it was Mackintosh who first alerted him to the idea of the staple, even though, as Mackintosh himself later generously conceded, a number of economic historians at the time were interested in the staples trades. It was possible also that Innis had learned much from Adam Smith's famous comments on commodity specialization in the political economy of new countries, on which his colleague C.R. Fay drew heavily.

The second scholar who anticipated—perhaps even prompted—a main theme in Innis's economic history was the Scottish geographer Marion Newbigin. After a visit to Canada in 1924 she wrote a survey of French colonization in the St Lawrence valley from the explorations of Cartier to the British conquest, emphasizing particularly the interaction between land forms, institutional life, and historical events. Her *Canada: the Great River, the Lands and the Men* (1926) raised the large questions of why and how Canada had come to be and why it was a distinct entity from the United States. From her contemporary vantage point, three-fifths of the Canadian population lived on the narrow strip of fertile land from Quebec to the Great Lakes, a territory that comprised only one-per cent of the country's area. Modern Canada seemed to be an enlarged New France, and Newbigin sought the explanation for the country's existence in the history of the French régime.

Newbigin's approach was in the possibilist tradition of geographical thought: 'man', she wrote, 'can modify the lands in which he dwells; in other respects he must follow where nature leads.' The two most powerful natural factors at work in the development of New France were the St

Lawrence River and the Pre-Cambrian Shield, and she examined the ways in which this geographical background affected discovery, exploration, settlement, and the eventual military collapse of the colony. She pointed out, for example, how the narrowing of the river at Quebec enabled the rulers of New France to control the activities of the settlers and how geography reinforced French authoritarianism. Her general conclusion was that the French were the first to confront the thrust and grain of the land and that their experience established patterns of activity and modes of responses that influenced later stages of development. The entire history of Canada hinged on the solution to the twin problems of maintaining access to the sea and internal expansion based on products that could find their natural outlet by way of the St Lawrence. The parallel between the fur trade and the river with the wheat economy and transcontinental railways was neither fortuitous nor insignificant. Canada was essentially what New France had been.[28]

Though Newbigin's book rested on no original research, her conclusions and manner of analysis were thoroughly suggestive. Mackintosh thought her work especially important for the examination of competition between the St Lawrence and the drainage basins of Hudson Bay and the Hudson-Mohawk river system.[29] Innis, who invariably described himself at this time as an 'economic geographer', and was familiar with the books of Vidal de la Blanche and Ellsworth Huntington, was critical of Newbigin's undue concern with military strategy, her excessive reliance on Parkman, and her insufficient treatment of the economics of the fur trade. He judged the book only 'a partially successful attempt to show the influence of the St. Lawrence on Canada's development' and contended that the possibilities of the combinations were not as endless as Newbigin had made them out to be—indicating that he leaned towards a more rigidly deterministic point of view.[30] One suspects—and it is a suspicion borne out by his study of the fur trade—that Innis was ready to push the case for geographical and technological determinism much further than the possibilist tradition permitted.

Newbigin's historical geography and Mackintosh's discussion of the role of the export staple clearly anticipated and foreshadowed some of the major themes of Innis's economic history. It may also well be that Innis's conception of the centrality of the St Lawrence system to Canadian development was a reflection of the contemporary popular interest in the deepening of the St Lawrence Waterway, a project that was the subject of considerable public debate and some historical analysis throughout the decade.[31] In 1924 he thought of working on the historical background of the Waterway, but the subject was dropped. Innis's conception of Canadian economic development was a blending of ideas drawn from various sources. Newbigin and Mackintosh may have stimulated his imagination, but his justly famous book on the fur trade was far more than a synthesis of pre-existing insights.

III

The Fur Trade in Canada: An Introduction to Canadian Economic History (1930) was an interpretative study of the dynamics behind the expansion of the trade from the early sixteenth century to the 1920s. In contrast to the previous historical literature on the subject, most of it heavily indebted to Parkman and accentuating the activity of heroic figures and the adventure of exploration, Innis's account fixed on the interplay of geographical, technological, and economic forces. At every turn the tempo and direction of expansion, the very efforts of men involved in the trade, were depicted as reflections of inescapable and anonymous forces.

Innis was not primarily interested in describing the history of New France in all its aspects and complexity, in the sense that historians sought to recreate a vanished age. He was mainly concerned with isolating the major factors that affected its evolution, and the manner in which the character of the fur staple shaped institutions and patterns of activity, in order to establish unusual tendencies in Canadian economic development generally. His work was an introduction to Canadian economic history in that the patterns revealed in the economic history of the Old Régime and in the fur trade were persistent and cumulative and were connected directly to the Canadian economy of his own day.

The main determinants of expansion of the fur trade were the demand for beaver fur in Europe, the increasing dependence of an Indian stone-age culture on the manufactured commodities of a more highly developed society, and the rapid extermination of the non-migratory animal. Extension of the fur trade along the southern edge of the Pre-Cambrian Shield was facilitated by the interconnected system of rivers and lakes and by the Indians' mastery of the canoe. But this drive into the interior not only brought on competition with the Iroquois to the south, and later the Hudson's Bay Company in the north, but it also increased transportation costs. Competition was most severe on the heights of land separating the three major drainage basins in northeastern America. The French response was military aggression and the initiation of vast encircling movements into the Lake Winnipeg and Saskatchewan country and the Ohio and Mississippi valleys.

The fur trade was the economic basis of New France and in Innis's judgement the trade severely weakened the colony and ultimately accounted for its collapse. The pursuit of furs drew men away from the settlements at precisely the time of year when they were most necessary to agriculture. True to his essentially liberal and anti-statist outlook, he believed that the authoritarian institutions of New France, and the control of the external trade by monopoly, were incompatible with economic diversification. The fur trade reinforced the dependence of the colony on the mother country, increased its vulnerability, and strengthened institutions that were inadequate to deal with the challenges of changing economic conditions. Compulsive expansion into virgin and untrapped areas deep in the interior was vital to the profitability of the trade in overcoming overhead costs, but by the mid-eighteenth century the outer limits of expansion, with the transportation technology then available, had been reached. 'French power in New France', he wrote, 'collapsed of its own weight.'[32]

The post-Conquest period saw the formation of the North West Company, a combination of Anglo-American capital and French technique, and by 1820 the trade was extended into the Athabaska area and to the shores of the Pacific. Following the lines of least resistance and the lure of the most valuable fur in the northern localities, the French had penetrated along the St Lawrence and Great Lakes into the Prairies; the North West Company extended this range and functioned for a time as a truly transcontinental organization. In spite of its more sophisticated organization the new company was subject to the same relentless necessities as its predecessors. Its organization reflected the same division between the centralized and monopolistic control in the external trade and the reliance on individual traders in the interior. The competition of the Hudson's Bay Company, which enjoyed shorter trade routes, and the mounting pressures of overhead costs led to the amalgamation of 1821. Though absorbed by its rival, the failure of the North West Company was qualified: the far-reaching area of control it had established was retained by the Hudson's Bay Company. In the sense that the boundaries of modern Canada were simply the limits of the effective dominance of the fur trade, the North West Company was 'the forerunner of confederation'. 'The present Dominion,' Innis wrote—and this became the epigram that summed up the entire book—'emerged not in spite of geography but because of it.' Canada was not merely a political creation, as he had once assumed it to be, but a logical unity based on the Shield and the river systems and historically defined by the fur trade. The Canadian Pacific Railway, and indeed the wheat economy, had reinforced and reasserted a solidarity that had been established by the fur trade.[33]

Though this contention was an important conclusion, it represented only one link in the argument that Canadian economic history could be understood only in terms of the dominance of a succession of staple exports. The main problem of settlers in the new world, Innis argued, was to discover a readily available staple commodity that they could produce and that could be traded for the manufactured goods of Europe. The range of such commodities that could be exploited in northern America was limited to fish, fur, timber, wheat, and minerals. 'The economic history of Canada', he explained, 'has been dominated by the discrepancy between the centre and the margin of western civilization. Energy has been directed toward the exploitation of staple products and the tendency has been cumulative .... Agriculture, industry, transportation, trade, finance, and governmental activities tend to become subordinate to the production of the staple for a more highly specialized community.'[34] The physical characteristics of each staple, the geographical background, and technology moulded the patterns of growth and institutions. The close relationship between government and economic activity throughout Canadian history was a direct consequence of the dependence on staple exploitation and transportation over long distances. So too was the tendency towards centralized control in such institutions as the fur-trade companies, the Canadian Pacific Railway, and the Bank of Montreal.

The foundations of Canada were laid in the symbiotic relationship between staple exploitation and European demands. Throughout its history Canada was dependent on more highly developed economies and, Innis insisted, it 'has remained fundamentally a product of Europe'. He rejected emphatically the notion that there were profound dissimilarities between Europe and northern America arising from the expansion of the frontier. Though he recognized the degree to which the established 'social heritage' was incidentally modified by vast land areas, he held that dependence on Europe through the mechanism of staple production enabled civilization to persist in Canada with the least possible 'depreciation'. 'Canada', he said, 'remained British in spite of free trade and chiefly because she continued as an exporter of staples to a predominantly industrialized mother country.'[35] By suggesting that the British connection was at bottom an economic relation, Innis was a world apart from constitutional historians like Chester Martin, who envisaged Canadian association with Britain as a thing of the spirit, a sentiment, and a moral union.

Canada's traditional dependence on Europe implied its vulnerability as a marginal supplier of staple commodities in world markets that were subject to fluctuations beyond its control. A trivial change in styles of beaver hats in France had drastic repercussions in the backwoods of North America. But to Innis vulnerability meant much more than mere shifts in demand and supply. In a number of essays published at about the same time as *The Fur Trade in Canada* he stressed that the development of Canada had been dramatically affected by the changing configurations of industrialism and technology throughout its history, and that the closer one moved towards the present the more sudden and unpredictable such changes became. 'No country', he wrote in 1930, 'has swung backwards and forwards in response to such factors as improvements in the technique of transport, exhaustion of raw materials and the advance of industrialism with such violence as Canada.'[36] Development was frenetic because the total range of modern technology was brought at once to bear upon areas of untapped resources. Stages of growth that in older societies had taken generations, even centuries, were telescoped, and growth was so sudden that it could only be compared in unpredictability and intensity to the onset of a cyclone. As Robin Neill has pointed out, the concept of 'cyclonics' was as central to Innis's thought at this time as the idea of the staple thesis of which it was a corollary.[37]

The development of western Canada and the North were outstanding instances of the way in which new areas came under the influence of modern industrialism almost at a single stroke. 'No one', Innis wrote, 'can travel down the Mackenzie river without realizing the importance of the economic cyclone on the Klondike to that area.'[38] Within a generation, from the 1890s to 1929, the North had witnessed the gold rush, the competition of traders who had come as prospectors and stayed to challenge the monopoly of the Hudson's Bay Company over the fur trade, the discovery of oil at Norman Wells in 1920, and the completion of the Hudson's Bay Railway, which in turn facilitated the development of mining in northern Manitoba. Innis, who travelled extensively and followed northern development very closely, saw with his own eyes the results of such cyclonic growth. The economies of railways and mines, fur traders, prospectors, Indians, and bush pilots coexisted in a jumble and not in neat and separate stages.

Though it took fifteen years to sell the first printing of one thousand copies,[39] Innis's *Fur Trade* was one of the few books in Canadian historical literature that truly deserve to be described as seminal. Together with his essays of the thirties, it had widespread implications and ramifications for economic historians and, later, for the theoreticians of economic development. But historians of Canada, most of whom had little formal training in economics, were quite selective in what they chose to emphasize in his teaching. The *Fur Trade* caught the attention of younger scholars at a moment when their dissatisfaction with constitutional and political history was most pronounced and when the Depression made the economic interpretation of the past seem more appropriate than the Britannic idealism of the previous generation. The sense of fatalism and determinism in Innis's economic history, moreover, suited the mood of the early thirties when people felt themselves at the mercy of overwhelming forces beyond their control.

Perhaps the main idea that historians took over from Innis was the belief that Canada developed not in spite of geography but because of it, and that there was a naturalness and solidity to the very structure of the country that lay far deeper than political arrangements. The notion that Canada consisted of five distinct geographical regions separated from each other by immense obstacles, and that these regions were northern projections of American ones, was an old and familiar truism. Goldwin Smith, for example, had employed it for his own critical purposes as far back as 1891. It followed from this idea that Canada was a fragile political creation and that its existence represented the triumph of human will and determination over the barriers and impediments of nature. What Innis argued was that behind the pattern of separate regions—an obvious fact that he never denied—there existed a countervailing tendency towards unity, based on the river systems and the Shield, that explained why the various regions were politically united in the first place. Confederation was, in a sense, a political reflection of the natural coherence of northern America.

There was another way in which his work strengthened the conception of the unity of Canada. In the attention he devoted to New France and to suggesting how the fur trade established patterns of activity and affected institutions, Innis accorded at least to the economic history of the Old Régime a far more prominent and significant position in Canadian history generally than the constitutional historians had done. For him, as for Newbigin, the period of New France was the real beginning of the country's history because French experience in the fur trade revealed regularities that were enduring and cumulative in that history. But while Innis underlined the inter-connectedness of the Old Régime with what came afterwards, at the same time he downgraded and blurred the significance of any but the economic, geographic, and technological features of that history. The implication of his analysis was that cultural, linguistic, and religious differences were not important determinants of activity. The main determining causes of events were material realities, not the language men spoke, the religion they professed, or the social beliefs they had brought from Europe. His history, as history, was dehumanized.

Sometimes, when it suited his immediate purposes, Innis spoke as though the geographic coherence of the country was still a cardinal fact of Canadian life, as when he told the Royal Canadian Institute in 1930 that an understanding of Canadian history was 'a certain antidote to the hysterics of those who worry about American investment . . . . Historically Canada is an economic unit and not a series of provinces.'[40] But even in the early thirties Innis became preoccupied with staples that, unlike fur and wheat, had divisive and centrifugal effects on Canadian development, and with the shifting trade patterns in the 1920s that were weakening the east-west orientation. While his study of the fur staple had a unity of form that reflected the impact of the trade, his two subsequent books, *Settlement and the Mining Frontier* (1936) and especially *The Cod Fisheries* (1940), did not. The attempt to analyse the international economy of the fisheries from 1497 to 1938, covering six regions, challenged Innis's powers of synthesis and defied his ability to impose an order on the material. Significantly neither of these publications had anything like the influence on historians as his work on the fur trade. As he moved away from this subject in the thirties, Innis focused his attention on the exploitation of staples that led to unbalanced growth and disequillibrium and that had different effects on regions. It is a gross oversimplification to associate the body of Innis's work with the argument for geographical unity.

There was one further aspect of Innis's economic history that held profound implications for historians of Canada generally. This was his analysis of the changes and disturbances that followed on the shift from one staple to another. Unlike fur, timber was a bulky export commodity that favoured a large return cargo and thereby provided a stimulus to immigration and agricultural settlement. It created a demand for labour and for agricultural produce. British reliance on Canadian wheat and the introduction of steam transportation on the St Lawrence intensified the need to overcome the natural obstacles of that route by the building of canals. Canal improvements in Upper Canada, however, could not proceed without similar improvements in Lower Canada, and the result was that pressure was built up to unify the two colonies and share the costs of transportation improvements. As Innis put it in one of those summary statements that bewildered the uninitiated and confirmed his reputation as a bad stylist: 'Eventually pressure from Upper Canada resulting from the handicap of high costs on the up-stream traffic of manufactured goods contributed in part to the Rebellion of 1837, to the Durham *Report*, to the Act of Union, and to a determined effort to build the St Lawrence canals.'[41]

The canalization of the St Lawrence system was completed at almost the same moment that the protective system was abolished and free trade was introduced. During the 1850s Canadians turned to railways as more efficient and cheaper supplements to the canals; this strategy in turn brought on new problems of raising sufficient revenue for capital investment. Alexander Galt's tariff of 1859 was justified on the grounds that duties on imported manufactured goods were necessary in order to enable the state to meet the interest charges on the debt incurred in subsidizing transport improvements, which in turn would reduce the costs of both exports and imports. Galt's tariff had been traditionally viewed by even historians like Skelton, who fully understood the economic history of the period, as an assertion of Canada's powers of self-government—another instance of the slow unfolding of the principle of responsible government. Innis penetrated beneath the political explanation and saw it as an effort to come to grips with the financial burdens of transportation improvements and he argued that the fixed charges led to renewed expansion, Confederation, and ultimately the National Policy. Changes in the technology of transportation and the necessities of changing staples were for him the crucial causes of changes in politics and fiscal policy. The connections he drew, while often abrupt and unelaborated, nonetheless provided clues to a reinterpretation of the very period—the first half of the nineteenth century—that had been so fully explored by the constitutional historians. Innis was primarily concerned with patterns of economic development, and he tended to comment on the political effects of such changes only incidentally and rather cryptically. Nevertheless it was precisely these connections between the underlying economic alterations and political and constitutional developments that were suggestive to historians. The effects on the economy of the St Lawrence of the change from the fur to the timber staple in the early nineteenth century provided one of the most illuminating examples of the way in which Innis's insights pointed towards a general reinterpretation of Canadian history.

One of the most striking features of the intellectual scene in the thirties was the close co-operation of scholars from the various social sciences. This was symbolized by the joint meetings of the Canadian Political Science Association and the Canadian Historical Association and it was partially due to the relatively small number of political economists and historians in the country. But it also expressed both Innis's personal influence and the usefulness of the historical economics of the staples. The staples thesis contained immensely suggestive implications not only for historians like Donald Creighton but for others in less mature disciplines. Innis, for example, placed Indian culture at the centre of his study of the fur trade and was the first to explain adequately the disintegration of native society under the thrust of European capitalism. The displacement of the Indians' non-competitive, communal economic system and the resulting psychological turmoil were examined further in one of the pioneer studies in Canadian historical anthropology, Alfred G. Bailey's The Conflict of European and Eastern Algonkian Cultures, 1504-1700 (1937). The same concern with social disorganization underlay the historical sociology of S.D. Clark.

IV

The practical implications of Innis's political economy for government policy were drawn out during the course of the thirties and early forties. The Depression had the immediate effect of intensifying, and in certain respects deflecting, the main impulses of the cultural nationalism of the twenties. The collapse of the economy strengthened the determination of scholars to concentrate on the material factors in history. To the pan-Canadian nationalism of the twenties and the search for generalizations embracing the entire country was added a greater sense of social collectivism. The LSR's advocacy of greater centralization of power in the hands of the federal government was widely shared in academic circles, even among those who were critical of socialism. That great inquest into the workings of the federal system, the Rowell-Sirois Commission, which was appointed in 1937 and submitted its report in 1940, came down heavily in favour of centralization, and its case was buttressed by extensive investigations into Canadian economic history. With the outbreak of the war the pressures on the social scientist to move out of the academy into government service, or more generally, to plan for post-war reconstruction, became intense.

Innis stood against the rising tide of demands on scholars to participate more directly in the political life of the country. He was critical of the LSR and the case for centralization of the Rowell-Sirois Report, and he came to see the participation of academics in radical politics, or even their joining the state bureaucracy, as disastrous threats to Canadian scholarship. The debate over the question of whether the social scientist should participate more actively in public life, or whether, as Innis thought, the university scholar should, with certain exceptions, deliberately insulate himself from the pressures of the present in order to attain a sense of perspective, was characterized by more noise and rhetorical flourishes than philosophical profundity, and more than one wise observer came to the conclusion that it all boiled down to individual differences in temperaments and aptitudes. Innis's own position, however, was based on three distinct though interrelated convictions: his recognition of the large role of hard, immutable elements in history; his personal distaste for centralization and his opposition to centres of power, monopoly, and bureaucracy; and his conception of economic history as a genuine 'science'. These three ideas underlay his defense of what he saw as an imperilled Canadian scholarly tradition and the integrity of the university, which he customarily referred to as an 'ivory tower'.

Innis was far more concerned with contemporary problems than his aloof attitude and elliptical judgements superficially suggested. 'The study of economic history', he wrote in that fateful year, 1929, 'should enable Canadians to see more clearly the course of the economic growth of Canada and possibly guide it with more intelligence and should aid them in determining their own destinies from an economic point of view as they succeeded in gaining control over them from the constitutional standpoint.'[42] Innis recognized the need for government planning, but he was also impressed by the baffling difficulties of interpreting and predicting events in a country so exposed to rapid change and the intervention of 'cyclonic' outside influences. His writing stressed the primacy and potency of the deterministic factors of geography, staples, and especially transport technology; in the thirties his published views verged on a hard technological determinism. His books and essays are filled with a profusion of details describing specific staples and technologies of exploitation; the habits of the lowly beaver, techniques for preserving cod-fish, and gold-mining processes were all related to very large effects. The political control of Newfoundland, for example, was attributed to Britain's lack of salt supplies, which made it necessary for her fishermen to land and dry their catch on shore. Other European fishermen with more adequate salt supplies preserved their fish in barrels aboard ship. Perhaps it was Innis's iconoclastic sense of humour that led him to juxtapose in a causal relationship the prosaic facts of primitive technology with grand political results, or to describe Confederation as a credit instrument. But it was characteristic of his economic history that one factor was isolated and its impact traced in a variety of directions—or, as he put it, the analysis was pushed to the breaking point. The net impression created was one of human helplessness in the face of brutal limitations imposed by nature and the intervention of blind uncontrollable forces. There is a sombre determinism, even fatalism, in his work, and one is struck by the prominence of the material environment that constrained and channelled human effort. Innis was in this respect a 'determinist'. But, paradoxically, to understand the magnitude and character of deterministic elements was for him to establish the margin, invariably narrow, in which men were free to make their own history.

Innis saw the role of the economic historian precisely in this light. Any effort to alleviate the effects of the Depression had to begin with a recognition and acceptance of the intractable elements and the fragility and complexity of the Canadian economy. He noted that the traditional Canadian reaction to fluctuations had been expansion, the tapping of fresh resources, capital imports for improvements in transportation, and the financing of those measures through the tariff. In the context of the thirties, when prospects for expansion were drastically limited, Innis predicted that traditional policies would become increasingly ineffectual and that more government planning would be inevitable. The immediate problem, as he saw it, was to reduce the unequal incidence of the tariff and adjust the burden of the debt.[43]

In a larger context Innis envisaged the Canadian economy in the thirties as subject to intense strains that were the product of the growth of new metropolitan demands and the exploitation of new staples. The staples trades had historically accentuated Canada's dependence on Europe, and in the case of fur and wheat had reinforced the country's unity. In the postwar period, however, the decline in the expansion of the wheat economy, the insecurity of European markets, the growth of the pulp-and-paper and mining industries, and the increasing significance of the American market and capital combined to weaken the St Lawrence as a centralizing factor in the Canadian system. These new staple resources were under provincial jurisdictions and the results were uneven development and complications of political control. 'The extension of the American empire, the decline of its natural resources, and the emergence of metropolitan areas, supported capitalist expansion in Canada and reinforced the trend to regionalism,' he wrote in 1937. 'The pull to the north and south has tended to become stronger in contrast to the pull east and west.'[44] This was a natural and inevitable consequence of the shift to different staples. Innis, who saw all of Canadian economic history as the puppet of various economic imperialisms, simply pleaded that American policy-makers consider the effects of their policies on Canada.[45]

Innis often seemed more impressed — one might almost say overwhelmed — with the intractability of the forces at work than with the prospects for precise solutions. His contribution to the report of the Royal Commission of Inquiry for Nova Scotia in 1934 consisted of a dissenting essay on the economic history of the province that revealed the roots of the problems and advanced no dramatic gestures in the direction of reform. In a book of essays that Innis co-edited, *The Canadian Economy and its Problems* (1934), the articles underlined Canada's traditional dependence on staple exports and foreign capital, and described the situation in which Canadians found themselves rather than ways they might change it. The University of Saskatchewan economist, George Britnell, whom Innis treated as a favourite disciple ('He is a Catholic but the most liberal I ever met'),[46] published an examination of the standards of living in rural Saskatchewan that was typical of such an approach. In *The Wheat Economy* (1939) the historical perspective was lucidly delineated, but Britnell stressed the variability and uncertainty of production and income, the limited alternatives to prairie producers, and doubted the ability of any provincial government to maintain social services over a period of adversity. Readers of such books were struck by the depressing preoccupation with difficulties, and one reviewer who expected more heroic remedies in a moment of exasperation labelled Innis and those who shared his views as the 'garage mechanics' of Canadian capitalism.[47] For reformers, Innis appeared to dwell excessively on what men could not do. His political economy, in its recognition and preoccupation with deterministic features of economic life, had an anti-reformist bias.

The second consideration that affected Innis's critical view of reform in the thirties was his attachment to responsible government, which he equated with local control, and his inveterate suspicion of centralization of power. One of the ironies of Innis's reputation was that, while no one had done more to reveal the profound historical tendencies contributing to unity within Canada and to centralization and monopoly in its institutions, few were temperamentally and by conviction more opposed to the centralization of influence. In his view concentrations of power were to be exposed and resisted. He habitually referred to the centralized character of Canada's institutions and patterns of metropolitan dominance within the country as distorted and warped. William Mackintosh was convinced that so strong was Innis's antipathy to centralization that he seemed unwilling to acknowledge the substantial reasons, advanced in his own books, that had brought on extensive state involvement in the economy.[48]

Innis was a strong individualist, a pluralist, and an old-fashioned liberal whose family's political tradition was Grit. 'Our differences probably go back to religion,' he told Arthur Lower in a moment of self-analysis, '—the Methodists are always anxious to control things—the Baptists are always suspicious of control .... The Marxist interpretation probably also applies—the background of farm life plus a training in economics leaves me very sceptical about methods of control—heretofore, they have been largely new methods of exploitation.'[49] He also recognized that his war experience had left him with a permanent aversion to dictation by those self-important servants of distant power, the bureaucrats. 'After eight months of the mud and lice and rats of France in which much of the time was spent cursing government officials in Ottawa,' he explained in 1943, 'I have without doubt developed an abnormal slant. I have never had the slightest interest since that time in people who were helping in the war with a job in Ottawa or London. The contrast between their method of living and France made it simply impossible for me to regard them as having anything to do with the war and I continue to look upon them with contempt.'[50] He hated pretension and pomposity and to a degree he always associated the military and civilian officialdom that had pushed the soldiers around in the First World War with all government agents. There are few figures who are treated with more scorn in Innis's writings, unless it is the academic who aspired to become a bureaucrat.

Innis assiduously attacked all schemes that involved the strengthening of the Ottawa government at the expense of the provinces. He was convinced that local governments were far more responsive to local needs and that the provinces or regions should co-operate more closely in order to check the defects of central domination and 'remote control'.[51] In criticizing that part of the report of the Rowell-Sirois commission that advocated the transference of jurisdiction over unemployment to the Dominion, he contended that the 'provinces and municipalities have shown greater capacity for administrative improvement than the federal Government.'[52] He was critical of the report for its pretensions to finality, because it disregarded the connection between the federal civil service bureaucracy and party patronage, and because it said so little about the iniquities of the tariff. He favoured adjustments within the constitution as it then stood rather than the more radical reallocation of powers that were proposed as options. But at bottom Innis was utterly opposed to the transference of additional taxing power to the central government. By the mid-1940s, when the war emergency and social welfare legislation had inflated both the civil service and the powers of Ottawa, Innis expressed his reservations about the efficacy of monetary policy to ensure full employment. 'My own view has always been', he advised Angus Macdonald, the premier of Nova Scotia, 'that the federal government people have always been too optimistic as to what could be done by monetary measures. They have been carried away by their enthusiasm for the possibilities of the Bank of Canada by Keynes and Hansen, by their own bureaucratic interest, and by the necessities of a war programme. The problem is not one of financial manipulation—it is one of getting down to brass tacks and considering in each case what can be done by cooperative effort . . . .'[53] He suggested that, since Nova Scotia had unique problems, it should not agree to any transfer of revenue until the Dominion signified some interest in working at these specific questions. Innis almost instinctively sympathized with regions like the Maritimes, as he had long before sympathized with western Canada, which had paid so heavily for the national policies.

The third dimension of Innis's rather sceptical response to reform in the thirties, and one that was ultimately to impel him into his explorations of the biases of various forms of communications, was his conception of the social sciences as scientific. His understanding of the problems of the social sciences was one of the main reasons why he was so critical of planning, manipulation, and centralization. Far from regarding economics as an established and certain body of knowledge, as one might expect, Innis in fact thought economics a frail instrument for understanding. The chief difficulty with all the social sciences was that their practitioners were bound up with the very social complex they sought to analyse. Various influences constantly impinged on their work and subtly prompted the very questions they raised. But there were limits to Innis's relativism, just as there were limits to his determinism: for the very influences that seemed to preclude a truly scientific and objective point of view could themselves be analysed and become the substance of self-knowledge. Innis believed that the social scientist should make a deliberate effort to sharpen his awareness of the bias of the times in which he worked and appraise his own limitations. He would thereby attain, if not an ideal position of detached objectivity, at least a sense of perspective and perhaps a more penetrating insight into the determining forces in social development.[54]

His almost automatic response to propositions and conclusions was to ask why men do the things they do when they do them, and why they believe the things they believe when they believe them. To raise such questions of one's own convictions—and Innis did ask them of his own work—could lead to paralysing doubt about everything. But Innis made the search for bias the main end of the social sciences. 'It is the essence of the philosophy of the social sciences,' he declared, 'that concern should be given primarily to their limitations.'[55] His admiration for both Veblen and Marx was based on the fact that these thinkers had suggested ways in which the economist could at least partly disengage himself from his immediate context. 'Marx', he wrote, 'contributed much in building the ladder to escape from his enemies, his followers, and himself.'[56] The ladder was the economic interpretation of economic history: the search for meaning in economic phenomena had to begin with the preliminary appraisal of the economic biases of one's own time.

If Innis was aware of the controversy among historians over relativism that Beard and Becker had inaugurated in the United States, he gave no indication of this in his writing. In any case his interest in the limitations of the social sciences arose far more from the claims of the intellectual radicals in Canada in the 1930s who alleged that, since an objective science of society was impossible, a scholar was left only with the prospect of declaring his own social faith. In the milieu of the Depression decade Innis had a much harder case to defend. No one appreciated more fully the difficulties of the social scientist in Canada. As Innis saw it, the weaknesses of the discipline stemmed from the importation of foreign-trained scholars who studied Canadian society, when they studied it at all, with concepts derived from other countries and quite different societies; and there were the ever-present and insistent requests that scholarship, especially historical scholarship, be abandoned in the search for immediate remedies for social problems. Innis cynically queried why economists were in such demand during economic crises. His equally cynical answer was that, since the politicians had no solution, they called on economists to provide a window-dressing of expertise, activity, and decisiveness. Some of his choicest epigrams of dispraise were reserved for those academics who, far from retaining a tentativeness about their subject bred of an awareness of limits, proceeded to expound final solutions. There were, Innis insisted, no last words in the writing of economic or any other variety of history.

Innis did not deny that the economist had an obligation to advise governments; he did so himself on a number of occasions. What he insisted upon was simply that the economist should not pretend to know more than he did, and that he should bring to government policy not nostrums but the awareness of intractable and long-range forces. The economist should not rush to supply solutions addressed to the needs of the moment, but should attempt to correct the biases that saw the needs of the moment as of paramount importance. About all he had to say on the subject, he told Lower in 1935, 'was that you cannot hope to discuss with an illiterate population (an illiterate from the standpoint of the social sciences) the complex problems of the social sciences but that it was important to continue with democracy—to save one from something worse—and that discussion should continue on an unabated scale but that it should at least attempt to be artistic. Perhaps more than all this that we know very little about the solution to so-called economic problems, and thus there is little point in concealing our ignorance by loud talk . . . .'[57] It was an index of Innis's anti-bureaucratic spirit, his individualism, and his scepticism about economics and history that he was convinced that intellectuals must accept the limits of their own understanding as well as the aims of the organized society in which they worked, and not pretend to determine and dictate those ends. The notion of the social scientist as social engineer in a planned society was completely alien to his outlook; in this respect he remained a traditional liberal democrat who could, in 1946, cite with tacit approval the political credo of Goldwin Smith.[58]

Innis's concern with limitations, his inveterate tendency to search out biases, and his feeling for the tentativeness of his subject were all to a certain extent reflected in his style of writing. Or, more accurately, it may be said that his distrust of the dogmatic reinforced an elliptical form of expression. There must have been few readers of his books who could not have agreed with his high-school teacher's remarks on his essay on Laurier—'You say many excellent things, some well phrased, but you say them in a very haphazard order.' His doctoral thesis was one of those exercises in monographic scholarship that G.M. Wrong and W.S. Wallace had in mind when they decried the decline of literary history. It may be that Innis learned his trade in a bad school; once he justified himself by saying that a person in his position had to put things in a deliberately ambiguous fashion in order to avoid annoying prominent members of the community. Innis was aware of his deficiencies, and after his marriage in 1920 to Mary Quayle, a Chicago graduate in literature who became a respected writer in her own right, he resolved that she should help him overcome his ignorance of literature by making a list of books he should read. But in his attitude to imaginative literature there was the temper of one who ransacks it for quotations rather than experiencing and assimilating it. He typically attributed the accuracy of detail and atmosphere of Leacock's *Sunshine Sketches of a Little Town* to the fact that Leacock was a trained economist![59] Innis's exposure to humanistic literature was narrow, and the zeal with which he threw himself into economic history, and his single-minded and ascetic dedication, left him time for little else. Scientific economic history had been born in revolt against romantic and literary history and Innis continued that revolt. Bartlet Brebner, who knew Innis well, said he possessed 'a tremendous inner drive to get things published which makes him a difficult person to deal with along ordinary business lines, and which . . . has had some sad effects on the expository technique of his writings.'[60] Innis seemed impatient, and his impatience increased as he retraced the steps in an argument to a conclusion he had already arrived at.

Sometimes, as in his cod-fisheries book, he seemed to think that quotations from the sources piled upon each other over several pages would reveal a pattern. This picture, of course, can be overdrawn: Innis had a partiality for epigrams, which he described as half-truths that infuriate those who believe the other half.[61] But it is probably fair to say that his mode of expression was at best awkward, and that as his philosophical concern with bias and limitations deepened, he was conscious that the things he wanted to say simply could not be said in a style that itself implied completeness and finality.[62] It did not seem possible to describe 'cyclonic' developments in a language appropriate for the description of evolutionary stages.

V

A preoccupation with the deterministic elements in history, opposition to remote central power, and concern for the limitations of the social sciences were the more negative sides of Innis's conception of the role of the intellectual in society. Yet for all his quizzical scepticism, which in the later 1940s was to bring him to the brink of a bleak pessimism, Innis possessed a firm and unshakeable faith in scholarship itself and in the institution of the university in which it was nurtured. His bitter and often apocalyptic denunciations of those individuals and social forces that threatened either of these twin loyalties can only be understood in terms of his total commitment to the ideals of scholarship and the university as he understood them and in relation to his own unique position within the social-science profession.

Innis's dedication to Canadian scholarship was total and selfless—though in his case there was a certain egoism of selflessness. His appointment as the first Canadian-born chairman of the prestigious Department of Political Economy at Toronto in 1937 and his position as Dean of the major centre for graduate training in the country after 1947 were formal acknowledgements of his status within his profession. There was scarcely a co-operative project in the thirties and forties to which he did not contribute a volume, or introduction—or, more dubiously, editorial advice. From 1940 to 1948 he was chairman of the Grants-in-Aid Committee of the Canadian Social Science Research Council, through whose hands passed applications of scholars for research funds; for fifteen years he was also one of the chief councillors of the Division of Social Sciences of the Rockefeller Foundation, and a frequent contributor of evaluations of scholars applying for grants from the John Simon Guggenheim Memorial Foundation. Innis was a jealous guardian of Canadian scholarship and he understood the frustrations of academics working in isolation from each other in a period when pure scholarship was being questioned even by those who should have been its chief practitioners. He not only knew what nearly everyone in the fields of political economy and history was doing but he was invariably encouraging. In the promotion of manuscripts that he thought worthy he was unflagging in his zeal. When he was pressed to go to the University of Chicago, he explained his refusal to his wife by saying: 'I can't leave Canada. I have all the threads in my hands.'[63]

On large matters and small Innis was a prickly nationalist who could become incensed at aspersions on Canadian scholarly effort. When the claim was made that the Ryerson Press did not have sufficient expert resources to edit several volumes in the Carnegie series on Canadian-American relations, Innis angrily told Lorne Pierce that the 'suggestion that the editorial work be handled by Yale is disquieting and should be resisted as a reflection on Canadian scholarship as well as on myself and the Ryerson Press.'[64] As this remark suggests, Innis was not above occasionally identifying his personal interests with the cause of 'Canadian scholarship'. He knew that he was an indispensible figure in the scholarly associations and his university and he was not immune to the resulting temptations. His favourite device for getting his own way was the blunt tactic of resignation, or the threat of resignation. It had worked in 1929 when he wrote a letter of resignation in a huff because a colleague was promoted above his head. In 1939 he caused considerable consternation among his friends and the fellows of the Royal Society of Canada by resigning as the secretary of Section II of that body because the Lorne Pierce medal was given to Wilfrid Bovey in recognition of his contribution to Canadian letters and for furthering French-English understanding through his *The French Canadians To-Day* (1938). Innis indignantly protested against certain allegedly irregular procedures in the decision and he told Pierce that, though Bovey might merit some kind of *bonne entente* award, this should in no way be confused with literary or scholarly distinction. (Privately he informed Lower that Bovey was given the prize 'as a result of French Canadian influences'.)[65] Innis even went so far as to find funds from an anonymous donor to be given for distinguished writing aimed at the improvement of cultural relations, on the condition that the Lorne Pierce medal not be awarded to Bovey.[66]

The pattern was confirmed a few years later when Innis tendered his resignation as chairman of the School of Social Work because of plans to appoint Harry Cassidy. Cassidy had been a member of the LSR and had, in Innis's indictment, committed the cardinal sin of the scholar in campaigning for a CCF candidate while still a civil servant in the British Columbia government. 'One perhaps should not take exception to this but the whole point of view is fundamentally false from the standpoint of research as I have looked upon it, in the social sciences. Research starts with recognized ends—and is warped to meet those ends whereas in my view it should be primarily concerned in the search for truth. The CCF to my mind and as far as research in a University is concerned sins against the light.' 'This step', he wrote of his resignation, 'will avoid embarrassment to you and me in case the plans with regard to Dr. Cassidy are carried through. It will also make it easier for me to withstand the increasing pressure from Chicago.'[67] This was not the last time such a card would be played.

Innis's determination to defend the integrity of the Canadian social sciences was obviously tied up with his own personal position, but there was much more in it than that. At the bottom of his faith in scholarship and the university lay his essential liberalism and his obsession with individual freedom. The war had intensified pressures that had been threatening enough in the Depression. Students enlisted in the armed services; practical men contended that the arts courses and even the annual scholarly meetings were luxuries that a nation at war could not afford; and the ranks of the social scientists were depleted by the insatiable demands of the government for advisers and administrators. This, to Innis, was a fatal drain on the community of scholars, if not an outright prostitution of their disciplines. The proper place of the scholar was to attend to his own business, strengthen the position of the university as a place where discussion about, and research into, the long-range problems of civilization could be carried on, and at least demonstrate some faith in those liberal values for which the war was being fought. It is not accidental that Innis coupled the necessity to preserve scholarly standards and a steadiness of purpose with democracy. For him the purpose of knowledge—culture itself—was to break the hold of the present. When he wrote that the 'universities must concern themselves with the living rather than with the dead',[68] he had in mind precisely the opposite of what a later generation would call relevance. There was great value in what did not immediately appear relevant in relation to the needs of the present because only by the study of the past and its broad problems could the individual attain a more independent perspective on his time and on himself. To know nothing but the present was to be a helpless victim of the debased myths of one's own immediate time. Scholarship, fragile though Innis understood it to be, was the corrective to the biases of the present, and it was through the search for truth that individual freedom was enlarged. The university for him was the crowning glory of a pluralistic democratic society. Innis was entirely consistent in defending academic freedom in the Underhill case in 1940-1, even though he otherwise rejected almost everything else Underhill stood for.

To see Innis's belief in these liberal terms is to gauge the extent of his rejection of that kind of research that was addressed to immediate solutions with pre-selected ends in view, as well as the depth of his despair over the almost irresistable forces that bore down on the scholar who was concerned with the limitations of his subject in the early forties. At this time Innis's main interest shifted to the examination of spatial and temporal biases in various forms of communications media, a change that will be examined later in this study. The major impulses that impelled him in that direction were implicit in his concern with limitations and the staples thesis.

For Innis a steady adherence to scholarly work and a consciousness of the bias of history and of the present were not only indispensable ingredients of human freedom but the touchstone of the status of a nation. His was a passionate nationalism that had for long been masked by irony, humour, and cynical comments on the clichés of his day. Innis had more in mind than the Canadian discipline of political economy that he and his contemporaries had worked out in the previous decade. 'Canada', he wrote in 1943—and here he revealed the substance of his faith—'cannot become a nation with a cultural development comparable to that of the United States and Great Britain without a sustained interest in the development of its universities. The political spirit will cease to hamper their activities only after colonialism has been defeated. Only then will Canada emerge as a nation with universities that can be compared with those of the United States and Great Britain. Scholarship provides the essentials for that steadiness and self-respect by which Canada can become a nation worthy of those who have fought and given up their lives in the last war or in this.'[69]

It must have seemed to Innis's critics that his view of scholarship amounted to intelligence ever raising questions of itself in an endless introspective search for the limits that defined what it could not do. F.R. Scott, the renaissance man of the left, might have had Innis in mind when he wrote—in a poem entitled 'To Certain Friends'—of those whose wills were broken by the rain of facts and whose knowledge of how to use knowledge grew smaller and smaller.[70] It is easy to criticize Innis's negativism and his encouragement of an apolitical stance for the intellectual in society.[71] But to see only the negative side of his outlook—his economic determinism, relativism, and apoliticism—is to miss a positive central thread that runs through his work, from the investigation of the fur staple to his defence of scholarship, and, later, his explorations in the biases of communications: to understand limits is to enhance the freedom of the nation and the individual.

5 | ARTHUR LOWER AND A NATIONAL COMMUNITY

Arthur Lower was the most nationalistic of English-Canadian historians. His historical writing from the mid-1920s to the end of the Second World War possessed a certain unity based on two interrelated concerns. The first was his original work on the role of the forest and the timber trade in Canadian development, published in the 1930s and generally regarded as a complement to Innis's exploration of the place of the fur staple. The second was a general preoccupation with some of the central questions of Canadian nationalism as these issues were suggested both by his own experience and the striving for an indigenous and authentic culture, which was so pronounced in the 1920s. Lower's most profound desire was that Canadians share a sense of living in a national community, one that was united by unspoken assumptions and tacit understandings such as those that unite a family. His major preoccupation in his polemical essays—and even, up to a point, in his more detached excursions into economic history—was with those forces in the Canadian past and present that impeded and frustrated this emergent sense of nationality. Such an orientation involved a very broad approach to history and an especially personal one. History for Lower became a search for a nationalist creed that would at once satisfy his own deep-seated need to belong to a homogeneous community, a 'motherland', and be an instrument that would aid that community in its ongoing process of self-definition. If history was an act of faith—the substance of things hoped for, as he wrote in his most famous book, *Colony to Nation* (1946)—then the duty of the historian was to reveal to people the reasons for the faith that was in them.

All written history is, in a sense, a form of autobiography and an essay in self-knowledge. Some of Lower's contemporaries tried to mask this personal element with detached irony, an involuted and desiccated prose, or the jargon of scientific objectivity. But with Lower a personal approach to history writing was undertaken without inhibitions, indeed with enthusiasm. It is not only that he peppered his articles and books with the kind of opinionated judgements and personal asides that Innis, for example, eschewed; or that he frequently alluded to episodes in his own life to illustrate a point he was making. It is rather that the most persistent questions he raised and his most original ideas about Canadian history were prompted by his own experience in a direct, immediate fashion.

Lower was born in Barrie, Ont., in 1889, the child of immigrant English parents. According to his memoirs his early family life was not unmarred by tension and difficulties. He recorded that 'my parents' association did not have much happiness about it' and that there were elements of 'bitterness'. His father, 'an English exile to the day of his death', was almost a stranger to him and a negative influence on his formative years.[1] The tensions in his home were accentuated, Lower later believed, by the misunderstandings between immigrants and their children. His parents possessed customs and memories of an established way of life that they sought to impose on their children; their offspring responded to the demands of a different society and discovered that their parents' ways were not the ways of their world. The parents recalled the place they had left; the children knew only the country in which they had been born.

This divergence within the family was further emphasized by Lower's education. He passed through Barrie Collegiate, taught school, and in 1909 entered the Faculty of Education in the University of Toronto. Later he enrolled in University College and took the courses in English and History. No one in his family had been to university before, and it was there that Lower discovered the costs exacted, at least in cultural terms, of those who move from a relatively humble background across a class line. The transition cut him off from his boyhood friends and widened the 'gulf' between himself and his parents.[2]

One wonders whether Lower's fixation on the nation as a familial community—homogeneous, stable, and undivided—did not have a little to do with rather bitter memories of his own home. Few other analogies are invoked more frequently in Lower's history and social criticism than that of the 'family'. Canada was the unwanted child of divorced parents, he wrote of the upheaval of the American Revolution, and he condemned Canadian immigration policy because it had introduced too many 'strangers' into the 'family'. He was later to explain, in reference to the bad effects of immigration, that he stood for a unity of culture because until a homogeneous society was achieved neither the individual nor the group could live a satisfactory and reasonably harmonious life. 'As a social animal, man's most powerful motives for action are those that spring from his relations with his fellows. He wishes their approbation and good will . . . . Now if instead of a close-knit group, there are just various people dumped down in the same geographical area, a good many of these incentives disappear and life becomes an unhappy matter of every man for himself.'³

Lower was raised in the stern discipline of the Methodist communion. Though he was never formally converted, never experienced the onrush of the conviction of salvation, Methodism imparted to him an irresistible drive to work and the wish to succeed. He has said that the Methodist church pounded into you the idea that you must not simply sit idly by and speculate and dream, but that you must do something. Perhaps his involvement in public debate derived from the same impulse; certainly his conviction that knowledge, especially history, had to have some direct imprint on men and society did. Nothing could be further from Lower's thinking than the notion of scholarship as an exercise in idle curiosity. The utilitarian and essentially emotional role of history was to illuminate and inspire a national 'faith'; the 'vocation' of the historian was to provide this social cement.

Lower remained loyal to the essentials of his mother's religion; he never publicly challenged it and never attacked the church as an institution. But he did manage to extricate himself from some of its more irksome social prohibitions, and to detach himself sufficiently to be able to see Methodism as a historical force. Perhaps more than any other historian of his generation Lower was alert to the role of religion in Canadian history and was willing to explore and speculate on the religious influence in national development.

'One of the strongest tendencies is my love for nature,' he wrote in a composition essay in 1914, '—so strong, I take it, that it is hereditary.'⁴ This love became almost religious in its intensity. As a boy he roamed the countryside around Barrie and sailed on Kempenfeldt Bay; he collected plants and insects, mastering their Latin names; and, like Innis, he enjoyed the animal stories of Ernest Thompson Seton. Wordsworth's poetry made a deep impression on him; Francis Parkman's books on New France, in which the wilderness figured in all its romantic majesty, first attracted him to history. While he was a university student Lower spent several summers working as a fire-ranger in northern Ontario and learned the crafts of paddling a canoe, packing, portaging, baking bannock, extinguishing forest fires, and other bush lore. For the first time in his life he was taken out of the provincial town and thrust into the strange world of the immigrant railway workers, Indians and half-breeds, French-Canadian priests and fur traders. He developed an intense and lasting love for the northern wilderness and for its sparkling waters with their unfamiliar names: Wabinosh River, Ombabika Bay, Lake Neboquazi. Much later he would recollect that when he stood on the shores of James Bay, where two and a half centuries before the English and French had played out the rivalry of the fur trade, he was gripped by a feeling for the immediacy of history that his own environment had been unable to evoke.[5]

This experience of the North was one of the crucial episodes in Lower's intellectual development and he was to return to it again and again. His attachment to the wilds sometimes expressed itself as a pantheistic feeling for the mystery of the forest, at other times as a simple enjoyment in the physical exertion that came from canoeing or chopping wood. 'To go into the "bush" in the spring, soft from a city winter', he wrote in 1932, 'and come out hard as nails in the fall, rejoicing in your ability to carry a canoe over a two-mile portage without setting it down, or to paddle at racing speed up the length of a twenty-mile lake ... to learn tolerance of others with whom you must live at very close range, to acquire the adaptableness and self-reliance which only the woods and their counterpart, the sea, impart: these are matters which must leave their mark [upon countless Canadians].'[6] Lower's response to the North affected both the history he would write as well as the style of life he would lead. While working on the Board of Historical Publications at the Archives in Ottawa in the early 1920s, he and his friends explored the surrounding rivers, camped, and fished as the poets Archibald Lampman and D.C. Scott had done a generation before. During his years at Wesley College in Winnipeg, from 1929 to 1947, he made for his cottage near Kenora as soon as the last examination had been marked in the spring and rarely returned until a few days before classes resumed in the autumn.

'I suppose I have always lived a double life:' he later reflected, 'by winter an academic and in the summers, reverting to some form of the primitive.' And out of this combination of the sophisticated urban culture and the simplicities of nature, the university and the bush, Lower distilled a vision. Canadians, he wrote,

> will always have this northern window through which to let fresh air into our civilized room. If we heap ourselves up in festering cities, that will be partly our own fault—for just beyond the pavement's end, stands the open, unfenced north. And if we can ever produce a way of life in this country which will be uniquely our own, it will arise from this combination of the simple and the sophisticated, from the complex skills and worldly wisdom of an urban civilization joined to the heritage of space and the clear untroubled eyes of a world which is eternally young.[7]

Only slightly less significant than Lower's admiration for the northern wilderness was his strong identification with the sea. He grew up in a household where the imperial faith was robust; some of his earliest recollections were of the stories of G.A. Henty; and he loved the little steamers on Lake Simcoe. From 1916 to 1918 he served as an officer in the British Navy on patrol duty in the English Channel. Though this experience was not to leave as much of a mark on his historical writing as did his engagement with the forest, still it represented a similar commitment to spaciousness and to the natural elements.

II

There was a certain tension between the kind of historical training Lower received and the variety of history he felt he had to write. He served a severe apprenticeship under Adam Shortt at the Board of Historical Publications between 1919 and 1925. Lower assisted Shortt in putting together a collection of documents relating to early Canadian currency and also did some preliminary classification of the *Montreal Gazette*. His M.A. thesis on the trade in square timber, done officially under the auspices of G.M. Wrong and the University of Toronto, was in fact supervised by Shortt. Shortt undoubtedly confirmed Lower's interest in economic history, but the master's rigid factualism and self-defeating dream of finality influenced his disciple only negatively.[8] Lower's own appetite for history had been whetted by the great literary historians of the nineteenth century, especially Macaulay and Parkman, and compared to them Shortt's perfectionistic scientism and the distrust of literary elegance must have seemed arid indeed.

The research Lower did for his doctoral thesis at Harvard, completed in 1929, laid the basis for three of his major contributions to Canadian economic history published in the 1930s: *The Trade in Square Timber* (1932); *Settlement and the Forest Frontier in Eastern Canada* (1936), published in one volume with Innis's *Settlement and the Mining Frontier*; and *The North American Assault on the Canadian Forest* (1938).[9] These were set within the familiar framework of the staples thesis that had been suggested by William Mackintosh and elaborated by Innis. A decade after Mackintosh had drawn attention to the significance of staple commodities for Canadian economic history, Lower wrote that 'New countries which rise rapidly to wealth and civilization invariably depend for their progress on the exploitation of some readily available natural resource.'[10] For two centuries the forest had provided the basis of Canada's existence. In his extended essay on the trade in square timber, Lower presented a straightforward account—replete with statistical tables and graphs—of the impact of the preferential duties legislated by Britain during the Napoleonic Wars. He paid special attention to the transference of British timber merchants' operations to Canada, the conduct of the industry in the St Lawrence and Ottawa valleys, the techniques for floating logs, and the degree of incompatibility between logging and agriculture. His second work was a socioeconomic study of the exploitation of the forest and agricultural lands in New Brunswick, northern Ontario, and Quebec from the early nineteenth century to the 1920s. He dealt with geographic controls on settlement, government administration of forests, and, very effectively, with the influence of cultural traits on northern settlement. His third book of the 1930s traced the reorientation of the timber industry from the British to the American markets.

These histories were invaluable additions to the burgeoning literature on the various staples trades, but they were quite different in character from Innis's work on the fur trade. Though Lower co-operated with Innis in editing two volumes of documents relating to Canadian economic history before 1885, their association was not intimate and their aims were not identical. Lower was fascinated by the human side of the timber trade, especially with the social life and the dress, food, and manner of work of the camboose men. Innis was preoccupied with revealing the direct connections between the nature of the staple and the economic and institutional effects that followed from its exploitation. Far more than Lower's, his interpretation of history veered towards technological and geographical determinism. Innis concentrated on the technology of mining while Lower dealt with religious and cultural factors in the successful settlement of the Shield country.

Both emotionally and intellectually Lower felt as constrained by Innis's economic history as he had been by Shortt's factualism. 'I always feel', he wrote Innis in 1933, 'that economic investigations really take me away from what should be my more proper concerns, and indeed from subjects in which I have a more instinctive interest.'[11] The topics that increasingly engrossed Lower's attention during the late twenties and throughout the thirties took him well beyond the confines of Innisian economics. All were related to his concern with the emergence of the sense of a national community in Canada. While previous historians had traced the growth of nationhood in the constitutional terms of the rise of self-government, Lower devoted himself to delineating the evolution of the feeling of community. His studies of the timber trade were but entrées into far-ranging speculations on the major themes that had shaped Canada. The New World's history, he wrote, 'has been largely the story of man's struggle with nature. It is the war with the wilderness which has been the ever-present factor, the constant influence shaping the mentality and the conduct of every inhabitant.'[12] For Lower the forest was not merely the scene of operations of staple exploitation: it became for him what the 'west' and 'frontier' were for Frederick Jackson Turner. Lower was as interested in the influence of the wilderness on communal life and institutions as he was in economic history. The impact of immigration, the role of the forest frontier in nurturing social democracy, the ever-recurrent antithesis between settlement and exploitation, and the persistent antithesis between French- and English-Canadian ways of life were Lower's central themes in his most creative period. They dominated his thought in the thirties and were synthesized in his most characteristic work, *Colony to Nation*.

III

Lower was one of the first Canadian historians to respond positively to Turner's thesis concerning the role of the frontier in American history. He encountered Turner's ideas while he was a graduate student at Harvard and was especially impressed with a course on the westward expansion of the United States given by Frederick Merk, who had replaced Turner on his retirement in 1924. Long afterwards Lower described Turner's famous essay of 1893 as 'the most formative piece of writing in modern history.'[13] Turner's paper was both a lyrical celebration of an agrarian myth that had been central to American nationalist thought since the Revolution and a hypothesis advanced to suggest the effects of three hundred years of western expansion on the institutions and character of the United States. 'The existence of an area of free land, its continuous recession, and the advance of American settlement westward', Turner had written, 'explain American development.' The true point of view for investigating the distinctive features of American history was not the Atlantic seaboard but the continuously moving line of settlement in the interior. The concept of the 'frontier', as Turner himself employed it, was identified with 'the hither edge of free land', 'the meeting-ground between savagry and civilization' and 'that zone of settlement nearest the wilderness, wherein society and government are loosely or incompletely organized.' The frontier in fact was not so much a specific place as a process in which institutions and social customs were transformed as people moved west. The migration of population attracted by free land emancipated people from the institutional controls of a complex and settled society, obliged them to do things for themselves, and thereby fostered individualism. Turner held that the frontier promoted nationalism because the pioneer looked to the national government to adopt measures he needed. Above all, the frontier promoted American democracy. Turner did not attempt to account for the development of modern democracy in general but only for the distinctive features of American democracy, nor did he ever deny that the institutions of self-government originated in Europe. What he insisted upon was that American democracy, which he equated with social equality and a social order based on fair play for all, had been conditioned by the frontier.[14]

Canadian historians who began a critical appraisal of Turner's ideas in the late twenties realized that the concept of the frontier could only be applied to Canada with a careful selectivity and an acknowledgement of major differences between the two North American nations. It was obvious, for instance, that whatever might have been true of the United States, the frontier in Canada had not unfolded in one continuous and unbroken line. In addition, as John L. McDougall pointed out in 1929, no society in North America had been more thoroughly exposed to the influence of the frontier than that of French Canada, and yet in spite of the penetration of her explorers and traders into the interior and of prolonged warfare with the Indians, the French had maintained 'an excessively stable, unadventurous, society . . . . They created on the banks of the St. Lawrence a replica of the French society which they had left.' The *coureurs de bois* had of course pursued the rough life of the typical frontiersman, but they were reintegrated into their society without fundamentally altering it: they drew up no petitions of right and drafted no theoretical defences of liberty. Perhaps the strongest case against the identification of pioneering with individualism and the breakdown of social cohesion, however, was the example of French-Canadian colonizing efforts in northern Quebec and Ontario in the later nineteenth and early twentieth centuries. The whole movement was initiated and conducted by the Church. 'Nothing could be farther from the American experience—what is arrived at is not a haphazard response to the call of free land, but a carefully pre-arranged building of new communities.'[15] The social cohesiveness of French-Canadian settlements in the North appeared to be a major exception to Turner's generalizations.

Another was the deeply held Canadian conviction that western settlement had been more orderly than was the case south of the border. Even supporters of the Turner hypothesis had to admit that the Canadian frontier was 'never so lawless as the American frontier', as was demonstrated by the enforcement of law and order by the North West Mounted Police on the Prairies and during the Yukon gold rush.[16]

Lower was aware of these exceptions and was to suggest others. Yet in the later twenties he found Turner's views attractive and compelling. Turner not only alerted Lower to the role of geographical factors in Canadian history but also, by fixing on the development of North American democracy, showed him how the historian might get behind the idea of responsible government to the qualitative changes in a people's social conditions that affected political behaviour. There was, moreover, a striking parallel between Turner's original intention in the 1890s and Lower's concern with Canadian nationalism in the 1920s. Turner's paper was directed against the stress that American historians had previously placed on the origins of the institutions of American self-government in northwestern Europe and their transplantation to the eastern seaboard. In underlining the way the frontier experience had changed these institutions, he was appealing for an American history that emphasized the distinctiveness of American experience and the role of the West in that history. Similarly, a generation later Lower found in the frontier thesis a way in which the qualitative differences between British self-government and Canadian democracy might be expressed.

Still, Lower insisted that Turner's thesis had to be applied in only a modified form. In both the United States and Canada, he contended in 1929, 'democracy has been a condition, not a theory. It has been the spontaneous product of the frontier and the forest.'[17] 'There can be little question', he added the following year, 'but that American democracy had a forest birth and there also can be little doubt of the validity of the larger thesis that the frontier environment, or life lived on the margins of civilization, tends to bring about an equality of which the political expression is democracy.' It seemed to him doubtful, however, that 'social equality could work out into political democracy unless the society possessing it had not possessed certain theoretical positions as to its nature before it was projected into its frontier surroundings.' Contrasting New France and New England before 1763, Lower noted that both colonial societies confronted similar frontier conditions and responded to them in similar ways. Both exhibited a larger degree of social equality than their respective motherlands, adaptiveness and initiative in meeting the demands of forest life, as well as restiveness with control. The French, who had come from a land that had known little else but authoritarianism in church and state, were far more independent and assertive than their Old World counterparts.[18] It was 'a tribute to the essential truth in Turner's analysis', Lower elaborated in 1946,

> that French life and society in America departed considerably from authoritarianism and in spirit approached English life and society in America. Where conditions were so uniform as in the settlers' attack on the forest, and where it was the worth of a man as a man, as an axe-swinging, forest-clearing, crop-sowing, animal, that counted, the same qualities came to the fore, the same scale of values tended to prevail .... North American democracy was forest-born. It carried with it a stubborn attachment to the rights and privileges that come from an independent life and a disinclination to coercion that was a strong defence against arbitrary authority.[19]

The frontier in New France seemed to Lower more a check upon authoritarianism than the seed-bed of political democracy. He doubted whether the French Canadians, if left to themselves, would ever have devised democratic political institutions; indeed, he suspected that once the temporary conditions of frontier life had passed, the old controls would probably have been re-established. The crucial distinction between New France and New England was that the English colonists possessed a conception of themselves as free men along with rudimentary representative institutions, while the French did not.

Lower accepted Turner's association between the peculiar features of American democracy and the frontier experience. Democracy, he emphasized, was a product of the frontier: 'You cannot make class distinctions of any permanence in a country where there is not much wealth and where everybody had started in the race for its accumulation from approximately the same point and started very recently . . . society in a new country is almost necessarily egalitarian and democratic, and therefore sooner or later politics must become so.'[20] Lower identified this democratic impulse with the United States — or sometimes more generally with North America — and he depicted it as locked in a continuous struggle with 'aristocracy' and 'privilege', which was represented by the British tradition. One of the major themes of his *Colony to Nation* was 'the constant struggle . . . between privilege and democracy, between the old world and the new, between history and geography.'[21] It was a conflict that for Lower went to the very core of Canadian experience because it mirrored the antithesis of two forces within the country's history. The outstanding characteristics of 'the American ways of life' were 'individualism, freedom of a rather anarchic type and a sense of equality'; the 'English tradition' was identified with 'privilege and differentiation of rank'.[22] The success of the American Revolution was the victory of the frontier, but to Canada it brought the United Empire Loyalists who imparted an anti-republican flavour to Canadian life. Of the rebellions of 1837, Lower judged that they 'struck a blow at privilege from which it was never to recover, and had opened the doors to the free play of those continental forces of equality and liberalism which time has revealed as our very life-blood . . . .'[23] Though Canada's frontier experience was not as intense or prolonged as that of the United States and its democracy was not as thorough-going, behind its monarchical institutions Lower found the same essentially egalitarian and socially democratic spirit that he, following Turner, attributed to the frontier.

IV

The frontier may have nurtured social democracy but it also encouraged other values against which Lower recoiled. His history and his social criticism rested on a hankering for a certain equilibrium, a settled state of things, and on a sense of realism about Canada's prospects. He despised the boomster spirit of the pre-war period and the 1920s and the ingrained restlessness and excessive mobility of modern North America. His revulsion against the shoddy materialism of Canadian life—fostered by the frontier and pioneering experience—and his condemnation of the fetish of economic success informed and underlay everything he wrote. 'The one preoccupation of a pioneer people', he said in 1937, 'is to better their condition. Inevitably everything tends to be sacrificed to material ends.' The social restraints of European society were loosened and New World societies were contemptuous of anything that might curb the appetites of individuals.[24] The 'frontier' encouraged a careless and exploitative attitude to economic life generally and to the use of natural resources. For Lower the forest industries were apt illustrations of the 'get-rich-quick' mentality at its worst. He was no romantic lamenting the disappearance of the forest in those areas suitable to agriculture, but throughout his studies of the timber staple ran a subdued revulsion against the indiscriminate and wasteful assault on the wilderness. It seemed that the main task of the lumberman was to destroy the forest as quickly as possible and extract the maximum profit. The assault on the forest, he wrote, 'so long sustained and waged on so vast a front, has provided a unique spectacle of fierce rapacity and crude energy . . . . The sack of the largest and wealthiest of medieval cities could have been but a bagatelle compared with the sack of the North American forest and no medieval ravisher could have been more fierce and unscrupulous than the lumberman.'[25] Brebner, who read the manuscript of Lower's *North American Assault on the Canadian Forest,* caught his meaning exactly when he suggested that the title might include words like conquest, demolition, ravage, plunder, and exploitation; he suggested as an appropriate subtitle 'A History of International Plunder'.[26] For Lower, lumbering, and indeed most other forms of staple economics, seemed vivid illustrations of a gambling spirit.

Lower's criticism of the indiscriminate ravage of the forest was based less on wistful nostalgia than on a desire for some source of control that would curb atomistic and selfish individualism and conserve natural resources. It was animated also by his knowledge of the human wreckage that had been left in the wake of the ignorant efforts to settle the Shield country. 'There was little sense of limitation in the Canada of the first half of the nineteenth century,' he wrote of the misguided assault on the poor pockets of soil in the forested lands of the Laurentian barrier. 'A generation in which the settler sat enthroned could not be expected to rise to the conception of a vast national estate rigorously conserved for the purpose for which it was best adapted, the growing of white pine trees . . . .'[27] There could be no question of the folly of encouraging settlement in the area, though Lower did not accept the depressing picture of the inhabitants of the Shield country drawn by Merrill Denison in his plays contained in *The Unheroic North* (1923), where the one-time men of the north were revealed to be hopeless yokels leading stultified lives.

The other aspect of lumbering as a typical example of careless exploitation related to the metropolitan forces that lay behind the expansion of the forest frontier. Lower clearly understood the relationship between British and later American demands for Canadian forest products, and he devoted a good deal of attention to analysing the way in which the shifts in demand and special legislation affected the timber trade in Canada. He described the crux of that relationship as 'demand centres calling on supply centres'. This conception—'metropolitanism', as he called it—was implicit in the staples approach to Canadian economic history, and by the time Lower elaborated it in the context of his synthesis of Canadian history, various formulations of it had been elucidated and applied by other historians. N.S.B. Gras, a Canadian-born scholar teaching in the United States, had advanced as early as 1922 a theoretical description of the four stages that urban centres passed through on their rise to metropolitan status.[28] The nature of metropolitan dominance had been examined by Robert Park and the Chicago sociologists in the same decade. And Lower's colleague at Wesley College, D.C. Masters, had analysed the financial rivalry between Toronto and Montreal; in 1947 Masters was to publish *The Rise of Toronto, 1850-1890*, which applied Gras's stages theory to the development of the Ontario metropolis. In *Colony to Nation* Lower described at considerable length the role of the London metropolis in the mercantilist system in the late-eighteenth and early-nineteenth centuries, and paid special attention to the rivalry between Montreal and New York and, later, to the struggle between Toronto and Montreal for the western hinterland.

But 'metropolitanism' for Lower meant more than an economic relationship; it was loaded with connotations of colonialism and exploitation. He insisted that British institutions and habits of thought—again equated with privilege and differentiation of rank—were strengthened in Canada by its historic reliance on the overseas metropolis, and that the staples trades in the period before the end of mercantilism in the 1840s were conducted to enhance England's national interests, or at least certain interests in England. The exploitation of North America was not only a characteristic of the frontier; Lower made it quite clear that its impulse came from the metropolis itself. 'The methods used might be wasteful,' he remarked, 'the natural product in question might be exhausted, the inhabitants used up, exploited or enslaved, the country might at last be squeezed dry and thrown aside like a sucked orange, but "the business had to go on".' [29] So persistent was this pattern in the past that Lower came to see the tensions between the determination to exploit nature and tear out her treasures for the maximum profit, and the desire to settle and possess the land, as one of the profoundest antitheses in Canadian history.

The exploitative attitude to nature was nurtured not only by the pioneer experience and the metropolitan relationship but also by Canada's Protestant religious heritage. Like other cultural critics of the 1920s whose outlooks were shaped by the revolt against 'Victorianism', Lower chastized 'puritanism' because of its dourness and philistinism, its suspicion of the emotional life, and its anti-intellectualism. The rigid taboos of late-nine-teenth-century Methodism were part of his own adolescence, and his criti-que of puritanism—which he equated with Calvinism—was also a revolt against his own past. There was nothing original in Lower's identification of the puritan heritage with the ethic of material success that underlay capitalism. It was an association frequently made by the younger intellec-tual critics in the twenties who had been influenced by the works of Max Weber, Ernst Troeltsch, and R.H. Tawney; the academic radicals in the League for Social Reconstruction had alluded to those virtues inculcated by the Canadian Protestant churches—industry, thrift, sobriety, and temperance—as precisely those values lauded by an aggressive and suc-cessful capitalism. It may well be, as Lower himself insisted, that his per-ception of the close association of the Protestant ethic and the spirit of cap-italism was not so much prompted by his reading of this literature as confirmed by it.[30] For one of the clichés of late-nineteenth-century Protes-tantism in English Canada, frequently invoked when disparaging contrasts were made with French Canada, was the equation of Protestantism and progress. Lower in a sense simply turned this identification on its head. By criticizing the faith in material expansion and 'progress', he was inevitably led into questioning what had been held to be its religious impulse.

In any case Lower's indictment of puritanism for encouraging, if not ac-tually sanctifying, material achievement as an outward sign of one's status as a member of the elect ran in conventional grooves. 'Wherever Calvin-ism has prevailed', he explained in 1943, 'societies largely committed to the acquisitive way of life have arisen.' Calvinism presented man with the question of whether he has been called to salvation; since there could be no certainty about the answer, the visible sign of his election was that he prospered. The Calvinist type of religion placed a tremendous burden on man to succeed, acquire, and sacrifice all to those ends. Stripped of its reli-gious phraseology, this 'Calvinist-individualist-success conception of life' degenerated into 'mere selfishness', and even into hedonism and paganism.[31] It had coloured the Canadian character and, Lower was con-vinced, endangered the very survival and domination of Canadians of Brit-ish stock. But above all he condemned it because it had fueled the ener-getic but essentially anarchic assault on virgin resources that in turn had produced a socially atomistic collection of individuals rather than a coher-ent community.

V

The antithesis of English-Canadian materialism and lack of coherence was

French Canada. For a historian so obsessed with Canadian unity, even with the issue of whether Canadians possessed a 'national soul', Lower necessarily had to come to terms with the historical relations between French- and English-speaking Canadians. In 1925 he referred to the presence of 'two nationalities' in the country and underlined that what held them together was the geographical and economic unity of the St Lawrence valley and the common possession of British political institutions. 'Sooner or later will not our vigorous climate, working on sterling stock, hammer out a vigorous and distinctive people, the "men of the north"?'[32] Such remarks had been commonplace in English-Canadian nationalist discourse for at least a generation. Hackneyed too was Lower's genuine admiration for French Canada as a tightly knit community that stood as a counterpoise to the aggressive acquisitiveness of English-Canadian capitalism. Like G.M. Wrong and other well-meaning writers who had tried to explain French Canada to English Canadians, Lower isolated those characteristics of Quebec that stood out most clearly in contrast to what he found most disturbing about his own society. He gave this familiar theme a novel twist, however. He set the contrast between French and English ways of life into the framework of the Weber-Tawney thesis on the relationship between religion and economic action.

The contrast between French and English social principles was most clearly visible on the northern frontier. In his *Settlement and the Forest Frontier* Lower examined in detail the profound differences between church-promoted colonization in northern Quebec and the individualism of Anglo-Saxon settlement in Ontario. The *habitant*, he explained, 'has his family, his church, his own people around about him, plenty of food (of a crude sort), the fresh air, and the freedom of the woods . . . . Living, to him, is more than achievement. To his priest, it is much better that he should lead a quiet, simple, self-contained life than that he should get caught up in the meshes of English industrialism, for the simple life is the good life.' Though Lower conceded that there was considerable evidence of difficult living conditions, he found the simplicity and naturalness of French-Canadian pioneer life thoroughly admirable, in contrast to that of English-speaking people who had elevated 'a high standard of living' into a shibboleth. 'What we really have to deal with', he wrote, 'is the clash of two completely different philosophies, the English philosophy of materialism and efficiency, the French-Canadian and Catholic philosophy of simplicity and spiritual satisfaction. They cannot be reconciled.'[33]

The roots of the French-Canadian way of life, he argued in his Presidential Address to the Canadian Historical Association in 1943, were to be found in medieval Catholicism, a peasant culture, and the experience of conquest. The religion of New France was paternalistic and sacramental and it nurtured and sanctified a manner of existence that stood in complete opposition to the frenzied activity to establish the symbols of one's election that had been stimulated by the Protestant Reformation. The life of the Catholic peasant, Lower elaborated,

> is a series of ritual occasions—planting and harvesting, being born, coming of age, begetting, dying. The land has always been there and it always will be. Man's occupancy is transient and the individual is only one in a long chain from forefathers to descendants. All are one family, inter-related if not in this generation, in the last or the next. All give unquestioned obedience to the great mother goddess, the earth-mother, who can easily be made to wear a Christian dress . . . . Man is subject to nature and to nature's moods: he learns to acquiesce in the drought and flood, the good years and the bad. As his animals and plants grow and come to harvest, so he grows and comes to harvest.[34]

Completely missing from this mentality, at least as Lower characterized it, was the restless striving for material success, and the desire for change, improvements, and progress so characteristic of the English-Canadian Protestant mind.

It was the fate of these two peoples, embodying two ways of life, to begin their shared history with a military conquest. Few English-Canadian historians made a greater effort to communicate what they imagined to be the psychological impact of conquest and occupation, mild though these may have been by eighteenth-century standards. The whole social structure of the conquered is laid open to their masters and they become a second-rate people. Lower wrote:

> Wherever they turn, something meets their eyes to symbolize their subjection: it need not be the foreign military in force, it need not be the sight of the foreign flag, it may be some small matter—a common utensil of unaccustomed size and shape, let us say, taking the place of one familiar. And then there is the alien speech, perhaps not heard very often, but sometimes heard, and sometimes heard arrogantly, from the lips of persons who leave no doubt that the conquered are in their estimation inferior beings. Even the kindness of the superior hurts.[35]

The Conquest was to give to French-Canadian society a cohesiveness, a determination to preserve the medieval, Catholic way of life, and the memory of a bitter wound. From it Lower dated the most enduring antithesis in Canadian history, a vast 'conflict of philosophies', that underlay the relations of French and English from that day to his own.

This 'conflict of philosophies' was at the bottom of the clashes between the elected assembly and the British oligarchy in the early nineteenth century. Lower saw the 'racial conflict' that led to the Rebellion of 1837 primarily in terms of a cleavage between a dynamic Anglo-American commercialism and a static, feudal agrarianism. 'On the one hand stand those who are close to the soil; irrevocably committed to the land in which and by which they live; and on the other, those who simply regard Mother Earth as a source of good things, who cut down its forests and tear up minerals regardless of its future, and then, if opportunity offers, rush off to pleasanter places.'[36] Like Creighton, whose *Commercial Empire of the St. Lawrence* (1937) had dwelt on the conflict between commercial and agricultural economies, Lower interpreted the Lower Canadian troubles in socio-economic terms. But where Creighton celebrated the achievements of the dynamic North American commercial class, Lower shared the point of view of French Canada as he saw it.

French Canada seemed to him to embody an altogether admirable social cohesion and solidarity based on an ethnic homogeneity, a sense of isolation from its revolutionary mother country, and its deep experiences of history. French Canada not only stood as the antithesis of the restlessness, mobility, and individualism of English Canada; it also represented for Lower the kinds of group feelings that English Canada might possess if its excesses were curbed and chastened. But he was not unmindful of some of the blemishes: a complacent self-satisfaction with mere survival, grinding poverty, a 'lack of initiative', certain emotional deficiencies, and—an important qualification for a staunch civil libertarian—a weak civic sense.[37] Nor was Lower oblivious to the important question of what would happen to those admirable anti-capitalist peasant values in the industrial and urban society that French Canada had already become. He did not feel that the primary antithesis of Canadian history could ever be resolved completely. The best that could be hoped for was that English Canada, once it outgrew its sentimental ties to Britain, and once its excessive materialism was checked by countervailing loyalties, would some day find in French-Canadian life values more acceptable to itself. The two peoples were bound together by the unbreakable bonds of geography, economics, and history—even if it was a political history of expediency.[38] The antithesis would partly resolve itself, but Canada would always remain a dual nationality.

Lower's portrait of French Canada was sympathetic, romantic, and sentimental. He seemed unaware of the possibility that the allegedly anti-commercial, anti-business spirit of that society might have been accentuated by the Conquest itself or by the nature of Quebec's resources. By rooting his explanation of these values in religion, transplanted from Europe and embedded in New France at its beginning, he seemed to overemphasize the continuity and uniformity of everything that followed. There is a fixity and sameness in the values he identified with French-Canadian civilization that hardly alter, even marginally, over time.

Yet if his assessment of the primary antithesis of Canadian life appears in retrospect highly selective, it should be remembered that Lower was one of the very few English Canadians to attempt any kind of analysis of French Canada in the later 1930s and early 1940s. Serious investigation of Quebec society on the part of English-speaking observers outside that society was carried on by American sociologists and historians. English-Canadian intellectuals seemed uninterested in any serious historical study of Quebec or French Canada on its own terms, unless one excepts Hugh MacLennan's *Two Solitudes* (1945). Whatever might be said of the adequacy of Lower's insights into French Canada, he at least fixed on one of the central themes in Canadian history at a time when few of his academic contemporaries devoted much sustained attention to it at all.

VI

French Canada's ethnic homogeneity stood in striking contrast to the heterogeneous character of English Canada, which had been produced by immigration. Lower's interest in problems of population and immigration provided the subjects of his earliest essays and recur persistently throughout his writing. The platform of the students' Conservative Party at the University of Toronto, which he led in 1913, advocated restricted immigration.[39] He was thereafter consistently critical not only of the assumption that immigration throughout the nineteenth and twentieth centuries had actually increased the absolute numbers of the Canadian population but also of the effects on the fibre of Canadian nationality of unselective immigration, especially of non-French and non-British peoples.

During Lower's lifetime the ethnic composition of Canada's population changed dramatically. In 1901 its people were almost entirely of British or French origin; by 1940 the population was '50% British, 30% French and the remainder of some alien stock'.[40] Lower had grown up in a provincial town that possessed a high degree of ethnic homogeneity, and his first encounters with the new immigrants who came to Canada in large numbers before the First World War occurred during his summers in northern Ontario. The Ukrainian and Polish railway labourers struck him as a strange and utterly alien people. Later, while a student at Harvard, Lower wrote an essay on the migration of French Canadians to New England, and in preparing it he read some of the major criticism of immigration produced by Americans who had been associated with the cause of restriction since the turn of the century. Among these works were some of the classic critiques of the new immigration: John R. Commons's *Races and Immigrants into America* (1920), H.P. Fairchild's *The Melting Pot Mistake* (1926), and Francis A. Walker's *Restriction of Immigration*, a pamphlet published by the Immigration Restriction League.[41] In the early 1920s American immigration laws were severely tightened to limit the influx of southern and southeastern Europeans.

Lower's residence in Winnipeg strengthened his hostility to the unselective nature of Canada's immigration policies, and the mixture of nationalities in that city left him alarmed. The so-called 'foreign question' was most pronounced on the Prairies. J.S. Woodsworth had sounded a warning about the consequences of indiscriminate immigration policies in *Strangers Within Our Gates* in 1909, though by 1916 he also lauded the valuable cultural resources the immigrants brought with them. The anti-foreign feeling that had been heightened during the war had by no means vanished in the later 1920s and 1930s.[42] But during the 1920s some people displayed a far more sympathetic attitude to immigrant cultures—sympathetic, that is, within the framework of assimilation. Robert England, Superintendent of the Department of Colonization of the Canadian National Railways, appealed in his *Central European Immigrant in Canada* (1929) for a greater toleration and understanding of the Slavic settlers, praised their contributions to the economic development of the West, and urged a positive appreciation for their art and crafts. Some of the nationalistic intellectuals in the twenties—Arthur Lismer, for instance—pointed to the folk cultures of Quebec and of the Slavic immigrants in the West as authentic arts to be preserved and treasured.[43] In the thirties Watson Kirkconnell, a colleague of Lower's at Wesley, drew attention to poetry in the Icelandic and Ukrainian languages through translations and anthologies. But even to these suggestions of a more tolerant approach, Lower remained indifferent. His contribution to the discussion about immigration and population in the late 1920s was to reject the myth that massive immigration had increased the Canadian population. He had nothing but disdain for those boomsters who were always predicting that Canada's population was destined to reach the hundreds of millions and was even more sceptical of the proposition that European immigrants were, or had ever been, necessary for the country's economic development. The main determinant of Canada's economic growth was foreign demand for its staple exports and the availability of land for settlement. The number of people the staple economy could absorb was strictly limited and depended in any case on the outside market. The land suitable for large-scale agricultural settlement had virtually been occupied. Canada, Lower believed, had in fact reached its optimum population size. In 1927 he wrote that Canada in 1919 was 'an overpopulated country'[44] and he added subsequently that it was probable that its population would be sixteen million in 1970.

Lower came to the conclusion that, in spite of the periodically large influxes of people during the nineteenth and twentieth centuries, Canada's population had not grown any faster than it would have done by natural increase. The increase in population had over the long run been fairly consistent at an annual rate of 1.91% from 1861 to 1921. In the period 1901-21, 3,230,000 immigrants came into the country and just under two million people left it. What had in fact happened, Lower contended, was that immigrants with inferior standards of living had simply displaced Canadians who went to the United States in larger numbers than if there had been no immigration. Lower formulated a Gresham's Law of Immigration: cheap men will drive out dear men. 'The man with the higher standard of living cannot compete with the man with the lower,' he explained. 'In this sense, virtually all immigrants are "cheap" men for on arriving in this country they are not in a position to bargain for the sale of their labour . . . . ' The native Canadian could not compete, he was displaced, and sought a job south of the border.[45]

What bothered Lower about this pattern of population movement was not only the tremendous wastage of human resources involved, and the callous and exploitative attitude towards immigrants that it revealed, but above all its effects on Canadian nationalism. 'If Canadians wish to see Canada possessed of all the best attributes of nationhood,' he explained, 'and if the chief result of immigration is to drive out the native-born, it is evident that much evil must come from this constant renewal of blood; generation by generation . . . . ' A people had to be moulded slowly by the soil and the climate before they became 'true children of the fatherland'. Yet the population was shifting and unstable, immigration forced precisely those best adapted to Canada to leave and replaced them with aliens; people never got a chance to integrate and adapt to a fixed culture. Clearly massive immigration was one of the main impediments to the formation of a strong sense of national community.[46]

It was not only this permanent state of social dislocation that Lower criticized. At bottom he believed that a reasonable degree of social stability and ethnic homogeneity was necessary for any kind of society. The standard against which he measured European immigrants and found them wanting was the type of British immigrant who had pioneered in Upper Canada. Their descendants—and the 'best of the people who have come since'—laid the foundations of English Canada and were almost completely Canadian in orientation. Lower was obsessed not only with their displacement and migration to the United States but also with the declining birth-rate of the Anglo-Saxons. This had been one of the alarmist cries raised by the American restrictionists in the late 1880s: in 1925 Lower had assured himself that 'In the United States, the Anglo-Saxon stock is becoming diluted but in Canada it is scarcely touched.'[47] By the 1930s he had changed his mind. The future, he believed, lay with those people who would breed. Between 1921 and 1931 the various groups in Canada increased at vastly different birth rates: the British by 10.07%, the French by

19.36% and others by 41.5%. Our British stock, Lower warned, 'both native born and born abroad, is rapidly slackening its rate of increase and . . . , unless some unforeseen change occurs, it is destined to be outnumbered, not only by the total of all groups but by one of them alone, the French.'[48]

One of the reasons Lower so consistently denounced the Puritan success ethic and the gross materialism it nurtured was because he attributed this deliberate decline in the birth rate to the desire for economic success. Calvinism, commercialism, a fixation with high standards of living, lead directly to 'race suicide'.[49] The future lay with the 'earthly animalism' of peasant peoples who expected little of life and whose group cohesion was most pronounced. This obsession with stock, blood, and breeding affected even the language Lower employed to bolster his views on Canadian foreign policy in the later 1930s. Those who advocated that Canada participate in the next European war, he warned, by and large were anxious to keep Canada a British country—'dominated by British ideals, with British institutions, and predominantly British in population. These are objectives with which I am in hearty agreement.' But as in the last war, men of British stock would enlist first and be sacrificed and those of French and foreign birth would replace British Canadians. Participation in another war 'would hasten the process by which Canada is becoming less and less a British country . . . .'[50]

Lower's convictions regarding the need for a homogeneous society were formed in the 1920s and were never substantially altered. Yet in time he came to drop the racist overtones—the vocabulary of blood, stock, and fatherland. He understood very well, both from his own background and from his observations and reading, the tragic disorientations of the immigrant,[51] and knew too of the racial and religious intolerance of Canadians: ' . . . the typical English-Canadian Protestant has reflected complacently on his superiority to Frenchmen, Catholics, Jews, and "Bohunks".'[52] It was, in fact, precisely his awareness of these tragedies and animosities that led him to advocate restriction. But fundamentally he always believed in the need for a relatively homogeneous society as the essential precondition for Canadian nationalism.

VII

Given Lower's intense preoccupation with those antitheses that characterized the evolving sense of community in Canada, it was perhaps inevitable that he would be drawn into the debate over Canadian foreign policy after the mid-1930s. Ultimately he came to the position that Canada should avoid entangling alliances both within the League of Nations and the British Commonwealth, that its commitments should be strictly limited, and that it should remain neutral in the next European war. Neither these conclusions, nor the particular arguments that Lower advanced in support of them, were calculated to enhance his popularity, and there was more than one occasion when his public lectures and articles stirred up, as he said, hornets that nearly buzzed him out of his job.

Lower vehemently denied the appropriateness of the term isolationism to describe his views. He neither believed that Canada could magically insulate itself from international contacts, nor that it could repudiate its historic associations with the Commonwealth or its more recent membership in the League of Nations. In fact, in a categorization of the three major attitudes towards Canadian foreign policy in 1935—a rather oversimplified analysis that reveals more about Lower's own attitudes than it does about the alignment of opinion—he avoided the word isolationism altogether. In his eyes the three camps were the traditionalists, who were either satisfied with things as they were or wanted to forge even closer links with Britain; the supporters of the League and collective security, who were willing to limit national sovereignty in order to prevent war; and the 'nationalists', with whom he classified himself.[53] The prospects of a European war made it absolutely necessary for Canadians to think through their future course of action. What Lower dreaded most of all was that Canadians—or at least the influential majority of citizens of British origin—would emotionally identify themselves with Britain's involvement. Anyone, he wrote in an autobiographical passage, who looks back to the reasons for his own enlistment in the First World War 'knows very well that he did not enlist on matters of high principle so much as on an emotional impulse.'[54] Canada may have acquired the constitutional trappings of autonomy, but in a profound sense its people had not matured sufficiently to be able to see their country and its interests as separate and distinct. And it was here that the crux of the problem lay. It was not only education they required; if necessary, people had to be shocked out of those complacent illusions about Parliament's ultimately deciding what Canada would do. It was not good enough to say that decisions would be made at the appropriate time because there were in fact real commitments—not formal ones, of course, but commitments of sentiment and unconscious ancestral ties. Mackenzie King's foreign policy in the late thirties was partly based on a deliberate effort to gloss over the radically different points of view within the country; his critics, like Lower, wanted to expose and highlight these various differences and strip away the veil of obfuscating rhetoric that concealed them. Only then could one set about defining broadly the concrete and realistic basis of rational foreign policy. In a sense this suggested that legal autonomy, which meant both so much and so little, would be matched by a genuine psychological independence, which in turn would underlie an independent point of view.

As was the case with his friend Underhill, Lower's consuming fear of

Canada's involvement in a European war was based on a loss of confidence, or a deepening of disillusionment, with British leadership in the years after 1935 and cynicism about the inflated moralism of the First World War. Both men were suspicious of the capacity of Canadians to be taken in by great crusades; in fact they attributed Canada's support for the League partly to the appeal that a kind of missionary society had for a people steeped in the morality of good behaviour. Both insisted on the need to be realistic and hardboiled, by which they usually meant that foreign policy had to be based on geographical and economic factors and a sense of limitations. But where the socialist Underhill tended to stress the operation of capitalism and imperialist rivalries in international relations, and reiterated the rallying slogans of the American isolationists, Lower's analysis rested on slightly different grounds. True, he made much of Canada's geographical isolation from Europe and the peculiar character of its economy, as did Underhill: but he paid far more attention to the ethnic composition of its population, the ties of blood, and, above all, to the way another war would adversely affect the national 'community'.

Lower's assessment began conventionally enough. Canada, he believed, was in fact an island surrounded on three sides by water and on the fourth by the United States, from which a military attack was unthinkable. It was three thousand miles away from any potential foe on the other side of the Atlantic, and five thousand miles from any source of aggression from the other side of the Pacific rim. It was so remote from naval or aerial assault under the prevailing technology as to be almost invulnerable. 'Along with the United States', he noted—and he underlined that the chief priority of Canadian policy was to preserve good relations with the Republic—'we enjoy a private world of our own.'[55] But unlike the United States, Canada's economy was based to a large extent on staple exploitation. This had two consequences for its foreign policy. First, Canada was more dependent on world markets for its exports and was necessarily tied more closely to other states. Canada could never pursue as rigorous an isolationist course as the United States and its chief interest, obviously, was peace and the removal of trading restrictions. The second implication was that the dominance of extractive industries and the limits of good soil meant that Canada's population would remain relatively small and thinly distributed in pockets over an immense area. Canada was not—and could never be—a major force to be reckoned with in world affairs, and its voice within the League of Nations was only that of a small state. Contrary to what might be expected, Lower did not write off the experiment of the League completely. 'The League has its obvious defects and limitations', he wrote in 1933, 'but it at least is the partial realisation of an ideal, and the probability is, in spite of the setbacks and failures we are now witnessing, that as the size of the world goes on diminishing through the development of the various forms of communication, the power of the League will increase and will eventually become large enough to establish the reign of law.'[56] The success of the League depended, however, on the co-operation of the great powers—England, France, Russia, and Italy. It was foolish to pretend that Canada's role would be anything more than that of a minor country.

Lower's analysis of the basis of Canadian foreign policy was haunted by the memory of the First World War, not only its excess of emotional zeal and crusading spirit but also the internal divisions it exacerbated. Canada was not in any meaningful sense a community. The Canadian people, except the French, were too close to their foreign origins to possess a unity of purpose. The constant influx of new elements and the consequent exodus of the native born had impeded the shedding of older loyalties, the slow, organic growth of tradition and adaptation to environment. A war waged in a distant place, especially one entered into in a spirit of ancestral kinship with Britain, would end the chances of making a strong and homogeneous community in Canada. People of British descent were in a relative sense a declining force because of their lower birth-rate; the French and the other minorities were increasing in relative proportions. The French-Canadian attitude to Empire was practical and hard-headed. To the recent immigrants the imperial tradition could have no meaning. 'To many a Slav on the western prairie', Lower wrote, 'King George must be as obscure a figure as the Shah of Persia.'[57] The very diversity of the country dictated that the only possible policy in foreign relations was one of compromise, for only through compromise could that undesirable diversity be overcome. But what Lower meant by compromise was that English-speaking Canadians should not enter another war automatically and unthinkingly.

If Lower can be described as 'anti-British' at all, and this is debatable, he was anti-British for a very specific reason. It was the imminent prospect of England's involvement in a war in Europe that threatened Canada most directly, for it was entirely possible, he felt, that people of British descent would respond in the same way as they had responded in the last war. Those historians who wrote in the imperial tradition had singled out for praise the evolutionary and organic development of Canada within the Empire. Lower and Underhill saw as one of the main drawbacks of such a pattern of growth the lack of any profound break that might have come to signify decisively for Canadians, especially those of British descent, the line that separated them from their 'homeland'. It was precisely this sense of separateness that Lower's history, as well as his contribution to the debate over foreign policy, were meant to underline.

VIII

Lower's passionate advocacy of neutrality imparted an urgency to his consideration of the past. He wrote his personal synthesis of Canadian history,

Colony to Nation, during the war, and it represented the distillation of his teaching of the previous fifteen years. It was, as one shrewd reviewer pointed out, less a systematic history of Canada as a series of reflections on that history.[58] When Underhill praised Lower as 'our most philosophical historian',[59] he meant not merely that Lower's interpretation of the past acknowledged the significance of 'philosophies' or 'ways of life', but also that it was essentially philosophical in a speculative sense.

Colony to Nation represented in Lower's development a declaration of faith, an answer to the questions about community and nationality that motivated all his work. That book can be understood only in relation to his search for some principle, or body of doctrine, that would impart to English Canada a strong sense of solidarity. For Lower the crisis of the Depression was not so much the collapse of capitalism as an economic system as the breakdown of traditional values and certainties. The certitudes that Canadians had lived by for three generations—an aggressive Protestant commercial ethic, faith in the British Empire and its institutions, and the maintenance of utilitarian, popular education—were losing their hold. The energetic dedication to material tasks had produced a very loose society in English Canada that was hollow at its centre and hostile to things of the spirit. It was entirely typical of Lower that in a fanciful 'Five Year Plan', which he published in the *Winnipeg Free Press* in 1932, he addressed himself not so much to the problems of economic recovery and full-employment as to a nationalist program that involved strengthening the powers of the central government; abolishing appeals to the Privy Council; asserting public control (but not ownership) over the great resource industries; reforming the educational system; and public support for the arts and literature.[60] What the country needed was some principle of cohesion. But where was it to come from?

Lower was searching for a principle similar to that which the intellectuals in the League for Social Reconstruction and the CCF had already found in the co-operative commonwealth and the spirit of mutuality and economic planning. But he rejected this collectivism. He fully recognized that Protestantism had produced its own counterpart to the unfettered commercial ethic in the form of the social gospel, but perhaps because of his liberalism and angular individualism he dismissed the CCF's 'nebulous humanitarianism' and excessive zeal for planning. 'I don't think I am predisposed to individualism as you are,' he wrote Innis; 'at least individualism rampant has never appealed to me, although I admit the difficulty of controlling the individual. But can he not be controlled from within? After all, some communities do have an esprit de corps which others do not and which mitigates many things.'[61] For Lower this principle of control from within was to arise not from economic reconstruction but from nationalism.

He frequently spoke of nationalism in the language of religion, and it is clear he expected that a nationalist faith could be embedded in the consciousness of Canadians as deeply as the old Methodism. Just as Methodism had instilled into people impulses to action, so Lower saw nationalism as a source of individual certainty as well as of collective behaviour. ' . . . at what period in life does a man, after a middle age of vigorous scepticism, begin to become religious again?' he asked Innis. 'Sometimes I think I feel it creeping on:—not formal religion of course but a sor[t] of semi-religious spirit, one that requires affirmation or certainties, rather than self-assertion.'[62] This quest for assurance, and the resulting confusion between religion and nationalism, shaped Lower's history.

He had fixed upon certain fundamental antitheses in the past and hoped for their resolution in the future. He envisaged his historical writing as an influence that would affect the balance between those forces and felt himself bound up in the historical pattern he described. The sense of community in English Canada was of course incomplete, but in the crisis of the Second World War Lower saw its outlines taking on a clearer shape. His history was an act of faith in the sense that the future would bring that communal feeling for which he so ardently hoped. Written history was itself an instrument that would promote this end, if the historian's intuitive understanding and recognition of the experiences of the people were sufficiently penetrating and if the public could be reached. The demarcations between the historian and history—between the past, present, and future—disappeared.

Colony to Nation was a passionate declaration of Lower's faith that the impediments to the growth of a sense of community were being overcome. It was also a sustained essay in self-definition and self-revelation. For ultimately Lower justified nationalism, a common culture in English Canada, and a common concern for the dual nationalities, on the grounds of the needs of the human personality. 'It is', he wrote in 1943, 'as necessary to health for a people to integrate their personality as it is for the individual. Sometimes the individual sensitive to such things feels drowned in the immensity and depth of the general cultural heritage of the world.' At such times he searches for a little island, for recognizable peculiarities—for, in short, roots.[63] *Colony to Nation* was Lower's own search for and identification with the land whose shape and colours he lyrically celebrated in the closing passages of the book.

Lower never again attained that emotional fusion with his material that made this work so powerful and earned for him a reputation as, 'the Abbé Groulx of English Canada'.[64] In subsequent years he was to write more, qualify his judgements on some subjects, elaborate them on others, and develop his examination of the civil-libertarian tradition. But the master themes of his historical thinking had all been adumbrated and were to remain constant in his outlook.

6 | A NORTH AMERICAN NATION

The nationalism of the twenties and the economic disasters of the thirties riveted the attention of historians on the social and economic bases of Canadian history. Innis's staples thesis, Underhill's attempts to rewrite political history in Beardian categories, and Lower's concentration on the forest frontier were three distinct manifestations of the determination to penetrate beyond the constitutional framework to the underlying material realities. The rejection of an essentially Britannic orientation tended, in the case of Underhill and Lower, to emphasize the North Americanness of Canadian experience. This tendency had further ramifications for the study of the historical interrelations between the United States and Canada and Canadian-American relations. Though interpreters of Canada had hardly been oblivious to continental affinities, it was only in the later twenties that a systematic and determined attempt was made to explore in detail the interconnections between Canada and its southern neighbour. This was a general impulse, but its most concrete testament was the twenty-five-volume series on the relations between Canada and the United States published under the auspices of the Carnegie Endowment for International Peace between 1936 and 1945.[1] The shift in perspective away from the imperial focus was sustained by the conviction that Canadian history had ceased to be a parochial subject and that the most fruitful way of looking at the past was in the context of internationalism. Canada was a member of the British Commonwealth; it was also a North American country with complex relations and affinities with the United States. It was as necessary to understand the historical roots of the latter association as it had been to examine the transatlantic imperial relationship.

I

This concern with the North American dimension of Canadian history was a reflection of the increasing public consciousness of the importance of Canadian-American relations in the twenties. Of course the nature and extent of the economic interdependence of the two countries, the migrations of their populations, the similarity of social outlooks, and the extension of American organizations northwards had all been subjected to comment and analysis earlier. In his polemical *Canada and the Canadian Question* (1891) Goldwin Smith illustrated the ways in which economic and social tendencies were re-uniting two peoples who had been artificially separated politically by a boundary that was itself a relic of an unfortunate quarrel in the past. In 1907 Samuel Moffett, a journalist of wide experience, updated Smith's argument. His impressionistic *The Americanization of Canada* elaborated on those tendencies that were fusing English-speaking Canadians into the American pattern. He pointed out that, of all living persons of Canadian birth, one fifth resided in the Republic; that, despite the conventional view that there was a greater degree of decorum and stability in Canadian political life, the essential issues of politics in both countries revolved around the distributions of franchises, tariffs, subsidies, and bounties; and that Canadian reading material—books, magazines and newspapers—were, if not American in origin, American in spelling and spirit. Like Smith, Moffett, drew attention to the role of American capital in the development of Canadian industry and resources, pointed to the international baseball leagues and labour organizations, and noted that even in their use of slang—that 'most delicate test of a peoples' mental unity'—Canadians and Americans were one.[2]

The trends to which Smith, Moffett, and others had called attention were intensified in the post-war years. In 1923 'the economic invasion of Canada by the organized wealth of the United States', as one writer called it, had led to a substantial proportion of American ownership in Canadian industry—41% of all steel furnaces and rolling mills, 45% in the electrical industry, 52% in copper smelting, 52% in drugs and chemicals, and 70% in automobile manufacturing.[3] Ten years later the total foreign investment in Canada stood at $6,794,000,000: $3,967,000,000 was of American origin, $2,731,000,000 came from the United Kingdom.[4] Evidence illustrating the extent of American influence, especially statistical evidence, multiplied in the twenties. In 1926 the editor of the *Welland Telegram* visited two newsstands in Hamilton, Ont., and complained that in one he found eighty periodicals, seventy-eight from the United States; in the other, sixty-seven publications, sixty-six from across the border.[5] The average number of border crossings at the same time was thirty million a year, an indication of the success of the Canadian tourist industry and perhaps also a mark of the influence of prohibition south of the border.

Conventional Canadian criticisms of American institutions, government, and popular culture were reinvigorated by an increasing awareness of the impact of these figures. As early as 1920 Archibald MacMechan, Professor of English Literature at Dalhousie, protested that Canada was becoming a 'vassal state'.[6] 'Anti-Americanism' was nourished by America's late entry into the First World War and the subsequent glorification of American military exploits[7] in movies shown by the American cinema chains in Canada. Some Canadians still adhered to the deeply engrained belief that in their political and juridical order they enjoyed certain advantages over their neighbours. 'Canadians may be "slow",' wrote William Arthur Deacon, literary editor of Saturday Night, in 1926, 'but they have been influenced by the murders in Chicago, and the number of lynchings in the South, and the goings on of the Ku Klux Klan; and they show a marked partiality for their own system of the administration of justice, with its speedier simplified court procedure, under judges appointed (not elected) for life, and so independent of political influences and affiliations .... '[8] Certain interests like magazine publishers conducted campaigns to convince the government that special legislation was required to limit the inflow of American periodicals in order to preserve the Canadian publishing industry. In 1930 Graham Spry and the independently wealthy Alan Plaunt formed the Canadian Radio League to press for a state-owned national broadcasting system: one of their motives was the desire to free Canadians from the influence of the commercialized networks of the United States. A regular feature of comment on American broadcasting, movies, and magazines was that criticism was directed against democratic mass culture generally.[9]

Yet this critical and fault-finding temper was subdued and very seldom resembled the shrill and apocalyptic rhetoric of particular groups in the later nineteenth century, or even the electoral appeals in the election of 1911. Contemporaries were struck by the ambiguous nature of Canadian views. Though Canada's prosperity depended in part on American capital, there was a wave of sentimental lamentations when a well-known native firm or business passed into foreign hands; while American films were immensely popular, the sensationalism of the American press was widely denounced. Contemporary intellectual analyses of these attitudes were impatient with Canadian hypersensitivity and offered psychological explanations for it. Frequently it was traced to the great disparity of power and population.[10] 'Our material inferiority we will balance by our moral superiority,' wrote an anonymous observer, 'you are big, but we are better; you are great but we are good.'[11]

In spite of the undercurrent of censoriousness, there was a widespread feeling that relations between the United States and Canada had improved, that issues that had generated tension had been resolved, and that the tendency of history moved in the direction of a better understanding and trust. This was the first generation of Canadians, Chester Martin declared in 1937, 'for whom the spectre of annexation to the United States has never risen above the political horizon'.[12] This recognition of the United States as 'Canada's friend'[13] rested on the heightened appreciation for the historical significance of the interconnections between the two countries. It may also have reflected the mood of optimism of the twenties that was expressed in the self-confidence of the intellectual community and the hopefulness about creating a national culture. It was deepened, furthermore, by a renewed awareness of the peaceful existence of the North American nations in contrast to the plight of Europe, where 'country [was] set against country, race against race, frontiers watched by suspicious guardians, enclaves and fragments of peoples only tolerated of necessity.'[14] The United States had rejected the League of Nations and Canada had entered it mainly for reasons of status; but the parallels in their foreign policies in the twenties convinced many that there was a common North American approach to world affairs. With the aggravation of European problems in the early thirties, an isolationist tradition was reinforced. One of the symbols of North American concord was the International Joint Commission, which since 1909 had jurisdiction over two thousand miles of boundary waters. The Secretary of the Canadian Section of the Commission wrote an article in 1934 on this 'peace pact that worked' and illustrated it with two pictures: one of two Austrian soldiers adjusting a chain on a bridge that marked a real border, the other of the personnel of the International Joint Commission gathered around a table.[15]

II

Both the harmoniousness and the complexity of Canadian-American relations affected intellectual life and especially academic training. Most Canadian students who sought a degree higher than the M.A. went outside the country for it.[16] The universities of the United States had attracted Canadian students in increasing numbers ever since the mid-nineteenth century. The prestige of the German-inspired seminar was at its height, and until the thirties training at the postgraduate level in certain fields was unobtainable on a large scale within Canada. Canadian students, of course, still made their way to the seats of learning in Great Britain, but the United States was closer and graduate financial assistance generous. The path followed in the generation before the First World War by Charles Colby in history at Harvard, Archibald MacMechan in English at Johns Hopkins, and O.D. Skelton and Stephen Leacock in political economy at Chicago was pursued by increasing numbers of aspiring Canadian historians, political scientists, and economists in the twenties. In 1927 the editor of the

Canadian Historical Review listed 54 doctoral dissertations underway, or recently completed, on Canadian topics; 44 of these were being done in the United States, 32 by students whose first degree was Canadian. By 1933 the number of Ph.D. theses on Canadian subjects had increased to 109; seventy were being written for American universities and twenty for Canadian.[17] A good deal of this research work laid the basis for pioneering monographs in Canadian historical literature.

The growth of interest in Canadian history in American universities was also stimulated by a greater American awareness of the rest of the world in the decade since the war, by the curiosity aroused by a neighbouring country that had assumed international status without breaking with the Commonwealth, and by 'the dominating place taken by Canada as a field for external investment'.[18] Canadian history was usually taught in the context of courses on North American settlement and economic development or as a sub-theme in the evolution of the Empire-Commonwealth. By the mid-thirties there were more courses on Canada's past being given regularly in the United States than there were universities in Canada. The first satisfactory college-level text in the subject that dealt adequately with the economic and social developments since Confederation was *A History of Canada* (1928) by Carl Wittke, who had taught Canadian history at Ohio State University since 1918.

Some of the first suggestions for the systematic examination of Canadian history in a North American framework were made by Canadian-born academics attached to American universities. The academic migration to the United States was one aspect of an entrenched pattern that moved Canadians from all social classes and professional groups to seek a living south of the border. In 1905 there were over three hundred graduates of Canadian universities holding chairs in American universities, a fact generally regarded as attesting to the high standards of Canadian education; by 1925 nearly six hundred former students of Canadian universities held academic appointments across the line.[19] Only a small proportion of Canadian students who received advanced degrees in the United States could be absorbed into the Canadian university departments. In some quarters, moreover, there was a snobbish opinion of the allegedly fact-grubbing and unpolished products of the American seminar and a preference for Englishmen or for Canadians who had been exposed to the general culture of the mother country. George Wrong staffed his department with men from Balliol College until 1924, when George Brown, a Canadian graduate in history from Chicago, was the first North-American-trained Ph.D. to be appointed.

Canadian expatriates teaching in the United States were immediately conscious of the discrepancy between the clichés of Canadian editorializing on the subject of Republican institutions and other national differences and the degree to which Canadians and Americans shared a common culture and social aspirations. 'I am beginning to realize the significance of what you often said to us,' one student at Chicago told his mentor, Adam Shortt, in 1906, '—that the boundary line is imaginary, and that really the people of Ontario and New York State have far more in common than the people of Ontario and Quebec.'[20] In 1929 Douglas Bush, then a lecturer in English at Minnesota, claimed that the composite image of American civilization as the average Canadian saw it 'might be summed up in a brief catalogue of symbolic names, Henry Ford, Rev. William Sunday, A. Volstead, H.L. Mencken, W.J. Bryan, Mayor Thompson, Jack Dempsey, Gloria Swanson'. Canadians seemed unaware of the contradictions involved in decrying American materialism and calculating their own progress in material terms, or in railing against the vulgarity of cheap American magazines and movies and importing them in enormous quantities. The best cure for a parochial complacency, Bush suggested, was a more thorough acquaintance with the better side of American life, especially that aspect of it represented by the universities and élite journals.[21]

The expatriate experience underlined and confirmed the notion of the international community of letters and scholarship and the conception of the university as an institution that transcended national peculiarities. James T. Shotwell, who went to Columbia from Toronto in 1898 and was caught up in the intellectual world of Charles A. Beard and James Harvey Robinson, recalled that he was not conscious of having crossed a significant cultural boundary. 'I suppose', he later testified, 'that I think of the academic world as one that has no territorial frontier and that the chief thing is to have the opportunity to make one's full intellectual contribution to anyone, anywhere, who is interested in it.'[22] John Bartlet Brebner, who studied at Toronto and Oxford before going to Columbia, held the same internationalist conception of the world of learning. The differences that he found in these three institutions were minor and superficial compared with their essential tasks.[23] Even a Canadian student who remarked that of all 'Britishers' a Canadian feels most at home at Harvard still praised the heterogeneity and cosmopolitanism of that university's student body as a stimulant that merged localisms in a larger understanding.[24]

There was, of course, another side to this generous internationalism. It was emphatically a one-way street: compared with the number of Canadians who studied and taught at American institutions, very few American students came to Canada. Innis, who liked to puncture the mutual backslapping spirit of Canadian-American conferences, observed rather frankly in 1938 that they came 'because of a regulation against Jews in American universities'; and, always conscious of bias in scholarship, he noted that even those Canadians who did return to teach in Canada gave courses based on their American experience.[25] While in the twenties and thirties the academic exodus from Canada was often regarded as an example of intellectual internationalism and Canadians in the United States were seen as ambassadors of good will and understanding, the phenomenon was later described for what it really was: an exile of some of the nation's most talented people and a testament to Canada's material scarcity and cultural meagerness. Brebner said that Canada exported men and women just as it exported fish, fur, lumber, and wheat.[26] Some of those who remained in the United States displayed an impatience with traditional Canadian attitudes and a patronizing treatment of Canadians who remained in the Dominion. The 'commonest habit of Canadian expatriates,' wrote one who knew them well, was 'the almost irresistible desire to put a tack under Canadians who stayed at home.'[27] 'For some reason or other', added another, 'the expatriated Canadians in the colleges here whom I know seem to represent Canada as inherently a dependency of the United States.'[28]

Still, a number of these scholars retained an abiding affection for the country of their birth and it was a measure of Canada's hold on them that they sought to reveal the significance of Canadian history to their American students and to analyse the impact of the United States on the development of Canada. They were the first to suggest and to undertake studies of the historical interrelations between the two countries in order to broaden the framework of Canadian historical writing and break down compartmentalized national histories. One of the first efforts along these lines was *A History of English-Canadian Literature to the Confederation* (1920) by Ray Palmer Baker, a Canadian who did his graduate work at Chicago and taught at the Rensselaer Polytechnic Institute. He contended that political relations had obscured the fact that the foundations of Canadian literature were laid not by Englishmen but by men whom the New World had 'made American in habit and thought', and that the 'literature of the United States was the literature of Canada.'[29]

In 1929 William B. Munro, a Canadian-born Professor of Government at Harvard, advanced one of the central contentions of this group when he began a discussion of the American influence on Canadian government by arguing that the North American continent was, except politically, a unit in all respects and that the man-made boundary had no physiographic, economic, ethnic, or linguistic justification. He suggested that many of the most crucial events in Canadian history were heavily influenced by the actions of the United States: the Revolution and the migration of the Loyalists; the War of 1812, and the birth of Canadian nationalism; the rebellions of 1837, which were 'a resounding echo' of the democratic uprising that took place in the United States; Confederation, which was 'both inspired by the American example and dictated by the fear of American aggression'; the parallel and integral westward expansion; and the party systems, which were born in New World conditions. 'The West, whether in the United States or in Canada,' Munro wrote, 'is not merely an area but a state of mind, a form of society, a point of view.' And the frontier, 'a place of rugged individualism' that had such a liberalizing impact on the Republic in the first half of the nineteenth century, was exerting the same transforming influence on Canada in the early twentieth century.[30] In the same year Hugh Keenleyside, a Canadian graduate of Clark University then teaching at the University of British Columbia, published the first scholarly survey of Canadian-American relations in which he reiterated the contention that the boundary had no logic or rational explanation in physiographic terms and treated in summary all the main themes that the Carnegie series later examined in exhaustive detail.[31]

In a paper written in 1931 Bartlet Brebner, who was to play a large role in planning the Carnegie series, appealed for a 'continental interpretation' of North American history. He outlined not only those areas in which interactions were obvious—economics, the movements of populations, patterns of social life, and government—but also cases of divergence, such as the special position of French Canada, the conservatism of English Canada compared with the American zest for experimentation, the different treatment of the Indians in the westward movements, and the greater degree of public ownership and state involvement in Canada's economy.[32] Brebner's approach, unlike Munro's, was based on an internationalist view of the interpretation of the histories of nations rather than on Turner's frontier thesis, about which he had serious reservations.

From the beginning of his career Brebner had been predisposed to comparative history in an international framework. He left Toronto during the war to serve in the international force at Salonika and in the British Army. He made a fresh start at Oxford in 1919 and came into contact with Curtis's group of imperialists and the imperial historians, Hugh Egerton and Reginald Coupland. He returned to teach at Toronto in 1921 and began work on a study of the handling of the Acadian population of Nova Scotia, which was published as *New England's Outpost: Acadia before the British Conquest of Canada* in 1927, two years after he departed, or was forced by Wrong to depart, for Columbia. Brebner's interest in the fate of the Acadians as a point of comparison with the treatment of the French Canadians after the Conquest was an outgrowth of the more general concern of the imperial historians with the way in which minorities had been treated in the Empire.

Brebner was to publish two other major books in the thirties that reflected a similar fascination with broad internationalist forces. In *The Explorers of North America, 1492-1806* (1933) he showed how the unity of the continental design was revealed by explorers of various nationalities; and in his *The Neutral Yankees of Nova Scotia* (1937) he dealt with the question of why a colony that contained such a large proportion of settlers from New England did not join the Revolution; he concluded that, since Nova Scotia was not effectively invaded by the rebels, its people were not forced to make a decisive choice—their fate was decided by the superiority of British sea-power. Brebner's proposal of 1931 was not so much an appeal for a strictly 'continentalist' history as it was a suggestion for an internationalist approach to the histories of Canada and the United States, which had for so long been treated in isolated compartments.

Brebner's appeal for a continental interpretation of North American history caught the attention of James T. Shotwell, the director of the Division of Economics and History of the Carnegie Endowment for International Peace. As we shall see, Shotwell immediately grasped the significance of Canadian-American history for the lesson it would convey as a model of peaceful international relations. At first, however, the proposal to examine Canadian and American relations was justified as an extension of an already existing program devoted to surveying all phases of American foreign policy and sponsored by the Social Science Research Council of the United States. In 1927 this body had approved an intensive examination of the United States' involvement in the Pacific area under the auspices of the Institute of Pacific Relations. In 1932 Shotwell, who was also the Director of the Program of Research on International Relations for the Social Science Research Council, secured its formal approval for the Canadian and American series and in 1933 the Carnegie Endowment committed itself to underwrite the costs. The Carnegie series was originally planned in forty-four or forty-five volumes encompassing the historical, economic, political, cultural, and educational relations between the two countries and it was to be published jointly by the Yale University Press and the Ryerson Press. Shotwell was the general editor of the series, but his major function was in acting as a liaison with the Carnegie Endowment and in public relations. Brebner became his chief adviser and the planner of the historical volumes.

The writing of the series was paralleled by conferences held at Canton, N.Y., and Kingston, Ont., which were intended to provide forums in which scholars might report on their work and also be meeting places where journalists, educators, civil servants, and public figures from both countries could discuss current issues. The conferences were suggested and later largely organized by two historians: Albert Corey, a Canadian graduate of Clark who taught at St Lawrence University, Canton, and Reginald Trotter, a product of Queen's who had studied under Munro at Harvard, taught at Stanford, and then returned to Queen's. The studies on the economic relations of the two countries were partly supervised by Jacob Viner, a graduate of McGill and Harvard who was then at Chicago. The whole project was initiated, largely supervised, and partly written by Canadian-born scholars in the United States, aided by scholars who were American trained and living in Canada. There were, of course, participants whose backgrounds were quite different. While it would be misleading to draw rigid correlations between academic experience and precise historical views, Canadian-born academics in the United States were on the whole the most receptive to the idea of continental history, because its truth seemed confirmed by their own experience. The discovery of North America was in a sense a discovery of themselves.

III

The study of North American comparative history and Canadian-American relations was also reinforced by a general impulse to broaden the scope and framework of Canadian history. Not infrequently the case for a more intensive examination of Canada's historical ties with its southern neighbour was made in reaction against the preoccupation of the constitutional historians with imperial relations. Implicit in the claim that the North American orientation of Canadian experience was a most fruitful context in which to illuminate aspects of its history was the conviction that Canadian and American relations were at least as important as Canada's relations with the Empire-Commonwealth.

Yet these two frameworks were not regarded as mutually exclusive, not even by constitutional and political historians like Chester Martin and W.P.M. Kennedy. It was a matter of restoring a balance. The process by which Canada had attained national status in a transformed Empire had been fully explored and research on the topic was subject to diminishing returns. The North American influences on this development and the social, economic, and diplomatic relations had not received the same amount of attention. The link between the older constitutional scholars and the younger exponents of North American history was the shared belief that Canadian history was an internationalist history. Martin and Kennedy were convinced that Canada was a national unit within an English-speaking community that included the United States. George Wrong had made this idea the centrepiece of his series of lectures, *Canada and the United States: A Political Study* (1921), and this recognition that behind dissimilar forms of government lay a cultural and linguistic unity had deep roots in the liberalism of Goldwin Smith and the imperialism of Sir George Parkin and G.M. Grant in the late nineteenth century. There was therefore nothing contradictory in the impulse to trace the similarities and connections between Canada and the United States while emphasizing Canada's unique association within the Commonwealth. Indeed, it was essential to reveal these international affinities because they bolstered the Canadian conviction that Canada's mission in the world was to function as an interpreter between Britain and the United States. This notion too was an old one and had been revitalized by the vogue of internationalism in the twenties. It accorded Canada a strategic position in relation to the United States, just as the record of constitutional progress placed it at the very centre of the evolution of the Commonwealth.

In a sense, then, the impulse to inquire into Canadian and American interrelations was quite compatible with the imperial approach of the twenties. Chester Martin, who had traced the conflicts between elected assemblies and appointed governors and councils back to the New England colonies, became the chairman of the group of Canadian historians involved in the Carnegie project and was committed, in conjunction with John Dafoe, to writing a history of the influence of Canadian-American relations on the development of Canadian nationality. Perhaps the most insistent exponent of the internationalist view of Canadian relations with the United States and the British Commonwealth was Reginald Trotter. In his *Canadian Federation* (1924) Trotter elevated the achievements of responsible government and Confederation to a higher plane when he noted that Canada had been the principal exponent of national autonomy preserved within an internationalist commonwealth. Canada not only pioneered this process of transformation within the Empire; it was also a country in which a large ethnic minority possessed a genuine cultural autonomy and still participated fully in national life. It was a short step to seeing Canadian relations with the United States as pointing toward a more co-operative and peaceful international order and away from truculent and suspicious nationalism.[33]

If the interest in Canadian-American relations was a logical outgrowth of the imperial internationalist outlook of the constitutional historians, it was also in part a reaction against their preoccupation with the forms and principles of government and their rather reverential treatment of institutions. In the later twenties they were criticized for failing to penetrate behind inherited labels and cherished images to examine how North American democracy and interest-group politics had changed the operation of the parliamentary system. Underhill and Lower found in Beard's progressive historiography and in Turner's frontier thesis respectively suggestive points of departure for interpreting political history in a quite different fashion. What they and others were concerned with was the way in which British political institutions and attitudes to politics had been profoundly altered in North America by a different environment. This 'environmentalism' encouraged a tendency to take the European heritage for granted and to concentrate on the ways in which it had been changed.

In three lectures delivered at Columbia University in 1933-4, entitled *Canada: An American Nation* (1935) and dedicated to Shotwell, John Dafoe revealed how the central problem of the constitutional historians could be reformulated. He argued that the foundations of both Canada and the

United States had been laid by colonists who lived in America for four or five generations divorced from English influences and dealing with problems unaided by European experience. They brought the principles and the primitive institutions of self-government from the Old World, but it was only in America that English liberty evolved into a genuine social democracy. European notions of class and aristocracy were broken down: the North American environment favoured individualism, equality, and freedom. Dafoe attributed Canada's role in reshaping the Empire to this dynamic North American conception and made it clear that in the evolution of social democracy Canada and the United States shared a common achievement.[34] The crucial events in Canadian experience became analogous to decisive episodes in American history: the Rebellion of 1837 in Upper Canada, for example, appeared as an abortive northern version of the Jacksonian assault on privilege. The immediate effect of looking at Canadian history in terms of these identities was to blur the distinctions that had previously been emphasized between a British political tradition and American republicanism. Similarly the word 'Americanization' came to connote not deliberate imitation or influence, but similar responses to the American continent and modern industrial life generally.

The parallel histories of the countries of the New World were generalized into a Turnerian version of hemispheric history by Herbert Bolton of the University of California. Once a student of Turner's, an expert on the history of the northern Spanish borderlands in America, and a participant in the early planning of the Carnegie series, Bolton in the twenties had advocated the idea of hemispheric solidarity as a basic field for historical research. The conviction that North and South America possessed a common history and commitment to freedom had a respectable ancestry running back to the eighteenth century and was at the height of its influence in the isolationist decade of the Depression. In his Presidential address to the American Historical Association in 1932, entitled 'The Epic of Greater America', Bolton contended that all the countries of the hemisphere had been colonized and settled by European peoples; in all of them European habits, institutions, and cultures had been modified to suit new conditions, and there had been agitations and struggles against the remnants of European political ideas and Old World control. In one way or another the nations of the western hemisphere had broken with Europe and achieved political independence. This process had lasted for centuries, and though Bolton recognized that there were distinctive elements in the development of various nations, he insisted that there was a pattern that transcended individual national histories. The countries of the western hemisphere, including Canada, had been participants in a common experience comparable to the common elements that united the history of Europe.[35]

The framework of the Carnegie series was a rather mutilated and re- stricted version of Bolton's hemispheric history. The themes that Bolton found linking the nations of the hemisphere were to be examined only in relation to the two countries north of Mexico. Brebner found Bolton's ideas suggestive, and Shotwell, who sometimes spoke of the entire series in terms that had only a slight relationship to individual volumes, fre- quently proclaimed the objective of the project to be the portrayal of the epic of America on a large canvas—the spread of civilization westward and the conquest and joint development of the continent.

There were of course Canadian scholars who were involved in the Car- negie series and who participated in the conferences who remained scepti- cal of any attempts to separate Canadian history too sharply from its im- perial origins. Trotter noted that the popularity of Bolton's ideas was offset in Canada by a consciousness of the Dominion's membership in the British Commonwealth and the League of Nations. He objected also to Dafoe's stress on the North American origins of Canadian constitutional development in relation to the Empire. Even if there had been no older American colonies or a United States, he said, British North America would have demanded self-government in the nineteenth century.[36] But still the impulse to broaden Canadian history to include relations with the United States arose from the internationalism of the imperial school, and the popularity of environmentalism riveted attention on the processes that united the two North American countries.

IV

Shotwell's interest in the study of Canadian-American relations was an ex- pression of his life-long preoccupation with world peace and international order. His concern with the foundations of peaceful international relations was nurtured in the Quakerism of his family and in Gladstonian liberal- ism. A colleague of Beard and Robinson at Columbia, he had sympathized with the progressive movement and was profoundly moved by Wilsonian internationalism. Shotwell had been a member of the Inquiry, the team of academic experts from various fields that accompanied the American dele- gation to the Paris Peace Conference, and he became a strong supporter of the League of Nations and of the Briand-Kellogg Pact that outlawed war. From 1914 to the late twenties he planned and directed the writing of an impressive series, sponsored by the Carnegie Endowment for International Peace, on the economic and social effects of the First World War. It even- tually comprised no less than one hundred and fifty volumes, written by two hundred collaborators from fifteen countries, and included Adam Shortt's *Early Economic Effects of the War Upon Canada* (1918). The en- tire project was aimed at revealing the catastrophic costs of the war and at demonstrating that in the industrialized and scientific modern world, war itself could neither be limited nor controlled and could no longer be employed as the extension of policy. The Carnegie history of the war was a monument to the progressive faith in man's rationality, intelligence, and capacity to learn from the past.[37]

Shotwell envisaged the multi-volume study of Canadian and American connections as a logical sequel to this work. The investigation of the relations between the two North American countries, at peace with each other since 1814, would disclose the positive foundations of international co-operation between nations. There was nothing novel about looking at these two countries in this fashion: the myth of the unguarded frontier had been a cliché for at least a generation and the isolationist reaction to the First World War gave it renewed vitality.[38] During the 1920s Canadian representatives at Geneva never tired of reminding Europeans of this singular tradition. Neither Shotwell nor any of the scholars later involved in the series, however, accepted the notion that the border had been unguarded and that relations had been tranquil and undisturbed. That myth had been laid to rest by the historians; one of the projected volumes in the series, on armaments and disarmament in North America, bore the paradoxical subtitle, 'The Military History of the Century of Peace between Canada and the United States'. The myth of the undefended border, moreover, rested on the conviction that there were exceptional and unique circumstances in North America, the implication being that it could not therefore convey any meaningful example to other continents. Shotwell's point of departure was quite different: he recognized that throughout much of the nineteenth century Canadian-American relations were characterized by friction, suspicions, and controversies. Peace had been preserved not because it was never tested but 'in spite of grievances unredressed, of threats and policies filled with menace and of almost constant economic strain'.[39] There had been many occasions when war might have broken out, but peace had prevailed. Despite some potential sources of tension and a residual anti-Americanism within Canada, the two countries had co-operated more effectively, and arrived at a better understanding of each other, than any two other states in the world. Canadians and Americans had ceased thinking of their relations in military terms. With the breakdown of collective security and, in the later thirties, the threat of another world war, the reasons for the peaceful relations in North America took on a universal significance.

Those enlisted to write for the series may not have shared Shotwell's vision, and in any case what editors plan and what authors produce are rather different things. In fact one of the most arresting features of the twenty-five volumes that in time appeared was their diversity and individuality of viewpoint. One of the reasons for this, and for the success of the project, was the financial resources it commanded. American foundations had for a long time made substantial and generous donations to support Canadian scholarship and educational activity. Between 1911 and 1935 the Carnegie Corporation gave $6,241,126 to Canadian libraries, universities, museums, and research projects.[40] Almost the same amount came from the Rockefeller Foundation. The combined figure of between twelve and thirteen million dollars was about thirty per cent of the total endowment of Canadian universities. The Carnegie Endowment's sponsorship of the series was part of this pattern: it advanced research funds and subsidized the publication of scholarly books that might not otherwise have been printed at all. Nearly every professional Canadian historian was at one time or another involved in the project, and the series included a number of books that were conceived independently and appeared under its auspices because of convenience. The Carnegie enterprise also represented an alliance of historians, economists, sociologists, and legal scholars who brought quite different outlooks to the appraisal of North American relations.

The series, moreover, was written over a decade that registered profound changes in world affairs. It was planned and launched in 1934 at the high-tide of North American isolationism and completed during the Second World War, which made it impossible to conceive of even continental relations in continental terms. 'When we began the conferences, based upon an original series of researches in Canadian-American problems . . , ', Shotwell admitted in 1939, 'there was no thought that we should find ourselves in such a short stretch of years looking, not just north and south, but east and west as well.'[41] Perhaps most Canadian historians had never lost sight of the transatlantic dimension. Individual scholars produced works that were far broader in scope than the title of the series suggested. A.L. Burt's *The United States, Great Britain, and British North America From the Revolution to the Establishment of Peace After the War of 1812* (1940) was an extensive study of Anglo-American, not merely continental, history; Harold Innis's *The Cod Fisheries: The History of an International Economy* (1940) traced the complex background of a staple trade involving western Europe and North America over five centuries.

In his editorial prefaces and speeches Shotwell tried to relate these individual studies to the general significance of Canadian and American relations. He believed that the scientific principles of the social sciences and objectivity in history were quite compatible with a pragmatic purpose, and he neither impressed an ideology on the series nor distorted the discrete, limited conclusions others had arrived at. While it should be repeated that individual contributors saw themselves working on precise questions and may have been indifferent to the wider ramifications of their research, most of the volumes did support the generalizations Shotwell sought to establish. It is in this limited sense that the series — with some exceptions —

may be said to contain a certain unity of argument and a coherence of purpose.

V

The most persistent theme running through the volumes was the determination to reveal those processes of civilization that transcended national units and bound Canada and the United States together. Two such elements were regarded as particularly central: the interpenetration of economic activity and the interchange of populations. The volume on Canadian-American industry was the first of the series to appear, and in his explanations of the project Shotwell invariably accorded large space to this aspect of the relationship. 'From the standpoint of economic interest', he wrote in 1934, 'the most important foreign relations of the United States are those with Canada. Not only is our trade with Canada larger than with any other single nation, but we have almost four billion invested in Canadian industries.' One of the most urgent reasons for the series was the promotion of understanding and goodwill at a time when what Shotwell called 'maladjustments', by which he probably meant nationalist economic solutions to the Depression, threatened to disrupt the smooth interdependence of the 1920s.[42]

The enormous growth of American investment, particularly during the First World War and the ensuing decade, was invariably explained as natural and normal, a result of geography, culture, and opportunity: it was also attributed to the nationalist tariff policy of Canada, which served as the greatest inducement to the establishment of branch plants in the Dominion. It was considered inappropriate to refer to this as 'economic imperialism', and even the word 'penetration' was considered slightly provocative in some quarters. Though most analysts conceded that the impact of American capital had distorted Canadian economic development in certain directions and retarded the emergence of industrial science in Canada, the process was regarded as generally beneficent in accelerating growth and increasing prosperity. American direct investment did not constitute control over the Canadian economy, and it did not imply a loss of political independence because the banks, press, and transportation interests remained in Canadian hands. Above all it was widely believed that the relative extent of American investment was destined to decrease. Canada was rapidly becoming a creditor nation and Canadians had more invested in the United States on a per-capita basis than Americans had in Canada. The actual decrease in the number of American companies set up in Canada during the early years of the Depression also seemed to confirm that foreign investment would level off. The sober conclusion was that 'in the future Canada will depend less and less on capital imports for its national development. It is possible that capital imports by Canada on a large scale are entirely a thing of the past . . . .'[43] The size of American investment, in short, should cause no concern; and even if it did, it was bound to decrease anyway.

The extent and historical character of this economic interdependence were further illustrated by studies of the development of the forest and dairy industries, labour relations, and railway interconnections. The cumulative impression was to underline the essential unity of the continent and the superficiality of merely political designations in North American affairs. Furthermore, the existence of substantial economic interests of Canadians in the United States and of Americans in Canada was held to constitute a basis of trust and a guarantee of good relations. Canada's Deputy Minister of Finance, W.C. Clark, voiced the almost universal opinion when he told the assembled scholars in 1935 that 'these financial ties should contribute to a better understanding and a closer fellowship between the two countries.'[44]

The historical and statistical investigations of the movements of population in North America, in almost complete disregard of political frontiers, buttressed the same point. The migrations of New Englanders to Acadia and Nova Scotia, Loyalists and late-Loyalists to British North America, French Canadians to New England, Maritimers and Upper Canadians to the Mississippi Valley, and American farmers to the Prairies, were unplanned, haphazard, and prompted mainly by the search for economic opportunity. The American historian of immigration, Marcus Hansen, wrote that these people viewed the continent as a whole. 'It was not the United States and Canada. It was all America to them.' They had settled the continent jointly and in unison, not just in parallel movements, and they were, Brebner added, 'capable of allegiance to one country one day and to another the next'.[45] Their loyalty transcended nationality; their allegiance was to a common North American individualism. By the 1930s about one-third of Canadian-born stock lived in the United States; about one per cent of American-born stock lived in Canada. It was estimated that there were over thirty million border crossings every year. This interchange of populations and the creation of a complex web of family ties reinforced a better understanding and mutual sympathy.

The five studies in diplomatic history bolstered this optimistic impression in a different way. They were based on a wealth of fresh archival material, dealt for the most part with discrete questions in a technical fashion, and generally satisfied even the most fastidious adherents of dispassionate history. Far from dilating on the mythology of the undefended border, historians like Max Savelle, A.L. Burt, A.B. Corey, L.B. Shippee, and Charles C. Tansill concentrated on episodes and issues where conflicts of interest were sharp and intense. They ranged from the drawing of the boundary in the period 1749-63 to the Revolutionary Settlement and the War of 1812; from the crisis of 1830-42 to the unsettled period of the Civil War and Confederation; and they embraced the rancorous dispute over fisheries and trade policy down to 1911.[46] The overall impression that emerged from these studies was that the Canadian-American relationship was born in civil war and was characterized for almost a century afterwards by tension, suspicion, and hostility, but that gradually issues had been peacefully resolved and arbitrated until an unparalleled cordiality and friendliness prevailed. This pattern was attributed to a tradition of realism in politics, to the spaciousness of the continent, and particularly to the application of arbitration and conciliation techniques.[47] The development of self-government enabled Canadians to perceive that their interests were similar to those of their neighbours and it gave them a measure of self-confidence that in turn undermined their traditional suspicions of the United States.[48] Canada's attainment of national status, it was held, also modified the traditional American view of the Dominion as a pawn of British imperialism on the continent. But above all, this long progressive change was directly related to the intermingling of people and particularly to economic interdependence.

Three historical works were devoted to Canadian regions, or sub-regions, that had experienced intense and close inter-connections with neighbouring areas of the United States: the Western Ontario peninsula, the Red River Valley, and the Pacific slope. Perhaps the finest of these books, Fred Landon's *Western Ontario and the American Frontier* (1941), dealt with an area that jutted deep into the republic, had historically been crossed by American pioneers moving westward, and had been thoroughly exposed to American political ideas, religious and educational standards, and farmer and labour organizations. Landon's study convincingly demonstrated that Canadian-American relations had repeatedly been relations between people in all walks of life, not merely formal interactions between states.[49]

The series not only strengthened the assurance that relations between Canada and the United States had, over the long run, become more friendly and co-operative; it was dedicated to the purpose of making them better still. It appeared ridiculous in the light of common interests that attitudes born in another day still survived to distort the way these people looked at each other. In his introduction to *Canada and Her Great Neighbor*, essays on the opinions of Canadians about the republic, the Columbia sociologist Robert M. MacIver, who had taught at Toronto from 1915 to 1927,[50] revealed this bias against an exaggerated nationalism more fully than any other participant in the series. While Brebner recognized that anti-Americanism, that faithful consort of Canadian national feeling, was permanent and ineradicable, MacIver saw it as an infantile disorder and attributed it to insecurity and jealousy. It was not clear where he drew the line between anti-Americanism and Canadian nationalism. In fact he rejected both when he wrote in 1938 that 'We are still children when we think of ourselves in national terms.' Nationalism, invariably fostered by 'vested interests', warped the ways in which people viewed each other, particularly at a time when messianic nationalism once again threatened the peace of Europe. International conflict, he argued, was not caused by economic interests or different faiths but by false images. These had to be destroyed before men could understand the real world and control it.[51] The examination of Canadians' opinions of the United States conformed to this prescription; negative views were underestimated and explained away. The parallel study of American national attitudes affecting Canadian-American relations was never made. The volume that dealt with Canada's rejection of reciprocity in 1911 took a similar view of nationalism: the defeat of that mutually advantageous measure was traced in large part to the opposition of economic interest groups that magnified and cultivated unfounded nationalist fears for selfish reasons.[52] The tendency to treat nationalistic passions and ideas as mere subterfuge and insincere rationalizations was common among historians who had been nurtured in progressive history and were determined to get behind all façades to the economic 'reality'. It also conformed to the needs of the internationalist outlook.

Shotwell drew these themes together and in his editorial introductions and public addresses generalized about the significance of the individual studies for the benefit of a general readership. Though moved by impulses that the contributing scholars did not perhaps share, at least not to the same extent, he remained faithful to the history they had written. Shotwell believed that the genuinely creative forces at work in the modern world were science and industry and that they were knitting all nations into a single interdependent international community. There was a lag, however, between the reality and the facts of modern life and the regrettable tendency of people to think in terms of national sovereignty and national distinctiveness. On the one hand there were the rigid institutions and theories of sovereignty; on the other the activity of industry and business, which no longer confined its routine operations to states but followed the engineer and the inventor across national frontiers. In the same way that American historians in the 1930s interpreted the Civil War as the result of emotionalism and hysteria, Shotwell explained international conflict as the consequence of a failure to remove the precise issues in dispute from enveloping abstractions and outmoded emotions that made rational appraisal impossible.

For Shotwell the key to peace lay not so much in the formal renunciation of war as an instrument of policy, or in the application of judicial machinery to adjudicate disputes, important as these were. Peace could be attained by the application of 'intelligence' and a general recognition by public and statesmen alike of the forces that underlay co-operation. The contribution of history and the other social sciences was to reveal those processes of civilization that made all peoples one, and to undermine antiquated, nationalistic prejudices. 'We have the feeble instrument of intelligence', he wrote, 'to battle with the old appetites, with claws that have become hands, with minds that are the museums of long antiquities .... '[53] The history of Canadian and American relations became a model of how nations might live together peacefully if only the correct lessons were followed. International peace in North America, the Carnegie series revealed, was the outgrowth of economic interdependence and the unimpeded workings of liberal capitalism, the free interchange of populations, the embedding of fragments of one nation within another, and a rational, non-ideological approach to problems.

VI

History has not been kind to Shotwell's optimistic faith, and events after 1939 served to highlight some of the deficiencies in the approach of the Carnegie series to Canadian and American relations. The major bias of the project as it was planned in 1934 was the conviction that these relations could be examined on their own terms without equal reference to Canadian ties with Europe—a reasonable proposition at the time, since so much attention had previously been focused on the British connection. The English background of both American and Canadian political cultures was more or less assumed in this approach. As has been pointed out, Canadian historians like Martin, Trotter, and Brebner were fully aware that continental history could not by its very nature adequately reflect the total range of international forces that had played upon Canada. In 1938 Trotter protested that the principal tendency in the treatment of the history of the Americas in his generation had been 'to exaggerate the term *American*', and he later added that Canadian history would never be understood if it was thought of 'as a series of footnotes and appendices to the history of the United States.'[54] The outbreak of the Second World War was to deepen these reservations.

Between 1939 and 1941 Canada, alone of all the nations of the western hemisphere, was at war in Europe, and this fact highlighted the entrenched patterns of thought and action in its makeup that did not conform to, that were perhaps more important than, the North American tradition. At a symposium of the American Historical Association at the end of December 1941, three weeks after the Japanese attack on Pearl Harbor, the historians addressed themselves again to the problem of whether the Americas had a common history. 'It is not enough to say that Canadian culture, institutions and habits of living have American elements,' George Brown commented. 'No one would deny that. But today another standard of judgement forces itself upon us.' That standard was the future of world order and the war in Europe. The cardinal factor in American history was the common interest in the Atlantic world. The notion of hemispheric or continental history had obscured the truth that the infinite network of interrelations between the Old World and the New had never really been severed. The Americas did have a common history, but it was not one of isolation.[55] As F.R. Scott wrote in a primer on Canadian-American relations in 1941:

> the most important factor underlying Canadian-American relations today . . . is the new danger from abroad which both countries are facing . . . . Basically the threat is to the inner philosophy, the democratic tradition and the whole standard of human values on which Canadian and American society has been reared. Millions of men are being taught, and believe, that democracy is finished, that dictatorship provides a superior system of government, and that the individual life is valueless except in so far as it makes itself the Tool in the hands of the national leader . . . . This fact changes greatly the ideological basis of Canadian-American relations.[56]

This consciousness of liberal values under challenge was to alter profoundly the writing of history after the war and in the Cold War period.

This shift in perspective was mirrored on the individual level in Brebner's summary volume, *North Atlantic Triangle: The Interplay of Canada, the United States and Great Britain* (1945). When he laid out the plan for the historical volumes, only the interplay between the 'Siamese twins' of North America was included. In the late thirties he grew increasingly conscious of the necessity to extend this framework and to consider the questions of why Canada had not been absorbed into the United States and what were the distinctive features of Canadianism. Brebner's angle of vision was subtly different from that of most Canadian historians. He had intimate contacts with the community of Canadian scholars but also a certain detachment provided by his residence outside the country. Sceptical of nationalist claims that Canada was destined to function as the indispensible interpreter within the Anglo-American system, Brebner always emphasized the extent to which Canada drew the elements of its national life from abroad. He attributed Canada's survival in North America not to natural geographical divisions of the continent, nor even to its resistance to American manifest destiny. Canada remained independent because the internal tensions of American sectionalism had paralysed early annexation efforts, and because of the British connection and particularly British sea-power.[57] When in 1943 he set about writing the volume that was intended to synthesize the Carnegie series, he found that in order to do justice to the historical relations of Canada and the United States the third side of the triangle of relations had to be considered in more detail than he had previously allowed.[58]

Brebner never at bottom accepted the implications of another view of Canadian history that found expression in the Carnegie series and that became the basis for a rather different, more nationalistic conception of how Canada developed. The maps carried on the fly-leaf of all the volumes, showing the natural geographical unity of the continent, stood in direct contrast to the conclusions of Harold Innis. Innis had advanced the proposition that the boundary of Canada coincided approximately with the Pre-Cambrian Shield and the drainage basins of rivers that the fur traders had explored. The Canadian economy, at least in its origins, had evolved along different lines from that of the United States, and an entire institutional system had been built on the east-west axis based on fur and wheat. The most effective statement of Innis's point of view was Donald Creighton's *The Commercial Empire of the St Lawrence* (1937), which bore the Carnegie imprint, and, as will be seen, treated the two North American economies as competitors. Creighton saw the main point of Innis's work as a demonstration of the fundamental unity of Canada and its dependence on Europe; Brebner found in the same teachings an explanation of Canada's economic vulnerability and its receptivity to outside influences. Innis himself edited several volumes of the economics books in the series, a fact that suggests the variety of approaches that found a place within it. These differences were not then regarded as mutually exclusive or as profoundly different as they would later seem.

With the completion of the Carnegie series Shotwell turned his attention to the peaceful uses of atomic energy; the Carnegie Endowment continued its support (on a diminished scale) for the improvement of Canadian-American relations through the Canada-United States Committee on Education; and Brebner (who became an American citizen only after the United States entered the war) preoccupied himself with British history and the development of the welfare-state. The study of Canadian and American relations and comparative history ceased being the objects of such concentrated attention on the part of Canadian historians. The subject survived, of course,[59] but after 1945 the writing of the history of Canada was redirected into different channels.

Brebner, who had a sharp sensitivity to the transitory character of history, reflected on the significance of the Carnegie series in 1947 and noted that its main impact, and the influence of the point of view it expressed, was to free Canadian historical writing from parochialism and to show that the United States was as significant a factor in Canadian history as the

British Commonwealth. He made an accurate prediction when he stated that in twenty-five years students would consult the Carnegie volumes as sources of information and would also 'learn a great deal about our recent and present climate of opinion by considering the kinds of uses which the eminent historians made of their information.'[60]

7 | REORIENTATION

The fifteen years after 1939 were a period of transmutation and reorientation in Canadian historical writing. Substantial changes in Canadian intellectual life generally were set in motion by the Second World War, the cold war with Russia, and the renewed concern with a national culture expressed in the appointment in 1949 of the Royal Commission on National Development in the Arts, Literature and Sciences. Altered circumstances affected historical thinking in divergent, occasionally confusing ways. Sometimes these changes were simply logical outgrowths of attitudes of the thirties that were worked out gradually and almost imperceptibly; in other cases there were dramatic and novel departures. The forties were to leave as deep an imprint on Canadian historical literature as the cultural nationalism of the twenties and the economic breakdown of the thirties.

The decade saw the publication of several one-volume surveys of the past that synthesized and consolidated the more specialized monographic scholarship of the previous twenty years: D.G. Creighton's *Dominion of the North* (1944), A.R.M. Lower's *Colony to Nation* (1946), and Edgar McInnis's *Canada: A Political and Social History* (1947). It also witnessed an increasing impatience with the anonymity, impersonality, and implied determinism of economic history, sociology, and the economic interpretation of history. In 1944 the professional journal of Canadian historians canvassed one hundred and fifty people and reported that there 'was an insistent demand for new approaches, fresh interpretations, novel points of view'.[1] By the later 1950s the dominant form of historical writing was political biography; economic history was in almost total eclipse; and historians had reasserted the separateness and autonomy of their discipline as distinct from the other 'social sciences'. These major changes in historical writing were products of the internal dialectic of historical scholarship as well as responses to deep currents in national life. They will be examined from two distinct perspectives: first in terms of the new themes that emerged and the renewed emphasis on liberal institutions, culture, and the Atlantic civilization; and then, in the following chapter, from the point of view of the responses of Innis, Underhill, and Lower to the challenges of the forties and early fifties.

I

One of the most significant continuities of interest from the thirties to the later forties was the emergence of the historical sociology of Samuel Delbert Clark. Sociology, which Innis once called the Cinderella of the social sciences in Canada,[2] was a relative latecomer to the academic scene. An understanding of the particular twist that Clark imparted to it requires a preliminary digression into the background of the subject.

The study of social relations and institutions was first promoted in English Canada by clergymen and lay reformers inspired by a sense of obligation and service of the social gospel. Early advocates of social Christianity were horrified by the separation of ethics from everyday economic conduct and by problems associated with rapid urban growth, rural depopulation, intemperance, and immigration. They described and diagnosed the origins of these and other social maladies in the hope that conditions could be controlled and rectified. In 1897 the progressive businessman, Herbert Ames, published *The City Below the Hill*, a description of housing and living standards in a working-class quarter of Montreal. The technique of the social survey was later applied by J.S. Woodsworth in his tracts on immigration and urban reform, and in his 1917 report on Ukrainian Rural Communities for the Bureau of Social Research of the Governments of Manitoba, Saskatchewan, and Alberta. The first courses in the subject matter of sociology were taught before the First World War by clergymen in church institutions like Acadia University or Wesley College to candidates for the ministry. In other universities political economists like O.D. Skelton at Queen's regularly lectured on immigration and race relations, social-betterment schemes, charitable work, and city planning. The basis of sociological enquiry in French Canada was laid by Léon Gérin. In the mid-1880s he studied at L'École de la Science Sociale in Paris and came into contact with the followers of Frédéric Le Play, who had inaugurated research on family budgets. In the next fifty years Gérin produced a number of monographs on the structures and functions of the traditional *habitant* family and the parish as the fundamental institutions of French Canada.[3]

The chief pioneer of academic sociology in English Canada was Carl A. Dawson, who founded the Department of Sociology and Social Work at McGill in 1922. Born in Prince Edward Island in 1887, and a graduate of Acadia, Dawson was a Baptist clergyman who had worked with the Canadian YMCA during the war. Afterwards he studied both sociology and theology at the University of Chicago and was converted to the social ecology of Robert Park, who envisaged the city as a laboratory in which human conduct and social processes could be examined. Park and his colleagues applied the same techniques of enquiry to urban groups as anthropologists had used in their surveys of primitive peoples. Their work on immigrant communities, hobos, gangs, the ghettos and the slums, stressed locality, neighbourhood, and community structure. They focussed on immediate problems, employed the field survey and interviews, and made use of statistics compiled for administrative purposes. They concerned themselves with metropolitan communities and the patterns of relations between the city and the region it dominated. Park, who was once a newspaperman, was the first to suggest that areas of metropolitan control could be measured by the circulation of urban newspapers. Underlying the Chicago social-ecology approach to sociology was a faith in reform and an impatience with deviation from the norms of American life.[4]

Dawson's work for the Canadian Pioneer Problems Committee, which superintended the eight studies in the Canadian Frontiers of Settlement Series that were published between 1934 and 1940, was one incident in the application of this methodology to Canada. In the thirties the Prairies became for some Canadian social scientists what the city had been for Park—a kind of social clinic. The father of the series, Isaiah Bowman, the Canadian-born Director of the American Geographical Society, believed that the long period of undirected and wasteful expansion of agricultural settlement had ended. At the same time he rejected the notion of a closed frontier and maintained that there was still available for occupation enormous areas of land in Canada, Siberia, Manchuria, Australia, South Africa, and South America. These pioneer belts were of strategic importance as sources of future food supply and raw materials and also for relieving the congestion of population in older societies. Bowman conceived a grand design for comparative studies of the 'pioneer fringe' in various countries in the hope that certain principles of 'a science of settlement' would be established and that these in turn would inform state-directed agricultural settlement policies. The Canadian Frontiers of Settlement project originated in the same intellectual milieu as the Carnegie series on Canadian-American relations, and the organizers of both shared a faith in collaborative, inter-disciplinary research directed at practical ends.[5]

The group of books that appeared in the Canadian Frontiers of Settlement series comprised examinations of the geographical setting of prairie settlement and of contemporary economic problems by W.A. Mackintosh; a joint history of land policies by Chester Martin and of settlement patterns by Arthur S. Morton; a survey of standards of living and agricultural practices by the sociologist of rural life, R.W. Murchie; and studies of settlement on the mining and forest frontiers by Innis and Lower.[6] Dawson and his collaborators contributed three volumes. *The Settlement of the Peace River Country* (1934) presented a model of the life cycle of a pioneer fringe — from outpost, to isolated farming, to integration and organization as a region. *Group Settlement: Ethnic Communities in Western Canada* (1936) analysed the gradual integration into the western community of immigrants like the Mennonites and Doukhobors, who had originally settled in isolated blocs. Dawson had no reservations about the desirability of assimilation, which he attributed to the penetrative power of material, mainly economic, factors. *Pioneering in the Prairie Provinces* (1940) appraised the social aspects of the pioneering process, the creation of religious and educational institutions, and the emergence of local 'metropolitan' centres.

While Dawson's studies did much to sustain sociology's claim as a separate discipline, these books were the products of a particular methodology that Clark sought to qualify and amend. Social ecology, he argued, was excessively concerned with surface description; it was presentist in orientation, and conveyed a static picture of society. The bias of Dawson's writings on the Prairies was reinforced by the same techniques employed in examinations of the institutions of French Canada in a period of industrialization in Horace Miner's *St. Denis: A French Canadian Parish* (1939) and in Everett C. Hughes' *French Canada in Transition* (1943). Like Innis in economics, Clark sought to offset the fixation with current issues and to establish certain principles of social change by using the broader perspective of history. The historical detail of past Canadian social change, moreover, would make the academic teaching of sociological concepts and theories less abstract.[7]

Clark's prescription for a more historical sociology was made in reaction to a certain type of enquiry, and it also expressed his experiences and preference for history. He was born in 1910 and grew up on a farm near Lloydminster on the Alberta-Saskatchewan border. His parents, who had come from Ontario, were supporters of the United Farmers of Alberta, and he recalled that two of his early heroes were the progressive leaders Thomas Crerar and Henry Wise Wood. At the University of Saskatchewan he studied with A.S. Morton and completed a master's thesis on Saskatchewan settlement with special reference to dry-farming techniques, an undertaking that was supported by the Canadian Pioneer Problems Committee. He went to Toronto in 1931 with the intention of doing research on the history of farmers' movements, but was disappointed with the kind of history taught there. 'I must confess', he told Morton, 'that I am finding it very difficult to keep my interests alive in the work which I am doing. What with trouble looming in the orient and with our present Economic crisis, it seems almost ludicrous to spend hour after hour studying the contribution of Sydenham or Bagot to responsible government.'[8] After a year he proceeded to the London School of Economics where he took courses on politics from Harold Laski and on economic history from Eileen Power and R.H. Tawney. On his return to Canada he worked at McGill as a research assistant, wrote a thesis for Toronto on the Canadian Manufacturers' Association as a pressure group, and, after teaching one year at Manitoba, returned to Toronto in 1938. In that year sociology became a semi-autonomous body within the Political Economy Department.

Clark carried into sociology the economics of Innis, the sociologists' preoccupation with deviance and social pathology, and an enduring interest in the frontier. Innis and others had analysed the patterns of Canadian economic development based on a succession of staple commodities and new technologies. Clark built upon their conclusions and determined to explore the social consequences of new forms of economic enterprise over time. In one of the classic works of American sociology, *The Polish Peasant in Europe and America* (1918-20) by William Thomas and Florian Znaniecki, he found a suggestive clue that provided a link between staple economics and social disturbance. The life histories of these immigrants portrayed a people who had lost a sense of participating in society because their attitudes, shaped by one milieu, no longer corresponded to the economic structures of their new situation. A succession of frontiersmen in Canadian history experienced roughly similar disorientations as the immigrant Polish peasants.

The characteristic feature of Canada's social history, Clark argued, 'has been the recurrent emergence of areas of social life involving new problems of social re-organization and adjustment'.[9] These storm centres of social breakdown were identified with the 'frontier'. Clark's definition and use of this concept was somewhat ambiguous. At times he seemed to attribute to the frontier traits that Turner had identified with it. Frontier conditions, he argued, promoted democracy and stripped away inherited habits of thought and action that were inappropriate in the new environment. Writing of the United Farmers of Alberta in 1932, Clark had described the agrarian movement as 'an expression of the frontier; an expression of that rugged and enterprising individualism which is the mark of the pioneer of forest or plains.'[10] On the other hand he denied the usefulness of a conception of a Turnerian frontier defined as the furthest edge of settlement or free land. The frontier was rather an area in which new forms of economic enterprise were developed.[11] As such it could be urban as well as rural. Slightly later he would equate that zone of new economies and social disruption with 'the frontier of capitalism'.

From within this perspective the history of Canadian social development became the record of a succession of disturbances in social relations, habits, controls, and institutions caused by the intrusion of new forms of economic production. In the fur trade of the St Lawrence Valley, the fisheries of Nova Scotia, lumbering and farming in New Brunswick, farming in Upper Canada, mining in the Yukon and northern Ontario, wheat-growing on the Prairies, and manufacturing in the industrial cities, the specific modes of production determined the nature of social problems. On each of these frontiers traditional institutions were transplanted with difficulty; people tended to be independent and nonconformist and freer of social restraints. Furthermore, the imbalance between age and sex groups weakened the family, and religious controls were undermined by the inability of established churches to meet the needs of new occupational groups. Social apathy, deviant behaviour, prostitution, crime, and intemperance were thus the first short-run effects of frontier life. Clark was concerned not only with disorganization but also with the way in which institutions were reorganized by moral reform agencies and evangelical religion.

In *Church and Sect in Canada* (1948) Clark surveyed evangelical and revivalist Protestant movements that emerged on the margins of society between 1760 and 1900. The churches had repeatedly failed to respond successfully to the requirements of classes immediately affected by new economic developments. Frontier conditions destroyed old status relations and emphasized individual worth and equality. Those directly affected by the new environment were isolated and dispossessed of a past culture. In sectarian evangelicalism they expressed their protest against authority and found a sense of fellowship and a social place. This, Clark insisted, was the common experience that linked the followers of Henry Alline in Nova Scotia in the eighteenth century, the Upper Canadian backwoods farmers who supported early Methodism, the industrial working masses who responded to the Salvation Army in the late-Victorian period, and the prairie farmers who turned to the fundamentalist prophetic preaching of William Aberhart. For people in the hinterland, religious separatism was analogous to political revolts against outside control. The sects were conservative, however, rather than truly radical, for they served to focus and thereby legitimize the status of fringe groups. In due course sects tended to lose their initial separatist thrust and became instruments by which their members were assimilated into the social order. Evangelicalism also led to political indifference because it stressed the other-worldly.[12] Social and ultimately economic factors were held to be the determining influences in religious history throughout all of Clark's analysis. He was alert, however, to the reciprocal effects of religion on economic life, pointing out that religion had inhibited the free play of economic forces in Canada and that sectarianism functioned as a discipline to the labour force.

It was but a short step from these conclusions regarding the social history of sectarianism to an analysis of social credit, the main contemporary manifestation of aberrant evangelicalism and political protest. When Clark witnessed the Aberhart campaign of 1935, he could only compare its emotionalism, the absence of a rational program, and its intense appeal to insecure people, with contemporary European fascism. A series of ten volumes on the background and development of social credit in Alberta was begun in 1943-4 when the Rockefeller Foundation made a special grant to the Canadian Social Science Research Council. Innis conceived the general idea of using these funds to support a comprehensive study of agrarian protest in the west, and through his influence Clark was made editor of the series.

Like its predecessors in co-operative research, the Social Credit series,[13] which was published between 1950 and 1959, represented an alliance of social scientists and humanists who approached the same general problem from different angles. The historical contributions included W.L. Morton's history of the Progressive party, D.C. Masters' assessment of western labour radicalism and the Winnipeg General Strike, and Lewis G. Thomas's description of the dominance and breakup of the Liberal party, which ultimately led to the one-party tradition in Alberta. The historian of Canadian agricultural policy, Vernon Fowke, examined the national policy and the wheat economy, emphasizing that agriculture in Canada had always functioned as the basis for commercial and territorial empire, and that the Prairie economy was truly a colonial one. Employing a subtle Marxist analysis, the political scientist C.B. Macpherson revealed the relationship between the ideologies of the United Farmers of Alberta and Social Credit and the political economy of independent commodity producers. Another political scientist, J.R. Mallory, investigated the issues involved in the collision between the provincial legislation of Social Credit and the authority of the central government. John Irving, a teacher of philosophy, sought to explain the psychological appeal of Social Credit in the election of 1935 and contended that it fulfilled a need of people suffering from economic difficulties as well as deep-seated feelings of guilt at being unemployed and on relief. Two of Clark's own students, the sociologists Jean Burnet and William Mann, examined respectively the community life and tensions in the district of Hanna in central Alberta and the function of sects and religious cults in the province. With the exceptions of the study by Irving, and to a lesser extent the books by Mallory and Macpherson, the series concentrated on the background of the Social Credit movement rather than on the period in which it came to power.

This tendency was equally manifest in Clark's own contribution, a study of political protest in Canada between 1640 and 1840 that ended eighty years before the appearance of Major Douglas's heretical monetary doctrines in the West. Contending that there was really nothing fundamentally novel about Social Credit, Clark set his history of protest within a continental frontierist frame of reference. He argued that Canada, like the United States, had shared in a common frontier experience of successive revolts against authority. The frontier engendered an intensely localist, separatist, and anti-authoritarian spirit, and the common characteristic of all frontier peoples was their desire for autonomy and withdrawal from the infringements of outside authority. This spirit had been the driving force behind a variety of revolutionary upsurges in both the United States and Canada. But whereas these movements had been successful in the United States, leaving their imprint on the Constitution and influencing the drive to liberate adjacent territory from European control, in Canada they had been frustrated and defeated. The geography of the St Lawrence favoured centralized authority, and the very expansive revolutionary developments in the United States evoked a counter-revolutionary tradition north of the border.[14]

With a wealth of historical detail Clark traced these democratic liberation movements from the period of the American Revolution to the War of 1812 and the Rebellion of 1837. Behind the revolt in Upper Canada, he believed, lay the revolutionary philosophy of the continental American frontier, with its faith in direct political action and democratic practice and its distrust of central authority. The 'marginal elements' in the community, who supported Mackenzie, 'sought control over economic power, and this involved destroying forms of economic endeavour such as banks and large mercantile establishments and, perhaps, most important of all, bringing to an end the intervention of governments in economic life.' Mackenzie's draft constitution presented the clear trend of the popular will. 'Responsible government', Clark wrote—and here he completely inverted Chester Martin's understanding of the matter—'developed in reaction rather than in response to the true democratic spirit of the Canadian people.'[15]

In terms of political protest the prairie west became what Upper Canada had once been. What the West revolted against in the rebellions of 1869-70 and 1885, in the Progressive party and in the Social Credit crusade, 'was being taken over or being dominated by an outside power .... The West sought to be left to itself; it wished to withdraw from those allegiances which placed it in a subordinate position .... '[16] It was in this sense that there were no fundamental differences between the Upper Canadian uprising and Social Credit, or for that matter between Mackenzie and Aberhart. The resemblances were further affirmed by the fact that all movements of political protest contained within their ideologies a desire to return to some simpler state of affairs in the past.[17] They were restorative and conservative, and, like the evangelical sects to which they were allied, eventually accommodated themselves to the existing metropolitan structures.

Historians' responses to Clark's work, as distinct from the Social Credit series as a whole, illuminated both their views of historical sociology and their scepticism about the frontier thesis, however it was defined. Though the ever-generous Brebner said of *Church and Sect* that it was a milestone in Canadian historiography and that there was no need to worry whether it was historical sociology or sociological history, most historians were either hostile or indifferent. They wondered about the connection—some thought it an uneasy one—between Clark's theoretical disquisitions and the new and rich documentary evidence that filled his books. Traditionalists like A.L. Burt, who once dismissed sociology as the study of fallen women, thought that Clark was too preoccupied with departures from the norms of social conduct and that he had exaggerated incidents of extremisms, in both religious and political history, to the neglect of constructive achievements. A historian of religion faulted Clark for reducing the religious impulse to an almost automatic reflex of economics, and thereby depriving it of any self-generating powers.[18]

The twin dimensions of Clark's work that were most frequently challenged were, first, the aims of sociology itself and, second, his use of the frontier thesis. Clark was above all interested in the uniformities and the cumulative patterns in social development, religious sectarianism, and political protest. He stressed the constant and repetitive regularities of human experience. The Manitoba scholar W.L. Morton probably spoke for the majority of Canadian historians in the post-war period when he said that sociology and history were incompatible. In contrast to the social scientist, he elaborated, the historian was devoted to explaining human behaviour in specific situations and at specific times and his work was guided by sensitivity for the unique and the exceptional.[19]

Historians took issue with Clark's conception of the role of the frontier in history on both specific grounds—claiming, for example, that he had overestimated the impact of backwoods' opinion in America's declaration of war in 1812—and also in more general terms. For reasons that will be made clear in the following pages of this chapter, during the later forties and throughout the fifties historians turned away from the Turner thesis and subjected it to considerable criticism. The composite, ambiguous character of the frontier as it was defined in Clark's work was one source of the difficulties, but so too was the tendency of old established disciplines to resist the encroachments of new subjects on their preserves. Clark's major works, *Church and Sect* and *Movements of Political Protest,* appeared at precisely the moment when historians were least willing to listen to his case. His historical sociology was a logical extension of Innisian social science and it was from this tradition that historians were disengaging themselves. That his books had little immediate influence on historical writing was perhaps owing as much to the shifting interests of historians and to their changing perceptions of what history was all about as to a presumed incompatibility between sociology and history.

II

Canada's participation in the Second World War became almost immediately the subject of contemporary historiography. Since the days of Ernest Cruikshank's chronicles of the campaigns in the Niagara region and William Wood's reconstruction of the naval engagements of the War of 1812, the interest in Canadian war history had declined. There had been, it is true, a continuing effort under official auspices to describe the engagements of the Canadian Expeditionary Force in the 1914-18 conflict, but the Director of the historical section of the General Staff, Colonel A. Fortescue Duguid, had managed to complete only one volume of a projected eight volumes by 1938. Apart from a very few professional historians like George Stanley, who had paid a good deal of attention to the military history of the two Riel uprisings in his *Birth of Western Canada* (1936), scholars displayed little concern for the subject. Military history suffered from neglect partly because it was associated, especially by exponents of the 'new history', with 'drum and trumpet' romanticism and the preoccupation with heroes and the great ones of the earth.[20] Underhill, who had written an early account of the Canadian Corps, typified in an extreme fashion the revulsion against militarism and the anti-war spirit of the thirties. On another level Innis's economic history downgraded military events. He accounted for the collapse of New France, for example, mainly in terms of economic crisis, as though the activities of Wolfe, Montcalm, and the admirals were of hardly any consequence. Canadian historical writing in the inter-war years was engrossed first in constitutional studies, and then in economic history and the economic and social interpretation of politics. This thrust ran against what was patronizingly termed 'old-fashioned' military history.

One scholar who withstood this tendency and investigated the relationship between military policy and operations and episodes in the Canadian past was Charles P. Stacey. He was born in Toronto in 1906 and was educated at the University of Toronto, and at Oxford with the aid of a Sir George Parkin Scholarship. He had close connections with the part-time military and belonged to the Canadian Officer Training Corps; served in the ranks of No. 2 Signal Company, Canadian Corps of Signals, in which he obtained a commission in 1925; and was attached to the Officer Training Corps at Oxford. He received a Ph.D. from Princeton and taught there from 1934 to 1940.[21] During the early thirties Stacey published articles on defence policy at the time of the Rebellion of 1837, on the influence of the Fenian raids on Canadian national feeling, and on the second Red River Expedition. His first major work, *Canada and the British Army, 1846-1871: A Study in the Practice of Responsible Government* (1936), took an almost routine and exhausted theme and placed it in a fresh and unexpected perspective. By demonstrating how prominent considerations of military policy figured in British official thinking, he showed how one of the corollaries of responsible government, colonial self-defence, was worked out in British North America. More fundamentally his work suggested how Britain, reacting to the shifting balance of power in Europe and to the threat of hostilities with the United States during the Civil War, brought its considerable influence in support of the Confederation movement.

Stacey then proceeded to an examination of the so-called undefended boundary between Canada and the United States for the Carnegie series. Primarily interested in the process that had led to the demilitarization of the border, he argued that the period before Confederation was one of dangerous tensions and considerable military preparations, and that the era of good relations was of a very recent growth. The turning point in peaceful relations was not the conclusion of the War of 1812 but the withdrawal of the British garrisons from North America in 1871. After that date the two North American people gradually ceased thinking of each other in military terms. Though his study 'Armament and Disarmament in North America: The Military History of the Century of Peace between Canada and the United States' was not published, mainly because Stacey became involved in the official history of the Canadian Army in the Second World War, he did draw out its essential conclusions in a characteristically pungent article on the myth of the unguarded frontier.[22]

At the beginning of the war the Historical Section of the Central Staff was still at work on the official history of the conflict that had ended twenty-one years before. After General H.D.G. Crerar became Chief of Staff in 1940, he made arrangements to facilitate the more speedy completion of the history of the role of the Canadian army in the Second World War. Stacey had met Crerar while preparing a short study of Canada's military problems. In October 1940 he was appointed historical officer at Canadian Military Headquarters in London and was charged with the preparation of material and the securing of additional information from participants for some future official historian. A historical officer was later attached to each division in the field and was to summarize its activities in monthly war diaries. On the suggestion of the Canadian High Commissioner in London, Vincent Massey, ten war artists—including Charles Comfort, Will Ogilvie and Alex Colville—were appointed to depict the record of the army.[23] The sheer bulk of the documentary sources accumulated by 1945 was awesome: a thousand paintings and one hundred thousand war diaries that filled six hundred cabinets at Ottawa and hundreds more in London.

In 1946 Stacey was appointed Director of the Historical Section of the Canadian Army and Official Historian for the war of 1939-45. The decision had already been made to produce a general non-technical survey for a popular readership, to be followed by four comprehensive volumes dealing with over-all policy and the major theatres of action. The official history was designed to furnish an adequate record of military experience for professional soldiers, but it was also intended to provide the public with an intelligent basis for making decisions about future military problems. Stacey had always been acutely conscious of the implications of even remote military events. He had, for example, repeatedly criticized Canadians for their lack of military preparedness and their historic reliance on a volunteer system as against a universal-service militia, which made more men available in the event of war.[24] And few had been more aware of the curious paradox that, while Canadians generally paid little attention to military affairs—a penchant faithfully reflected by their historians—they had devoted considerable time and resources to waging war in the twentieth century. 'The people of modern Canada,' Stacey commented in 1946, ' . . . a country whose young men have fought two bloody wars within the space of a single generation, a country which claims the status of at least a "middle power" in world affairs, a country which has lately found itself obliged to increase its peace-time military establishment quite materially, now required to be far better informed than they have been in the past on military matters. They will', he warned, 'have to go on forming judgements on such matters for many years to come . . . . '[25]

The Canadian army in the Second World War was composed of a far larger proportion of Canadian-born than was the case with the Canadian Corps in the First World War. Circumstances compelled men from all regions and provinces to think of themselves as citizens of one country. The army was therefore not only a symbol of the nation; it was in a way the anvil of nationalism, a reforging of the commitments made in the First World War. To Stacey, Canadian participation was 'the greatest undertaking in our history', for unlike those moral equivalents for war that some had found in the building of the CPR, this was war itself, waged in 'defence of freedom against the bloodiest tyrannies of modern times.' It was, he confessed in words that evoked the emotion behind the project, perhaps presumptuous to attempt to write a history worthy of those who had made it,

worthy of the men who fought the lonely battle at Hong Kong and waged the grim encounter on the shingle of Dieppe; who routed the paratroops from the ruins of Ortona and beat the fanatical S.S. back mile by mile down the long road to Falaise; who broke the Hitler and

Gothic Lines; who opened the Scheldt and cleared the Hochwald; who battled in the mountains of Sicily, on the flats of the Lombard Plain and the polders of Holland, and through the German forests; who won too many victories to catalogue, and brought credit to their country wherever they set the print of their hobnailed boots.[26]

The writing of the official history was not unmarred by tension between the professional historian and the politicians.[27] The preliminary survey, *The Canadian Army, 1939-1945: An Official Historical Summary* (1948), and the more detailed studies that followed,[28] were characterized by a painstaking exactitude and a precision of expression that conveyed the meaning of this tremendous experience. In these books, and in his masterful piece of detective work, *Quebec 1759: The Siege and the Battle* (1959), Stacey revealed himself to be the country's finest practitioner of technical history.

The official history of the army, together with the official history of the naval services under the direction of G.N. Tucker,[29] were two major historical projects launched in the forties. At various stages they enlisted the aid of a number of professional historians: G.F.G. Stanley, J.B. Conacher, G.W.L. Nicholson, and Eric Harrison on the army, and J.M.S. Careless, Donald Kerr, and David Spring on the navy. This was perhaps one of the main reasons why the writing of the history of these armed services did not repeat the sad experience of the efforts to write the history of Canadians in the First World War.

The Second World War underlined anew the recognition that forces generated far beyond the confines of the continent had profound repercussions on Canadian development. With the publication of Stacey's history, as well as of Gerald Graham's *Empire of the North Atlantic* (1950), which illustrated how sea power was the controlling factor in shaping the political fortunes of North America,[30] and G.F.G. Stanley's *Canada's Soldiers, 1604-1954* (1954), the military and naval dimensions of the past took on clearer outlines. From the forties onwards, even where Canadian historians did not themselves actually write military history, their work was to show a greater awareness of military and strategic considerations that affected the country's past.

III

The experience of war refocussed attention on the Atlantic world and the British Commonwealth and deepened an appreciation for traditional freedoms and the institutions of self-government that underlay Canadian life. In 1940 George Brown, the editor of the *Canadian Historical Review*, commented that historians in the recent past had tended to take 'the history of the Atlantic world' for granted and had 'written history in terms of the conflict between the colony and the Mother Country rather than in terms of the greater cultural bonds which united the Atlantic world. Now that the bastions of this world are crumbling, we are beginning to realize its significance. We have been unwilling to show enthusiasm for it, but now we look and see that it was bigger than we had thought.'[31] Four years later Chester Martin reasserted the viewpoint of the constitutional historians of the twenties when he proudly noted that, between the collapse of France and the German invasion of Russia, 'the only nations in arms left standing against the axis were the nations of the British Commonwealth.' He proceeded to re-emphasise that Canada's participation in the war could be explained only in terms of its evolutionary development in association with the Empire.[32] For Martin, as for Brown and others like Reginald Trotter who had never really abandoned the beliefs of the imperial historians, Canada's role in the war reaffirmed the essentially internationalist character of its experience and reinvigorated their faith in the country's role as a mediator within the Anglo-American system and the United Nations.[33]

The cold war, which for Canada began with the Gouzenko spy case of 1945, reinforced the pertinence of the North Atlantic world. 'At a time when the idea of an Atlantic community is expressing itself through arrangements for mutual defence,' Brown explained shortly after Canada entered the North Atlantic Treaty Organization, 'it is well that we should also have repeated emphasis on the common ideas, aspirations, and points of view which alone give that community, or civilization, its reality . . . .'[34] A Montreal newspaper put it more forthrightly. In supporting an appeal for more studies of the three main countries in the North Atlantic triangle that were united by tradition, language, and political association, it pronounced this 'the immediate need of the free world alliance'.[35]

The war in Europe, and later the cold war with Russia, stimulated a questioning of the assumptions on which Canadian history had been written. There was hardly one reappraisal of the direction in which historical scholarship should move that did not recognize the contemporary crisis of values and beliefs in western civilization. Canada declared war a week after Britain in order to demonstrate its autonomy, but the fundamental principles for which it fought the war were the same. There was a widespread recognition that the historian had a duty to contribute to a more adequate understanding of the liberal institutions and democratic values that were at stake, and to demonstrate to Canadians how central these had been in the past. It was a measure of this faith that George Brown and a Toronto colleague, D.J. McDougall, who had been blinded in the previous war, gave lectures to German officers at the prisoner-of-war camp at Bowmanville on representative government, American history, and the Commonwealth.

'The social scientist', Underhill declared in 1941, 'had discovered that the community had values and that he must go out and take part in their defence.'[36] This may have been a 'discovery' for Underhill, but for most historians it was simply a heightened awareness of enduring traditions that had been taken for granted—or, worse, lost sight of in anonymous economic history that assumed a homogeneous appetite and missed the differences in the ways generations understood law, power, and force.[37]

This perception was sustained by the cold war. 'There is little need to remind ourselves', ran one defence of political history in 1950, 'how militant ideologies have affected the world in the last generation, and how they continue to do so . . . . You may, if you like, call the writ of habeas corpus a part of legal history, control of the pre̠s a part of literary history, and torture a result of technological skill. To the individual affected, however, these distinctions are unreal. The rule of law, the right of free expression of ideas, government as the servant of the people—these are basic freedoms which have been and are threatened, and without which all other freedoms are vain.'[38] These subjects too had their place in history.

This rejuvenated recognition of the common cultural history of the Atlantic civilization and the importance of liberal institutions had at least two direct implications. The first was a growing interest in the history of ideas, convictions, and political opinions, and in the way cultural baggage from the Old World was transferred and maintained in the New. Some pioneering studies had been made earlier on the political ideas of William Lyon Mackenzie by R.A. Mackay, of Egerton Ryerson by C.B. Sissons, and of George Etienne Cartier by J.I. Cooper. George Brown had explored aspects of early Methodism, Daniel C. Harvey had examined the intellectual awakening of Nova Scotia, and Underhill had analysed the political opinions of the Upper Canadian reformers.[39] While in a way marginal to the dominant economic history of the thirties, these essays represented the beginnings of more serious attention to individuals' convictions, feelings, and outlooks. This tendency was to underline the need for a history of religion that did not assume conviction to be the reflex of sociological changes. Even economic historians grew interested in the non-economic criteria that affected business and entrepreneurial decisions.[40] In general, however, this interest in ideas did not lead to a critical and systematic intellectual history but rather to biography.

The second, and in the short-run more substantial, implication of the Atlantic civilization concept was the qualified rejection of the frontier thesis on the grounds that it encouraged an isolationist, introverted view of Canadian history. Having never embraced the frontier hypothesis as unreservedly as the followers of Turner in the United States, Canadian historians did not so much repudiate it completely as seek a balanced assessment of its potential usefulness after American historians had questioned its appropriateness. Turner's generalizations about the role of the frontier in the history of the United States had only an indirect and a modified influence on the writing of the history of Canada since 1920. Innis had rejected it outright; Underhill had fused the frontier approach with the broader Beardian notion of the class and sectional bases of parties; and Lower had been at pains to note that, while North American democracy had a forest birth, its survival was conditional on the existence of certain institutions and laws of self-government. Turner's ideas about the American frontier had been applied selectively to explain certain developments and episodes in the history of a country that had never possessed a continuously receding line of settlement, had retained strong ties with Europe, and contained a substantial minority with a cultural background quite different from the Anglo-Canadian majority.[41] In the case of French Canada, A.L. Burt argued in 1940 that the wilderness interior and an abundance of land explained the extent to which the society of New France departed from the authoritarianism of the mother country.[42] And S.D. Clark had grounded his interpretation of the social development of the country on a redefinition of Turner's thesis in terms of the staples approach.

Criticism of the frontier thesis in the forties expressed impatience with the inclination to isolate frontier society from its larger context and with the underestimation of the way European institutions and traditions had persisted in the New World.[43]

Even for the history of the Prairies the frontier hypothesis was held to be useful for only certain limited themes. George Stanley had depicted the insurrection of 1869-70 and the rebellion of 1885 within the framework of the 'problem of the frontier, namely the clash between primitive and civilized peoples.'[44] His was not so much a Turnerian frame of reference as an imperial one that compared the destruction of Métis society with the fate of other peoples who unsuccessfully resisted the march of white civilization in Africa and Australia. In the larger view of western history Stanley conceded that, while significant adaptations were made to climate and land in agricultural techniques and economics, government, law, religion, and social institutions were less affected. As the North West Mounted Police and the sectional survey preceded agricultural settlement, problems of lawlessness and controversies over squatter rights were generally avoided. The agrarian movements, he argued, were not so much expressions of an indigenous frontier radicalism as simply protests of primary producers of agricultural commodities, who sold their products in a variable world market, against the closed and protected market in which they had to purchase manufactured goods. The prairie west possessed a 'personality' of its own, but that character was shaped by traditions and past experience as well as by the frontier: 'Environment has largely conditioned our economic; tradition, our political ways of life.'[45]

The most effective and positive reassessment of the frontier thesis was advanced by a younger historian, J.M.S. Careless. A Toronto graduate, Careless had done his advanced work at Harvard and been thoroughly exposed to the thinking of some of the leading critics of the Turner school in the United States. Arthur M. Schlesinger Sr. had taken up Turner's own suggestion regarding a study of the role of the city in American civilization, and both Dixon Ryan Fox and Louis B. Wright had appealed for a history that would treat the American frontier in the context of the edge of European civilization and in terms of the transference and modification of culture.[46] Careless's thesis on the mid-Victorian liberalism of George Brown and the *Globe*, completed in 1949, provided the basis for a comprehensive critique of the frontier thesis as it applied to Canada.

This critique was expressed on two interrelated levels. First, Careless showed that the Upper Canadian liberals looked to Britain as the fountainhead of all political wisdom and felt themselves to be participants in British political culture; that their ideas of the state, society, and economy were virtually unadulterated Cobdenite and Gladstonian liberalism; and that the Reform party of George Brown was a fusion of agrarian radicalism and Toronto business interests. Brown's reform party was not, as Underhill had portrayed it a generation before, an agrarian and frontier protest against the domination of big business, but rather a combination of both those groups, united by regional ties and a similarity of interest in railways and western expansion. Moreover, in his examination of the rivalry between the commercial and manufacturing interests of Toronto and Montreal, Careless demonstrated that 'business' was not the homogeneous and monolithic entity in opposition to liberalism that Underhill had often treated it as being. In the development of Upper Canadian liberalism the political convictions brought from Britain, combined with Toronto business interests, were at least as decisive an influence as the frontier.[47]

The second and more speculative level of Careless's re-examination of the frontier approach outlined a general interpretative scheme for Canadian history that incorporated the frontier idea into a more spacious frame of reference. Like others, Careless objected to the tendency of historians inspired by Turner's statements to fix values and associate the 'West' and 'agrarian democracy' with the forward-looking and the 'East' and 'business interests' with an imitative conservatism and self-interestedness. He traced the history of the frontier hypothesis in Canadian historical writing in the previous generation and illustrated how its qualified popularity was linked to the reaction against the constitutional historians and enhanced by the isolationism of the inter-war period. Careless then suggested that the shortcomings of the frontier approach to Canadian history could be offset by a closer attention to the role of urban centres, an approach that he called 'metropolitanism'.[48]

The notion that the metropolis was the organizing centre of business, politics, and culture, and that it had a determining influence over the hinterlands, grew out of the economic history of N.S.B. Gras, the Innis staples approach, and the Chicago school of urban sociologists. It had been employed by Lower in his books on the timber trade, by D.C. Masters, and by Carl Dawson in his attempts to measure the metropolitan influence of prairie cities through the circulation of newspapers.[49] When looked at closely, however, it was not a simple formulation. In Gras's original definition there were four successive conditions that were necessary to a city's achieving metropolitan status: the creation of a well-organized marketing system for a hinterland; the development of manufacturing; the linkage of the urban centre to its subsidiary hinterland through transportation improvements; and the emergence of a mature financial system. While Masters adopted this model of four stages in his study of Toronto, Innis had much earlier criticized Gras, and all others whose understanding of economic growth had been generalized from European experience. In the Canadian case, he argued, cities grew and took on the characteristics of metropolitan centres in a radically different pattern and order. They arose not in isolation, but out of the commercial dictates of staple exploitation and cyclonic growth.[50] Innis's perspective implied a rather different perception of the actual 'stages' of development and he looked askance at the monopoly position of metropolitan dominance.

The economic history of the staples trades provided the underpinnings of Careless's definition of a more appropriate framework to re-examine Canadian history generally. Metropolitanism, or the rise of cities, he wrote, was the obverse, neglected side to frontier expansion. Behind the unfolding of the frontier lay the city that supplied capital, marketing facilities, communications, transportation, and culture. Careless proposed that a substantial segment of the Canadian past could be apprehended more adequately if the relationship of cities to their hinterlands and to each other were explored in depth, and that the existence of relatively few dominant cities within Canada might, upon further analysis, deepen an understanding of the conservative, centralist tendencies in Canadian life. Similarly a more explicit recognition of the function of external metropolitan centres, like London and New York, would enhance our knowledge of the derivativeness of Canadian culture.

The metropolitan approach, which incorporated the frontier thesis and sharply delimited it, while melding the economic history of the thirties with the newer interest in culture and ideas, was itself indicative of the modest revisionism of the historians of the forties. More subdued and tolerant than the revolt against constitutionalism in the late twenties and early thirties, this search for fresh perspectives assimilated what was considered salvageable from the past and reformulated appropriate elements in more immediately useful terms. It was typical of the subtlety of the reorientation of the forties and early fifties that Careless could, in 1954, re-state in language appropriate to his generation one of the central proposi-tions of the historians of the twenties: that the pragmatic temper of the Canadian character and the national habit of compromise and maintaining opposites in balance implied certain qualifications for a fruitful participa-tion in international affairs.[51] The metropolitan hypothesis was a more pre-cise instrument of analysis than the nebulous idea of a common Atlantic civilization, but it pointed in the same direction: to the need for a more systematic study of the transfer of culture, especially from Britain. It called attention, concretely and specifically, to the study of ideas and convictions. Significantly, Careless's discussion of metropolitanism on balance laid more emphasis on the geo-political relations between cities and hinter-lands than on the internal character, class structure, and texture of urban society.[52]

IV

The desire to recover the transatlantic dimensions and cultural contacts was also affected by the impact of American policy on Canada in the late forties and the contemporary upsurge of concern with a national culture. In the crisis of 1940, when the fate of western Europe and Britain hinged on America's entry into the war, the defence agreements were accepted without criticism. In 1945 Canada emerged from the war as a major power, and its espousal of international responsibility and the United Nations was universally regarded with acclaim in the intellectual community. One indi-cation of this sustained interest in Canada's new position was the founding of the *International Journal* in 1946. The cold war and the polarization of the world into two power blocs, however, undermined Canada's freedom of action in relation to the United States, and the recovery of the European nations deflated its sense of status even further. By the outbreak of the Ko-rean war in 1950 many Canadians had come to resent being taken for granted by American policy-makers, and relatively minor issues involving trade, the behaviour of U.S. military personnel in Newfoundland, and the conduct of border officials compounded this annoyance.[53] So too did the ir-responsible tactics of Congressional Committees on un-American activi-ties, especially the investigations of Senator Joseph McCarthy.

This restiveness was muted and unfocussed, but one of its expressions was the revival of interest in a national culture, a concern that had been pronounced in the twenties and submerged in depression and war. An early indication of this renewed interest in the state of culture was Brebner's *Scholarship for Canada* (1946), a report commissioned by the Social Science Research Council. In many ways Brebner's far-ranging in-quiry into the conservatism of the academic scene, the status of research, and the tremendous loss to the intellectual community through immigration to the United States anticipated some of the findings of the Report of the Royal Commission on National Development in the Arts, Letters and Sciences in 1951. That Commission was chaired by Vincent Massey, and included Arthur Surveyer, a Montreal civil engineer, Norman Mackenzie, the President of the University of British Columbia, Georges-Henri Lévesque, Dean of the Faculty of Social Sciences at Laval, and Hilda Neatby, a historian from the University of Saskatchewan. The commissioners travelled nearly ten thousand miles in all ten provinces, received four hundred and sixty-two briefs from various social organizations and voluntary societies, and heard twelve hundred witnesses. The Commission not only registered but also aroused a real interest in cultural development. Its report was grounded on two clearly stated assumptions: that there were important spiritual resources in the nation that inspired its people and prompted their actions, and that national unity, while resting on material foundations, belonged ultimately to the realm of ideas. 'Canada', it was asserted, 'became a national community because of certain habits of mind and convictions which its people shared and would not surrender.'[54]

After surveying the mass media, the position of voluntary associations, institutions like the National Gallery, museums, universities, orchestras, and the plight of the artist and the writer, the Report expressed considerable apprehension at the extent to which Canada depended on foreign countries, especially the United States, for its non-material, cultural necessities. Though acknowledging the generosity of American foundations in supporting Canadian intellectual and educational effort in the past, it was critical of the 'American invasion by film, radio and periodicals' and called for a program of 'resistance to the absorption of Canada into the general cultural pattern of the United States.'[55] The Massey Commission made numerous recommendations, but the two central ones were the creation of an arts council that would directly subsidize cultural endeavours and federal aid to higher education. The Report stood for a rededication to the hopes of the twenties and also a profounder appreciation for higher culture at a time of unprecedented prosperity. The Canada Council was created in 1957 with a fund of $100 million. The interest on half this amount was to be used for scholarships and grants to cultural activities; the other portion was devoted to higher education. This was a substantial, if not revolutionary, departure in Canadian intellectual life. With the creation of the Canada Council, Canadian intellectuals finally achieved that state support for which many had pleaded ever since the late nineteenth century. They had attained, in fact, the intellectual parallel to the system of bounties that other social groups and classes had received since the inauguration of the National Policy.

The Massey Commission inquiry reflected an anxiety on the part of an intellectual élite over the pervasiveness of American mass culture. The tastes and standards of industrial and commercial democracy had, of course, been a common subject of comment within the United States for some time, and Brebner had reminded Canadian intellectuals of that fact. It was no less pronounced in certain quarters in Canada. Marshall McLuhan's *The Mechanical Bride: The Folklore of Industrial Man* (1951) was a sustained assault on the mass media and especially the misuses of modern advertising. In 1953 Hilda Neatby launched *So Little for the Mind*, a slashing attack on progressive public education, educational experts with their theories of life-adjustment, and the anti-intellectual and anti-historical legacy of John Dewey. In her appeal for a restoration of more aristocratic and selective standards in education, she was not unmindful of contemporary realities. 'We are defending our civilization . . .,' she wrote. 'It seems not unreasonable to suggest that one should know something of the nature of the civilization we defend.'[56] And in the later fifties the philosopher George Grant, the son of W.L. Grant, brooded over the implications of post-war economic prosperity and scientific mastery. While conceding that the technological society may have freed men from the vagaries of nature, he condemned the secular religion of material progress for deflecting attention away from the enduring and timeless moral order.[57] These reflections on 'mass society' were indicative of a more pervasive apprehension in the intellectual community that was to impinge directly on historical thought.

V

Of the various changing features of the intellectual landscape in the forties, the relative isolation of French and English traditions of historical writing seemed to alter least of all. The events surrounding the conscription crisis in the Second World War, and the fear that the experience of 1917 would be repeated, re-emphasized the urgency to understand French Canada and threw the isolation of the two historiographical traditions into high relief. Hugh MacLennan's novel *Two Solitudes* (1945) and the founding of the bilingual quarterly *Culture* in Quebec City in 1940 were indications of the former tendency. A sense of uneasiness over French-English relations lay back of the 1943 annual meeting of the Canadian Historical Association, which was devoted to papers on aspects of French-Canadian nationalism and politics. In the same year E.R. Adair, who taught the history of New France at McGill, remarked that 'a deep and almost complete cleavage exists between these two schools of historical scholarship, the English-Canadian and the French-Canadian . . . . '[58] Nine years later Hilda Neatby regretfully noted that, with some exceptions, French-Canadian historians confined themselves to the period before 1760, English-Canadian historians to the era after the Conquest.[59]

In spite of the hopes of G.M. Wrong, A.L. Burt, and other earlier exponents of the *bonne entente,* the two traditions of historical writing flowed in separate channels. From its beginnings the Royal Society of Canada institutionalized the split by segregating French- and English-speaking historians into two language sections. While a president of the Canadian Historical Association had explained in 1923 that one of its objectives was to promote a more perfect harmony of the two peoples, the Association itself remained a predominantly English-Canadian body. The major vehicle for the publication of scholarly articles in English was the *Canadian Historical Review;* in French it was the *Bulletin des Recherches Historiques.* The historians who contributed to both journals were rarities. It was not until the early fifties that the *Canadian Historical Review* agreed to publish articles in French. When in 1954 Careless surveyed Canadian historiography and suggested the new direction it was taking, he did not mention a single article or book by any scholar writing in the French language. In historical writing, as in other aspects of the life of the two peoples, the metaphor of the two solitudes seemed appropriate.

Even a cursory glance at the actual development of French-Canadian historical thought reveals the extent to which it diverged from English-Canadian problems and concerns. The two dominant figures in the early twentieth century were Senator Sir Thomas Chapais and Abbé Lionel Groulx, who were in quite different ways heirs to the tradition of the nationalist historiography of François-Xavier Garneau. In 1915 Chapais began teaching courses in Canadian history at Laval University and Groulx became the first occupant of the chair of Canadian history at the Montreal campus of Laval.

Chapais was a patrician in social outlook and a devotee of scientific objectivity. His eight-volume *Cours d'histoire du Canada,* which appeared between 1919 and 1934, paralleled the English-Canadian constitutionalists' preoccupation with political evolution from the Conquest to Confederation. He concentrated on the process by which French Canada had acquired protective guarantees for its cultural integrity and the right of self-government in association with the British majority, and he saw the safeguards enshrined in the Confederation agreement as a climax to these developments. He emphasized the role of the Church as the custodian and bastion of national survival and described the Conquest as a providential event that saved the French Canadians from the Revolution of 1789. Sympathizing with the pragmatic and well-intentioned political triumvirate of Baldwin, Lafontaine, and Elgin, Chapais praised the tradition of cooperation carried forward by Cartier and Laurier and stressed the liberality and the conciliatory character of British policy.[60]

Abbé Groulx wrote a different history based on different circumstances. Where Chapais had come to history from journalism rather late in his career, Groulx was trained in theology and literature, but history was at the centre of a life-long effort to sharpen and sustain the French-Canadian sense of separateness. He began lecturing in Canadian history at a time of great emergency and stress in French Canada. The compact of Confederation had been repeatedly violated by an insensitive English-Canadian majority: in 1885 with the hanging of Riel; in 1899 with the dispatch of troops to support the Empire against another 'little people' in South Africa; in the 1905 schools crisis in the new western provinces; and again in 1917 with the election on conscription. Groulx's *Nos Luttes constitutionelles* (1916), *La Naissance d'une race* (1918), and *Notre Maître le passé* (1944) were intended to supply a bracing tonic for a small national community that was more threatened than it had been since the early decades of the Old Régime. Groulx at bottom was devoted to the examination of the history of the moulding of a community, profoundly French and Catholic in character, and to so retelling that story that history itself would become an ever-present reality in the minds of his compatriots. The historian, like the priest, was the vessel of a mystical communion between the dead and the living. He must strive to understand, through all the means afforded by historical science, but he could never be a passive and neutral observer. Groulx was moved by a feeling for the mystery of the complex process by which a tiny people had sustained themselves in a wilderness, had become a 'nation', and continued, after military conquest, to survive. The explanation for this phenomenon lay in providence—the divine will in history.

Committed to a generally conservative and corporatist social doctrine, which he preached through the agency of the Action Française in the twenties, Groulx was attracted to the symmetrical and graded social order of New France. In contrast to Chapais, he treated the Conquest as a great challenge to the survival of the nation and insisted that the ultimate aim of the British, and British Canadians, never changed. Back of the twists and turns of policy, of concessions here and impositions of majority decisions there, lay the enduring desire to absorb the French Canadians spiritually.

At the centre of Groulx's vision of the past stood the figure of Dollard des Ormeaux and, in the background, his sixteen companions, who had been killed on the Ottawa River in 1660 by Indians intent on the destruction of the settlements on the St Lawrence. Dollard became a symbol of sacrifice in the protection of a national community in the same way that General Brock had earlier assumed the status of a national hero in the loyalist tradition of Ontario. Dollard became what Brock had been: a reminder of the duties that the past demanded of the present.[61]

Even this sketchy summary of the main lines of French-Canadian historical writing indicates how remote it was from some of the chief developments in English-Canadian historiography in the inter-war years. The constitutional approach was infused with a commitment to internationalism that found in French-English co-operation, and the Canadian imperial relationship, the model for a supranational state. The historians who wrote in this tradition were not only distrustful of extreme nationalism, whether in Ireland or Quebec, but they were also less interested in the internal texture of French Canada and its society than in the relations between the spokesmen for the two peoples in politics. The temper of the younger historians of the twenties and thirties was impatient of biography and the personal history of heroes and great figures. Academic history was born in rebellion against the late nineteenth-century romantic glorification of the heroic history of New France. Some delighted in revealing the sordid economic motivation behind activities once glorified as feats of adventurous explorations. The iconoclastic and acerbic Adair argued in 1932 that Dollard and his unfortunate associates had certainly not gone out to sacrifice themselves, that they were ignorant of the techniques of Indian warfare, and that their deaths probably encouraged further Indian attacks on the colony. As a saviour, Adair concluded, Dollard must be relegated to the 'museum of historical myths'.[62]

Even when Chapais's generally warm attachment to British liberalism and liberality commended him to the *bonne entente* historians, his constitutional approach seemed old-fashioned and excessively Whiggish to an exponent of the new history who wondered whether it had any immediate value to French Canadians worried over Anglo-American control of the economy of Quebec.[63] The economic interpretation of politics and economic history generally tended to blur the significance of cultural characteristics and local peculiarities based on language and religion. In Innis's study of the fur trade it seemed to matter very little whether traders spoke French or English; in Creighton's work on the commercial imperatives of the St Lawrence, French-Canadian society was described as a torpid feudal remnant resisting the North American spirit of enterprise.

There were, it is true, English-speaking Canadian historians who devoted themselves to the study of phases of the history of French Canada and who usually endeavoured to depict that society in a sympathetic light. But Lower's attempt to explain the philosophical and religious origins of the two outlooks and to represent what a conquest must have meant to the conquered people was rather untypical. So too, in a way, were A.L. Burt's *Old Province of Quebec*, a meticulous examination of the relations between the two peoples on the morrow of the conquest, and *The Administration of Justice Under the Quebec Act* (1937), a study by Hilda Neatby, one of Burt's students, that unravelled the tangled strands of a confusing period in legal history. Stanley Ryerson, a perfectly bilingual great-grandson of Egerton Ryerson and an educational worker and editorialist for the Communist cause in Quebec, laid the basis for a Marxist interpretation of the past with *The Birth of Canadian Democracy* (1937) and *French Canada: A Study in Canadian Democracy* (1943). Though signifying at least a more immediate curiosity about French Canada, these books made little impression on historians. There were others who tried to bridge the gap between the two histories: Gordon Rothney of Sir George Williams University; Abbé Arthur Maheux, who taught Canadian history at Laval; Gustave Lanctôt, Dominion Archivist and historian of French-Canadian immigration to New England; and Séraphin Marion, who also worked at the Archives. In the early forties George Brown and a Toronto colleague, Richard Saunders, were connected with the Visites Interprovinciales, a society devoted to bettering relations through the exchange of children between families in Ontario and Quebec during the summer holidays.

On the whole, however, English-Canadian historians did not concentrate on the inner resonances and complex internal texture of French Quebec. Such investigations of Quebec that were published in English in the late thirties and early forties were done either by American sociologists like Horace Miner and Everett Hughes or by historians in the United States like Elizabeth Armstrong, whose *Crisis of Quebec, 1914-1918* (1937) was an examination of the conscription issue from a viewpoint sympathetic to French Canada. The first synthesis of French-Canadian history in the English language, *The French Canadians, 1760-1945* (1955), was written by another American, Mason Wade, who had come to the subject by way of an appraisal of Francis Parkman.

When Adair remarked in 1943 on the cleavage between the two historiographical traditions and the reluctance or inability of English Canadians to enter into the sources of French history, he suspected that there was a psychological reason for this. 'No doubt in a large measure unconsciously', he explained, 'the English-speaking Canadian hates the idea of the existence of a large body of people in Canada who are quite unassimilated to his standards and to his point of view; he cannot do anything about it, but at least he can preserve the fiction of his cherished Canadian unity and Canadian nationality by pretending that they are not really there ... ,' salving his conscience 'by Rotarian clichés about the complete understanding that exists between the two races in Canada.'[64] Overstated, perhaps, and unfair to some well-intentioned scholars who were hardly unaware of the problem, but there was nonetheless an element of truth in this biting remark. The English-Canadian historian, like the community in which he wrote, did not fundamentally accept the French-Canadian group as anything more than a minority with certain rights within the Province of Quebec. The idea of two equalities was utterly foreign to his mind and would remain so until the revolution of opinion of the sixties.

The outbreak of the war and the referendum on conscription had the immediate effect of reviving the *bonne entente* spirit, of which Abbé Arthur Maheux of Laval, editor of *Le Canada Français*,[65] was an energetic exponent. He was firmly committed to the view that misunderstandings arose from ignorance rather than malice, and that history could be used to illuminate, from a terrible contemporary perspective, the real meaning of the Conquest. 'The monstrous conduct of Hitler and Mussolini,' he wrote in a study of relations between the English and French in the aftermath of the Conquest, 'the savagery of their war, the oppressive manner in which they have treated conquered, invaded, occupied and menaced peoples, make us look upon the picture of the years 1758-1760 as an idyll.'[66] His book of lectures, *Ton Histoire est une Epopée.* 1 *Nos Débuts sous le régime anglais* (1941), reaffirmed A.L. Burt's conclusions that the Conquest and the period that ensued was free from tribulations and was characterized by the respect that the military governors, especially James Murray, entertained towards the French people and their religion. The cover of the French edition of this work depicted a *coureur des bois* handing a torch upwards to a Canadian soldier of the Second World War period—a reminder, perhaps, of contemporary obligations.

Maheux's books were translated into English by Richard M. Saunders, who went on to articulate the central English-Canadian critique of Groulx and his followers. Groulx had accepted and reformulated the main task of French-Canadian historiography—the use of history to ensure national survival. Accepting the dictum that nations do not love each other, he had also, Saunders claimed, acted on the view that 'active cultivation of dislike and antipathy is an essential part of nation-building . . . . '[67] The notion that nationalism and historical scholarship could be mixed only to the detriment of the latter, and that the nationalist history of French Canada was inward looking and self-centred, if not downright self-pitying and parochial, was common in English Canada.

It was ironical that by the mid-forties a new generation of French-Canadian historians, who were beginning to reorient the historical writing on French Canada, drew their inspiration from Groulx and some of their insights into the past from the economic history that had prevailed in English Canada in the thirties. In 1946 Groulx initiated the establishment of the Institut d'Histoire de l'Amérique Française at the University of Montreal and began publishing the *Revue d'Histoire de l'Amérique Française* the following year. The Institut became the centre of operation for three men—Maurice Séguin, Guy Frégault, and Michel Brunet—who changed the direction of French-Canadian historical writing. They were representatives of the first generation of historians of French Canada who were professionally trained, secular in outlook, and mainly concerned with social-economic history. Maurice Séguin's thesis, *L'Agriculture et la Nation, 1760-1850,* completed in 1947,[68] Frégault's *La Civilisation de la Nouvelle France, 1713-1744* (1944), and Brunet's essays of the fifties[69] revised the entire perspective on Quebec's past. They contended that New France had not been the clerically dominated agricultural civilization that French Canada became, but a more complex commercial society, with its own urban bourgeoisie. The Conquest destroyed an integral society and decapitated the commercial class; leadership of a conquered people fell to the Church; and, because commercial activity came to be monopolized by British merchants, national survival concentrated on agriculture. This argument was advanced to explain the 'economic inferiority' of French Canadians, and it rested on certain assumptions about the bourgeoisie in New France, the mentality of the colony, and the origins of nationalism that subsequently became the subjects of a lively debate within the French-Canadian historical community.

These younger historians were greatly indebted to the economic history of Innis and Creighton. Groulx's own *Histoire du Canada français depuis la découverte*, which was published in four volumes in 1950-2, made frequent and favourable reference to the English-Canadian literature of the thirties. Brunet adopted a reformulation of Careless's metropolitanism to underline the consequences to New France of a conquest that cut it away from its French metropolis.[70] The changes in French-Canadian historical writing in the post-war period were related to the intellectual revolution that preceded the 'quiet revolution' in politics. French Canadian historians enthusiastically embraced the social sciences, and were exposed to the influences of the French *Annales* school, which had sought to reconstruct the life of past societies in their totality.[71] At the same time the English-Canadian historians were moving away from economic history towards biography.

8 | REORIENTATION AND TRADITION

The complex, subtle, and bewildering shifts of perspectives in Canadian historical thought that began in the forties were responses to the feeling that the literature of the past had to be transcended, and to profound changes within the society and the world in which the historian worked. These same promptings impinged immediately upon the minds of Innis, Underhill, and Lower, who represented the generation that had made its main contribution to the study of Canadian history in the thirties and early forties. For them the period was a time of reassessment, self-examination, reversals of opinion—and, in Innis's case, of a fundamental departure.

I

Beginning in July 1940, a month after the military collapse of France, Innis abruptly turned his attention to books on the technology and economics of the press, censorship, advertising, and propaganda.[1] By 1945 he had completed a 1000-page manuscript on the history of communications from which he drew his startling and exploratory essays on the ways in which various technologies of communication biased the cultures in which they were embedded. He had embarked with an almost obsessive determination on a stupendous task of demonstrating the centrality of communications to the way men think and what they think about. His interest in communications began with the conviction that advances in the techniques of communicating were the main determinants of economic change. It ended in perplexing essays that were loaded with contradictory *obiter dicta*; philippics on the pressures exerted by modern mass media on scholarship, the university, and Canadian independence; and arcane illustrations of the influence of the media of communication on art, literature, law, politics and on the rise and fall of empires, ranging over the Egyptian, Summerian, Assyrian, Greek and Roman civilizations, the British Empire, and contemporary society.

There was an inner logic in the development of Innis's thought from the economics of the staples trades to his communications studies. By 1940 the great enterprise of examining the history of the older staples had been virtually completed with the publication of the works by Lower on timber, by MacGibbon and Britnell on wheat, and by Innis himself on fur and fish. Moreover, the studies prepared for the Rowell-Sirois Commission marked the fruition of the economic interpretation of Canadian history. The overview of Canadian economic development from 1867 to 1939 contained in Book One of the *Report* and in individual historical studies—William A. Mackintosh's *The Economic Background of Dominion-Provincial Relations* (1939) and Donald Creighton's *British North America at Confederation* (1939)—traced in detail the relationship between underlying economic changes and the problems of federalism. To complete this survey of the staples trades, Innis turned to an examination of the modern pulp-and-paper industry. This investigation led immediately to his consideration of the market for newsprint, the history of the press, and the influence of printing on public opinion and communications monopolies.

There were strong elements of continuity between these new interests and Innis's early economics. The connecting link between his history of the Canadian Pacific Railway and *Empire and Communications* (1950) was the role of communications and technology as key factors in economic change. Moreover, Innis looked on the technology of communication in much the same way as he had looked on the staple. Technologies of communication—whether they be stone tablets, newspapers, or radios—influenced societies, institutions, and cultures in the same way that the exploitation of certain economic staples shaped them.[2] The communications studies also represented an intensification of his concern with the biases and limitations of the social sciences, which had to be detected and neutralized.

With a degree of over-simplification, Innis's contentions relating to the central role of communications to civilization and culture may be abstracted from the mass of illustrative historical allusions and restated in three propositions. First, he argued that the available media of communications strongly influenced the social organization, institutions, and cultural characteristics of society. The means used to convey messages were not simply the marginal appendage of a culture; they were the heart of a civilization that shaped attitudes and structures and subtly biased what was actually being transmitted.

Second, communications media possessed a bias in the direction of either time or space. In pre-print cultures a medium that was heavy, durable, and that was transported with difficulty, like clay tablets or stone, emphasized the time dimension. A medium that was light and easily transported, like papyrus and paper, tended to favour the dissemination of knowledge over space. Time-biased media favoured institutional decentralization and the sacred, religious, and historical. Space-biased media were associated with secularism, centralization, bureaucracy, state authority, territorial expansion, and technical administration. The discovery of cheap paper and the commercial application of machine industry to printing after 1800 accentuated a fascination with the ephemeral, the superficial, and the present, and destroyed the sense of time, permanence, and duration. The bias of paper and printing emphasized nationalism, the development of metropolitan centres, individualism, and monopolies that enjoyed 'freedom of the press'.

Third, various technologies of communications in history provided the bases for monopolies of knowledge held by particular groups, and this in turn led to the search for alternate forms of communications, rivalries between interests, and general social instability. Innis argued, for instance, that the invention of printing—which favoured the growth of vernacular languages, national separateness, and the nation state—destroyed the monopoly of knowledge of the medieval church. Conflicts over the control of communication systems became for Innis the clues to historical change.

Innis employed these propositions to explain the characteristics of entire cultures of the past and present and to account for the rise and fall of civilizations and empires. He had been stimulated by Oswald Spengler's *Decline of the West*, Arnold Toynbee's *Study of History*, and A.L. Kroeber's *Configurations of Cultural Growth*. Charles Cochrane's *Christianity and Classical Culture* (1940), which he called 'the first major Canadian contribution to the intellectual history of the West,'[3] had aroused his curiosity about classical history. But Innis's determination to investigate the implications of media was also sustained by his tremendous alarm over the effects of commercialized and mechanical means of communication in his own time. His discussion of the biases of communications were loaded with moralistic assaults on commercialism, science, and manipulative monopolies. The modern press and radio were indicted for pandering to the lowest common denominator and for making impossible any sustained thought about long-range questions.

The crux of Innis's position was his desire for balance and perspective. This balance was defined in various ways, depending on the particular features of various media and their effects that he stressed at any particular time. On one level it meant recapturing something of the spirit of the 'oral tradition'. Oral discussion, Innis wrote, 'inherently involves personal contact and a consideration for others, and it is in sharp contrast with the cruelty of mechanized communication and the tendencies which we have come to note in the modern world.'[4] The spoken word engaged all the senses and stressed memory and creative thought; writing, however, gave man a 'transpersonal memory'. 'Individuals', Innis explained, 'applied their minds to symbols rather than things and went beyond the world of concrete experience into the world of conceptual relations within an enlarged time and space universe .... The idea of things became differentiated from things and the dualism demanded thought and reconciliation.'[5] The commitment of writing to print and the mechanical transmission of knowledge encouraged a preference for the factual and the concrete, passivity, and the cult of the present. Science not only facilitated the dissemination of information but also selected the kind of knowledge distributed. In Innis's vocabulary mechanization meant standardization, the ruthless destruction of permanence, and the impossibility of genuine intellectual liberty. In economic thought and university teaching it led to over-specialization and the retailing of pre-packaged information. The oral tradition was central to the university and Innis pleaded that 'determined efforts to recapture the vitality of the oral tradition must be made.'[6] The university was an ivory tower in which men devoted themselves to a concern with the broad problems, constantly questioned assumptions, and sought to resist and weaken all trends to dogma and the presentism that were natural products of the communications monopolies.

Balance also implied an equilibrium between the biases of space and time, which Innis identified as the ideal condition for creativity and intellectual freedom. 'Culture,' he wrote, 'is designed to train the individual to decide how much information he needs and how little he needs, to give him a sense of balance and proportions .... Culture is concerned with the capacity of the individual to appraise problems in terms of space and time and with enabling him to take the proper steps at the right time.'[7] The tragedy of western culture, as Innis saw it, was that the sense of time had been pulverized by a flood of matter-of-fact scientific information and by the bias of modern mass communications that favoured the contemporary and the ephemeral. 'We must somehow escape on the one hand from our obsession with the moment and on the other hand from our obsession with history.'

The sense of urgency back of Innis's later apocalyptic pronouncements suggests a mind caught up in a kind of intellectual cyclone where everything impinged all at once and from all directions, and where there seemed to be no place for stability and contemplation. In the forties some of his deepest commitments to the social sciences were under challenge. Innis sensed that excessive specialization in economics, its presentist tendencies, and the desire for disciplinary autonomy implied a breakup of the political-economy tradition that had underlain his economic history of Canada. The approach of Innis and the so-called Toronto school in the thirties was emphatically historical in orientation and concerned with the interrelations of geography and technology over time: the staples thesis linked the history of Creighton, the sociology of Clark, and the political economy of Innis. This common approach was weakened in the forties; there were complaints about the subordination of political science to political economy, which had, in conjunction with other factors, favoured a descriptive, historical approach to the neglect of theory.[8] Changing fashions in economics also foreshadowed a very different style. 'The American cult of quantities', Herbert Heaton wrote in 1954, 'is no mere turning tide. It is a tidal wave, on which Clio's little craft seems likely to be sunk by the swarm of vessels manned by statisticians, econometricians, and macroeconomists who have been interested in the new theme, "Economic Growth" .... '[9] Innis's speculations on communications were partly responses to the conditions that were leading to a splintering of the 'social sciences'. Ironically, they were also his contribution to the dissolution of the political-economy tradition.

Innis understood well enough that his interest in communications in remote cultures reflected an intense involvement with Canada's present position and its future, especially in relation to the United States in the years after the Second World War. He had previously described how the entire Canadian economy had been gradually realigned under the impact of the rise of the 'American Empire' and its demands for new staples, but his response to this development in the thirties was one of resigned fatalism and a plea for consideration on the part of American policy makers. His passionate nationalism — held in check for so long and disguised by his critical comments on Canadian pretensions — was outraged by Canada's acceptance of a position of unquestioning supporter of the United States in the Cold War. Innis travelled to Russia at the end of the Second World War and lectured in England in 1948, and these trips intensified his growing cynicism about the nature of American foreign policy. Indeed, his stay in Russia increased his awareness of another dimension of the bias of communications: the problem of how so-called improvements in modern communications impeded mutual understanding between different cultures.[10] The polarization of the world into two power blocs and the diminution of Canada's freedom of action moved Innis to anger and bitterness because he saw clearly how the effects of propaganda, monopolies of knowledge, and mass-commercialized journalism and radio prevented a balanced, independent appraisal of Canada's options in foreign policy.

'Canada,' he wrote in 1948, in a parody of the title of Lower's history, 'moved from colony to nation to colony.' The nature of its resources dictated that it become a satellite to the American economy, just as it had once been an adjunct of British industrialism. Canada's fairly recent acquisition of autonomy within the Commonwealth had given it little time to develop a mature and independent foreign policy. The anti-revolutionary traditions of French Canada and the United Empire Loyalists predisposed Canadians to accept the anti-socialist, free-enterprise rhetoric of American policy. 'We complained bitterly of Great Britain in the Minto affair, the Naval Bill, and the like, but no questions are asked as to the implications of joint defence schemes with the United States . . . . ' American policy was itself determined by the exigencies of domestic politics, an unstable political system, and a tendency to elevate military leaders to high office—all of which confirmed the influence of the commercialized press and radio that played upon the present and the discontinuous.[11]

This indictment of the 'vacillating and ill-informed' American foreign policy and the 'crude effrontery of American imperialism' was paralleled by Innis's alarm over the fact that Canada was so vulnerable to the communications media of the United States. The overwhelming pressures of the newspapers and radio monopolies and their 'bombardment' of Canada, he argued, threatened Canadian national existence. This constant 'hammering' of English-speaking Canadians not only tended to separate them even further from the cultural life of French Canada, but also made the task of the Canadian author virtually impossible. 'The jackals of the communications system are constantly on the alert to destroy every vestige of sentiment toward Great Britain, holding it of no advantage if it threatens the omnipotence of American commercialism. This is to strike at the heart of cultural life in Canada.'[12] Canada could only survive, he wrote in general support of the recommendations of the Massey Commission Report, 'by taking persistent action at strategic points against American imperialism in all its attractive guises.'[13] In foreign policy this meant assisting in the development of a third bloc designed to withstand the pressure of the United States and Russia. In cultural policy it meant the general strengthening of cultural and communications agencies and recognizing that cultural strength comes from Europe. So strong had Innis's anti-Americanism become that when he set about writing an autobiography in 1952 and reread some of his letters from 1918 expressing a revulsion at Americans' bragging and boasting of their role in the First World War, he acknowledged that this 'antipathy, very acute at first, I suspect never really came to an end in spite of the extraordinary kindness of individual Americans.'[14]

There was something alien to Innis's spirit in these last jeremiads. He had sought balance and an appreciation of limitations, and had upheld the virtues of 'steadiness, steadiness, steadiness'. Perhaps the rationale for the extreme positions of his later years was that, in order to appreciate balance, things must be brought into perspective even at the expense of a single-minded concentration on a single cause. The pressures that moved him to abandon academic detachment must have been intense. Still, on the plane of practical policy there was an undertone of helplessness and qualified pessimism. 'All we can do in Canada is protest against *Time, Reader's Digest* and the like,' he told Brebner. 'We dislike them intensely but can do nothing about it.'[15] Brebner, who was taken aback by the anti-American nature of Canadian cultural nationalism in the early fifties, and believed that Innis had exaggerated both the commercialism of the communications systems and the monolithic character of American culture, found his friend's appeals for a third power bloc and a restoration of the European dimension 'insubstantial'.[16]

Brebner had been one of Innis's most candid critics for some time. 'I often think', he wrote him in 1949, 'about the confusing nexus of agreement and disagreement between us . . . you seem to be attributing exclusive causal force to a partial thing. It's odd in you because the roots of liberty for you are in pluralism. You pick some single agency of change, draw legions of satellites into its train, and launch it in uncompromising assault on the hated Colossus with a kind of wry despair about the assault having any appreciable effect. That is, neither of us is a true sceptic, probably because we've both inherited some one or two kinds of evangelistic religion.'[17]

Innis held out little hope in the short-run or the long-run and he seemed to be verging on a pessimistic anarchism. It was with an immense sadness that, after a visit to the Public Archives, an institution that had been at the centre of the hopes for a national history in the twenties, he confessed that 'I never realized before how desolate and sterile it has become.'[18] What always checked this gloomy tendency, however, was his faith in liberalism and in the university and the world of scholarship, which he called 'the growth hormone of civilization'. What also saved him from the darker pessimism towards which his relentless logic led was a sense of the ridiculous: ' . . . one cannot be a social scientist without a sense of humour in Canada and one is in constant danger of dying with laughter . . . .'[19]

One of Innis's closest friends in the forties was the irreverent newspaperman George Ferguson, with whom he traded stories and anecdotes about the pompous celebrities and the general inanities of the day. ' "What this country needs most", Ferguson once told him, "is a good 5-cent bull shit filter." '[20] That was precisely the spirit, if not the vocabulary, of Innis's attitude to those who took themselves too seriously and wanted to order others around. Were it not for his deep attachment to the life of the mind, and his cynicism about men in large groups, there were aspects of Innis's outlook that might have been mistaken for an old-fashioned democrat's populism.

When Innis abandoned Canadian economic history and turned to the larger field of communications in world history he entered a virtually unexplored territory where few of his friends in the historical fraternity were willing or able to follow. Their general impression of his later work was a mixture of admiration for his intellectual daring and courage and bewilderment over what he was driving at. His writings had never been models of lucidity and his speculations on communications were made even more difficult to follow when he read his concentrated papers at scholarly meetings. It became a cheap joke that this historian of communications had difficulty communicating in print. One can sympathize with the plight of his graduate students who were told that their essay topic was 'Contrast the economic implications of a written and oral language tradition,' and who were then informed that 'This is a good example of a lecturer hoping to learn something from a student's essay. I would have no idea of how to start it.' Innis had come to the history of the ancient world rather late in life. One of his friends has recalled that he mispronounced even the most familiar names from classical literature; another thought he had got out of his depth and over-reached himself. One of the minor refrains in the response to Innis's later career was a feeling of dismay that he had deserted the more direct study of Canadian society and regret that he was exposing himself to criticism from those who had nourished grudges. Even those knowlegeable in the abstruse field of communications criticized Innis on particular and general grounds. They were struck, as was Brebner, by the contrast between the complexity of the problems he undertook to examine and the simplicity of his conceptual scheme that hinged on the two dimensions of space and time. If standards and values were determined by economic and technological processes, was it possible to throw over certain patterns of behaviour and adopt others that were fashioned under different economic circumstances?[21]

It is suggestive of both the scientific limitations and the imaginative possibilities of Innis's ideas that the exploration of communications in Canada was carried forward not by the social scientists or historians who had earlier been closest to Innis but by the literary scholar Marshall McLuhan, and that McLuhan's own works were less an extension of Innis's ideas than an inversion of them. McLuhan responded to Innis's *Empire and Communications* by noting that the whole tendency of modern communications was towards participation in a process rather than the apprehension of concepts.[22] Where Innis was primarily concerned with communications technology and its effects on institutions and culture, and only marginally with its impact on the human senses, McLuhan's attention was mainly focussed on the way media became extensions of human senses and thereby affected the relations between them.[23]

The later preoccupations of Innis had little direct impact on the writing of Canadian history except in so far as his criticism of American policy and

Canadian difficulties expressed a more widespread sense of unease that was shared by other historians. They continued to regard the staples thesis as his major contribution to Canadian studies and were hesitant about accepting his speculations on communications as anything more than exploratory and suggestive beginnings. The virtual destruction of the dominance of the political-economy tradition in the fifties registered profound shifts in Canadian intellectual life, and to a degree Innis's changes in focus mirrored those changes. By the time he died in 1952, Canadian historical writing was addressed to questions and subjects that bore only a remote relationship to the kind of economic history he had expounded. It was left for another generation to begin to recover and build on the foundations he had constructed. But however confused his contemporaries may have been by his later works, they held a unanimous opinion of his selfless devotion to pure scholarship. Even those with whom he had disagreed acknowledged that he was the dominant figure in the Canadian social sciences in his generation. Lower, who confessed he did not see where the later writings led, called Innis the most outstanding historian devoted to pure scholarship. He was a man who, to paraphrase his wife, had done the things he really wanted to do, and whose way of living was to wear himself out in the pursuit of truth.

II

While at the end of his life Innis protested in uncharacteristically apocalyptic language against the increasing American pressures on Canada, Frank Underhill, equally uncharacteristically, was coming to accept the fundamentals of the *status quo*. He was fifty-one in 1940. In the next fifteen years he abandoned the democratic socialism of the CCF party, became the major academic defender in Canada of the American view of the cold war, and reluctantly embraced official Liberalism. At the core of his political outlook was a concern for the liberty and free development of the individual, and it was this conviction that provided the element of continuity in the changes of emphasis and direction of his thought.

Underhill always had a sensitive perception of the coming fashions in historical writing. As early as 1940 he anticipated the growing discontent with the concentration on economic history, just as in the later twenties he had voiced the most extreme criticisms of the constitutionalists. He noted that the best studies done for the Rowell-Sirois Commission and the Carnegie series were in the field of economic history, which conveyed an impression of fatalism, impersonality, vulnerability to outside forces—in short 'a ghostly ballet of bloodless economic categories'. This kind of history deflated Canadian self-esteem and tended to paralyse positive activity. Having once urged historians to treat politicians as the mouthpieces of economic interests, Underhill now appealed for a history that would deal with flesh-and-blood individuals and with Canadian political, educational, and religious ideas. In his Presidential Address to the Canadian Historical Association in 1946 he observed that Canadian historical writing 'had come to the end of an epoch' and that the time was ripe for a history of ideas that would analyse the conceptions that lay behind Canadians' actions and would explain how they thought in one way in one period and in a different way in another.[24]

Though in the early forties Underhill maintained his interest in the political opinions of the Upper Canadian reformers and in the career of Edward Blake, he was bedevilled by the vacuity and unoriginality of Canadian political discussion and by the apparent incapacity of Canadians to examine and probe the ideological bases of their communal affairs. Typically he drew his own analysis of the larger themes in the history of Canadian political culture from the books of foreign observers: Goldwin Smith, André Siegfried, James Bryce, Rupert Brooke, and John Hobson. Underhill attributed Canada's intellectual weakness and its citizenry's preference for living in a mental fog to the debility of its radical tradition. The founders of the country, he said, had turned their backs on the inquiring, rationalist eighteenth century; Canadians had always aped the more conservative trends in English life; and they had never fully realized the country's independence. 'It took us in Canada one hundred years to write our Canadian declaration of independence—from Lord Durham's Report to the Statute of Westminster. And, because of this fact, independence has not had the same effect upon our national consciousness as it has had upon the consciousness of Americans . . . . '[25] In his attempt to write the history of Canadian political ideas, which he identified almost exclusively with radical political and social criticism, Underhill was concerned with a subject that, according to his own settled conviction, was of marginal significance. Canadian history, he believed, was a history of the failure of radicalism.

Underhill's move away from an economic interpretation of politics was related to his re-evaluation of the history of the party system and his reappraisal of the leadership of Mackenzie King. Again he was stimulated in this direction by American political science, this time Pendleton Herring's *The Politics of Democracy: American Parties in Action* (1940), an apologia for the North American omnibus political party on the general grounds that in a continental country with diverse sectional and group interests it provided a forum within which all interests could arrive at a consensus. Underhill expressed some reservations about Herring's book, but the essential idea of major political parties as brokers, mediating the aims of diverse classes, ethnic groups, and economic interests, underlay his reassessment of the recent history of Canadian political parties and his new appreciation of Mackenzie King.

Underhill's main indictment of King's leadership was that the Liberal leader had no inspiring nation-building policy comparable to Macdonald's or Laurier's because of the conditions of Canadian disunity after the First World War. By the time King died in 1950, Underhill concluded that the secret of his political success was that he understood so acutely and practised so ably the two fundamental rules for political survival in Canada: it could not be governed without the consent and co-operation of French-Canadians; and political leadership consisted in securing the support of all regions and varied interests. The Liberal party itself reflected the federalism of the country. Underhill's final estimate of King rested on the brokerage view of parties, which was in a sense a logical outgrowth of the progressive conception of political history as the conflict of privileged and underprivileged classes. But where once Underhill had written of Canadian politics in progressive terms in order to justify the hopes for realignment, by 1950 he accepted and vindicated the brokerage system.[26]

This favourable estimate of King and Liberalism was perhaps facilitated by a more generous recognition, if not a more profound understanding, of the interests of French Canada. In the late twenties and during the thirties Underhill had treated French-Canadian political objectives as little more than an uncanny ability to be on the winning side; his stress upon economic factors had relegated cultural, religious, and linguistic characteristics to a secondary place. In the Depression the *Forum* paid little attention to Quebec except to decry incidents of 'clerical fascism' in that province and to denounce the anti-civil-libertarian activites of Premier Duplessis. Members of the League for Social Reconstruction were not a little impatient with the resistance of French Canada to suggestions for strengthening the powers of the Ottawa government over social and economic policies, even though they sympathized with that community's isolationism.

It was perhaps the war and another conscription crisis that served to move the problem of French-English relations closer to the forefront of Underhill's thinking. Certainly he learned a good deal from Lower's *Colony to Nation*, which made the conflict between the two peoples and ways of life the central theme in Canadian history and which Underhill called the 'most mature and philosophical history of Canada that has yet been written'.[27] In any case, when Underhill was asked in 1960 who he believed was the greatest of Canadian political leaders, he answered— Laurier.[28] Laurier, whom he had once charged with presiding over the betrayal of the Grit reform tradition, now became the most outstanding practioner of the delicate art of keeping French- and English-speaking Canadians working together.

These revisions in Underhill's understanding of the past were indicative of more deep-seated changes in his outlook. The fall of France in 1940 was a shock to his implicit assumption that Britain and France possessed sufficient power to contain Germany; the beastialities of Nazism made his isolationist rhetoric about the fraudulent appeals of 'freedom' and 'representative government' seem unfortunate and embarrassing reminders of the liabilities of sarcasm. The Second World War challenged his faith in human rationality, in the perfectability of institutions, and in the benevolent management of experts. He came to see his earlier conviction that political liberty automatically followed economic democracy as misguided. Then the cold war completely disabused him of an admiration for socialist planning in Russia. The 'deepest experience of our present generation', Underhill wrote in 1949, 'centres about the problem of freedom. We have just emerged from a great war which was fought for the preservation of free society; and we seem to be drifting towards another one. We have had a terrifying revelation of what totalitarianism means; and we have become acutely aware how weak is the position of the individual and how deep-rooted are the totalitarian potentialities in our contemporary society .... '[29] This 'North York Presbyterian Grit', as he called himself, later attested that he found the American theologian Reinhold Niebuhr, who stressed the reality of sin and frailty in human affairs, 'the most penetrating and illuminating writer on politics whom I read.'[30] He never went so far in this rediscovery of the old values, however, as to see much in the religious metahistory of Arnold Toynbee. 'Why has it not occurred to him', he asked, 'that Industrialism, by raising material standards of life, may also be making possible a higher intellectual and spiritual life for the great majority?'[31] But still, a measured pessimism about human nature and a concern with totalitarian pressures compelled a re-examination of the assumed identity of the liberal tradition and socialism.

Underhill's changing commitments were most emphatic on two fronts. The first related to Canadian foreign policy. The revolution of 1940 had transferred the leadership of the English-speaking world to the United States; with the Russian threat after 1945 Canada had no other choice but to support American policy. From the coup in Czechoslovakia in 1948 to the Korean war and beyond, there were few Canadian academic figures who were more insistent on defending the United States' view of the international conflict and on underlining the sameness of Canadian and American interests in the cold war. Underhill accepted without question and without reservations the dominant opinion that Soviet totalitarianism posed the most serious menace to the free world and that this challenge could be met only by military strength, not negotiation.[32] One suspects that his support for the Western alliance was a recoil against his misreading of the events of the later thirties.

The second aspect of Underhill's change of mind was his criticism of Canadian socialism. Underhill had hardly been uncritical of the CCF, even before the dissolution of the LSR in 1942, but by the late forties and early fifties his former associates became the objects of jibes that had previously been reserved for businessmen. His main concern was with the question of how excessive state power could be checked and held in balance, and he was merciless in his diagnosis of the failure of the CCF to amend its traditional reliance on state control and planning. He condemned the party for carrying a Depression mentality into an era of prosperity, for the growth of labour influence in its councils, and for its dictatorial bureaucracy and loss of interest in research.[33] Capitalism had not failed to the degree the socialists had hoped in the thirties. The welfare state, which owed so much to the prodding—and the electoral challenge—of the CCF, had worked to remove the cruder forms of insecurity of the Depression. The problem, as Underhill understood it, was not the abstract issue of the virtues of theoretically distinct economic systems; it was a technical question concerning the mixture of private and public enterprise. Underhill had never had much personal rapport with urban labour and he came to understand that the other interest on which the radical tradition had relied, the agrarian community, had revealed itself as only another conservative pressure group.[34] The chief obstacle to an egalitarian society, he said, was the ' "damned wantlessness of the poor" '.[35] By the time the CCF formally qualified the principles of the Regina Manifesto in 1956, Underhill was well on his way back to the party he had voted for in 1911. When he published a collection of his essays in 1960, *In Search of Canadian Liberalism*, he dedicated the book to Lester Pearson.

The central theme that Underhill returned to again and again throughout his career was the position of the intellectual in Canadian society. In the thirties the task of intellectual leadership had been defined in relation to social criticism, radical politics, and the realignment of parties. By the fifties Underhill, like the American liberals whose ideas he echoed in the pages of the *Canadian Forum*, looked to an élite of dedicated and enlightened men who would preserve the standards of a more aristocratic age amid the pressures towards conformity of mass culture. He too rediscovered in the writings of Alexis de Tocqueville and John Stuart Mill warnings about the implications of populism and the tyranny of majoritarian democracy. 'The emergence of the Social Credit movement and of the Diefenbaker Conservative movement,' he wrote in 1963, 'with their appeal to the little men in the towns and on the farms, to the more uneducated and backward sections of the population, with their suspicion of Civil Service experts and central bankers, with their fundamentalist anti-intellectualism in both religion and politics—all this shows how far we have gone in the direction of a simple-minded populist democracy.'[36] Having once celebrated the farmers and the urban working class as the only potential bases of radicalism, he now worried over the lack of intellectual distinction in a society that accepted the standards of the 'commonplace man'.

Those aspects of mass culture that the Massey Commission denounced as 'alien', and that Innis associated with the commercialized communications monopolies, Underhill saw as integral to modern democracy generally, not as some unique ailment of the United States. Nothing triggered his satire more quickly than the revival of 'anti-Americanism' in the fifties, especially when it played on the threat to 'Canadian culture'. 'I don't think it matters that much whether we are politically independent or politically amalgamated with the United States,' he told an interviewer in 1960. ' . . . If we are to be culturally distinct, then we have to produce a culture that is worthwhile.'[37]

At this time Underhill came close to resolving the tension between the intellectual who was critical of society and the social order itself. When he left the University of Toronto in 1955 because he had not been named chairman of the history department, Lester Pearson, Jack Pickersgill, and Kaye Lamb, the Dominion Archivist, found a position for him as curator of Laurier House in Ottawa, and he was paid by the Public Archives. Later he was given a sinecure as historical consultant to the National Research Council. This unique patronage system was an individual counterpart to the more generous acceptance of the intellectual and creative artist in society generally in the late fifties and the sixties. Underhill took a good deal of satisfaction in those products of constructive socialism that had been created to foster Canadian culture: the National Research Council, the CBC, the National Film Board, the National Gallery, and the Public Archives. Above all the Canada Council signified the greater recognition of intellectual effort and served to narrow the gap between the intellectual and society.[38]

Underhill occupied an ambiguous position in the history of Canadian historical thought and social criticism. His major interests were in political philosophy—in the way Canadians thought about, and conducted, their communal affairs. He raised penetrating questions about what he once termed 'Canadian civilization', and he tried to see contemporary problems in the perspective of history. At his best in the short essay and in his lectures, his iconoclasm and irreverence appealed to the young who were trying to free themselves from their elders. The word most often used by his admirers to describe the importance of his lectures in their own intellectual development was 'liberating'. But iconoclasm could degenerate into a corrosive negativism until it seemed that everything was satirized for the sake of satire itself or for the satisfaction it brought to the satirist. Underhill defined the essential quality of intellect as critical, but he apparently remained quite uncritical of his self-interested motives for establishing the position of intellectuals like himself in the community. He chastised Canadians for the derivativeness of their ideas, but there were times when he was the most 'colonial' of Canadians, expecting historians to rewrite the past in the categories of Charles Beard, to reconstruct politics on the model of the Fabian Society and the British Labour Party, and to appreciate the warnings of de Tocqueville, which American liberals had come to esteem in the early fifties. Yet he was in other respects his own best critic. He could confess in 1952 that when he graduated from Toronto in 1911 he had not even heard of Freud, Pareto, Sorel, Picasso, Matisse, or Stravinsky. It should be obvious by now that he had the habit of generalizing personal deficiencies and projecting his own failures onto Canada generally. What else could he have meant when he said that radicals of the thirties attempted to create a great politics and had failed because Canada did not possess a great culture, and that there could be no Canadian Parrington because Canadians had not written sufficiently incisive political speculations for him to interpret?

One of the tragedies of Underhill's career, measured against the standards he tried to emulate, was his failure to escape from his own negative and critical impulses. The writers he admired—Charles Beard in the United States and the Webbs in England—had behind their reputations as engaged intellectuals substantial works of scholarship that would outlive their more polemical and transitory journalism. But with Underhill all we have are the essays of the journalist, probing and illuminating though they may be, as a prelude and a preliminary to something that did not materialize. He committed himself to write a number of books that were never finished: a volume for Kennedy's projected eight-volume history of Canada, a book of essays on Canada at the crossroads in the early thirties, a study of political ideas in mid-Victorian Upper Canada for the Carnegie series, and a biography of Blake. (His later lectures, *The British Commonwealth* (1956) and *The Image of Confederation* (1964), were derivative and repetitious of earlier opinions.) Arthur Lower was correct in suspecting that the attractions of the occasional pieces for the *Forum* seduced his friend away from more permanent writing. As the English critic Cyril Connolly, who knew all about the temptations of journalism and the other 'enemies of promise', put it: 'A writer who takes up journalism abandons the slow tempo of literature for a faster one, and the change will do him harm. By degree the flippancy of journalism will become a habit and the pleasure of being paid on the nail, and especially of being praised on the nail, grow indispensable.'[39] Underhill was defensive about his shortcomings, saying that if he had not spent so much time and energy on practical politics he would have written learned books that everyone would praise and no one would read. This may be a reasonable position in itself, but it is not compatible with attributing the failure of intellectual radicalism to the paucity of a culture that must in part be built up and enriched by creative intellectual effort.

III

Compared with Underhill's deviation from his social democratic commitments and Innis's transition from the political economy of staples to the technologies of communications, Arthur Lower preserved the essentials of his views about Canadian history as these were set out in *Colony to Nation*. Written under the catalyst of war, that book itself represented his change from economic to general history. The modulations in Lower's outlook in the late forties and the fifties consisted of variations of emphasis, not of substance or direction. His early training, he admitted, had impressed him with the deterministic side of life, a tendency that had always been held in check by an awareness of the role of spiritual and religious forces in history. Lower never accepted unreservedly the full implications of Innis's conception of the geographical dictates underpinning Canadian unity, and by 1952 he reflected that 'if there is one country under the sun which does refute the geographical determinist it surely is Canada, for there is hardly a logical aspect about it.'[40] In his social and political thinking, moreover, Lower had not strayed far from the centre of Canadian liberalism in the thirties. He had never been attracted to the democratic socialism of the League for Social Reconstruction but looked instead to a heightened sense of national community as the source for social cohesion that others found in economic reform. Hence he felt no compulsion in the forties to abandon political allegiances or economic determinism. But in spite of the substantial differences that separated him from Innis and Underhill, Lower in his own individualist fashion responded to some of the same promptings and moved in the same direction.

In 1947 Lower left Wesley College and the West, where he had never felt completely at home, and moved to Queen's University. His *Colony to Nation* had been a resounding success: within ten years of its publication it had been printed five times in three editions. (One of the minor ironies of that work's own history was that Longman's filled orders from London because prospective purchasers in India, Ceylon, and Spain did not know where Toronto was![41]) In the dozen or so years after its appearance, Lower published three reflective studies on Canadian history. *Canada: Nation and Neighbour* (1952) sketched Canadians' attitudes to the outside world and attempted to explain the nature of the country's foreign policy; *This Most Famous Stream: The Liberal Democratic Way of Life* (1954) traced the institutional, religious, and historical roots of liberalism in the English-speaking world; and *Canadians in the Making* (1958) marked a return to Lower's consistent preoccupation with the sense of identity, this time focussed on the stages of the nation's social evolution. The element of commentary—intensely personal, frequently pungent, sometimes querulously cantankerous—had always been more prominent in his writing than narrative or dispassionate analysis, and in these books these features became even more pronounced. His later publications were based less on research than on insights that arose from a personal engagement with his times. By the late forties Lower's position as a national gadfly who could be relied upon for controversial opinions had been established by his numerous articles in *Maclean's* and *Saturday Night* on familiar subjects—the myth of mass immigration; if we joined the U.S.A.; what this country needs is ten new provinces; the forest-heart of a nation—and a few novel topics: class in Canada; why men fight; Catholic and Protestant differences as revealed in attitudes to pets; home thoughts from abroad.

Where Lower modified the main lines of his approach, at least in his substantive historical studies, was in his greater recognition of the liberal foundations of Canadian life and in his unfavourable reaction to what he called 'Canadian mass man'. These were extensions of older, not new, fixtures in his outlook. By the early fifties he sensed a special urgency in retracing the background of the liberal democratic way of life and in expressing disquiet at those pressures that threatened to drown the exceptional individual, as well as élite cultural standards, in a sea of mass consumption and conformity.

Back of his reconsideration of liberalism lay the painful memory of the Nazi gas chambers and concentration camps and the even more immediate apprehension that unless Canadians had a clear conception of the principles on which their institutions rested, 'we cannot face the mountain of dialectical conviction represented by Communism.'[42] And behind these considerations stood Lower's strong attachment to civil liberties. This had moved him to protest, through the Civil Liberties Association of Winnipeg, against the War Measures Act and the Defence of Canada Regulations, which at the beginning of the war had conferred on the state sweeping powers of arrest and detention, and in certain cases related to the war effort had suspended *habeas corpus*.[43] The espionage case of 1945 and the detention without trial of a number of people suspected of spying intensified his fear of arbitrary state authority and reinforced his support for a Canadian Bill of Rights. Lower was primarily concerned with the freedom of the individual against the state rather than with the rights of corporate groups. For him the 'quintessence of liberalism' was contained in the statement: ' "I wish neither to take nor to give orders." '[44]

Lower traced the origins of liberalism to the heritage of institutions rooted in history and fixed in experience, to the great petitions and charters of English freedom, and above all to Protestant Christianity. It was out of Christian belief that the commitment to the dignity and worth of the individual was born, and it was this precious faith in the individual that underlay the tremendous history of the emergence of Parliament, the revolutions of the seventeenth century, the spread of English-speaking civilization beyond the seas, the American Revolution, the Canadian struggle against privilege, frontier social democracy, and federalism. Not even in the days when he was most responsive to the Turner thesis had Lower ever believed that the social democracy promoted by space and frontier conditions could sustain itself without a heritage of law, institutions, and conceptions of freedom imported from Britain. Now his major preoccupation was precisely with those very traditions and convictions. At the heart of his rededication to liberalism lay the question of whether that faith could survive without its religious sanctions and the centuries-old discipline in Christian ethics. Lower did not think so. 'It seems . . . that the essence of the Christian scheme of things lies in a specific method for giving dignity and purpose to human life. This method consists in belief in Christ and redemption through him.'[45] Without this religious respect for the individual, liberalism would have no solid, sustaining core of conviction.

From the vantage point of 1954 Lower glimpsed a more positive side to puritanism than he had appreciated before. 'After the first world war', he reminisced, exaggerating a little, 'our rebellion went so far that it seemed as if we would not be content until we had utterly destroyed the society we had built. We turned on religion and made the church and its ministers figures of fun.' The inherited code of morals and traditional culture, civil institutions, the family, and politics had been held in contempt. This scorn, and the successive storms of prosperity, depression, and another war had severely tested democratic institutions. Perhaps, he added, the war was necessary 'to bring, not only our defeated foes, but ourselves back to simpler and healthier things.' Protestant Christianity and particularly the Calvinist tradition could rightly be indicted for many sins, but no society moulded by it had ever fallen to state-worship.[46]

The perspective of the early fifties brought a clearer recognition than was possible before that underlying the monarchical and parliamentary system of Britain and the presidential and republican government of the United States lay a common heritage of liberalism. The English-speaking people had given to the world something of enduring value: the institutions of freedom. The differing patterns of life that arose from the colonizing efforts of Britain, Spain, Portugal, France, and Holland 'made nonsense of the contention that society is but the reflection of its physical environment.' It was an older truth, more or less taken for granted by the younger historians of the inter-war years, but reasserted in the aftermath of the Second World War and the cold war. Like Underhill, Lower expressed no reservations about the degree to which Canada was integrated into American defence planning, though he remained critical of alien economic ownership and American mass culture.[47]

The other dimension of Lower's defence of liberalism against the state was his worry over the erosion of individual liberty by mass society and culture. This latter concern provided one of the more striking differences between his twin overviews of Canadian history, *Colony to Nation* and *Canadians in the Making.* In 1946 he felt that the country was on the threshold of national life. Twelve years later, encouraged by the absence of racial tensions in national politics, the end of appeals to the Judicial Committee of the Privy Council, the centralization of power in Ottawa, the recognition of the problems of a national culture in the Massey Commission Report, and Canada's acceptance of international obligations, Lower felt that the threshold had been crossed. The theme of the earlier book was the development of a sense of national community; the focus of the later one was ostensibly the stages in a community's evolution. The economic historian, Lower submitted, addresses himself to the question of what man does to the environment; the social historian examines what the environment does to man. Lower's subject was the attitudes, opinions, and feelings of Canadians in the past, but these were so drastically filtered through his own emotions that his social history became a series of judgements and comments rather than systematic analyses and re-creations. An uninhibited and engaging book, *Canadians in the Making* was filled with anecdotes about such matters as the fashionableness of freckles on ladies, ballads, and the incidence of venereal disease in the army. But the main themes that provided its structure were all permutations of his early ideas: the French-English dichotomy; the crucial impact of religion, particularly Calvinism; frontier and social democracy; the metropolitan-provincial relationship; the disturbing and unsettling effect of mass immigration; competing centres of loyalty; and, above all, the rise of an emotional commitment to Canada. Through it all ran Lower's declaration of attachment to the forest and the hope that the simple and wholesome values nurtured in the wilderness and the countryside would survive in urban society.

It was when Lower came to pronounce his opinions of society in his own time that his early ideas were submerged in fulminations against affluence, including the 'great god CAR' and his associated dieties, and against novelty and equality. The problem as he saw it was simply this: 'how to maintain a society with the equalitarian values of the pioneer and at the same time gradually build a national culture which in the distinctions it makes is not concerned overmuch with the shrine of Equality.' Great cultures were not built by Everyman but by a small élite of artists, writers, and men of taste.[48] 'My main concern', he had earlier written with reference to the university and the divorce between academic culture and national society, 'is as to how the university can be preserved for the elect and not at the same time cut itself off from the masses . . . . ' The kind of limited groups that had the respect of society at the time of Confederation had disappeared, in part because men no longer possessed a common body of knowledge. The educated were 'shoved off into corners by the great democratic public that storms against "culture-vultures" who like to have symphonic concerts on Sunday afternoons. This great public, coming up from below, its head full of sad American slave music and its belly full of Coca-Cola, has little respect for the academic "culture" of the class-room. What has got to be done is to create a new culture—a native culture, built upon the remains of the old, and let us hope, incorporating a good deal of it.'[49] At this point, as in the beginning of Lower's career, nationalism was the solution to all problems.

There was a vein of wistful sadness in Lower's concluding reflections on the failure of Canada to create a single metropolitan centre or to resolve, if only partially, the antithesis between French- and English-speaking Canadians. ' . . . how sad and sorry Canada must remain', he remarked, 'as long as it continues to be a pale imitation of the United States. How sad and sorry when the way out appeared so plainly: here was a country of two peoples, of two ways of life, of two cultures. That fact alone gave it any distinction it might happen to possess.'[50] It was a regret that would grow in the sixties.

Lower always believed that the historian should write of the past so as to bring about the future he desires. The indispensable quality of the historian to him was the commitment to the national community. There was an essential mystery about the past and it could only be assimilated—not understood through the intellect alone, but through a combination of empathy for the dead and immersion in the emotional experiences of the present. Lower despised the 'destructiveness' of historical scholarship, the constant uprooting and disinterring that killed necessary myths.[51] He defined the role of the national historian in the nineteenth-century tradition as the maker of myths by which national communities live. It was therefore hardly surprising that he spoke of the historian's 'avocation' in religious terms. The historian was the intermediary between the past and the present, an instrument of a mysterious dialogue. He embodies, in his own life, the meaning of that dialogue; the cycle is complete when he writes the history of himself. It is in relation to his peppery My First Seventy-five Years (1967) that one can see that all Lower's history was heavily autobiographical. Lower was the only historian of his generation to write an autobiography: the exception, of course, was Abbé Groulx. Neither mentioned the other.

It is a commonplace that historians change their minds and alter the main lines of their interests. It is of some significance, however, that Innis, Underhill, and Lower, for all their idiosyncracies, responded to the upheavals of the forties and fifties by returning to the problems of 'Canadian culture' and by reasserting their common liberalism. Each of them, however, perceived the threat to individual freedom somewhat differently. For Innis the task was to preserve the intellectual freedom of the individual in a world constantly bombarded and assaulted by modern communications that had destroyed the balance between the present and the past. Lower understood it to be the need to sharpen an appreciation for the tradition of self-government and individual liberty and to deepen an awareness of the fact that the origins of liberalism lay in religion. And Underhill saw the problem in terms of protecting the exceptional individual against the conformist pressures of mass society. Innis's approving citation in 1946 of the political credo of Goldwin Smith, Lower's *This Most Famous Stream*, and Underhill's accurate declaration, a few years before his death in 1972, that in his political philosophy he had never really got beyond John Stuart Mill, attest to the hold the old faith had upon them.

9 | DONALD CREIGHTON AND THE ARTISTRY OF HISTORY

No other Canadian historian was so concerned with history as a literary art as Donald Creighton. At the centre of his thought was the idea of the St Lawrence River as the inspiration and basis of a transcontinental economic and political system. His major works on commerce and politics from the Conquest to the mid-nineteenth century, on Confederation, and on the age of Macdonald not only recreated significant aspects of the past within variations of this framework, but did so with a kind of artistry that itself greatly shaped the resulting structure of the past. Moreover, the development of Creighton's thought and practice created a link between the cultural nationalism of the twenties, the environmentalism of the thirties, and the reformulation of history as biography in the fifties.

I

Like so many Canadian intellectuals of his generation, Creighton, who was born in Toronto in 1902, was a child of Ontario Methodism. A concern with the health of society ran deep in his family. His grandmother, Eliza Harvie, was a pioneer of the early feminist movement who worked for the Women's Christian Temperance Union and was an energetic inspector on behalf of neglected children. His father, William Black Creighton, was an ordained minister who held several pastorates, became editor of the *Christian Guardian*, and, after church union in 1925, editor of the *New Outlook*. Less a preacher in the evangelical tradition than a journalist, commentator, and reformer, the elder Creighton embraced a social-service Christianity and sympathized with the moral criticism of competitive capitalist society advanced by Ernest Thomas and Salem Bland. Like most other adherents of the social gospel he saw the sufferings of the Great War as a harbinger of the coming Kingdom of God and vigorously supported conscription. Though he turned to pacificism in the twenties, his faith in social Christianity never wavered. As editor of the *New Outlook* in the thirties he supported the Fellowship for a Christian Social Order, which included Eugene Forsey among its members, and was censured by conservative churchmen, especially those connected with the pietistic Oxford group, for turning the journal into a 'red propaganda sheet'.[1]

Donald Creighton's first love was literature. 'I was born', he recalled, 'into a household in which books, history, biography, literature were all about.'[2] His father frequently brought home bundles of books and Creighton read them; while still in high school he sometimes reviewed them for his father's journal. He liked the iconoclastic flavour of Lytton Strachey's assault on Victorian evangelism and the satire and sarcasm of H.L. Mencken's *The Smart Set*. He enrolled in Victoria College in the University of Toronto in 1921 and took the course in English and History, which then included ancient and modern history as well as languages. During the 1924-5 session Creighton was the editor of the college magazine, *Acta Victoriana*, in which he disrespectfully deflated the pomposities of the Student Christian Movement and the Students' Parliament. 'If I am to be castigated myself,' he wrote in response to criticism, 'I prefer to be castigated with an epigram than with a sermon . . . . After all, college parliaments and associations, though very laudable things doubtless, are not so majestically important that one must approach them on bended knee, with a countenance exhibiting the most profound reverence and veneration.'[3]

Creighton's sarcasm was invariably expressed in the orotund language of religiosity. In a cutting rebuke to an article by Douglas Bush, who had censured Canadian parochialism and held up the classics as the touchstones of beauty and intelligence, Creighton began: 'Among the many militant orders, sects and societies of the world, not the least pugnaciously confident is the unorganized association of the Classicists. No faith-healer from California, no reformed cattle-stealer evangelist from Wyoming, armed though they be with gilt-edged divine inspiration, can ever approach, except in their moments of superlative inspiration, the calm, the unshakable assurance of the Classicists.' While not excusing the credulousness and lack of discrimination of some of the literary nationalists of the twenties, Creighton denied the appropriateness of the universal standard. The literature of other countries and ages, he wrote, may broaden one's tastes and sharpen critical faculties, but it contained no standards against which Canadian literature should be judged.[4]

Pelham Edgar and E.J. Pratt doubtlessly confirmed Creighton's attachments to literature, but his tutors in history—J.B. Brebner, Hume Wrong, and especially George Smith—turned him towards history. At Balliol College, Oxford, he read mainly in the European and British fields and deliberately avoided those specialized courses on imperial constitutional history that touched on Canada. (One don called him 'a thorough Canadian rubber neck'.)[5] After his return in 1927 to the Department of History in the University of Toronto, where he was to spend his entire professional career, Creighton taught a course on the French Revolution and resolved to make that subject his speciality. In the summer of 1928 he went to the Sorbonne and began research under the supervision of the great socialist historian of the revolution, Albert Mathiez. Though Creighton was more attracted to the moderates of the revolution than his teacher, who had rehabilitated Robespierre, he found Mathiez's treatment of the crisis as a social and economic upheaval and a conflict of classes a breath of fresh air. His plan to write on French history was frustrated, however, because of the impossibility of financing future trips to Europe, and there was no alternative but to turn to a field where the sources were more easily accessible. On the suggestion of W.P.M. Kennedy he began to read the papers of Lord Dalhousie, governor-in-chief of Canada in the 1820s, that had recently been acquired by the Public Archives. Thus, unlike a number of historians whose determination to work in Canadian history was fired by emotional commitments made in the First World War, Creighton came to the history of his own country by accident, almost by default.

II

Kennedy anticipated that Creighton would do a monographic study in constitutional history, a counterpart of George Glazebrook's life of Bagot, but Creighton's interests moved in a rather different direction. He grew bored with Dalhousie, who never seemed to come alive in his official correspondence, and felt that there was little genuinely new to say about the contentions between the reformers in the elected assembly and the nominated council in Lower Canada. Moreover, his lack of interest in a constitutional history that dealt in forms and enactments reflected a general dissatisfaction with what a preceding generation had done and a desire to penetrate beneath words and acts to the underlying economic and material basis of politics.

Creighton became increasingly fascinated with one group that had never really been examined — the merchant community and its political allies—and he resolved to explore the tensions from the point of view of the merchant class. He quickly found that behind the familiar constitutional exchanges lay a more profound conflict over land tenures, taxation, immigration, tariffs, canals, and commerce. In two papers published in 1931 and 1933 he advanced an interpretation of the rebellion in Lower

Canada that hinged on the 'contrast between two classes, between two ages of economic and social development, between the France which the political revolution had destroyed and the England which the industrial revolution had created.' On the one side stood the French—'a pastoral people dominated by professional groups'. Their leading characteristics were an 'inherent economic conservatism' and a 'petty prudence'; they offered the 'sullen, inert opposition of men who accepted unquestioningly the purposes, pursuits, and habits of their forefathers'. They saw Lower Canada as a fixed community and they sought to preserve its feudal society and all its institutions. On the other side were the Anglo-American merchants and bureaucrats, imbued with the 'American spirit' of enterprise and aggressiveness, concerned with material expansion, commerce, and prosperity. They envisaged the whole of northern North America as a vast network of lakes and rivers that could, by artifice and improvement, attract the commerce of half a continent. The clash between these two groups, representing such radically different outlooks, could not be seen exclusively in terms of race, at least not in any ethnological sense; nor could it be regarded as a struggle over the preservation of linguistic and religious values. Its roots lay in different responses to the opportunities offered by the North American environment. 'It was', Creighton stressed, 'a straight conflict between an aggressive mercantile body and a dormant peasantry.'[6]

This conclusion reminded Creighton's contemporaries of Charles Beard's recent reinterpretation of the American Civil War as the culmination of an irrepressible conflict between different economic systems,[7] and it was in keeping with the general determination of younger historians to interpret the traditional themes of cultural conflict and responsible government in economic terms. Creighton's approach, however, was far closer to Lord Durham's view of the conflict in Lower Canada—a view that was frequently repeated in histories of Canada published in the nineteenth century. Creighton's purpose was to examine the tensions from the perspective of the commercial class, and it was exactly that point of view that Durham had incorporated in his celebrated *Report*.

Creighton pursued his researches along these lines. In 1935 he described his work-in-progress as an inquiry into the emergence of the business communities of Montreal, Quebec, and Toronto, and with 'the development of Canada as a field for foreign investment'.[8] But *The Commercial Empire of the St. Lawrence*, which appeared in 1937, was far more than a prosaic study in business history. It stated a theme that was to become fundamental to all of Creighton's work: the belief that the St Lawrence River and lakes system was the inspiration of transcontinental dominion. The conception of the empire of the St Lawrence was discovered through a subtle interaction of Creighton's own research and his intuition and imagi-

nation, which eludes precise analysis. But it was also rooted in the intellectual life of the 1930s. It drew upon the work of other scholars and it was
shaped by Creighton's essentially literary approach to history.

Creighton's greatest debt was to the economic history of Harold Innis.
Innis admired Creighton's articles on the conflicts of agriculture and commerce in Lower Canada and took a personal interest in his work. He suggested, for example, that Creighton read Marion Newbigin's *Canada: the
Great River, the Lands and the Men* and in it Creighton found a lesson on
how to write a study around a geographical entity. He was especially taken
by Newbigin's description of the natural geographical divisions of North
America in terms of river valleys and their drainage basins and by her arguments that these natural divisions were not separated from each other
by impassable barriers, that at critical points the divisions could easily be
surmounted. This left room to calculate the effect of human will and effort
as well as the determinism of nature. Creighton reviewed Innis's *The Fur
Trade in Canada* in his father's journal in 1931 and found particularly intriguing the conclusion that Canada became a political reality not in spite
of economic laws and geography but because of them.[9] Innis's study of the
formative role of the fur trade in shaping Canadian development was the
most important single intellectual influence on the evolution of
Creighton's own views of Canadian history. The themes that Innis had
isolated—the organization of the nation around the waterways, the centralized character of Canada's institutions, the crucial place of staple commodities, Canada's dependance on metropolitan markets, the instability
and vulnerability of her economy, the North West Company as the predecessor of Canada itself—were all eventually incorporated in Creighton's
own work. Though he built upon the foundations that Innis had laid, however, the resulting structure was different in many ways. It is true that
Creighton made the conceptions of Innis literate and dramatic, but his
contribution was far more than an extended and elegant footnote to Innis's
economic history. Innis was the economic historian searching out the patterns and dynamics of economic development; his concern was with the
peculiar effects of the trade in various staples and with the broad interrelations between geography, technology, and the pulls of British, and later
American capitalism. His ultimate interest was in generalizing about the
unique patterns of the economic growth of new countries that had developed in relation to old countries. Creighton, on the other hand, had come
to Canadian history not through economics but from literature and history, and he retained the historian's traditional concern with government
and politics. His main stress was on the interplay between politics and
commerce, on the clash of interest groups and the political alignments of
such groups. While Innis sought in economic history a contribution to a
more adequate theory of growth, Creighton advanced an economic interpretation of politics.

Creighton was indebted to Newbigin's geography as well as to Innis's economic history. But it was his artistry and his literary conception of history that fused what he borrowed with what he discovered into a book that was uniquely his own. *The Commercial Empire of the St Lawrence* was a triumph of literary art—not just in the superficial sense of being pleasingly and evocatively written but rather because its essential design and shape derived from literary models. As the economic historian Herbert Heaton shrewdly pointed out, it was in fact a play in three acts.[10] The geography of northern America—the stage—was described at the outset and the main protagonist introduced. For Creighton the St Lawrence River, the only great river that led from the eastern seaboard into the heart of the continent, was not just another feature of the landscape that invited, deflected, or defied human effort. It was a sentient and active participant in the story, the chief actor in the drama of history. From the river, Creighton wrote,

> there arose, like an exhalation, the dream of western commercial empire. The river was to be the basis of a great transportation system by which the manufactures of the old world could be exchanged for the staple products of the new. This was the faith of successive generations of northerners. The dream of the commercial empire of the St Lawrence runs like an obsession through the whole of Canadian history; and men followed each other through life, planning and toiling to achieve it. The river was not only a great actuality: it was the central truth of a religion. Men lived by it, at once consoled and inspired by its promises, its whispered suggestions, and its shouted commands; and it was a force in history, not merely because of its accomplishments, but because of its shining, ever-receding possibilities.[11]

The dream the river evoked in the minds of those who responded to its promptings was the desire to build a commercial empire in the interior of the continent—an empire that was based on the river system and on the metropolitan markets in Europe, and that was in direct competition with the southern routes.

The first act ran from the Conquest to the reconstruction of the fur trade by the Anglo-American merchants and then down to 1783, when the treaty that concluded the American Revolution artificially cut away the Ohio and Mississippi Valleys from Canada and thereby destroyed forever the 'natural development of the . . . commercial state'.[12] The second act began with the attempt to extend the trading system in the Northwest and with the migration of the Loyalists and the efforts to rebuild the trading system on the new staples of wheat and wood. But again the dream was frustrated by the political division of the colonies in 1791, which flew in the face of their geographical unity; by the emergence of the conflict between agriculture and commerce; and by the unification in 1821 of the two fur-trade companies, which broke the connection with the West. In the third act the conflicts in the Canadas intensified and exploded in the rebellions. One final and concerted attempt was made to reassert the primacy of the St Lawrence system and to capture the trade of the middle-west through the union of 1841, the building of canals, and a political campaign to maintain the protected imperial market and free trade in the interior of North America. But this strategy also failed. It was defeated by the abolition of the old preferential system, the triumph of the American trade routes and railways, and the loss of the merchants' political power. 'The years 1783 and 1821', Creighton wrote, 'had each brought down the curtain of an act; but 1849 meant the conclusion of an entire drama.'[13] The finality of this termination was highlighted by the flames above the Parliament buildings in Montreal and by the annexation manifesto in which the merchants turned their backs on their own past.

The men of commerce were overcome by many forces, but Creighton made clear that their efforts had been mainly obstructed by the river itself, which had inspired their ambitions and captured their imaginations. For the river had a fatal defect: 'It was like a great, healthy, powerful organism spoilt by an incongruous weakness.'[14] For miles it moved slowly and easily, and then its course was broken by rocks and rapids. It was vulnerable also to invaders from the south, for the barriers that separated it from the Hudson Valley were easily surmounted. As in classic tragedy the St Lawrence was defeated by a flaw in its own makeup.

In Creighton's book the river was a colossal presence, men were Lilliputians in comparison. Living on its shores and responding to its dictates, they were but frail instruments of its purposes. Ultimately their hopes were dashed on its rocks. The feeling that pervaded Creighton's narrative had much in common with that evoked by the paintings of the Group of Seven. The landscapes of a northern terrain, for the most part without human figures, moulded the national character. What the painters had only implied, Creighton (and Innis) documented historically. The landscape of river, lakes, and Shield was the matrix of Canadian institutions, economics, and national hopes.

Very soon after completing his study of the commercial empire, Creighton elaborated on its meaning for the founding of modern Canada. Reviewers had pointed out that the finality and conclusiveness of the collapse of 1849 had been exaggerated by Creighton's dramatic technique.[15] Creighton himself was fully aware that, though mercantilism had been destroyed, the business class continued to exist, and that in the 1850s it substituted for the older strategy based on canals the building of railways. What had happened in 1849, he explained, was that the 'irrepressible urge to territorial expansion and material conquest, which the St Lawrence had planted in successive generations of its sons, had . . . been frustrated in its original course . . . .' But there was another channel in which these impulses could move, and after a period of groping, that new direction was found. The connecting link between the death of the old commercial empire and the creation of Canada in 1867 was the political instrument of the merchant class, the Tory party shorn of its anti-French bias and dedicated to a different variant of the ancient theme. 'The new Tories', Creighton explained, 'helped to create a new and different variant of the old conception of the St Lawrence as a unified and competitive entity in North America .... They substituted economic nationalism for international commercialism; they replaced the old colonial economy by a federal union of the provinces.'[16] The new dominion, like the old commercial state, had its financial and commercial focus in the cities of the St Lawrence, and the railways, western settlement, and tariffs were the three agencies designed to forge its unity. The imperialistic ambition for western dominance was the driving force of the new country, just as it had been characteristic of the St Lawrence since the fur trade. In short, Canada was a substitute, or a kind of successor state, to the commercial empire that had come crashing down in 1849. This belief was to remain fundamental to all of Creighton's subsequent writing.

There were other implications in Creighton's work in the later 1930s that were of particular significance to that decade and were rooted in its particular problems. Creighton was not typical of a number of politicized social scientists and university intellectuals in the thirties who debated the reform of the capitalist system in the League for Social Reconstruction; or Canadian foreign policies in the Canadian Institute for International Affairs; or both at Couchiching conferences and on the talk programs of the CBC. Of course Creighton was interested in the larger issues of national policies. Like Innis, he leaned towards an isolationist position in foreign affairs and believed that Canada's contribution to collective security should be limited. Generally Creighton remained aloof from direct participation in political discussion, partly because of temperament, partly because of Innis's advice. But even though he did not editorialize in his publications, his work had an indirect bearing on two major questions of the Depression period.

The problems of the Canadian colonies in the 1820s and 1830s that Creighton analysed at length were not remote and unfamiliar to Canadians in the thirties: they were in fact easily recognizable and immediate. The political division of the old province of Quebec in 1791 had defied its physical and commercial unity; the difficulties of divided jurisdiction had frustrated efforts to improve the St Lawrence system. That river was the basis for Canadian unity, and those who had responded to its needs had always worked, as did the merchants in 1821 and 1840, to align the constitutional system with this reality. The situation Canadians confronted in the 1930s was not unlike that of a hundred years before. At a time when there was an obvious and pressing need for a strong central government to deal with the economic collapse, the powers of the federal government were weak and inadequate. Creighton's book—in which he stressed the incompatibility of a divided jurisdiction and geographical unity—appeared in the same year that R.B. Bennett's new-deal legislation was declared beyond the sphere of authority of the parliament of Canada. What was implicit in Creighton's account was elaborated in a study he prepared for the Rowell-Sirois Commission in 1939. Unlike Innis, who had an almost instinctive aversion to concentrations of power, Creighton made the strongest possible case for the view that the Fathers of Confederation had intended the national government to possess the full panoply of power and had envisaged provincial administrations as mere municipal councils. Their clear intentions had been subverted mainly by the English jurists on the Judicial Committee of the Privy Council, and in all of Creighton's work there are few who are treated with more irony and scorn than these pathetic creatures who misread the unambiguous language of the Confederation debates and the British North America Act. The case for centralization was a popular one with intellectuals in the 1930s, and it was to remain at the core of Creighton's view of Canadian history. For him it was obvious in the records of Confederation, but even more importantly it was sanctioned by the needs of the St Lawrence empire.[17]

The other inference in *The Commercial Empire of the St Lawrence*, and one that was to remain equally central to Creighton's later work, was the belief in the creative role of the business class. In the atmosphere of the Depression, when everything took on political connotations, it was possible to see Creighton's history as reformist history because the economic interpretation of the past was so frequently allied with the outlook of the left. Herbert Heaton confessed that he found in Creighton a perfect practitioner of the Marxist approach and thought of recommending his book to the Left Book Club. The burden of Creighton's case, however, was rather different. He had begun his work with the deliberate decision to examine the tensions in Lower Canada from the perspective of the commercial class, and that original decision had cumulative effects. He not only analysed and explained the aims of that class; he embraced and celebrated its purposes. Through their daily encounters with the material realities of northern America, members of the business community became essentially modern Canadians. 'At that time', Creighton wrote of their reaction to the treaty of 1783, 'the merchants were the only Canadians in the modern sense of that term; they alone thought in terms of a distinct and continental northern state.'[18] The merchants were the creative and progressive group who imparted élan and direction to their society. It followed that those who opposed their aims—the Upper Canadian agrarian community or the spokesmen of French-Canadian nationalism—were not only reactionary in rejecting the commercial state but were also either indifferent or hostile to the larger implications in the programs they resisted. In Creighton's pages the reformers cut ridiculous figures; it was appropriate, he commented on Mackenzie's insurgency, that a rebellion concocted in a brewery should end ingloriously in a tavern.

Creighton's point of view set him apart from those historians who attempted to link the radicalism of the thirties to its antecedents. Frank Underhill sought to give the CCF a sense of place and legitimacy by tracing back the reform tradition to its nineteenth-century origins. And Stanley Ryerson attempted to give the Communist party a historical position in Canada by going back to the Mackenzie-Papineau radicals and depicting the revolts of 1837 as the beginning of the overthrow of feudal remnants by a rising capitalist class.[19] It was significant that, while Underhill was delivering his interpretation of the history of Canadian political parties to LSR and CCF groups, Creighton made one of his few public appearances to lecture the Canadian Bankers' Association on the economic crisis of 1837 and its consequences.[20] The thrust of Creighton's argument was that the business class not only represented a higher form of economic enterprise but was the bearer of the national idea.

By the early forties Creighton had established the conception of the St Lawrence system as the ancestor of modern Canada. In his survey, *Dominion of the North* (1944), he extended the idea backwards into the French régime, portraying the Intendant Talon as yielding to the invitations of the St Lawrence, and advanced it into the period after Confederation. At this point he thought of either writing a history of New France or pursuing the theme into the later nineteenth century. Innis, who perhaps suspected that Creighton's treatment would resemble Parkman's, suggested that the Old Régime had been done and urged Creighton instead to take up the life of Macdonald. Macdonald appealed to Creighton's imagination mainly because his career satisfied the literary demand for a central and important character acting on a wide stage, and also because Creighton had come to see Macdonald as the custodian of the idea of the empire of the St Lawrence. 'Back of him,' he wrote of Macdonald in 1944, 'was the ancient urge, which had persisted in the St Lawrence region ever since the French régime, towards a strong and centralized political union—a union which would be allied with Great Britain and independent of the United States.'[21] The French fur traders and Talon had responded to the solicitations of the river; the merchant class had tried and failed to erect a commercial empire; the makers of Confederation reconstructed the old commercial system in political form; and Macdonald gave it substance in his national policies. The biography of Macdonald, which engrossed

Creighton's attention for over a decade and appeared as *The Young Politician* in 1952 and *The Old Chieftain* in 1955, was a direct and logical extension of his early work.

III

The life of Macdonald was a strategically significant work both in the development of Creighton's historical thought and in the evolution of Canadian historical writing generally. Above all it marked the beginning of a revival of interest in a type of historical literature that had been disregarded in the past and that was later to become the dominant form in Canadian historiography. Since 1920 the main task of the biographer—the revelation of character and personality in history—had been neglected for a variety of reasons. Some of the early professional historians associated biography with all the shortcomings of the stuffy, panegyrical, and commemorative life and times written in the Victorian period. Alexander Mackenzie's glorification of George Brown, or Castell Hopkins' deferential life of Sir John Thompson were typical of an entire genre. Both writers were reticent about the private lives and inner feelings of their subjects; they commemorated rather than explained their heroes and aimed at exemplifying 'character' for the edification of the young. In the late nineteenth century the writing of biography was constrained by a mania for good taste, respectability, and decorum. Custodians of family traditions jealously stood guard against even moderately critical appraisals of their ancestors, as William Le Sueur discovered when he was prevented through threatened legal action from publishing his study of William Lyon Mackenzie by the rebel's grandson. The twenty-volume Makers of Canada series, written by an assortment of journalists, literary men, amateurs, and a few professional historians, and published between 1903 and 1908, was the climax of the Victorian practice of biography in Canada.

In the two decades after 1920 the writing of lives suffered a curious fate. On the one hand the careers of a number of political figures were examined. Those who wrote of men involved in the struggle for responsible government, however, were more concerned with the biography of the state than with their subjects' own natures. The personal character of Skelton's Laurier was subordinated to the history of the Liberal party and the politics of compromise. Even later, Longley's *Hincks* and Wilson's *Baldwin* were not so much evocations of character as examinations of political history contained within a biographical framework. 'Are there really biographies of Baldwin, Hincks, and Laurier,' Creighton asked in 1948, 'or are these merely lives of Robert Responsible-Government and Francis Responsible-Government, and Wilfrid Responsible-Government?'[22] While the inter-war period in some way witnessed a continuation of the Victorian tradition, it was also touched by a more sceptical spirit that was hostile to romantic hero-worship. Lytton Strachey's *Eminent Victorians* was admired in certain circles for its irreverence and iconoclasm and its merciless exposure of the real motives of the idols of a discredited generation. In the United States and Europe debunking biographers endeavoured to undermine the fame of history's heroes and, sometimes, to build up the villains. 'They tried', wrote one historian of the craft, 'to make the intelligent seem stupid, the dignified foolish, the earnest hypocritical, and the humble vain. They dwelt upon petty idiosyncracies, physical ailments, inconsistent or eratic behaviour . . . . '[23]

This iconoclastic temper expressed itself in Canada in a more tepid and limited fashion, leading in most cases not to full-scale biographical works but rather to revisionist essays. The first people to be closely scrutinized in this manner were figures whom the late-nineteenth-century romantic nationalists had put up on pedestals. W.S. Wallace challenged the legend of Laura Secord. Two McGill historians—William Waugh in his *James Wolfe, Man and Soldier* (1928), and E.R. Adair—deflated the reputation of the dauntless hero, showing him to have been snobbish, rash, and untrustworthy, possessing no special military abilities, few social graces, and, in Adair's words, suffering from a 'social inferiority complex'.[24] The literary scholar J.A. Roy refused to pass silently over Joseph Howe's earthy gusto or his interminable and unseemly importunities for imperial recognition and position.[25] As we have seen, the hypercritical Adair subsequently examined one of the most cherished myths of the French-Canadian nationalists and found Dollard, the saviour of French Canada, to have been an ordinary mortal, a fur trader, who through mismanagement and bad luck was accidently slaughtered by avenging Iroquois. It was A.L. Burt who best summed up the thrust of this new impulse when in a paper on Guy Carleton, Lord Dorchester—whom he characterized as autocratic in disposition, treacherous in temper, and unscrupulous in concealing his own mistakes—wrote that 'Tradition made Carleton divine; research makes him human.'[26]

The economic interpretation of history was even less hospitable to biography. In the thirties the interests of historians and other social scientists converged on the large, impersonal factors that played upon the past and relegated a concern with individuals to a subsidiary position. Moreover, the interplay between economic forces and politics suggested a way of reinterpreting the motives behind the behaviour of politicians. One historian complained of the 'conspiracy of silence' with which John A. Macdonald's biographers passed over the relationship between political activity and economic reality.[27] Another, J.B. Brebner, explained that patronage and the struggle for the spoils of office had much to do with the politics of responsible government, a struggle that Chester Martin had made appear as the unfolding of a great ideal through the activities of pragmatic men.[28]

The reaction against history as the sway of impersonal forces and the tendency to search out the foibles and ignoble motives of men set in during the late thirties and was enormously strengthened in the forties. Underhill, who had once dismissed politicians as the mouthpieces of economic interests, turned to a study of Edward Blake. In 1937 the classicist C.B. Sissons published the first volume of *Egerton Ryerson: His Life and Letters*. Scholarly interest in biography represented a determination to delimit the dominance of material forces and a desire for a more intimate, human, and vivid experience of the past. 'History', Creighton wrote in 1945, 'is not made by inanimate forces and human automatons: it is made by living men and women, impelled by an endless variety of ideas and emotions, which can best be understood by that insight into character, that imaginative understanding of people which is one of the great attributes of literary art.'[29] The growing respectability of biography implied not merely a shift from one mode of writing history to another but a profound change in the way the past itself was conceived. Biography became a vehicle for reasserting the ability of men to make their own history. Fascism and then Communism were threats to the democratic belief in the importance of the individual, and these challenges may have contributed to a renewed concern with the single person in history.[30] Perhaps the intensification of cultural nationalism in the late forties and early fifties may also have affected biography, for it was a perfect instrument for recapturing those traditions and values that the Massey Commission said were as necessary for the defence of the west as armaments.

In Creighton's case biography was also associated with the assertion of the autonomy of history as a distinct form of intellectual enterprise, with its own procedures and modes of understanding. In the early stages of his work on Macdonald he read R.G. Collingwood's *The Idea of History* (1946) in which the English philosopher advanced a strong case for the distinctiveness of history in relation to the social sciences. The autonomy of history was defined by the chief task of the historian: the reconstruction and reënactment of past thought and activity in his own mind. Collingwood became one of Creighton's favourite philosophers of history because he sharpened his perception of the literary quality of history and its separateness from economics, sociology, and political science. Ironically the growth of biography was the historian's contribution to the break-up of the social-science tradition.

When Creighton spoke of all history as being contemporary history he meant this not only in Collingwood's terms, that the historian rethinks past thoughts in relation to his contemporary world. The contemporaneity of history implied that it must be so constructed that at any given time actors in the past were faced with a future that was as opaque and unpredictable as our own futures. To recreate the unknown future as men in the past knew it would make their world, imaginatively, our own. Such was the distinctive role of historical biography.

During the fifties and early sixties some of Canada's leading historians, and younger scholars as well, devoted their best efforts to political biography. Creighton's *Macdonald* was followed by William Kilbourn's study of the fiery and mercurial William Lyon Mackenzie and the tragicomedy of 1837; by Kenneth McNaught's life of J.S. Woodsworth, the saintly conscience of reform in Canadian politics; and by John Gray's *Selkirk*. William Eccles continued the anti-romantic tradition of his mentor, E.R. Adair, in his appraisal of Frontenac, who always seemed on the lookout for the main chance to recoup his fortunes and restore himself in courtly favour. After discovering George Brown's family papers in Scotland, J.M.S. Careless turned to a full-scale life of the editor of the *Globe* that brought together his concerns with the intellectual history of mid-Victorian liberalism, party politics, and the metropolitan influence of Toronto. A survey of the career of Mackenzie King by the veteran journalist Bruce Hutchison was followed by an iconoclastic book by H.S. Ferns and Bernard Ostry, who found in the Liberal leader's early career little to admire and much to censure, and then by the official and more formalistic biography by the political scientist R. MacGregor Dawson. Roger Graham devoted three volumes to King's great rival and antagonist Arthur Meighen. In George Stanley's life of Riel, the Métis leader appeared not simply as the misguided exponent of a frontier revolt but also as a tortured conscience visited by incredible visions, teetering on the edge of madness. With these and other studies, and with the launching of the monumental *Dictionary of Canadian Biography* in 1966, biography became a dominant form in historical studies.[31]

The best of these biographies synthesized detailed studies of political history, ideas, and attitudes with sensitive portraits of character. The new biography highlighted the fortuitous, the unexpected, and the vagaries of human nature. None of these books was directly informed—or marred—by any explicit application of psychological theories, Freudian or otherwise, though historians were probably alert in a general fashion to the truth that for the interpretation of personality, nothing—no statement or detail—was irrelevant. Creighton paid a good deal of attention to Macdonald's domestic tragedies and to the pressures that lay behind his drinking. Careless attributed the transformation of Brown from an uncompromising sectional voice of Upper Canada into a mellower, more constructive advocate of federal union to his marriage to Anne, the 'mother of Confederation'.

Biographies made history more human and colourful and thereby brought historical scholarship closer to the reading public. One student of Canadian culture was surprised to learn that Hutchison's *The Incredible Canadian* had sold fifteen thousand copies within its first year of publication, and that ten thousand copies of Creighton's first volume on Macdonald had been printed. He was led to wonder whether the Massey Commission's rather bleak estimation of the prospects of the writer in Canada was entirely justified.[32]

Biography, like all historical writing, both illuminates and distorts. It is a branch of history but it is not the same thing as history. History deals in generalizations about groups, institutions, and movements in time and is more than a mosaic of lives. Biography deals with the particularities of a human being and seeks to simulate, through narrative, an individual's life.[33] The 'historian who writes biography', wrote one practioner, 'may have to compromise some principles if he is to succeed in his avocation.'[34] The task of revealing a single life may subordinate and therefore oversimplify the complexity of historical controversies.[35] The necessary empathy with one's subject that the form demands may lead to the assimilation of a single perspective and outright partisanship. To the apologist for biography, however, history conceived as innumerable lives contains its own checks and balances because the re-creation of many biographies restores and recaptures the conflicts of wills and personalities. Because biography is precluded from answering certain questions about mass action and social patterns, it may well be the kind of history that a people untroubled by deep social divisions or economic problems prefers to read.

Creighton's *Macdonald* was not only an early indication of the revival of biographical writing in Canada but it contributed to the growing respectability of the genre and became the standard against which succeeding lives were measured. It was more than a political biography, for in the writing of these two volumes Creighton brought together his most intense convictions about Canadian history as well as his personal vision of history as a literary art.

The life of Macdonald was at once a study of character and a way of carrying forward into the later nineteenth century the analysis of the interrelated nation-building policies inspired by the St Lawrence: the political creation of Confederation, the transcontinental railway, the tariff, the strong central government, and the Anglo-Canadian alliance. The biography was also a demonstration of Creighton's belief that history's true kinship was with imaginative literature. His own allegiances had never been given completely to the social-science tradition of Innis. His affinities were rather with modern English historians like G.M. Trevelyan, who had protested against the dull scientism of modern historiography; with those nineteenth-century novelists—Dickens, Balzac, and Zola—who were secretaries of their age; and with the modern Americans, Faulkner and Dos Passos. Back of all Creighton's work lay a creative impulse that could never have been satisfied with monographic analytical studies of discrete problems. His profoundest desire was to be a writer; he experimented with writing fiction throughout the thirties and early forties and later described himself as a 'novelist manqué'. In many respects Creighton's work most closely resembles not that of his Canadian contemporaries but the romantic history of Francis Parkman.

The romantic movement had given an enormous impetus to the development of the historical imagination and to efforts to comprehend the past in its own terms. The romantic historian did not start with a question that led to analysis; he thought of history as a drama and he sought to tell a story. He searched for a significant theme in which a large number of interesting individuals acted on a wide stage and he tried to communicate the drama of the story through narrative. He thought of himself as a literary artist painting a canvas with pictorial fidelity and re-creating the past in all its vividness and vitality. The romantic historian had a strong sense of locality, a feeling for the association of events with specific places, and he was alert to detail—the weather, the character of rooms, the angle of the sun—that imparted an authentic setting to his tale. He did his research as assiduously and as exhaustively as any devotee of the cult of scientific history, but the facts and impressions were put into a mould derived from imaginative literature.[36]

In his *Commercial Empire of the St Lawrence* Creighton borrowed the device of the stage play that unfolded in terms of plot, character, scenes, climaxes, interludes, and resolutions. He appropriated from the naturalistic novelists the idea of an organic entity or symbol that gave unity to a segment of reality. And he had been inspired also by the pithy and succinct summaries of character in the biographical essays and books of Lytton Strachey and Philip Guedalla.

Though his biography of Macdonald was set within the historical biographical framework, Creighton's attempt to recreate a life and milieu owed as much to techniques derived from romantic history and literature and music as it did to contemporary academic historiography. The most arresting feature of his two volumes was that an entire age and its political history were not merely ordered around Macdonald, but that readers saw the whole scene through his eyes alone. (After Macdonald imbibes too much, we even share the unsettling sense of the floor shifting.) As in the romantic histories and Wagnerian opera, which Creighton greatly admired, characters were not merely human beings; they personified elemental forces, principles, and ideas. Macdonald was above all the custodian of the dream that the St Lawrence River inspired. In the *Commercial Empire of the St Lawrence* the river was the chief protagonist, at once prompting, inspiring, and frustrating the purposes of men; in the biography we catch only fleeting glimpses of the River of Canada, but images of it recur, like the leitmotif in an opera, sufficiently often to remind us that it is the ultimate source of the national design that Macdonald promoted. The action takes place on the level of thought, conscious intentions, and the conflicts of individuals; the impulses the river inspired have become embedded in the instincts, emotions, and habits of men. The theme of the empire of the St Lawrence is the same, but it is carried to a new movement and transformed.

The chief protagonist is thus not a politician like the others. 'Macdonald', Creighton wrote, 'represented Kingston; and Kingston stood at the head of the St Lawrence River, at the foot of the vast inter-connecting system of the Great Lakes ... the main task of Macdonald's entire career was to defend and enlarge the political union which the St Lawrence required and to realize the possibilities which it seemed to promise.'[37] Those who placed themselves in opposition to Macdonald's program—Confederation, which he alone had grasped in its totality; the strong central government; the protective tariff; the CPR—were therefore depicted as having turned their backs on the design he represented. We come to see his enemies as he saw them: dangerous opponents, men of narrow vision fundamentally at odds with the building of a transcontinental nation. Their defence of local interests, or their criticisms of the costs of the nation-building policies, are not so much explained as dismissed. The chief bias of biography—the oversimplification of the complexity of political action—was in this case reinforced by the identification of Macdonald with transcendent purposes. The vignettes of the secondary figures are strongly drawn: Brown is 'an awkward, red-haired, extremely tall, extremely serious young Scotsman of firm views, great ambitions, and superabundant physical energy ... a passionately serious dogmatist to whom all compromise and accommodation were alien and difficult.'[38] Blake is 'a legal and constitutional nationalist, deeply concerned about the remaining badges of Canada's subordination to the imperial Parliament and government. But for the other form of nationalism, which emphasized the territorial expansion and integration of the country, he had little more than a parochial Ontario suspicion.'[39] Joseph Howe in 1864-5 'brooded, his big face, with its rather coarse features, once ennobled by vitality and conviction, now dulled and heavy with care and disillusionment and fatigue.'[40] Of the rebellion in the West in 1885, Creighton's Macdonald wondered: 'Had Riel determined to pull down the heavens because his own private demands for money were ignored?'[41]

It was with some justification that Underhill noted that, though the biography was an artistic triumph, he found too little on the cut and thrust of Victorian partyism that had so alienated his intellectual hero, Goldwin

Smith. He would have been more impressed with it as a work of history if he did not so often discover 'that those political leaders who collided with Macdonald were not only intellectually deficient and morally delinquent but also physically repulsive.'[42] Macdonald seemed too elevated, too cerebral, and Underhill did not recognize the old chieftain who was alleged to have defined the politician as the little boy who climbs the tree to shake down the acorns to the hogs below.

In the pages of Creighton's biography the warfare between the intellectuals of the twenties and the Victorian era was prolonged. A typical romantic hero, Macdonald was at once representative of his age, knew Canadians better than anyone would ever know them again and expressed their inmost desires, yet he was isolated and not completely accepted. Creighton emphasized that Macdonald's lack of earnestness, his enjoyment of life, and his utter lack of moralizing led Victorian Canadians to misunderstand him and to refuse to take him seriously. It was perhaps this curious blending of Creighton's obvious sympathy for the old chieftain and his sarcastic treatment of those who considered him as only a gifted manipulator that provoked Hilda Neatby's criticism that Creighton compensated 'for a vein of cynicism by a vein of sentimentalism.'[43]

IV

The decade in which Creighton was absorbed with Macdonald was a time of reorientation in Canadian historical studies and change in Canada's international position. The world of Sir John A. Macdonald that he was imaginatively reconstructing and the Canada of the late forties and early fifties intersected, touched, and melded together. The historian who immersed himself in the past until he saw the texture of his subjects' clothes and heard them talking, even predicted what they were going to say, came to see his present in conjunction with another age, as vital and in some ways as contemporary as his own. The Macdonald biography was the result of this complex interaction: it embodied a relived past and also conveyed implications for the period in which it was written.

Creighton turned to Macdonald as a rewarding subject for historical and literary, not partisan, reasons. In the forties, as in the thirties, he was, if not completely indifferent to contemporary politics, at least not actively and emotionally engaged in either current affairs or political commentary. Certainly he was no devoted adherent of the Tory party. He recalled that he voted for Mackenzie King in 1935 and again in 1940: in 1944 he was at the Public Archives in Ottawa beginning his research at the climax of the conscription controversy, and, as historians are wont to do, wondered how future scholars would interpret the episode.

During the Second World War Creighton's public attitude to Canada's participation and its closer associations with the United States was unexceptionable. When Underhill was in trouble at the University of Toronto over his speech on the significance of the Ogdensburg agreement of 1940, Creighton told him that his was a pretty temperate analysis of what seemed the obvious implications.[44] In 1945, like most thoughtful Canadians, Creighton was moderately hopeful that Canada would maintain its newly established position in the English-speaking world, co-operating with the two roughly balanced forces that had shaped all its history: the United States and the British Commonwealth. The Dominion, he then wrote, was a North American nation, separate and distinct from the United States but linked to its southern neighbour by economic interests and social bonds, attitudes, and values, and countless ties of friendship. The Permanent Joint Board of Defence of 1940 was based not on American hegemony but on common convictions about security and the acceptance of equality. The other side of the balance, the Commonwealth, had come into existence as an *entente* of sovereign states in large part because of Canada's efforts. Balanced between these twin historic forces, Canadian policy in the future was expected to mediate between, and further the co-operation of, the English-speaking peoples in the world at large.[45]

While Creighton may have had private reservations about the economic and military agreements with the United States at the time—as he later insisted—it was nonetheless only in the late forties and especially in the early fifties that his criticisms became vocal and explicit. Together with Innis, he became more and more apprehensive about the curtailment of Canada's freedom of action in foreign policy and by the infringements on its sovereignty that cold war military co-operation entailed. 'Good relations with the republic must continue to be a most important objective of our foreign policy,' he said in 1953, 'but good Canadian-American relations will not necessarily enable Canada to make its own contribution to the solution of the world's crisis, and may actually prevent it from doing so.' The notion of the solidarity of the free world led by the United States was a specious slogan based on 'hysterical dogmatism'. Canada's own foreign policy, Creighton advised, should be based on the acceptance of communist régimes where they prevailed and a desire to seek accommodations with them, a recognition of the implications of the revolution in Asia, and a determination to work through the alliance with Western Europe, the Commonwealth, and the United Nations.[46] What bothered him most of all was the pliant and generally unquestioning acceptance by Canadians of American leadership and the excessive moralism of redemptionary internationalism. 'In Europe', he wrote, 'NATO is a collective defensive enterprise; but in North America it is a two-power organization in which Canada can accept only the assistance, and the direction, of the United States. In the north, Americans build and man our radar installations, and in the east, in Newfoundland and Labrador, they hold and occupy military bases. The foreigner sits firmly astride the eastern approaches to our country; and the base, a primitive form of military imperialism, grimly questions Canada's claim to control her own destiny.'[47]

Creighton's strictures on American imperialism were based on his wish that Canada would pursue a more independently minded external policy, not on any sympathy for communism with which some, including John Diefenbaker, charged him. In Creighton's mind an independent foreign policy had to rest on a more adequate perception of Canadian history and a reassertion of principles that had guided its leaders in the past. This, in fact, was exactly what the work of Macdonald provided. Lest the full import of Macdonald's purposes was obscured by the luxuriant detail of the biography, Creighton explained how Canadians of the fifties might find in his career 'a tract for the times'.[48] Macdonald's 'fundamental aim', Creighton wrote, 'was to protect Canada from the dangers of continentalism; and it is the dangers of continentalism, economic, political, military, which now seem to be pressing in upon us steadily and from every side.'[49] Macdonald's experiences in forestalling American designs on the west, his difficulties in the negotiation of the Treaty of Washington in 1871, and his battle with the continentalist Liberal party over the issue of freer trade with the United States, were recognizable to those perplexed by Canadian-American relations in the 1950s. Creighton hoped that a more general awareness of the fact that all Canadian history was a struggle for survival in North America, and that Macdonald had devoted his political career to ensuring independence from the United States, would impart to Canadians a more vigorous determination to ensure their separateness along lines consonant with tradition.

There was no doubt in Creighton's mind about the lesson to be drawn from Macdonald's foreign policy. The achievement of Canadian nationality, he argued, had been a dual process: emancipation from British imperial control and the maintenance of a separate political existence on the North American continent. The first goal had been achieved peacefully through compromises and adjustments, the second had been more difficult and was won through armed struggles in the American Revolution and the War of 1812. Creighton contended that the only great foreign policy Canada ever had was Macdonald's creation: the preservation of an autonomous nationality within North America by balancing the British connection—the Anglo-Canadian alliance—against American pressures. During the twenties and thirties, however, those who appropriated the title of Canadian nationalists deliberately departed from this historic prescription in an exaggerated and misguided pursuit of 'autonomy'. Theirs was a work of destruction which, in conjunction with the decline of Britain as a major influence and the end of the balance of power within the English-speaking world, only furthered the identification of Canada's interests with those of the United States.

It was from this vantage point, and with the outcome of recent history uppermost in his mind, that Creighton launched a comprehensive indictment of English-Canadian historical writing. His concern with isolating the various points of view that expressed themselves in literature relating to the past began in 1948, and ten years later his revisionism had assumed full form. In some respects his writings ratified and carried forward the changes in historical thinking that had occurred in the forties. Creighton insisted on disentangling history from its previous associations with the social sciences and restoring its autonomy. He appealed for a closer and more positive treatment of the ideas and values of Canadians who had built the country. In affectionately appraising the teachings of Harold Innis, he not only stressed that Innis had broken down the notion of the North American continent as an undifferentiated mass and emphasized Canada's dependence on Europe, but he also highlighted his mentor's distrust of the United States. In another way, however, Creighton's engagement with historiography was unique, personal, and followed directly from the conclusions he had reached during the course of his study of Macdonald.

Creighton directed his main complaints against what he called the 'Liberal interpretation', sometimes 'the authorized version', of Canadian history. The joint product of journalists like Dafoe, political scientists like Skelton and Dawson, and some historians, notably Arthur Lower, this interpretation had allegedly concentrated on a single theme: the growth of freedom from Britain through responsible government and the attainment of Dominion status. It reduced the history of the country to the tale of a 'stupendous crusade, mainly constitutional in character, by which Canada ascended from the degraded status of dependent colonialism to the serene heights of autonomous nationhood.'[50] This view, Creighton contended, was narrowly partisan, really a species of hagiology, and pernicious in its effects. It flourished in the inter-war period and expressed a dislike of Britain and a respectful admiration of the United States. At that time, Creighton wrote, Canadian writers 'sought instinctively to depress the importance of Europe as the source of Western civilization and to exalt the creative power of North America. . . . North America had become a faith; and what was needed was a cultural Book of Genesis which could serve as a first chapter in the new religion's Holy Writ.'[51] Creighton lampooned the resulting devotion to the frontier thesis (which he dubbed an American version of the myth of the noble savage) for its crude environmentalism, its glorification of the periphery of civilization, its parochialism, and its manifest inability to account for certain decisive episodes in the Canadian past, such as the rebellion in Upper Canada. He protested also against some of the volumes in the Carnegie Series for neglecting, or taking for granted, Canada's survival in North America, and for overemphasizing continental affinities. For another theory of historical change borrowed by colonially minded intellectuals in the thirties—the Marxian notion of class conflict—Creighton had even less patience.[52]

The liberal version of Canadian history, Creighton charged, misrepresented the main outlines of the past that appeared so clearly in the fifties. British military and diplomatic support had guaranteed Canada's survival in North America against American Manifest Destiny. Creighton believed that history written as an anti-imperialist struggle for responsible government blurred the sharp clashes within North America and so obscured Canadians' sense of their own distinct and quite separate interests on the continent that they had no basis for judging American claims objectively. It appeared enormously significant to Creighton that those who had been so exercised about autonomy and British imperialism in the thirties accepted the American version of the place of Canada in the 'free world alliance' and would not bestir themselves to question the implications of such 'cooperation' except to write the newspapers 'to denounce some misguided Canadian who has dared to criticize the Truman doctrine, or the Munroe doctrine, or the Hickenlooper doctrine, or some one of those policies with theological titles by which Americans like to indicate the intimacy of their partnership with God.'[53]

Creighton's dissent from a substantial strand in Canadian historiography, registered with a sarcasm reminiscent of H.L. Mencken, was at least as polemical as it was historical. He was not so much concerned with explaining the origins and evolution of this so-called liberal nationalist history as with the destructive frame of mind it represented. His own standard of judgement was the conception of Canadian history as a struggle for survival in North America, an idea that was rooted in his early work on commercial rivalries and pervaded his books on Macdonald. At times Creighton's treatment of Canadian historiography bore a striking resemblance to his accounts of Macdonald's encounters with his enemies.

Creighton's disapproval of the tendencies in Canadian foreign policy and of the historiographical tradition that rationalized the course of modern Liberalism was bound up with a growing uneasiness about the long domination of the Liberal party in national affairs and the critical reappraisal of the legacy of Mackenzie King. Creighton had an intellectual affinity with a small circle of people who shared anxieties about certain features of Canadian politics. These included Eugene Forsey of the Canadian Labour Congress; the younger philosopher George Grant; the Toronto journalist Judith Robinson; two historians, William Morton of the University of Manitoba and Roger Graham of the University of Saskatchewan; and John Farthing, whose Freedom Wears a Crown (1957) sought to restore an appreciation of the constitutional monarchy and the British heritage of freedom as central to Canadian life. They were drawn together less by personal ties than by a common revulsion against the stagnation of political life in the early fifties and what they saw as the destructive nature of King's work. Their complaints touched many issues, but the central one was that, under King's leadership, traditional Canadian institutions had been undermined and traditional orientations abandoned.

It was Forsey, the constitutional expert, who most effectively documented the indictment that King had weakened the parliamentary system. A democratic socialist who had played a part in the League for Social Reconstruction and the founding of the CCF, and was a confidant of the former Conservative leader, Arthur Meighen, Forsey possessed both an immense knowledge of the constitution and a fastidious regard for the observances of customary practice. In 1943 he had published a detailed study of the 1926 constitutional crisis, *The Royal Power of Dissolution of Parliament in the British Commonwealth*, in which he demonstrated that Meighen, not King, had followed the correct constitutional precedents. Forsey had admired Meighen since the early twenties, and in the course of preparing his book their acquaintance ripened into a close friendship that was subsequently nourished by their mutual regard for the constitution and by their detestation of Mackenzie King. 'I do not know anyone except myself', Meighen told Forsey in 1941, 'who quite realizes the moral turpitude of Mackenzie King as you do . . . . One really gets discouraged about democracy in Canada when such sanctimonious and slimy sinuosity is crowned with success.'[54] By 1951 Forsey came to the conclusion that King had not really believed in parliamentary responsible government, and that through his resort to plebiscites, and his practice of governance that was presidential in all but name, he had subverted the position of Parliament. Forsey believed that King was moved by a profound contempt for the past and had developed a 'special talent for inventing fictitious precedents and disregarding real ones.'[55]

A vigilant guardian of constitutional proprieties, Forsey was also a kind of editor-at-large to the academic community. No one could rise to such heights of indignation over slipshod—or malicious—usage on matters relating to the constitution, the English language, or historical facts. He became legendary for book reviews announcing that he had compiled dozens of pages of errors, and for his letters to newspaper editors rebuking any lapses in correct practices. He was angered by the use of the word 'federal' to refer to the Government of Canada, and in 1952 he campaigned against dropping the designation 'Dominion of Canada' and the words 'Royal Mail'. Arthur Lower was tempted to think of Forsey as possessing a neat, secretarial type of mind typical of Canadians, but for Forsey these phrases were not mere words. They denoted a historical tradition and a mode of government that had been undermined by King and his successors. In 1952 Meighen, Farthing, Forsey, and some others thought of compiling a book of essays on the British tradition in Canada in protest against the 'Americanizing' tendencies of the St Laurent administration. Creighton was asked to furnish an article for it but on second thoughts concluded that his Macdonald was the best contribution to the cause.[56]

Forsey's censure of King's legacy was amplified in Roger Graham's three-volume biography of Arthur Meighen, which was begun around 1952 and completed in the next decade. Meighen was depicted as a man of principle who stated forcefully and unambiguously where he stood on major national issues. He tended to idealize political life and believed that the function of leadership was to clarify issues so that the electorate could make intelligent choices. Meighen was King's great antagonist and he was defeated, not because of the rigidity or inappropriatness of his thought or tactics, but because King had deliberately blurred issues, had sought to accommodate all varieties of interests and opinions into an omnibus and therefore meaningless party, and frequently invoked the cause of preserving national unity while deceitfully playing on anxieties for his own ends. In contrast to Underhill, who had come to see King's practice of consensus politics as the only kind of leadership possible in Canada, or the Ferns and Ostry critique of King's ambition and the essential fraudulence of his pretensions as a social reformer, Graham was critical of King's tendency to downplay real but divisive questions and to obscure rather than to clarify. The end product of King's style of politics was the creation and maintenance of a large national party that suffocated the vitality of political debate and the definition of policies.

The condemnation of King's bequests—the diminution of the status of Parliament, the stifling one-party state, and a wrong-headed foreign policy—were all related to the revival of the fortunes of the Conservative party of John Diefenbaker in the elections of 1957 and 1958. Forsey's essays, Creighton's recovery of forgotten alternatives, Farthing's lofty defence of the Crown, George Grant's association of the philosophy of liberalism with mass society, Graham's rehabilitation of Meighen, and the historical work of W.L. Morton (to be examined later) were to some degree responses to the mood of disaffection that lay behind Diefenbaker's appeal. These men were attracted to the Conservative leader not from simple and crude partisan feelings, but because he promised a deliverance from dull, aimless management and a return to tradition. Especially after the Liberal party's use of closure in the pipeline debate, which confirmed all of Forsey's observations about the disregard for parliamentary primacy, and after the Suez crisis revealed how far Canada had drifted from Britain, Diefenbaker appeared as the defender of the rights of Parliament and the Commonwealth association. The resonance between his appeal and the past—suggested at one level in his personal cult of Macdonald—led one journalist to observe that the Conservatives 'have taken power on a wave of a rediscovery of history'.[57]

Creighton had contributed a great deal to this rediscovery of another dimension of Canadian experience. His views, of course, were not identical with those of Forsey or the others, and he had come to his convictions by a different route. He did not, for example, exhibit to the same degree that combination of an interest in preserving traditional institutions with a concern for the well-being of the working classes that marked the outlook of Forsey and was to suggest to one political sociologist a 'red tory touch' in Canadian conservatism.[58] But for Creighton's admirers—like George Grant, who in 1965 called him 'the leading contemporary theorist of the conservative view of Canadian history'[59]—as well as for his critics, his works were associated with a party point of view. His books gave the Conservative party an ancestry and reinstated it in the mainstream of Canadian political history. This had not been his original intention and was hardly his main achievement. But by describing a pattern of interpretation as 'Liberal', Creighton himself identified some history—and, by implication, all history—with partisan commitments.

Yet the affinity between Creighton's literary imagination and his predispositions was far deeper than politics and in a way transcended parties. In essays where he made the meaning of his history most explicit, Creighton declared his rejection of self-sufficient and exclusive rationalism. The mysteries of human behaviour and history, he believed, could not be understood by constantly tearing up roots, subjecting the past to clinical dissection, or applying all-embracing ideologies. He spurned ideologies because they began with vast oversimplifications of human character and conduct. He employed religious imagery—'hot gospellers', 'authorized version', 'revelations'—to lace his sarcasm for theoreticians, doctrinaires, reformers, classical liberals, and all who judged by universal standards. He celebrated men like the Fathers of Confederation, who contented themselves with experience and the heritage at hand and did not attempt to plumb the depths of political theory or speculate on the rights of man. His Macdonald was neither a crusader with a mission nor a believer in abstract ideas. Macdonald 'was not a rationalist who believed that government was a series of general objectives which could be attained by the application of timeless and universal rules. He thumped no tubs and banged no pulpits. He was far too concerned with the intricate details of concrete complexities of human situations, to follow an ideal faithfully or to settle everything by scrupulous reference to a given set of rules. For him government was neither a quest for political justice nor an exercise in arithmetic.' It was a craft that was worked within tradition and conventions. The politician, Macdonald believed, 'should never aspire to the alien role of prophet, philosopher, or engineer.'[60]

In speaking of the role of humanistic education in the democratic state, Creighton sounded the authentic notes of Burkean conservatism. According to Creighton, Burke's view of society as a partnership between the generations was central to any understanding of the place of the humanities in the modern world. For the humanities 'exhibit humanity's hard-bought experience, its slowly gathered wisdom, its irreplaceable riches . . . . Their emphasis is necessarily and inevitably upon conservation rather than innovation; it is their business to guard, against the nihilism of rootless and disinherited marauders, the great traditions of a culture and the great traditions of a state.' Humanists know 'that in the interests of the future, a reconciliation will have to be made between the past and the present; but they believe that reconciliation is something in which the dead, the living and the unborn are all involved.'[61] Change must preserve continuities and must be instructed by experience—by history, not ideology. In this ongoing process the historian is the spokesman to the living on behalf of the dead.

This conviction is perfectly integrated in Creighton's conception of history. History will yield no understanding if it is approached as a problem in mechanical engineering; historical events are unique and therefore incomparable; the past has to be relived in relation to time, place, and circumstance; history is scientific at the research level, but in composition it is literary and artistic. Out of the encounter between character and circumstance comes experience—the only reliable guide in human and national affairs. History is thus a substitute for universalist ideology, and the historian becomes a mediator between generations.

V

In spite of Creighton's anxiety about the direction in which Canada was moving, he remained generally sanguine about the future. Like others whose hopes for a genuine Canadian culture were nourished in the twenties, he saw the Massey Commission and the Canada Council as concrete promises of a more vigorous creativity in literature that would give Canadians a stronger sense of identity and purpose. In 1957 he told an American audience that, though immediate circumstances had increased insecurity north of the border, 'our political survival is probably more certain now than it ever was before.'[62] No doubt Creighton's confidence was also sustained by the Diefenbaker victories of 1957 and 1958. He concluded his *Story of Canada* (1959) with allusions to Canada's first Elizabethan Age and the reuniting of the country in the election of 1958.

The period after the publication of Macdonald also marked Creighton's recognition as Canada's foremost historian. He won all the major literary awards and prizes and received numerous honorary degrees. In 1957 he was named joint editor of the multi-volume Canadian Centenary Series, and in 1960 he was appointed, by Harold MacMillan on Diefenbaker's nomination, to the Moncton Commission on the constitution of Rhodesia and Nyasaland. He wrote a section of the Commission's report that urged a decentralized federal system. In 1965 Creighton was appointed to the Ontario Advisory Committee on Confederation and in 1967 he was made a Companion of the Order of Canada.

In *The Road to Confederation. The Emergence of Canada: 1863-1867* (1964) Creighton told the story of how the movement for the union of British North America had succeeded in the face of an ever-present possibility of failure. Confederation was anything but an easy and automatic political achievement. An air of uncertainty hung over the whole enterprise; its successes were partial and provisional; and the setbacks it experienced might have permanently checked lesser leaders. The dramatic tension in Creighton's account derived from the rigid timetable that the Canadian coalition had placed on agreement for a general union. When obstacles and defeats impeded and delayed the drive for Confederation, the prospect was very real that the coalition would be forced back upon the more limited amalgamation of the Canadas alone. Creighton admirably succeeded in fulfilling one of his own demands of the narrative historian, that of making the world of actors of the past as unpredictable and open as the present and future seemed to his readers. There was, he said, nothing fixed and settled about Canadian nationhood.

Soon it appeared to him that the whole future of the country was in doubt. Like Grant and some other intellectuals, Creighton had been attracted to the Conservative party almost by default, and Diefenbaker's failure to live up to all their expectations was followed by a tremendous sense of lost opportunities, even of betrayal. Those who had hoped that the triumph of the Conservative party meant a return to, and a renewed respect for, those institutions and inheritances that liberalism had denigrated, felt baffled and thwarted by the Conservative leader's defeat. So great was the heartbreaking contrast between the hopes they had invested in him and the tribulations of his downfall that the result could only have been either a questioning of those fundamentals of Canadian nationalism that lay at the heart of Creighton's history or a gloomy pessimism about the capacity of Canadians to live up to them. George Grant expressed this mood perfectly in *Lament for a Nation* (1965), which was both an essay on recent Canadian history that explained Diefenbaker's contradictions and the continentalist forces arrayed against him, as well as a philosophical discourse on the insufficiencies of modern liberalism. Liberalism, with its definition of 'man as freedom' and its exaltation of material progress, was, he argued, the mass religion that led inexorably to the erosion of all historic loyalties and allegiances and to social and national 'homogenization'.

Creighton's *Canada's First Century* (1970) was, as W.L. Morton commented, the full orchestration of *Lament for a Nation*. A self-indulgent, brooding, and at times spiteful book, it was an impious parody of the whig-liberal history in which the present was invariably judged as a desirable culmination of past progress. In Creighton's narrative exactly the opposite was the case. Canadian history since the age of Macdonald culminated in the achievement of nationhood in the First World War—'the greatest experience that the Canadian people had ever known, or would ever know'[63]—and had since been characterized chiefly by the steady abandonment of those institutions and convictions that ultimately derived from the St Lawrence. The independent east-west transcontinental economy, strong central government, the Anglo-Canadian alliance, the understanding that cultural and linguistic rights were subordinate to survival, had all been betrayed or eroded by circumstance. Just as the commercial empire suffered from certain geographical obstacles and inadequacies that in the end defeated the merchants, so too the very physical character of Canada led to the integration of its economy with that of its historic competitor.

Like other English-Canadian historians of his generation, Creighton had always regarded separatist French-Canadian nationalism as retrogressive and undesirable. This did not mean that he had no sympathy with the preservation of a distinctive French culture within Canada as he understood it, or that he was unwilling to entertain the idea that, within certain limits, an attempt should be made to recognize bilingualism along the lines of the Preliminary Report of the Royal Commission on Bilingualism and Biculturalism. But he stressed the narrow limits within which the Fathers of Confederation had accorded the French language official recognition, and dismissed the idea of a bicultural compact underlying Confederation and extending westward as a myth. For implementing any constitutional reform that would accord Quebec special status, Creighton had nothing but contempt. At bottom he believed that the concern with linguistic rights and culture had been exaggerated out of all reasonable proportions, and that the 'obsession' with the Quiet Revolution was distracting attention away from dangers that threatened the nation as a whole.[64]

Separatist French-Canadian nationalism was an extreme form of provincialism. In all his works Creighton concentrated on the centre, not on the periphery of the country. The history of the commercial empire and the Macdonald biography were organized in relation to over-arching themes and patterns that enclosed and transcended groups, classes, or sections. He viewed with sarcastic disfavour both the growth of provincial powers and scholarly efforts concentrated on regional history. One can only contemplate with awe, he wrote of W.L. Morton's study of the Progressive party in the Social Credit series, at the monuments being erected to Henry Wise Wood and William Aberhart. 'In comparison with these gigantic literary edifices, the memorials of the trivial radicals and sectional leaders of the East will have all the appearances of a row of perfunctory little tombstones in a pauper graveyard.'[65] Provincialism and internationalism were the twin millstones between which national commitments and national history were being ground down.

What was so striking about *Canada's First Century* was the extent to which Creighton's pessimism rested on a moral revulsion against the long range effects of those commercial and business drives that he had once associated with the origins of the nation. 'The rapid growth of industrialism and urbanism in Canada and the increasing dependence of the Canadian people on the proliferating marvels of technology will gradually weaken and break down the native Canadian moral standards and cultural values, and undermine the inherited Canadian belief in an ordered and peaceful society and simple way of life.'[66] Like Grant, Creighton identified this heresy of progress with the United States. 'The Americans have escaped completely, or almost completely, from the mythical and religious explanations for existence which consoled the ancient and medieval world of Europe. They have come to believe, with fewer qualifications than any other people on earth, that progress is the only good in life, and that progress means the liberation of man through the progressive conquest of nature by technology.' It was this religion that Canadians accepted and for which they were willing to 'endure all the hideous evils of modern industrialization and urbanization'. The collapse of Creighton's Canada involved much more than the weakening of this or that national policy: the causes were in our minds and in our acceptance of the values of modernity and hedonism. We have met the enemy, he said, and it is ourselves.[67] Creighton wrote in the prophetic mode, as his father once did, recalling the moral standards from which Canadians had departed as well as the national policies they had abandoned. The hope for survival, he advised, lay in the reassertion of Canadian nationalism in its first integral form, but this seemed impossible. His readers appeared to be left with only the consolations of nostalgia.

Canada's First Century was the logical climax to certain tendencies in Creighton's thought, not some aberration produced by immediate and disappointing circumstances. It was a perfect fusion of his convictions, his conceptions of history, and his search for literary organizing principles that would give symmetry and shape to the past. Processes and ideas in history were identified with individuals. Goldwin Smith, O.D. Skelton, and above all Mackenzie King represented the obverse of Macdonald's design, which was carried to fruition by Borden. In each of his major books Creighton sought to give artistic form to a segment of the past, and taken together they possess a cohesive unity. The idea of the commercial empire of the St Lawrence is born out of man's responses to the geography of North America; it becomes the inspiration for the building of a nation under Macdonald; and then the nation is destroyed. The pattern is reminiscent of another book, also the product of pessimism, which Creighton greatly admired: Oswald Spengler's *The Decline of the West*, in which civilizations, like natural organisms, follow each other through the remorseless cycle of birth, flowering, decay, and death.

Creighton's histories were, if not entirely closed universes, at least self-sufficient ones in the same sense that a novel or a play is self-contained. Taking his models from the fiction, history, and music of the nineteenth and early twentieth centuries, he gave his books an internal richness, a dynamic, and a finality and completeness that, to some tastes at any rate, did not provoke wonderment and questioning but rather satiated the reader. There is little room in them for sceptically savouring the ironies of human intentions—such as the fact that it was in part the national policy of protection that invited and successfully attracted American branch plants into Canada—or indeed for questioning whether the precedents of history are so inviolable as virtually to prohibit adjustments to contemporary needs that men in the past did not anticipate.

Creighton's history was a monument to the belief that history was akin to drama, that it moved in accordance with the deeper truths contained in the very forms of literature and music—that history, in short, imitated art. And it is with this proposition that any comprehensive assessment of his achievement must begin.

10 | WILLIAM MORTON: THE DELICATE BALANCE OF REGION AND NATION

William Lewis Morton was one of the first major historians of Canada who brought to his field of study a perspective moulded by the cultural milieu of the prairie west. Of the leading modern historians of English Canada, Innis, Lower, and Underhill came from a rural or small-town setting in Ontario and Creighton from Toronto. Morton—along with his near-contemporary, Alberta-born George Stanley—possessed an exceptional feeling for the integrity and legitimacy of the western region and its localities; his sense of the plurality of Canadian life informed and shaped everything he wrote.

I

Morton's early associations were not with the old Canada of the St Lawrence Valley and the Maritime provinces but with loyalties that were English, imperial, and western. He was born in Gladstone, Man., in 1908. His grandparents had settled in 1871 on what was then the outer limits of the new province, an uninhabited area that within a decade became a settled society, dominated by the Ontario-born, with only a sprinkling of English, Scottish, and Irish immigrants, and overwhelmingly Protestant in religion. Though Morton was a third-generation Manitoban, he has recalled that in his home all points of reference and all standards were English, tempered only by a local variant of an intense imperial patriotism.[1] Other peoples—like the French, whose linguistic and school rights were swept away by the Greenway Liberal government that Morton's grandfather had been elected to support; or, later, the European settlers—were not accepted as equals.

Morton was educated in local schools, and for two years—between the ages of seventeen and nineteen—he worked on the family farm as a hired hand for one hundred dollars a month with room and board, and broke land with a horse-drawn plough. 'I was fortunate', he remembered, 'because I was among the last of millennial generations of men who followed the plough ... whose work fed household, village and city, and carried the fabric of civilisation on their sweating shoulders.'[2] In his last year as a farmhånd his father was elected to the Manitoba legislature as a Progressive and later supported the Bracken coalition in the thirties. The great outburst of agrarian protest that sent sixty-five members to the House of Commons in 1921 took place during Morton's most impressionable years. When he was twenty-two, the long-standing issue that fueled prairie resentment against Ottawa, the control of natural resources, was finally settled—only to be succeeded by Depression-generated protest movements that promised to destroy eastern economic dominion. The intensification of the prairie tradition of grievance, the feeling that a distant government treated the western farmer unjustly, left a deep imprint on his mind and was to sharpen his appreciation for western separateness.

The imperial orientation of his home and his education, however, kept that sense of separateness from degenerating into a mere parochialism. He entered the University of Manitoba as an older student and in 1932 was awarded a Rhodes Scholarship. At Oxford he took a course with the imperial historian, Vincent Harlow, on the expansion of the British peoples overseas, and completed his first foray into historical research: a study of the regulation of the Newfoundland cod fishery in the late eighteenth century. Partly inspired by John Dafoe, the editor of the *Winnipeg Free Press*, Morton at this time looked forward to a career in public life, preferably in journalism. He spent the summer of 1933 in Germany with an American fellow-student, Dean Rusk, in order to learn the language, and wrote an article for Dafoe's paper on the sense of purpose and direction that the early national socialist régime had given to the German people. Throughout the thirties he remained an isolationist, sceptical of British imperialism and convinced, as were many others, that Britain and France could contain Nazi Germany.

Morton returned to Manitoba in 1935, and after a succession of short appointments at the university and its affiliated colleges, Wesley and St Johns, as well as at Brandon, he found in 1942 a secure niche in the history department at the main campus, where he was to remain for almost twenty-five years. His keen interest in foreign policy drew him into the Winnipeg unit of the Canadian Institute for International Affairs. The war made him a complete convert to Dafoe's teachings on collective security. It also heightened his anxiety about the preservation of civil liberties. One of the few other organizations Morton joined was a local branch of the Canadian Civil Liberties Association. It was a measure of his profound concern with the rights of the individual that, in response to the King government's handling of the Gouzenko affair and the administration's apparent indifference to the legal traditions for which the war had been fought, he abandoned his family's and his own allegiance to the Liberal party and thereafter voted Conservative.

Morton's deep ancestral roots in Manitoba on the one hand, and the imperial flavour of his home, his education, and his concern with foreign policy and civil rights on the other, form the perimeters within which his thought evolved. His sensitivity to the imperial relation and to the larger world outside further strengthened his appreciation for the inwardness and separateness of the history of his province and region. Some of the best literature on western Canada was the product of scholars who at least partly stressed the British imperial framework. Nova Scotia-born Chester Martin, who had taught at Manitoba and came to sympathize with the cause of 'western rights', once declared that 'Western Canada ... is, in fact, the oldest continuously British area on the continent'; [3] he proceeded to treat the history of the west as a recapitulation of eastern colonial experience in gaining self-government. George Stanley's *Birth of Western Canada* (1936), partially based on his Oxford thesis, set the Riel uprisings into the spacious imperial theme of the clashes between native peoples and expanding 'progressive' civilizations.

The industrious Arthur Silver Morton (no relation to W.L. Morton) wrote his encyclopedic *A History of the Canadian West to 1870-71* (1939) from a similar imperial perspective. He had turned to the history of western Canada both because the First World War cut him off from the source materials for his original field of interest in church history and because he believed that, as a teacher in a provincial university, he owed special obligations to the people of Saskatchewan. He possessed 'warm feelings of gratitude'[4] to the Hudson's Bay Company, which had given him unrestricted access to its archives in the early thirties, and he was instrumental in creating the Hudson's Bay Record Society, which reprinted selections from those holdings. His book luxuriated in the picturesque detail of the fur trade. Revelling in controversies about such matters as the route taken by Henry Kelsey into the interior, A.S. Morton was fascinated by the problems of establishing the exact positions of old fur-trading posts. Entirely typical of his outlook and manner of approach was his account of efforts to locate the remains of Fort à la Corne:

> I headed off the Historic Sites Board from putting up a monument on the traditional site at La Corne, telling them that the fort would be

found forty miles farther down the River at Nipawin. A friend of mine located the remains of Forts within the radius in which I expected to find it and we were up and were able to delineate a large Fort 200' x 150' at what David Thompson calls Finley's Falls. This must be Finley's Fort of 1773. Forty yards east of it we located a smaller Fort 36' x 130' about, whose lines of whose palisade were for the most part very definite. In the middle of the palisade was a stump of a spruce tree about two feet across. An expert of the Forestry Department gave the growth of the tree one hundred and thirty-nine years and allowed twenty years for the rotting of the stump. We hunted out the man who cut the timber on the river flat and he said he had cut it twenty-two years ago. The tree therefore began to grow in 1770, on a conservative estimate, and as the palisade had to rot before the tree could grow we got well beyond English times into the French regime. Thus my interpretation of the Documentary evidence is justified by the discovery of the ruins of the Fort.[5]

A.S.Morton's history of the west and his biography of George Simpson, which appeared in 1944—the year he died, at the age of seventy-four—advanced no generalized interpretations of Canadian history. But his concentration on the activities of an imperial trading monopoly underlined the independent origins of western Canadian history.

W.L. Morton was an inheritor of this tradition.

II

W.L. Morton's sense of western separateness provided the independent basis from which he launched an appraisal of the prevailing conventions and interpretations in Canadian historical writing. Canadian historians, he wrote in 1946, had dwelt on a few fundamental themes: the survival of French Canada; the history of Ontario and the development of self-government; and an economic history that explained 'the metropolitan destiny of the St Lawrence River ... to exploit economically and unite politically the northern half of the continent'. In the works of Innis and Creighton, central Canada was conceived as the dynamic heart of a commercial imperialism that, through Confederation and the National Policy, incorporated and exploited subordinate hinterlands. With the accuracy of this description of the past Morton did not quarrel; what he objected to were its corollaries and its implications for those Canadians who lived in the hinterlands. The 'Laurentian theme' rested on an economic interpretation of history and implied a homogeneous view of Canadian experience; it relegated the history of the west to a peripheral position; and, above all, it was indifferent to questions of justice and equitable relations between the four sections and two races in Canada. Morton not only protested against an economic interpretation of the past at a time when other Canadian historians were virtually abandoning it, but he also identified the Laurentian approach with the very metropolitan dominance it explained. 'Confederation', he charged, 'was brought about to increase the wealth of Central Canada, and until that original purpose is altered, and the concentration of wealth and population by national policy in Central Canada ceases, Confederation must remain an instrument of injustice.'[6] The history of western Canada possessed an individuality that transcended its tributary relationship to the national economic policies; it therefore constituted a decisive field for historical investigation on its own terms. Morton's critique of the state of Clio in Canada was, in terms of broad cultural history, an exact though belated counterpart of the traditional western indictments of the dominance of eastern Canada over national policies and economic life.

If the history of western Canada was to be interpreted in a fashion that was at once faithful to the local identity and still remain united to national history, where was one to start, what questions were to be pursued, and what instruments of analysis employed? Through his reading, and possibly also through the influence of his teacher, R.O. MacFarlane, who had been a student of Frederick Jackson Turner at Harvard, Morton was familiar with the way in which American historians had used the frontier thesis and the notion of sections to establish a respectable basis for western history. In the early thirties he had been excited by Walter Prescott Webb's *The Great Plains* (1931), which described how the implements of an agricultural civilization that had evolved in the humid, forested areas of the east had been adapted and altered in the settlement of the arid and treeless plains west of the 98th meridian. Moreover, no one who had witnessed the succession of natural disasters on the Prairies in the Depression, and who saw at first hand so total a collapse of the wheat economy that sober social scientists wondered whether capitalist agriculture could survive in that region, would have remained unimpressed with the effects of environment in history. Morton felt that the distinctive geography of the prairie provinces, the harsh and hazardous climate, and the inflexible and vulnerable economy must have changed the way people thought and modified the institutions they received. Yet he was conscious also that the history of the west could not be adequately comprehended and recounted in terms of a clash between the 'hereditary culture' brought by the settlers and some homogeneous 'domineering environment'.[7] Like George Stanley—who discounted the relevance of the frontier thesis for explaining the culture of the Prairies, as distinct from its agricultural practices—Morton remained critical of the simple dichotomy between frontier and inheritance, geography and culture. His own experience contradicted any such elementary formulation. In a study of the local history of the Gladstone district that he completed in the mid-forties, Morton showed a sensitive awareness of the continuity of institutions in newly settled areas. 'A great heritage has been brought in and transplanted with singularly little loss,' he summarized, 'the church sprung from a far distant Palestine, local government going back to Robert Baldwin's Ontario, and the New England townships and beyond the seas to Norman and Saxon times; and self-government as the English-speaking people had developed it over the centuries and in new lands.'[8]

It was clearly not in any one-dimensional application of the frontier thesis or geographical environmentalism that the implications of the Laurentian theme could be offset, or the peculiarities of prairie life explained. The key was rather to be found in the 'metropolitan-hinterland relationship' and the interplay between favoured economic centres and subordinate areas. This conception, as we have seen, had been outlined in the writings of N.S.B. Gras in the early 1920s; it was embedded in the Laurentian approach of Innis and Creighton; and it had been employed by two of Morton's colleagues at nearby Wesley College: Arthur Lower in his studies of the timber trade, and more generally in his *Colony to Nation* (1946), and Donald C. Masters in an analysis of the rivalry for financial control between Toronto and Montreal. For Morton the chief advantage of the metropolitan-hinterland idea was its flexibility: it dealt not in antithetical dichotomies of environment versus culture but in graduated relationships.[9] It allowed a place for the deliberate adaptation of practices to a peculiar geography, while not underplaying the cultural inheritance as Turner had done. It recognized the transplantation of economic, political, and social institutions from older settled areas to the frontier, and still enabled one to escape the implied interpretation of Canadian history as simply the imperialist expansion of central Canada. The main determinant in the development of the Prairies after 1870, Morton pointed out, was the area's integration into the metropolitan system and industrial order of the east. The technology of modern capitalism—railways, banks, and marketing and distributing facilities—was rapidly built up, and metropolitan controls over social, religious, educational, and political institutions were extremely effective. The history of the west—at least after 1870—was to be written within this framework of metropolitanism.[10] From the middle-forties onwards Morton was thus attempting to define and refine a general concept of the metropolitan-hinterland relationship that would be appropriate to his purposes and that would provide the framework for analysis of the interplay of a distinct region in a federal state.

At the same time he had already initiated an examination of the roots of western agrarian protest. His *Progressive Party in Canada* (1950) was in a way a retrospective engagement with his own heritage and the people among whom he had grown up, as well as a contribution to regional and national history. With a generous though not uncritical sympathy, he broadly drew the outlines of the Progressive party—illustrating its affinity with the campaigns for prohibition, female suffrage, and the democratization of politics; analysing the weakening of the two-party system in the First World War that opened the door to independent political action; examining in detail the fate of the Progressives in complicated manoeuvres in the House of Commons; and, above all, lucidly revealing the fatal ideological split between the liberal followers of Thomas Crerar and the supporters of the group-government idea of Henry Wise Wood. The Progressive party was àn expression of rural protest against the increasing urban dominance of Canadian society; an episode in the transition from a *laissez-faire* to a managed economy; and, most profoundly, a rebellion of the wheat-growing west against policies that were designed to benefit chiefly central Canada and the political system that was the instrument of metropolitan interests. So much emphasis did Morton place on the western, sectional dimension of progressivism that he was criticized—by Creighton, for one—for underestimating the importance of the Ontario farmers' protest movement. Morton's book was a study in the pathology of sectional radicalism and defeat. The Progressive revolt achieved only marginal benefits for the western constituencies; the structure it sought to overthrow remained intact.

Morton accepted the substance of the Progressives' indictment of the National Policy and the party system. Stripped of the millenarian anticipations and extravagant rhetorical embellishments in which it was enclosed, the Progressive challenge was the simple claim that, 'in a federal union of free citizens and equal communities, there must be such equality of economic opportunity and such equality of political status as human ingenuity may contrive and goodwill advance.'[11] Morton's analysis of progressivism was undertaken within the confines of the same liberal categories that the movement represented. More generally, he was concerned with the way in which the original and unavoidable position of inequality of the west in Confederation produced a tradition of revolt and apoliticism. The initial bias of prairie politics was imparted by the struggle for equality that was inaugurated by Riel and that lasted until control over natural resources was transferred to the provinces in 1930; the second phase, exemplified by the Progressive party, hinged on agrarian sectionalism; and the third, the utopian and the experimental, was represented by the Social-Credit and CCF movements. By 1955 it seemed to Morton that this tradition was not one of rejection of Canada. 'The Prairie West', he wrote in a paper which, ironically, was read to the Royal Society in his absence by Creighton, 'has been defined as a colonial society seeking equality in Confederation. That equality was sought in order that the West should be like, not different from, the rest of Canada.'[12] Morton's assessment of the Progressive tradition deflated its separatist implications and reconciled the regional identity with the national community. In his own mind the equality for which the West had striven was recognized in the recommendations of the Rowell-Sirois Report and was practically implemented in 1947 with the beginning of equalization grants to those provinces that benefited less from national policies than their contribution to the country's prosperity warranted.

One aspect of Morton's interpretation of the Progressive revolt that was to have a more general application in all his other writings was the significance he attributed to the forty-ninth parallel as a real dividing line in western history. For the American historian Paul Sharp, whose *Agrarian Revolt in Western Canada* (1948) anticipated Morton's analysis of the Progressives by two years, the close parallels and relationships between the Canadian and United States' farmers' movements—suggested, for example, by the role of the North Dakota Non-Partisan League in prairie politics—indicated the meaninglessness of the political boundary. Not only had the Canadian west been a northern extension of the agricultural frontier of the United States, but 'the fundamental similarities in environment . . . produced the same agrarian protests on both sides of the international boundary.'[13] While Morton did not explicitly reject this line of argument, the entire thrust of his own work was quite different. He set the Progressives in the context of the metropolitan-hinterland relationship and the east-west economic system. Though he acknowledged the affinities between American populism and Canadian progressivism, he discerned variations in the style and intensity of expressions of agrarian discontent in the two countries that 'arose from the different metropolitan orientations, the different political controls, and the graduated environmental differences . . . . ' The metropolitan controls in Canada, Morton argued—and here he was indebted to S.D. Clark's historical sociology of the failure of protest movements north of the border—were stronger, more centralized, and 'the Parliamentary system less responsive than the congressional to local pressures'.[14] These remarks, of course, were not based on an intensive comparative study of the two patterns of agrarian politics, but they do indicate the distinctive orientation of his work. Indeed, he would subsequently trace the profoundly different character of western-Canadian history more extensively and come to see that, behind the divergent tendencies of twentieth-century agrarian radicalism, lay an obscure clash of peoples—the Métis of Red River and the Sioux Indians. Such a 'blind and primitive working of history with geography' had laid the basis for the different histories in western North America.[15]

Morton's *Progressive Party* was preoccupied with the question of justice and fairness in the relations between the regions of a federal state. *Manitoba, A History* (1957), by far his most finely crafted work, was his answer to a problem of recognition he had posed in 1946. He had then wished for a history of the West written with such fidelity to the inner texture of local experience and so evocative of the sense of place that it would immediately trigger a recognition in those who had been moulded by that history. The cultural nationalists of the 1920s had confronted a similar problem: how to convey in literature, art, and history the distinctive features of Canadian life so that a people who had previously perceived their country only through borrowed concepts could finally recognize it through the rich allusiveness of their own art. So too had the novelist Hugh MacLennan at a later date. The writer dealing with universal themes in a Canadian setting, he said, could not take a knowledge of that setting for granted; he therefore had to become a historian and a sociologist. Manitoba — the West—was a colonial society, as all Canada had once been in a far deeper sense than economic metropoltanism implied. Manitoba evoked no literary landscape; imaginatively and in art it did not exist.[16] For this reason Morton deliberately set out to establish the general patterns that moulded Manitoba society and attempted to portray the land as vividly as possible by drawing on fur traders' and other descriptive accounts as well as on his own observations. In *Manitoba*, a work of great emotional involvement, Morton resolved the discrepancies that had existed in his mind between the locality he knew and the 'unreal' world he had assimilated from a distant literary culture, between his commitments to a society that he believed possessed a character and authenticity of its own and a historiographical tradition that consigned it to the margin of national development.

The central theme of his narrative was the development of a distinctive variant of Canadian society within the province. Centuries previous to the incorporation of the West into Canada, Manitoba's history had been connected, not only to the St Lawrence Valley but also directly to Britain through the English voyages of discovery, the fur trade from Hudson's Bay, and the implanting of Selkirk's settlement. In the generation after the defeat of the North West Company in 1821, during which the Red River colony was isolated from the Canadas, the primary characteristic of the colony was the balance that existed ethnically between the Métis and English-speaking settlers and economically between the buffalo hunt, river farm lots, and the canoe brigades of the fur trade. Following a number of predecessors, most recently the French sociologist Marcel Giraud—whose *Le Métis Canadien* (1945), written in Paris during the German occupation, recreated the way of life of a people of two cultures—Morton stressed the central role of the indigenous Métis, whose power and institutions, particularly the buffalo hunt, strengthened their sense of themselves as a corporate entity, a 'new nation'. After a fashion the Métis became the archetypal westerners—misunderstood by an uncaring and ill-informed government in distant Ottawa and provoked into protest by policies that adversely affected their vital interests and about which they had not been consulted. Viewed from the Red River, Canadian expansion westward threatened an admirable and balanced society, a community weakened by internal contradictions but a community nonetheless.

Morton's assessment of the resistance of 1869-70 in his *Manitoba* and related studies departed from the interpretation established by George Stanley some twenty years before. Though sympathetic to the inhabitants of Red River, and critical of the Dominion's failure to explain its own intentions, Stanley had regarded both this uprising and the Northwest Rebellion of 1885 as incidents in the conflict between peoples at different stages of development similar to ones that had occurred in Africa, Australia, and on other imperial frontiers. The Red River Rebellion, he wrote, 'was fundamentally the revolt of a semi-primitive society against the imposition of a more progressive, alien culture . . . . ' The uprising had primarily to do with the response of a primitive frontier to imperial expansion, not with the ethnic relations between French and English in eastern Canada. According to Stanley, Riel led the Métis on a futile protest against the inevitability of their national extinction, for they were 'bound to give way before the march of a more progressive people'.[17]

Because Morton saw the Red River society as a civilized community, he necessarily came to a different evaluation of the resistance. Red River, he believed, was not a frontier settlement in any meaningful sense of that term. It was 'an island of civilization in the wilderness'[18] and had possessed a government, churches, courts, and schools for nearly fifty years. The Métis took the initiative in resisting Canadian expansion because they sought a guarantee for their rights as civilized people. Theirs was not a blind reaction against a 'progressive' civilization; what they opposed was not incorporation into Canada but rather becoming an adjunct of Anglo-Saxon Ontario. It seemed to Morton that to relegate the resistance movement to the status of a foreordained failure was to diminish its true significance. Red River was a dual society, based on the approximate numerical balance between the French-speaking Catholic Métis and the English-speaking Protestant settlers. The Manitoba Act embodied the principle of duality in its definition of the province as officially bilingual, with a dual denominational school system. Morton had written long before that Manitoba 'was in many respects autochthonous, the offspring of the fur trade, the missions, and the deep soil of the Red River Valley. The Dominion recognized rather than created.'[19] At the bottom of the troubles Morton saw an issue of profound significance for Canada generally because the resistance had 'challenged Ontario to recognize that the dual character of Canadian nationality was not a temporary concession to necessity, but the foundation and framework of the federation.'[20]

The great tragedy of Manitoba's—and Canada's—history was that this principle of duality, ratified in 1870, was gradually undermined by the migration of settlers from Ontario who tipped the demographic balance, and it was then overthrown with the abolition of bilingualism and state supported separate schools in the early 1890s. What the Grit-inspired majoritarian and intolerant democracy of Ontario had begun, the massive influx of continental European immigrants forced to a conclusion. The settlement of the Manitoba School issue in 1896 permitted the teaching of any mother tongue in the classrooms; by the First World War this privilege threatened to turn Manitoba into an Austria-Hungary of the New World and was abolished in 1916.

Manitoba became a British-Canadian province and in the process abandoned its heritage of duality; but it never became merely a transcript of Ontario. The great immigration of the Laurier years made Manitoba and the West generally a more ethnically diverse society than Canada as a whole until after the Second World War, and in this cultural pluralism Morton found another strand of experience that made his province unique. During the years when his book was gestating, the Manitoba Historical and Scientific Society sponsored a series of studies on the province's ethnic communities: Poles, Mennonites, Icelanders, Jews, French-Canadians, Ukrainians, and Hutterians. Morton shared the underlying assumption on which this project was based—that Canadian life admitted, indeed was predicated upon, a balance between cultural diversity and membership in a common political community. In *Manitoba* he was more concerned with delineating the common and shared feelings that brought these groups together than in dealing with them on their own terms. His view of ethnic relations was therefore consensual and the picture he drew was, on the whole, one of a tolerant pluralistic society. Life in Manitoba, he wrote,

> forces a common manner, not to say character on all its people . . . . Few Manitobans can pass a day without meeting at least one person of different background. It is not an easy way for ordinary folk to live, dependent as we are on our prejudices to sustain and comfort us; it is lived in Manitoba in the deliberate belief and profession that a sound, satisfactory, and enduring society can be based on no more than the profession of common country, a common political allegiance, and the maintenance of personal freedom and equality under the law. In short it is perhaps in Manitoba that the Canadian experiment in political binationalism and cultural plurality is at its most intense.[21]

The two other outstanding features in Morton's account of Manitoban history were the agricultural society and the interplay between the south and the north. He defined the central theme of his book as the progress of agricultural settlement and in one romantic passage celebrated the common environment and way of life. 'The fundamental rural life of the province', he wrote, 'was the great moulder of its people, and its influence was for uniformity, a uniformity not superficial, but deep, because founded on attachment to the soil and the home. Whether a Ukrainian pioneer in the bush frontier of the Swan River or a son of Ontario stock on the well-cultivated terrace lands of the Pembinas, whether a druggist in Beausejour or a bank manager in Dauphin, the typical Manitoban was a country man, at home with country ways and at ease in the steady rhythm of countrylife.'[22] The other persistent feature in Manitoba's past was the interplay between the agricultural areas of the south and the northern Shield. The fur trade had been based on the symbiosis of the food-producing Red River Valley and the canoe brigade. With the extension of Manitoba's boundaries northward in the twentieth century, the building of the port at Churchill, and the development of mining, this interior rhythm was restored. 'The plains which fed the fur trade now fed the mines, and where the fur brigades had filed down the river the grain cars now rolled into Churchill.' In this, as in other respects, Manitoba's character was quintessentially Canadian because it was a response to the challenge of the north and because 'its life was the action and reaction of settled south and wilderness north, the Plains on the Shield, and the Shield on the Plains.'[23]

The limited autonomy of Manitoba's past, then, lay in its historical combination of cultural pluralism and bi-nationality with a single political allegiance, the interplay of north and south, and the agricultural economy. While not uncritical of the province's insufficiencies—the materialism and excessive pragmatism of its people and their distrust of the intellectual life—Morton's history celebrated positive achievements. It possessed literary unity because Morton deliberately sought out the general and overriding themes that embraced the circumstances of all the people of the province. *Manitoba* was his answer to those who had allegedly thought or implied that the West was a *tabula rasa* upon which metropolitan forces freely played to make a replica of the East, or a mere tributary dependency in an economic relationship, or a record of 'protest' parties to which the social scientists had almost reduced it. Yet in a mysterious, even enigmatic way, the fundamental determinants of Manitoba's history, while operating in a specific locale, were also those that had worked upon all of Canada. Manitoba, for Morton, was the most Canadian of all the provinces in the sense that the factors that had moulded its people were but variations of the factors that had shaped Canadian history generally. Manitoba was a microcosm of all Canada also in that it had been one of the storm centres of the national past—in 1870, 1890, 1916, and 1919. The things Manitobans had done were not pale reflexes of the operations of profounder forces originating elsewhere but were in themselves of great national significance. Morton had accused the metropolitan historians of projecting one legitimate view of Canadian history, the notion of central-Canadian economic imperialism, onto all of Canadian history and thereby depriving those who lived on the hinterlands of a sense of their own self-respect. In *Manitoba*, and in his later works, he generalized a view of the past and present that had become fully explicit in his passionate engagement with his native province and made it apply to the entire Canadian identity.

III

By 1957 Morton had completed his major contributions to western Canadian history. Thereafter his writings broadened to encompass Canadian history generally. His lectures on *The Canadian Identity* (1961), his textbook survey, *The Kingdom of Canada* (1963), and his study of the Confederation movement, *The Critical Years: The Union of British North America, 1857-1873* (1964), were logical outgrowths of his tendency to see national developments from a regional perspective and regional history in relation to broad international developments. A historian who traced the origins of responsible government in Canada to late eighteenth-century Irish politics, and who described Confederation in the context of a vast alteration in the balance of power in North America that included the failure of Emperor Maximilian in Mexico, was hardly a regional scholar with narrow segregated preoccupations. There were strong continuities, moreover, between his 'western' and 'national' studies—for example, in the persistence of his conviction that the chief characteristic of Canadian nationality consisted in its diversity and pluralism; or in his equally insistent contention that the thrust and grain of Canadian experience lay in its northern position and the interplay between the agricultural south and the Shield. In his Presidential Address to the Canadian Historical Association in 1960, he argued that Canada had been profoundly shaped by the existence of the North—a perpetual frontier along the line that separated the farm from the wilderness, the territory beyond which cereal crops could not be grown. 'Canada', he wrote, 'is a northern country with a northern economy, a northern way of life and a northern destiny.'[24] It had been discovered and explored as the edge of a northern maritime frontier. The country's economy depended on the exploitation of resources found in the North; and this fact, as Innis had earlier pointed out, reinforced its dependence on more highly developed societies, not only economically but culturally. In this as in other respects Canada was Manitoba writ large.

Still, if Morton's transition from a 'regional' to a 'national' historian was subtle and gradual, it was an alteration in focus nonetheless. At one level it was signalized by his designation as joint editor with Creighton of a sixteen-volume history of Canada, announced in 1957. In its original prospectus the Canadian Centenary Series was to contain nine volumes covering the regions before 1857, one on Confederation, and six on the national period—a distribution of emphasis that clearly indicated the executive editor's conception that the Canadian past could be comprehended only in relation to the existence of distinct sections that were enclosed in a federal state but whose fierce localisms and particularities were not obliterated by it. Morton's own contribution, the volume on British North American union, had been planned around 1950 as an analysis of the West and Confederation, but it evolved into a more comprehensive study—an indication of his shifting interests.

At another level Morton's altered perspective was counterpointed by his more intimate involvement in national affairs—through his position on the Board of Broadcast Governors, for example—and his departure from Manitoba to Ontario. Though in 1963 he was made Provost of an élite affiliate of the University of Manitoba, University College, he held the post only until 1966, when he became the first Master of Champlain College at Trent University, Peterborough. Ironically it was in the Ontario heartland that he wrote an epilogue to his *Manitoba*. His strong but angry words about the Winnipeg establishment—'canny, reactionary, untravelled, fearful of ideas and of imagination'—that had blighted the prospects of the city, the province, and the university, and his allusions to the status of the province's two best writers, Margaret Laurence and Jack Ludwig, as 'expatriates', suggested the depth of feeling behind his move.[25]

Morton's writings in the decade after 1957 were heavily coloured by the revival of Conservatism in Canadian politics, its growing respectability in a segment of the intellectual community, and by the beginnings of the Quiet Revolution in Quebec. Morton was identified with a small group of intellectuals who were united less by strong personal relationships or partisan ideological ties than by a common aversion to the long Liberal hegemony in national affairs and a shared solicitude for traditional institutions. Along with Creighton and Eugene Forsey, George Grant and John Farthing, Morton became disgusted with the Liberal party's high-handed tactics in the pipeline debate and with its alleged disregard for the rights of Parliament, traditional procedures, and symbols.

Morton personalized the cause of the malaise in Canadian politics in the fifties in the figure—and legacy—of Mackenzie King. King's distrust of Parliament and his resort to 'plebiscitary democracy' had contributed to the erosion of parliamentary government and to an unprincipled régime that 'rots Canadian life as fungus rots a log'.[26] Reiterating an accusation made some time before by Creighton, Morton also condemned King and Skelton, 'that evil genius of Canadian external policy', for destroying Canada's relationship with the old British Commonwealth without attempting to offset the influence of the United States with a European counterbalance. Theirs was a work of negative destruction and isolation that led to the present condition of Canada in which the country—Morton's anger found its best expression in analogies of organic decomposition—was 'so irradiated by the American presence that it sickens and threatens to dissolve in cancerous slime'.[27]

For Morton, as for Creighton, this decline in national life was associated with attitudes to the past that had contributed to the weakening of Canadian self-confidence. He criticized Lower's historical work because it conveyed the 'colonial fixation' of an entire generation. 'They love the nation Canada, but they hate it also. They hate it because they hate its colonial origins, which they wish to deny but cannot, and must therefore trample on endlessly in ever less meaningful frenzy.'[28] Underhill was censured for maintaining that the British connection had been an incubus and that Canada's colonial history revealed only the reasons for its anaemic life. Morton was remonstrating against specific judgements and particular interpretations of events, and against the destructive, negative, and corrosive intelligences these men brought to their investigations. Some twenty years previously he had attested that the historian and the poet had much in common: 'Each is a maker of myths, only the historian has neglected his job of making myths in this decadent, analytical age.'[29] He wanted a history that recreated and recalled the great creative achievements of the past and thereby strengthened the country's awareness of its distinctive heritage. In this he drifted further from Underhill, whose writings on economic and class interests in politics had underlain his work on the Progressives, and moved closer to Creighton, the bias of whose commercial empire he had once protested.

A positive set of 'conservative principles' underlay Morton's aversion to the undermining of parliamentary institutions and his uneasiness about the decline of Britain as a world power and the rising influence of the United States. Making these explicit in a speech to a conference of Western Canadian University Conservatives in 1959, Morton simply reiterated those conservative tenets that the American writers Clinton Rossiter and Russell Kirk had recently disinterred and rehabilitated. He also attempted to locate the roots of Canadian conservatism in the British background, in the determination of French Canada to preserve its society, and in the Loyalist concept of a community of allegiance. But what was so arresting about his definition of the mission of modern conservatism was not his rehearsal of the traditional precepts—respect for the continuities of history, society conceived as a partnership between generations, the rejection of the belief in human perfectability—but rather his statement that the old philosophical individualism of the extinct Liberal now found its true dwelling place in conservative minds. This did not mean that Morton en-

dorsed a *laissez-faire* economic policy; in fact he asserted that 'the welfare-state is not in any conflict with Conservative principles, of which laissez-faire and rugged individualism are not part.' At the very centre of the
cluster of convictions that composed his political credo was the belief that
values existed only in relation to people, that 'people are themselves of absolute value.' In a society that was becoming more bureaucratic and corpo-
rative, where all too much power was being concentrated in administrative
boards and in the office of the Prime Minister, the role of conservatism was
to preserve and, if necessary, to renovate those institutions that protected
the individual from unrestricted state authority.[30]

Morton had always been suspicious of majoritarian democracy and had
earlier found an ideal prescription for Canadian nationality in Lord
Acton's dictum that freedom was most efficaciously protected by diversity.
As far back as 1939 he had criticized the Tory and Liberal traditions in
Canadian and Manitoban politics—the one for divorcing property from
social obligation, the other for regarding a mere numerical majority as the
only solution to delicate and complicated questions.[31] In an essay published in 1943, and undoubtedly written in the atmosphere of the national
plebiscite on conscription, Morton noted that only in the provinces and
local societies did there exist a sufficient degree of consensus to enable un-
restrained parliamentary democracy to work. At the federal level the simple majority principle could be used only with reserve, and on some subjects not at all.[32] Civil liberties could be preserved only if certain restraints
were imposed on the democracy. The monarchical tradition was the source
of one such restraint.

The monarchy assumed for Morton a dominant position in the Canadian identity. Few aspects of his later writing have been more misunderstood or subjected to such sceptical review. Esteem and reverence for the
Crown in Canada, generalized in the title of his textbook survey, may have
been nurtured in his English home in Manitoba and by his self-confessed
romanticism. But when Morton wrote of monarchical institutions he did
not mean a sentimental royalism but a set of constitutional principles
rooted in Canadian history and the practice of government. At the time of
Confederation the monarchical idea was understood to involve a balanced
social order, a tradition of authority, and above all a rejection of popular
sovereignty of the American type.[33] The rejection of popular sovereignty
meant the repudiation of majoritarian democracy. Confederation was the
creation of a political nationality, not a nationalist state. Sectionalism and
communal diversities were not obliterated by union; they were incorporated into it and subtly transformed such institutions as the cabinet. The
focus of political loyalty lay with the monarchy, not with the state as the
expression of the general will. In this sense Canadian nationality did not
demand conformity, as did the American—only political allegiance. The

'moral core of Canadian nationality', he averred, 'is found in the fact that Canada is a monarchy and in the nature of monarchical allegiance. As America is united at bottom by the covenant, Canada is united at the top by allegiance. Because Canada is a nation founded on allegiance and not on compact, there is no process of becoming Canadian akin to conversion, there is no pressure for uniformity . . . . '[34] Monarchical institutions were indispensable to a pluralist society and pluralism and diversity were the source of genuine freedom.

The implications of this view of Canadian democracy and character were further amplified in Morton's personal confrontation with the issues raised in the early phase of the Quiet Revolution. Though his western upbringing provided him with a measure of intuitive sympathy with the striving of another community for equality—he recalled in 1966 that he had once been a political separatist in his all-too-indignant youth[35]— Morton found *séparatisme* very disturbing. In 1960 he had treated the historical experiences of Canada's two main cultural groups as variations on a common way of life, a shared engagement with the northern position of their country, and a common allegiance to the Crown and monarchical institutions. By the spring of 1963 it seemed that these and other certitudes that he had casually accepted no longer enjoyed popular support. The period, he confessed, was one of profound depression in his life, a time in which the British-Canadian world he had known and taken for granted had collapsed.[36]

Though Morton admitted that Canada was composed of two cultural entities, he emphatically denied that this necessitated a division of sovereignty through some form of associate-statehood or separatism. Separatism, he insisted, should be resisted by force of arms if necessary. Institutional duality had been tried before and had been abandoned by those men of experience who had made Confederation. If Canada were forced into political duality, he told a French-Canadian journalist, then it would be best for Quebec to secede completely.[37] 'Canada is not a dual community, French and English . . . . It is a society of free individuals, equal in civil and political rights, equal in religious and cultural rights, and equal in the common citizenship of all members of the community.'[38] All French Canadians — not only the eighty-three percent residing in Quebec — 'should have their right to their own culture guaranteed by the federal constitution throughout Canada in the same way that the same rights are guaranteed to the English minority within the province of Quebec.'[39] French linguistic rights should be broadened across the entire country wherever that was practicable; the powers of the federal government should be strengthened and the Bill of Rights made fundamental law so that the central government could return to its proper function as the protector of minority rights and civil liberties.

The sanction for this prescription lay in the past. In *The Kingdom of Canada* Morton wrote of a nation built on a northern economy and on cultural diversity. He described the union as 'in effect and in law a pact between the two peoples and two cultures.'[40] And he treated the conflicts of cultures in the late nineteenth and early twentieth centuries as clashes of British-Canadian and French-Canadian nationalisms, each striving to imprint its own image on the entire country, each learning, slowly and painfully, that the Canadian state could not become the nationalist state of either group. His assessment of the critical years from 1857 to 1873 bore the imprint of the current concern with French-English relations even more deeply. He deliberately set out to underline the role played by French Canadians in the formation of the union, and, where once he had judged Confederation as an instrument of 'Laurentian imperialism', he now asserted that in the partnership between French and English to extend their union across the continent lay the 'moral purpose' of Canada.[41]

According to Morton's understanding of the meaning of Confederation, the heart of what he termed the 'conservative principle'—or sometimes, more cumbersomely, the 'Macdonaldian constitution'—consisted of the belief that the central government was to be the supreme custodian of the welfare of the entire country and the chief protector of the rights of minorities. In the thirty years after 1867 this power was destroyed, partly by judicial decisions, partly by the commitment of the Liberal party to provincial rights. The settlement of the Manitoba schools question signalized the end of the federal government's willingness to guarantee minority rights.[42] This 'disaster of 1896' destroyed the Macdonaldian constitution. In 1964 Morton urged that the province take the lead in rectifying the injustice of 1890 and restore the old duality of cultures; the next year he told a public hearing of the Royal Commission on Bilingualism and Biculturalism that it was highly desirable that Canadians go back to the principles that had been overturned in 1890.[43] The central government must be made strong again precisely because it was the protector of local diversity and minority rights.

Back of Morton's support for official bilingualism projected across the country lay the conviction, gained through his earlier studies of the western resistance of 1869-70, that this was in accord with the original intentions of the makers of the federal union. In 1967 the historical case for biculturalism was challenged by Creighton, who argued that the Fathers of Confederation had narrowly delimited the official recognition of the French language and that provisions of the Manitoba Act relating to separate schools and provincial status were not generally accepted principles but *ad hoc* concessions, implemented prematurely, before the character of the West was determined by the settlers who would go there. Morton accepted what he took to be the gist of Creighton's historical case, that the duality embodied in the Manitoba Act was provisional and the consequence of political expediency, not the recognition and application of a general principle. The federal government seemed neither to deny nor affirm duality but only tolerated its practice pragmatically. Still it appeared to Morton—and here his disagreement with Creighton was profound—that the general principle of bilingualism must be asserted on the ground of principle, for if there were no guarantees for the French outside Quebec, there could be scant grounds for minority guarantees for the English inside Quebec.[44] One of the minor ironies in Morton's position was that western public opinion on the bilingualism issue was closer to Creighton's sympathies than his own. Not surprisingly he wondered whether the almost uniformally critical response evoked by the Royal Commission on Bilingualism and Biculturalism 'revealed that in fact Manitobans had never accepted the idea of a dual nationality', or whether Manitoban society was more conformist and egalitarian than he had earlier supposed.[45]

IV

Morton's major intellectual achievement was perhaps not in the arena of advocacy but in the successful effort to construct a framework and find a vocabulary to convey his attachments to both Canada and the West. He rediscovered in the writings of Lord Acton, neglected by Canadian historians since the twenties and recovered again by liberal critics of nationalism after the later fifties, a formula by which loyalty to the one was reconciled with affection for the other. One of Morton's most enduring preoccupations was with the acceptance of pluralism as the guarantee of freedom, civil liberties, and justice. He believed that no historian could remain clinically neutral when dealing with moral issues—an Actonian principle.

Throughout his work Morton was concerned with balance—between local and general, between region and nation, between the rights of individuals and minorities and the demands of political communities; perhaps too between what he was fond of calling the head and the heart. The indictment of majoritarian democratic impulses runs like a red thread—perhaps one should say a blue one — through all his work. His sympathies were always with the variegated and the plural, with small communities and the concreteness of their ways of life. Morton's feeling for the local was stronger than the so-called nation-building approach to the Canadian past allowed, and this brought him perhaps closer to a younger generation of historians who would accept as common wisdom Northrop Frye's statement that the tension between a political sense of unity and the imaginative sense of locality was central to whatever the word Canada meant.[46]

Because Morton's history was so bound up with his own first-hand knowledge, as is all written history, the passage of time disclosed slightly different perspectives that suggest the limitations of his work. 'How', Morton once asked, 'is any central thesis of historical interpretation in Canadian history to be reconciled with the need to develop regional and provincial history if Canadian history is really to be understood?'[47] To attain an imaginative grasp and insight into the particularities of one community, and to communicate those elusive feelings that are not always explicitly stated in the documents, requires such a rare combination of talent that one despairs of any single mind's writing a history of the entire country as convincingly as Morton wrote *Manitoba*. He admitted his own difficulties in evoking the regional outlooks of Ontario and British Columbia with the same sureness of touch that he brought to the history of his native province, a fact that may explain why the admirers of his history of Manitoba found his study of Confederation too clogged with detail and a vaguely disappointing book. Paradoxically his own difficulties only confirm his general teaching.

Particularities like regions or provinces always turn out to contain even more limited identities. Cultural and ethnic pluralism was central to Morton's Manitoba and he chose to stress common, not divergent, experience. He was not concerned with the impact of assimilation on the newcomers and conveyed little appreciation for the harsher conformist demands of the dominant British Canadian society, such as are mirrored in John Marlyn's novel *Under the Ribs of Death*, a story of an immigrant boy who changes his life and loses everything, or in Fredelle Brusser Maynard's sensitive and moving memoir, *Raisins and Almonds*.[48] The contrast Morton drew between the American tendency towards eradicating cultural distinctions and the Canadian pattern of a tolerant mosaic has gained little confirmation in subsequent studies of the treatment of eastern and central-European immigrant groups during the First World War, the surge of support for the Ku Klux Klan in Saskatchewan at the end of the twenties, or the subjection of the despised minority of Orientals in British Columbia. It has been argued that the idea of a pluralistic mosaic may well be as inappropriate a description of the present as it is a one-sided generalization about the past. For all intents and purposes, and despite the retention of languages and folkways, most of the children of the older immigrant communities, with the possible exception of the Hutterians, have been completely integrated into the social and economic environment. The mosaic may be 'more of an exercise in nostalgia than a description of current reality.'[49]

Morton's glorification of the land and of agricultural life as the primary factors that moulded the people of Manitoba has also been criticized. He once admitted this bias and his tendency to romanticize a life lived close to the natural elements by declaring that urban backgrounds and cityscapes never really excited his imagination. The city-bred historians who condemned his respect for environment, he wrote, 'have what I call the pavement mentality . . . they know neither the revolution of the seasons nor the relevance of time and place, but live contained and self-impelled lives.'[50]

There is finally one further pattern that revealed itself in Morton's intellectual development. He described restrospectively a dichotomy between the late-Victorian British milieu and the literary romanticism to which he was exposed and the landscape of the West that he struggled to come to terms with and express. In some respects his observations parallel those of another western writer, Wallace Stegner, who diagnosed, perhaps in words too strong to apply with complete fidelity to Morton, a curious kind of intellectual schizophrenia that was produced by being brought up on a frontier—a place that had not been mentally assimilated and therefore had no history. 'The lateness of my frontier', Stegner wrote, 'and the fact that it lay in Canada intensified the discrepancy between that part of me which reflects the folk culture and that part which reflects an education imported and often irrelevant. The dichotomy between American and European that exists to some extent in all of us exists most drastically in people reared on frontiers, for frontiers provide not only the rawest forms of deculturation, but the most slavish respect for borrowed elegances.'[51] In his best work Morton managed to bring these twin poles of reference into creative equipoise. But Stegner's remark may explain the curious blending in Morton's outlook of an intense attachment to an agricultural region defined as pragmatic, experimental, and democratic on the one hand, and his romanticism and his allegiances to the monarchical tradition and Anglo-Canadian toryism on the other.

11 | TRADITION AND THE 'NEW' HISTORY

The outstanding features of Canadian historiography in the two decades after the mid-1960s were a sudden acceleration of research and publication, broadening of the scope and subject matter of history, and destruction of interpretations that had once given meaning to Canadian experience as a whole. Though much of the literature extended and amplified the tradition of national political history, a sense of the coherence of Canadian history was lost and historians no longer agreed upon what was central to their field of study and what was peripheral. This transformation in historical writing was hardly a unique feature of the world of Canadian scholarship. 'Modern historiography in general,' wrote the American historian Bernard Bailyn in 1982, 'seems to be in a stage of enormous elaboration. Historical enquiries are ramifying in a hundred directions at once, and there is no coordination among them. . . . Fields and problems that were once discrete and rather easily controllable merge, lose definition, reveal depths below depths. . . .' The shapelessness of contemporary historical literature was due at least as much to the changed commitments of historians as to the sheer proliferation of publications. What an Australian said of historians of his country applied up to a point to their Canadian counterparts: 'Historians, with one or two illustrious exceptions, no longer see themselves as the interpreters of national character or purpose. If they champion a cause it is more likely to be that of a class, a party, an ethnic or racial group, a locality or a gender than that of the nation as a whole.'[1] The severing of nationalism and history, in Canada as in Australia, was one of the most significant developments of the period.

I

Canadian historians had once concentrated upon explaining how a national community had come into being, and they had fixed upon the evolution of self-government, the distinctive patterns that had emerged out of the interplay of geography and economics, and, in the fifties, on biographies that highlighted the importance of personality and will over material forces in political development. While Donald Creighton and William Morton brought sharply differing viewpoints to their studies of the past, they nonetheless agreed that their subject was Canada as a nation state and that history was supremely important in promoting a community's self-understanding and definition. This belief about historical enquiry and the mission of the historian was, of course, an old claim, no doubt sincerely held; it was also a contention that had served to justify the existence of the historical profession.

By the early sixties pastmasters like Creighton and Morton were joined by members of another generation, born between the wars, who assimilated, perpetuated, and modified the prevailing modes of history. Three representative figures—H. Blair Neatby, P.B. Waite, and Ramsay Cook—all took their senior graduate degrees at the University of Toronto, were drawn to political biography, and assumed that history was concerned with unique events and conscious intent and behaviour. They wrote no economic history and retained an abiding suspicion of the determinism of the social sciences. In their first books they described such events as the union of 1867 or examined, usually in a biographical framework, such important themes in political history as the rise of liberalism, or the accommodation of western Canada's special interests within Confederation.[2] Though they accepted the nation state as the necessary framework of analysis they were hardly unaware of regional diversities: pluralism was in fact fundamental to the political history they wrote. Canada to them was a political creation in which conflicts of races, religions, and economic interests had been mediated, on the whole successfully, through the political process. Their sympathies were with the moderate men of the centre—the architects of Confederation, or the conciliators of the middle way, Laurier and King—and they would have shared the judgement of a slightly older scholar, Gerald M. Craig, who in *Upper Canada: The Formative Years, 1784–1841* (1963) judged that the rebellion of 1837 had complicated, not facilitated, the resolution of the colony's political problems.

Though they wrote 'national history', these historians were hardly nationalists like Lower or Creighton. In fact, during a decade that witnessed an upsurge of cultural and political nationalism in both English and French Canada, Ramsay Cook warned that all attempts to turn the country into a nationalist state had historically endangered liberal values. Drawing upon the teachings of Lord Acton (as had the imperially minded critics before him) Cook depicted both nationalist traditions as misguided and retrogressive.[3] While they eschewed the passionate patriotism of some of their predecessors these historians shared a quiet satisfaction about the country's past—and future. One of their contemporaries, Margaret Prang, spoke for a generation when she said that her own confidence in Canada had been inspired by the facts that the country had survived the enormous strains of the Depression, managed to avoid another destructive conflict over conscription, and extended to all its citizens a humane social security system. These historians were typical of the Canadian intellectual elite of their time in that they were not intensely engaged *social* critics.[4]

Though these individuals and their near contemporaries shared a general consensus about what was important in history they hardly subscribed to a monolithic party line, nor was tradition simply a static body of knowledge. As will be seen, Neatby, Waite, and Cook would in the following decades expand considerably an understanding of Canada's past, sometimes in surprising and unpredictable ways. Others who published important studies in the early sixties considerably altered inherited views. William Eccles, for example, challenged interpretations of New France that had survived intact in the romantic histories of Francis Parkman and the economic history of Harold Innis. Eccles put into a far more favourable light exactly those features of the colony that had been previously most condemned: where Parkman and Innis had equated state paternalism with weakness, Eccles argued that without government initiative and direction New France would not have survived as long as it had. In addition, he wrote appreciatively about the military-aristocratic ethos of the colony, its humane legal system, and above all its social welfare practices.[5] From an equally original angle, Morris Zaslow was at work reconstructing the history of Canada's northern expansion as a fully integrated strand of the nation's story.[6] And intellectual history, which had been cultivated by F.H. Underhill, J.M.S. Careless, and Ramsay Cook, was projected beyond the study of political opinions by S.F. Wise, who located the religious and philosophical roots of Upper Canada's conservative tradition, and by Carl Berger, who analysed the convictions and feelings of the advocates of imperial unity.[7]

A few historians in the sixties, moreover, subjected the tradition in which they had grown up to searching criticism. J.M.S. Careless joined Ramsay Cook in condemning the undue emphasis on national history and unity. The 'nation-building approach to Canadian history,' Careless wrote in 1969, 'neglects and obscures even while it explains and illuminates, and may tell us less about the Canada that now is than the Canada that should have been—but has not come to pass.' Region, culture, and class, he argued, were as legitimate forms of group identity as the nation state, and in Canada, where nationalizing forces had been weak and regional interests powerful, these might be more appropriate frameworks for examining the past. The 'distinctive nature of much of Canadian experience has produced a continent-wide entity identifiable in its very pluralism, constraints, and compromises.' Significantly, Careless did not repudiate the nation state as the proper subject of historical investigation: rather he appealed for a more pluralistic history of Canada.[8]

II

The transformation of Canadian historical writing after the mid-sixties was the consequence of profound changes in the country's educational and intellectual life. At the beginning of the boom in higher education and the virtually uncontrolled expansion of university systems there were some 160 historians in all fields in all colleges and universities in the country; by 1976 there were nearly 1,000. In the decade after 1966 the numbers of doctoral and masters' theses being written increased from 350 to some 1,200. This growth in the number of scholars expected to explore new subjects or revise old ones and increasingly hired as specialists in certain aspects of Canadian history rather than as generalists was the primary impulse behind the tidal wave of publications. The effect of this impetus, moreover, was compounded by the ever-increasing emphasis placed upon research and publication in universities that justified themselves as pioneers opening up new frontiers of knowledge rather than as transmitters and conservers of it. To those whose memories ran back to the fifties the triumph of the research ideal within academe was one of the most striking features of the changed environment in which scholars worked.[9]

Along with the enlargement of the historical profession came modifications in its character. Once the relatively small gentlemanly community of historians was dominated by a few outstanding individuals who wrote biographies of other outstanding individuals; now the profession had become a more anonymous collectivity, internally divided into subgroups of specialists who tended more and more to write of anonymous groups and classes. Growth brought into the ranks of academic historians people of more varied ethnic and cultural backgrounds, with a diversity of experiences, perspectives, and attainments.

Experimentation was further encouraged by the significant proportion of young historians who had been trained outside the older Canadian centres of graduate instruction in which a mastery of past literature was a prerequisite for research. This enhanced diversification; but it also weakened the links between certain types of history published in the seventies and others that represented extensions of tradition. The profession was decentralized as historians were dispersed in relatively strong departments across the country, exposed more fully to Canada's regional variety, and encouraged to explore more local subjects. The existence for the first time of significant numbers of historians who lived and taught regional histories in the universities of the west and the Maritimes provided the initiatives for the founding and sustenance of such important institutional supports for reinvigorated regional history as the annual Western Canadian Studies Conferences held in Calgary since 1969, and the revival of *Acadiensis: Journal of the History of the Atlantic Region* (1971).

The historical profession, moreover, became more varied and mature through the university recruitment of scholars who specialized in fields other than Canadian. A generation ago it was rare for a historian living in Canada to conduct research abroad; in the seventies, thanks partly to generous funding of both research and publication by the Canada Council and then by the Social Sciences and Humanities Research Council, books on the histories of European countries, the third world, and the United States, as well as such topics as the histories of science and the family, abounded in a rich profusion. While this literature was addressed primarily to an international community of scholars it impinged upon the writing of Canadian history by broadening the context in which Canada's history was studied and, in some cases, presenting alternative models of how history could be written.

The expansion of the profession coincided with deep, bewildering changes in Canadian society which impinged upon the consciousness of historians. The later sixties witnessed an intense questioning of the direction in which the country was moving and the dissolution of the post-war feeling of relative self-confidence. The rise of French-Canadian nationalism, the increasing vitality and assertiveness of provincial governments, and Canadian economic dependency were only three of the more highly visible challenges. In *The Forked Road: Canada, 1939–1957* (1976), Donald Creighton, the country's greatest nationalist historian, continued his personal war against these powerful currents and denounced those who led Canada down the road to subservience to the United States. Written when he was ill with cancer (Creighton died in 1979), it never did demonstrate that there existed another fork in the road at the crossing, and his book was savagely condemned by most historians. Even those who shared his sense of nationalist outrage were at a loss in coping with his attacks on the welfare state.

Where Creighton was driven to bleak despair, others were more hopeful about the possibilities of change that were indicated by the loosening of the hold of older British-Canadian norms, the feminist movement, the native peoples' rejection of their 'colonial' position in Canadian society, and, above all, student activism. Nowhere was this restlessness and intellectual ferment more pronounced than among the supporters of the 'New Left' in the universities.[10] In Canada as elsewhere this was less a movement than a mood—amorphous, sometimes incoherent, preoccupied with the Vietnam War, civil rights, and the bureaucratic organizations of the multi-university. In so far as it possessed a consistency of feeling the new left was hostile to hierarchy and authority (including interpretations of history that seemed to justify the flawed present). Those who shared its sentiments were disillusioned with electoral politics, instinctively sympathized with the rebels of the past—William Lyon Mackenzie, Louis Riel, and Norman Bethune—and identified, despite their own predominantly middle-class backgrounds, with the victimized and dispossessed—blacks, immigrants, workers, women, and native peoples. In some respects the new left was profoundly antihistorical and showed little appreciation for evolution and continuity. 'The future,' Northrop Frye wrote of this age of hysteria, 1968 to 1971, '... cannot be the outcome of the past: it is a brand new future, which may be implicit in the present but it is to be built out of the materials of the present by an act of will, which cannot operate until it has been released from the past.'[11] At least a few students, however, were driven to search out studies in Canadian history that were critical of what had happened and that would furnish the counterculture with its own independent and authentic roots in the past. Just as over a generation before Frank Underhill had turned to progressive historiography in order to trace the antecedents of the social democratic protest of the thirties, so too some students in the late sixties found exciting perspectives in Stanley Ryerson's Marxist histories of Canada, The Founding of Canada (1960) and Unequal Union (1968), and in Clare Pentland's 1960 'underground classic', Labour and Capital in Canada, 1650–1860, finally published in 1981. And some discovered in the vigorous British neo-Marxist literature, best exemplified by Edward P. Thompson's The Making of the English Working Class (1963), models of how anti-capitalist traditions and alternative histories could be recovered.

Reform movements which seek to change the future have always tried to rewrite the past. In the late sixties and early seventies representatives of groups rejecting their subordinate positions in society called for new histories that would give them greater recognition. These appeals invariably came from outside the historical profession, or occasionally from young historians just securing a foothold within it. One of the earliest books of essays on women's history, compiled by a feminist collective, declared that 'History and political economy courses in schools implied that women, alongside immigrants and the working class in general, had no role in Canadian history. Our involvement in organizations addressing themselves to women's oppression made us realize the urgent need to uncover a history which would challenge the conclusions of existing texts and establish women's rightful importance in Canada's past.'[12] A stinging indictment of white supremacy from a radical native point of view maintained that the fabrications of traditional Canadian history had to be overthrown in the struggle for decolonization. 'Those in power,' Howard Adams charged, 'command the present and shape the future by controlling the past, particularly for the native. A fact of imperialism is that it systematically denies native peoples a dignified history.'[13] The new history, as we shall see, involved more than the sympathetic study of previously neglected groups, but it owed not a little of its critical spirit to contemporary reform movements that were questioning institutions and practices. For some, history became a force for remedial action and moral criticism, a weapon for attacking the abuses of the present by exposing their sources and pointing to better alternatives not taken in the past. And Canadians in general were compelled to come to terms with moral wrongs in their historical experience by demands for an apology for the removal of Japanese Canadians from the west coast during the Second World War, by legal cases involving aboriginal land rights, and by requests for the posthumous pardon of Louis Riel.

III

The growth of the professional study and teaching of history was only one dimension of an upsurge of cultural nationalism and an unprecedented popular fascination with the past. Inspired by the celebrations of the centenary of Confederation and sustained by a universal search for roots, this wave of nostalgia expressed a hankering for direct contact with a visible, tangible 'living history'. It was the taproot of countless private ventures in genealogy, the retrieval of memorabilia and memories, the creation of hundreds of local museums, and the vast outpouring of local history. Local histories were populist in the sense that they dealt with the activities, people, and interests that general readers could readily comprehend and identify with. One of the most successful of these ventures into the past was *The Island Magazine*, published since 1976 by the Prince Edward Island Heritage Foundation; its first issue sold almost six thousand copies, and later numbers attained a readership of 3,500 to 4,000[14] (the subscribers to the *Canadian Historical Review* numbered about 3,000). This magazine combined essays by academic historians on outstanding figures with local roots—Sir Andrew MacPhail and Lucy Maud Montgomery—or on early governors or politicians, as well as pieces on folklore, appreciations of church buildings, lists of passengers on immigrant ships, songs once taught at school, accounts of soapmaking, cutting hay, and recipes, and, in one instance, a denunciation of daylight saving time. The printing of books on local history was facilitated by the proliferation of regional publishers—Breakwater Books in St. John's, Ragweed Press in Charlottetown, or Western Producer Prairie Books in Saskatoon. This last company, owned by a group of farmers who were members of the Saskatchewan Wheat Pool, brought out its first book in 1954 and thirty years later had a backlist in print of over 150 volumes on western Canadian history, landscape painting on the prairies, Ukrainian folk stories, and the social life of the one-room country school.

This retrospective impulse was expressed, too, in such CBC television serials as 'The National Dream' (based on Pierre Berton's history of the building of the CPR), 'Riel', and 'The Newcomers', the latter a series of seven one-hour historical dramas on the Tsimshian Indians and immigrants from France, Scotland, Ireland, Denmark, Ukraine, and Italy. Historical figures caught the attention of novelists: Heather Robertson's *Willy* fictionalized an already unbelievable world of Mackenzie King. The composer Godfrey Ridout evoked in the music of 'No Mean City: Scenes from Childhood' (first performed in 1984) the remembrance of the symbolic dates of old British Canada—May 24, July 12, and November 11. And Barry Broadfoot, whose faith in the reliability of human memory exceeded that of most historians, recorded in several volumes the recollections of people who experienced prairie settlement, the Depression, and the Second World War.[15]

This vogue of the past was above all addressed to the recovery, preservation, and in some cases the interpretation of artifacts. Of the hundreds of handsome picture books published in the period, some of the most informative and attractive conveyed both through illustration and prose the beauty—and function—of everyday things in the material culture of the past, everything from quilts and bedcoverings, iron-fences, stoves, and even manhole covers, to illustrations on pottery.[16] Commercial incentive and civic improvement combined to refurbish whole groups of buildings in city cores—Historic Properties in Halifax, the market district in Winnipeg, and the waterfront of Victoria—and entire settlements and villages were renovated or reconstructed. If such places as King's Landing in New Brunswick, or the Motherwell Homestead

National Historic Park at Abernethy, Saskatchewan, offer accurate indications of what contemporaries found attractive in the past, it was more graceful, more human in scale, than their own grey surroundings of the high-rise, the supermarket, and the expressway. (It was also sanitized and antiseptic.) The promotion of tourism—the selling of the past—was one of the major reasons for the expansion in the activities of the National Historic Parks and Sites Branch of Parks Canada; in the process of assembling accurate information for authentic restorations, researchers unearthed an enormous body of data on material culture, living conditions, and historical events. By 1981 Parks Canada had published over fifty volumes in its 'History and Archaeology' series, among them an altogether engrossing book with the unpromising title of *Grist and Flour Mills in Ontario: From Millstones to Rollers, 1780s to 1880s* (1981), by Felicity L. Leung. The restoration of Fortress Louisbourg, a project launched by the federal government in 1961 to relieve unemployment and promote tourism in Cape Breton, generated a small library of research reports that provided the basis for several books, including Christopher Moore's *Louisbourg Portraits: Life in an Eighteenth-Century Garrison Town* (1982) and A.J.B. Johnston's *Religion in Life at Louisbourg, 1713-1758* (1984), both of which applied insights from modern French historiography to Canadian subject matter. Johnston in particular went far beyond the usual treatment of religion in a sensitive chapter on faith, morals, and popular customs.

The writers of history who have responded best to the popular curiosity about history have come from the world of journalism, not the university. Academic historians whose books were printed in one or two thousand copies condescendingly relegated those writers whose works sold in the tens of thousands to the status of 'amateurs'. In reality, of course, it was the academic historians who devoted themselves only part-time to writing history and the popular writers who depended on the sales of their books for a living. In any case the appeal of 'popular history' rested on the telling of a gripping story, entertaining narrative, vivid characterization, a sense of drama, or the exposure of human foibles and frailties. Sometimes it could also serve the purpose of national feeling. Pierre Berton treated the building of the Canadian Pacific Railway as a great national undertaking and achievement, and his two volumes on the War of 1812 rendered the immediacy of the conflict by using the present tense throughout.[17] Sandra Gwyn's *The Private Capital: Ambition and Love in the Age of Macdonald and Laurier* (1984) resembled a delightful gossip column. It was filled with anecdotes and personal detail (twice we are told that Sir Sandford Fleming liked marmalade in his porridge) and breathless revelations about Laurier's long affair with his law partner's wife or the social rounds at Rideau Hall and the sexual escapades and preferences of some of its residents. One of the very best books of this type was *The Lumberjacks* (1978) by Donald MacKay, a journalist who had worked for United Press, and who recovered and conveyed graphically the ways of life of the woodcutters, their methods of work and camp life, unique language, codes of conduct, songs and folklore, food, and the technology they used from the cross-cut to the chain saw.

The expectations of the reading public regarding a work of history and the practice of most academic historians were closer a generation ago than in the last decade. Historians in general no longer regarded the art of narrative biography as a model for their work, and they have outgrown—or abdicated—the role of interpreters of the national character. Academic scholars have increasingly occupied themselves with anonymous social patterns, with groups and classes rather than with individuals; they prize analysis over narrative and description; their most original books do not tell a story but answer questions; and they frequently take as their points of departure evaluations of the corpus of existing literature and its shortcomings. All this tended to make access to the past difficult for the general reader; it was almost as though the historian had interposed himself or herself between the reader and history. These contrasts might be illustrated in an exaggerated way by noting that in a decade when Berton's books on the War of 1812 and *The Dionne Years: A Thirties Melodrama* (1977) were on the bestseller lists, the brightest young historians were beginning to explore subjects that were scarcely comprehensible to most readers of his works or for that matter to not a few historians. Some seventy-five papers were presented at the annual meeting of the Canadian Historical Association in 1981 and ten were selected for publication in that organization's *Historical Papers*.. Of these the four in Canadian history judged the most original and important were: 'Unwed Motherhood in Nineteenth-Century English Canada', 'Paupers and Poor-Relief in Upper Canada', 'Canada's Post-War Re-armament: Another Look at American Theories of the Military-Industrial Complex', and 'Fur Trade Labour and Lower Canadian Agrarian Structures'.

These divergencies in subject matter and approaches should not obscure the fact that there have been a very few scholars who have written highly original works of history which have found a wide readership beyond the academic profession. Michael Bliss took on the difficult task of recreating the inner history of a scientific breakthrough and in *The Discovery of Insulin* (1982) reconstructed the series of experiments and the clashes of personalities in such a compelling and scintillating fashion that his efforts were praised by the most demanding historians of science as well as reviewers who loved an exciting story.

Writers outside the academic establishment, moreover, have written original and indispensable works of history. There was more to be learned about life in western Canada between the wars from James Gray's *The Winter Years: The Depression on the Prairies* (1966) and *The Roar of the Twenties* (1975) than from any two academic treatises at the time they were published. A practising lawyer, Patrick Brode, advanced immeasurably an understanding of both the Loyalist tradition and legal practice in nineteenth-century Ontario in *Sir John Beverley Robinson: Bone and Sinew of the Compact* (1984); and Murray Peden, in *A Thousand Shall Fall* (1979), drew upon his service in an RAF squadron to give us an account of the air war against Nazi Germany that deservedly received the ultimate accolade from Charles P. Stacey, who wrote that it was the best book any Canadian has written about his war experiences and one of the best books about the war that has been written anywhere. Such generous praise was rare. The responses of most academic historians to the surge of popular history was uneasy and critical, as though the confines of a craft guild had been violated. Historians who would hardly accept at face value the special pleadings of, say, manufacturers advocating a tariff, have never subjected the claims of their own profession to close scrutiny. They have, in fact, for all the growth in numbers and publications, become more isolated from the society in which they lived and in general have failed to respond to the enormous popular interest in the past—either in satisfying it, or educating it.

IV

A generation ago the biography was the dominant form in Canadian historical writing and its continuing vitality was manifest in the *Dictionary of Canadian Biography* which, under the general editorship of Francess Halpenny and Jean Hamelin, comprised nine plump volumes by 1986. This project was an outstanding undertaking in Canadian historiography—for its scale (the volume on the 1881–90 period contained 586 biographies by 382 contributors) and for the quality of the generally meticulously researched and authoritative entries. The organization of entries according to the chronology of death rather than alphabetically drew together information on persons who lived in approximately the same periods and thus these books were relatively self-contained, collaborative works of history that were much more than the sum of their parts. They were, in effect, portraits of a succession of ages. It must be a reader of exceptionally limited curiosity who has not found himself or herself, hours after taking up one of these works to check a particular person, still immersed in the complex web of many intersecting lives. There is in fact no more effective way to escape from the categories that historians impose upon the past than to plunge into one of these volumes which so faithfully convey so many perspectives and life-paths simultaneously. Though predictably the largest proportion of biographies was given to administrators, political figures, businessmen, and clergymen, the editors have cast their net widely enough to include also artists, artisans, and architects, slaves and native peoples, labour leaders, and women (now identified by their maiden names rather than their married names by which they were recognized by their contemporaries). By using the index to identifications, moreover, it is possible to see patterns that linked particular social groups, the seigneurial class in Quebec in the late eighteenth century, for example, or the business or academic communities of Victorian Canada. The *Dictionary* has been aptly called a 'great cathedral to the biographical tradition', a structure built over many years by generations of craftsmen.[18]

Like the cathedral, however, the art of biography seemed to belong to another age. Many valuable biographies continued to appear but the bulk of them by historians were more notable for the information they contained about such matters as past politics than for enlarging our comprehension of human behaviour. This was to be expected in those originally composed as doctoral dissertations, for their authors' experiences of life were limited; but it was more generally true also of books about people who were no doubt of great historical significance but who left few revealing records of their personal lives. Such studies as John S. Galbraith, *The Little Emperor: Governor Simpson of the Hudson's Bay Company* (1976), Robert Bothwell and William Kilbourn, *C.D. Howe: A Biography* (1979), or John Kendle, *John Bracken: A Political Biography* (1979), were important contributions to our knowledge about—respectively— the management of the fur trade, Canada's industrial mobilization in the Second World War, and Manitoba politics in the inter-war years. But the private lives, let alone the private thoughts, of these people were still mysteries. Only very seldom did a writer of insight, literary skill, and luck with sources manage to render penetrating and memorable glimpses of human beings. Maria Tippett, in *Emily Carr: A Biography* (1979), a sensitive study of the relation of art and life, managed to convey lucidly and sympathetically the influence of a devastating childhood experience upon the woman's personality. And P.B. Waite, whose relish for the telling and amusing anecdote was unsurpassed among contemporary historians, presented in *The Man from Halifax: Sir John Thompson, Prime Minister* (1985) a political career in all its amplitude and a singular study of a Victorian marriage and family.

Biographers became somewhat defensive about their craft. Robert Craig Brown, the author of a life of the uninspiring but dedicated wartime leader, Sir Robert Borden, confessed that within the historical profession the biographer was apt to feel 'something like an eccentric cousin: a bit old fashioned in his insistence that individuals can and do shape the historical process.... Biography is becoming ever more internal and individualistic, history more collective.'[19] The rising current of social history not only emphasized groups, classes, and the experiences of common people: its exponents dismissed biographies of elite figures, especially politicians, as propagating a false consciousness about historical change. Yet social history also provided an incentive to reinterpret even political leaders in new ways and to retrieve the life experiences of the obscure.

Brian Young, in *George-Etienne Cartier: Montreal Bourgeois* (1981), treated this Quebec politician as a social type. We learn much about his taste in wines, the magazines he read, his long extra-marital affair, and his anglophilia; but the core of the sketch consisted of an examination of his law practice; investments in real estate, railways, and banks; the politics of his constituency; and his conservative purposes in reforming the Civil Code, ending seigneurial tenure, and supporting the new federal state. Christopher Moore in *Louisbourg Portraits* successfully employed the experiences of ordinary people—a widow, merchant, sea-captain, fisherman, soldier turned settler, and a drifter accused of theft—to bring into sharp relief the character of the society in which they lived, their strategies for survival, marriage and child-rearing practices, the operations of the judicial system and the world of commerce. In a tentative analysis of the criminal records of the 'jailbirds of Victorian Halifax', Judith Fingard depicted an unusual gallery of unique personalities, discerned some common patterns in crime and punishment, and wisely resisted explaining away the vagaries of human behaviour as social protest. An equally surprising aspect of life in the lower reaches of society was revealed in Peter DeLottinville's profile of the career of Charles McKierhan—'Joe Beef'—whose Montreal canteen (a combination of tavern, menagerie, boarding house, and private welfare agency) catered to transient workers.[20] One of the most positive effects of this interest in the lives of ordinary people has been to show how truly unconventional they actually were.

While these writers pursued biography into unfamiliar directions, most other historians who wrote lives were uncomfortable with the psychologists' truth that people are driven by forces of which they are unaware, or that patterns of behaviour are shaped by buried childhood experiences. The problem of relating the inner life to the public role arose with striking clarity in 1976 with the appearance of *William Lyon Mackenzie King, Volume III, 1932-1939: The Prism of Unity* by H. Blair Neatby and *A Very Double Life: The Private World of Mackenzie King* by Charles P. Stacey. Drawing upon King's diary, which recorded in profuse detail his views of political problems, moods, thoughts, doubts and dreams, Stacey exposed King's early contacts with prostitutes, his obsessions with money, rich women, and dogs, and his belief in spiritualism. So naive did King's own faith in the messages from beyond seem that Stacey was left with the impression that he was dealing with a rather limited intelligence. Stacey justified his approach on the grounds that this information had been self-censored by the official biographers and that it was necessary to bring it to light for a fuller understanding of the whole person, even though he came to the conclusion that what King received from the spirit world was reassurance, not advice. For Neatby the issue was whether all this evidence provided about King's personality in the diary was of any use for explaining him as a political being; after considerable reflection he concluded that it was not, that the historian could account for King's political decisions and his leadership style in exclusively rational terms. He believed that King's spiritualism was important—but mainly as an indication of the extent of his isolation from other human beings.[21]

It says something for the common sense (or conservatism) of historians that the only sustained attempt to employ psychological insights to King's formative years and to show how his personality traits did influence his political activity was made by a political scientist, Joy Esberey, in *Knight of the Holy Spirit: A Study of William Lyon Mackenzie King* (1980). In the first part of the book, Esberey presented a convincing interpretation of the origins of King's neurotic personality in his inability to break out of the suffocating embrace of his family, to accept his mother as a human being, and to establish his own individuality. The second part, which illustrated his pattern of behaviour in political life— in, for example, his dealings with such figures of authority as the governors-general, or with his views of the British Commonwealth as a family—was less effective. Esberey was less interested in explaining King's political career as a whole than in linking the two levels of his life together, but few, if any, historians thought the exercise entirely convincing.[22]

V

While political biography went into relative decline, historians and social scientists rediscovered and rehabilitated the political economy tradition that Harold Innis and his contemporaries had developed in the thirties. This renewed concern with the material foundations of society and politics was partially a reaction to the neglect of economic history by the preceding generation; it owed much also to the resurgence of nationalism. At a time when American influences in the social sciences were decried by some as irrelevant to understanding Canada, Innis came to exemplify an indigenous scholarly tradition which offered penetrating explanations for the country's dependence upon Britain and the United States and insights into economic disparities among regions. Some of his new admirers even attempted to fuse his approach to economic history with Marxism. Innis, however, had centred his analysis upon trade relations, on the physical properties of staples of the pre-industrial era, and on the ways in which each commodity had shaped structures and patterns. For the Marxists, on the other hand, the crux of the matter was the process and means of production and the social relations of capital and labour.[23] The marriage of Marx and Innis was a barren union: so much time was expended by the political economists of the left on clarifying paradigms that little economic history was written. Nonetheless, Innis became a cult figure: social scientists attempted to rescue him from the communications theorists, subjected his writings to considerable analysis, and reprinted even his inscrutable notebooks.[24]

One of the major studies inspired by the debate over foreign ownership, Tom Naylor's *The History of Canadian Business, 1867–1914* (1975)—in two volumes—owed much to Innis, nothing to Marx, and a little to Gustavus Myers, the turn-of-the-century muckracker who had set out to expose the shady origins of Canadian wealth. Naylor argued that Canada's reliance upon staple exports had fashioned a set of commercial institutions and patterns of behaviour that stultified industrial entrepreneurship. Despite the adoption of the national policy of protection, the economy had not substantially diversified between Confederation and the First World War; the country continued as a supplier of raw materials and relied upon imported American manufacturing. Naylor's case was illustrated with a profusion of new information about the banking system, patent laws, and the practices of municipalities in bonussing companies to locate within their boundaries. While some economic nationalists hailed his study as comparable in importance to those of Innis or Creighton, most historians were, to say the least, sceptical of both his methods and his identification of merchants as the enemies of manufacturing. Even when they recognized that he had fixed upon important problems in Canadian economic history, such as the extent to which banks had actually underwritten industrial ventures, they condemned these volumes as demonologies of the business world, filled with distortions and factual errors.[25]

Naylor's assertions regarding the anti-industrial bias of the merchant class received little support from two less controversial studies. Gerald Tulchinsky, in *The River Barons: Montreal Businessmen and the Growth of Industry and Transportation, 1837–53* (1977), investigated entrepreneurs of various ethnic origins who were involved in the forwarding trade and ocean shipping, built railways to American ports, and also developed manufacturing around the water-power sites on the Lachine canal. And John McCallum, in *Unequal Beginnings: Agriculture and Economic Development in Quebec and Ontario until 1870* (1980), contended that Ontario's economic lead over Quebec was due to the superior productive capacity of its agriculture: wheat production had brought very high returns which stimulated other sectors of the economy, including transportation and industry. Quebec's more limited industrial growth was due more to lack of virgin land and external markets than to the traits of classes, merchants, or farmers.

One of the most important books of the last two decades, H. Viv Nelles' *The Politics of Development: Forests, Mines and Hydro-Electric Power in Ontario, 1849–1941* (1974), resumed the study of staple production where Innis and others had left off and carried the ramifications of an old subject into unanticipated directions. This work was both a detailed history of the natural resource industries and the entrepreneurs who developed them, and an incisive and critical appraisal of the provincial government's development policies. The extension of government activity through regulation and conservation, the promotion of the processing of resources within the province, and the creation of a publicly owned hydro-electric power system were, according to Nelles, instigated by pressures from certain segments of the business community, not in opposition to business in general. In fact, he claimed that the state became a client of the business community though he did not establish convincingly that feasible alternatives to what he condemned existed at the time. Still, his study was immensely instructive for explaining Ontario's ascendancy within the Canadian economy, continental integration, and what can only be called Ontario's 'national policy'.

Nelles' book contained many new points of reference on state-business relations, some of which were carried forward by others. In an official history of the Ontario Northland Railway, Albert Tucker offered both a straightforward account of the construction and operation of the line and an extended analysis of an experiment in public ownership that rested on the common interests in efficiency and development that were shared by politicians and businessmen. Tom Traves assessed the unsuccessful efforts of the newsprint, sugar, steel, and automobile industries to use the state to solve problems of competition and uncertainty of markets in the twenties.[26] And John Richards and Larry Pratt, *Prairie Capitalism: Power and Influence in the New West* (1979), took up the theme that provincial governments have acted as entrepreneurs in staple-led development and examined the efforts of Saskatchewan and Alberta in promoting the exploitation of natural gas, oil, and potash. Despite the apparently large ideological differences between the social-democratic CCF and the right-wing Social Credit parties, both governments entered into similar arrangements with foreign companies; in the seventies, both provinces, again governed by parties with different names, became more activist in attempting to establish diversified industrial economies based on staples.

Historians who wrote of individual businessmen and firms tended on the whole to be more sympathetic to their subjects than those who examined state-business relations. They were more sympathetic both in the sense that they attempted to recreate from the perspective of an individual or a group the insecure worlds in which they operated and made decisions,[27] and also in that some writers set out to rehabilitate people whose very names had passed into historical folklore as synonyms for greed and manipulation.

In *A Living Profit: Studies in the Social History of Canadian Business, 1883-1911* (1974), Michael Bliss reported on the opinions of the business community towards success and failure, workers and unions, political questions, competition, and justifications for the restriction of competition. In his *A Canadian Millionaire: The Life and Business Times of Sir Joseph Flavelle, Bart., 1858-1939* (1978), Bliss replied indirectly to criticisms that he had examined attitudes divorced from practice, and presented on a very broad canvas a richly detailed portrait of a self-made man, his business activities in meat packing and finance, and public service as chairman of the Imperial Munitions Board and in church, hospital, and university. One of the very best Canadian biographies, this study escaped the restrictions of the genre to explore the texture of the business culture of turn-of-the-century capitalism—its religious origins in Methodist perfectionism, its complex networks, and its sense of social obligations. Ted D. Regehr, in *The Canadian Northern Railway: Pioneer Road of the Northern Prairies, 1895-1918* (1976), took on a more difficult task in attempting to refurbish the reputations of William Mackenzie and Donald Mann. Painstakingly researched, scrupulous in unravelling complex financial dealings, and cautious in interpretation, this work claimed that these entrepreneurs were less interested in accumulating wealth than in using their formidable business skills in building something permanent, and—more convincingly—established that their railway (which suffered bankruptcy in the Great War and was taken over by the government) fulfilled real needs of the prairie settlers. Duncan McDowall told the uncommon success story of a well-rounded and profitable company that stood in striking contrast to the pattern of dependency upon foreign ownership in *Steel at the Sault: Francis H. Clergue, Sir James Dunn, and the Algoma Steel Corporation, 1901-1956* (1984). Delineating the background of the company from the visions of the founder of an industrial complex to the authoritarian management of the financier who took it over in the Depression, this analysis highlighted the interplay of the industry and the three levels of government and was especially effective on the state-regulated and controlled capitalism of the Second World War period under C.D. Howe whose presence in the volume seemed as prominent as the two figures mentioned in the title. It was Howe who created the Crown corporation examined in *Eldorado: Canada's National Uranium Company* (1984) by Robert Bothwell, who recorded the discovery and early exploitation of uranium in the thirties and the nationalization of the private company in war, and presented a well-drawn picture of the inner workings of the Crown company and its struggles for international markets.

VI

Historians of politics, external affairs, and military policy have almost forsaken the nineteenth for the twentieth century and have intensified their investigations into two distinct eras—ages identified with Laurier and Borden, and with Mackenzie King. Robert Craig Brown and Ramsay Cook, *Canada, 1896–1921: A Nation Transformed* (1974), drew upon over sixty theses initiated in the 1960s to produce a masterful synthesis, a 'progress report' on contemporary Canadian historical scholarship that was supplemented by their own independent research. This survey emphasized economic development, urbanization, western settlement, social movements, and, above all, the demands of the war emergency on the social and political system. Thus their analyses of French-English relations, tensions between east and west, the conscription crisis of 1917, and the upsurge of wartime idealism and reform were all intricately related to social changes and group interests. John English put wartime political change into a novel perspective in *The Decline of Politics: The Conservatives and the Party System, 1901–1920* (1977), which showed that the unionist coalition of 1917 was the climax of efforts pre-dating the war to modernize the political system, diminish the undue influence of local interests, and establish a national consensus based on the ideal of national service and a homogeneous British-Canadian nationalism.

Three of the country's most prolific historians collectively expanded our understanding of how profoundly the experience of war shaped Canada's development. In 1970 Charles P. Stacey completed his official history of Canada in the Second World War with *Arms, Men and Governments, 1939–1945: The War Policies of Canada* and then turned to a survey of foreign relations, the first instalment of which, *Canada and the Age of Conflict: A History of Canadian External Policies, Volume I, 1867–1921* (1977), centred upon the Dominion's ambiguous status within the

Empire, her struggle for autonomy during the war, and efforts to consolidate a co-operative imperial foreign policy. Desmond Morton, who worked in the early sixties in the Canadian Army Historical Section, seemed to write faster than most of his colleagues could read and published voluminously on the political history of the militia; on the military events of the North-West Rebellion; and on the career of a relative, General Sir William Otter, who had commanded troops in the Boer War and who was in the First World War in charge of the internment of enemy aliens.[28] In *A Peculiar Kind of Politics: Canada's Overseas Ministry in the First World War* (1982), Morton demonstrated that the recognition of Canada's nationhood depended not only on the fighting capacity of her soldiers, but no less on the development of effective administrative control over their disposition in Europe. This was, he made abundantly clear, a Canadian triumph over their own amateurism and unfocused enthusiasms. Like Morton, J.L. Granatstein nurtured his interest in conscription in the mid-sixties in the Army Historical Section (then in the process of becoming the Directorate of History, Department of National Defence) where he co-operated with J. Mackay Hitsman on a study of manpower policies in both world wars. In *Broken Promises: A History of Conscription in Canada* (1977), these two authors showed scant sympathy for those who had supported compulsory military service as a military necessity, and they censured the military and the politicians for miscalculating manpower needs. In addition, they attributed conscription to overzealous patriots—bigots really—set on forcing French Canadians to do their share.

Mackenzie King and his times became an academic growth industry as historians explored from many angles national political life in the Depression, the Second World War, and the decades of the Liberal party's hegemony. This had a great deal to do with the release after thirty years of government records previously closed to researchers and to the lifting of restrictions on the use of King's diary. In contrast to the earlier tendency to blame King for subverting parliamentary government, or eroding the British connection, or posturing as a reformer, the literature of the seventies was much more favourable to him as a political leader. A generation that was itself more acutely conscious of the fragility of Canada seemed more appreciative of his difficulties in preserving national unity. The sheer size and luxuriance of King's papers and the prolixity of the diary may also have exerted a subtle and irresistible enchantment, enticing writers into sharing King's perspective and assimilating his point of view.

That sympathetic understanding was not always the enemy of detachment should be clear to any reader of Blair Neatby's third volume in the official life. Its subtitle, *The Prism of Unity*, perfectly conveyed

King's deepest conviction that Canada was an association of diverse cultures, regions, and interest groups and that the task of statecraft was to promote a sense of partnership among all of these. For King, politics was an endless effort to avoid division, even at the expense of clarity or consistency, and to encourage a sense of commonality: and it was this positive belief, combined with his superb sensitivity to the twists and turns of politics, not simply luck or opportunism, that guaranteed his improbable success. Neatby was hardly uncritical of King: in fact, he devoted so much attention to R.B. Bennett's reform programme that he left the impression that King was incapable of responding creatively to people's needs in the early years of the Depression.

In J.L. Granatstein's *Canada's War: The Politics of the Mackenzie King Government, 1939-1945* (1975), the activities of the prime minister form the central thread of a massively documented account of the conscription crises, the beginnings of the welfare state, fiscal policy, external relations, and the enlargement of the powers of the central government. Granatstein did tend to give King the benefit of the doubt and accentuated the positive consequences of what his critics perceived as evasion or lack of imagination. Where King had once been reproached for his timidity in advancing Canada's claim for recognition within the councils of the allied powers commensurate with her actual economic and military contribution, Granatstein attributed the country's marginal position more to the unwillingness of Britain and the United States to share authority. Indeed, among the most arresting features of his account of war policies were the difficulties in dealing with the British. This admiration for King's political skills was, somewhat surprisingly, no less evident in Stacey's *Canada and the Age of Conflict: A History of Canadian External Policies, Volume II, 1921-1948: The Mackenzie King Era* (1981), which was liberally peppered with the author's own reminiscences of the mood of the times. Though Stacey highlighted King's misunderstanding of Hitler, he, like Neatby and Granatstein, emphasized that Canada's declaration of war in 1939 with a minimum of internal discord was King's major political achievement.

These positive appraisals of King's contribution to national unity have been complemented by extensive examinations of his early career as a labour relations expert, his social thought, and his position as a reformer. While Paul Craven's *'An Impartial Umpire': Industrial Relations and the Canadian State, 1900-1911* (1980) was concerned with the development of a distinctive labour relations system and with the state as mediator of competing class interests, it also presented the most convincing analysis of King's intellectual development, the nature and sources of his convictions about society, and his activities as a conciliator in the

Department of Labour in the Laurier period. Similarly, James Struthers' *No Fault of Their Own: Unemployment and the Canadian Welfare State, 1914–1941* (1983) was a complex survey of government policy relating to the jobless from reliance upon local poor relief to the adoption of a national unemployment insurance scheme. Though much attention was devoted to the role of the social work profession and to federal-provincial conflict, the book also offered telling insights into the reasons for the King government's initiation of unemployment insurance and the limited, indeed conservative, purposes this measure was intended to serve.

One supremely important work that managed to escape the King-centred view of the age was the richly descriptive *The Government Party: Organizing and Financing the Liberal Party of Canada, 1930–58* (1977) by the political scientist Reginald Whitaker. This was by far the best historical examination of the makeup and mundane operations of a major political party and a perceptive inquiry into the political culture that made possible the virtual identification of the Liberal party and the state. In Whitaker's work, historical detail and analysis took precedence over the application of theoretical models of how parties were supposed to function and the result was a brilliant elucidation of party structure, patronage, financing, and the important role of advertising agencies. The study was most effective also in showing how the politicians relied upon the civil service for new ideas and initiatives, a point taken up in Granatstein's group portrait of some twenty bureaucrats who exerted an influence disproportionate to their numbers upon the creation of government structures, external policy, and the welfare state, *The Ottawa Men: The Civil Service Mandarins, 1935–1957* (1982).

Some of the veterans of this golden age of the civil service published valuable memoir-histories that were based on research as well as reflection. In one of the most attractive and informative of these—*The Shaping of Peace: Canada and the Search for World Order, 1943–1957* (two volumes, 1979 and 1982)—John Holmes considered the aspirations and ideas that formed part of his own thinking as a career officer in External Affairs and examined what became of them in the encounter with a darkening and dividing world. Among its many charms are the under-stated presence of the writer who took seriously the duty to escape the implications of his own epigram: 'Recollections in tranquillity of untranquil times tend to excessive clarification.' Escott Reid recalled the making of the North Atlantic Treaty and A.F. Wynne Plumptre chronicled Canada's relations to the world monetary system.[29] The poet-diplomat Douglas LePan evoked the magnetic personality of General A.G.L. McNaughton and told of a memorable encounter with J.M. Keynes in his beautifully written but reserved *Bright Glass of Memory: A Set of Four Memoirs* (1979). Reserved is a word no one would use to describe

Charles Ritchie's *The Siren Years: A Canadian Diplomat Abroad, 1937–1945* (1974), a delightful and sardonic diary of his official—as well as very personal—experiences in London during the Blitz.

Those like Holmes or Reid who had actually witnessed the transactions they described were apt to emphasize the narrow range of options that were open to Canada during the Cold War, and they were sceptical of later accounts by historians who either decried Canada's growing dependence upon the United States or minimized the reality of the threat of Russia. Robert D. Cuff and J.L. Granatstein—in *Canadian-American Relations in Wartime: From the Great War to the Cold War* (1975) and *American Dollars and Canadian Prosperity: Canadian-American Economic Relations, 1945–1950* (1978)—explored both these themes. In the first they examined several wartime agreements that unintentionally constricted Canada's freedom of action; in the second they thoroughly documented the country's economic dependence upon the American purchases of raw materials and defence requirements.

Apart from these investigations in Canadian-American relations and Stacey's survey, historians of Canada left the writing of the history of external policy, at least in book-length studies, to political scientists. This was the case even with such relatively remote topics as *Canada and the League of Nations* (1975), by Richard Veatch, who was as interested in the machinery of policy formation and the influence of ministers and civil servants, parties, and pressure groups as in the actual contents of policy, most of which was very well known (the only major surprise in this book was a bizarre case in which the Six Nations Iroquois unsuccessfully took their grievances to the League). The most impressive instance of a single-minded steadiness in the writing of the history of diplomacy and defence policy has been James Eayrs' series *In Defence of Canada*, conceived in 1953 when he was a research assistant on the official biography of Mackenzie King and which, by 1984, constituted five volumes ranging from national security policy in the early twenties to Canada's involvement in the background to the Vietnam War. In all of these Eayrs was the resolute enemy of moralism as well as pretensions to realism: his studies were brilliantly written, sparkled with striking vignettes of personalities and ironical observations (sometimes at his subjects' expense), and solidly grounded in seemingly boundless documentation.[30] Like Eayrs' work, Denis Stairs' *The Diplomacy of Constraint: Canada, the Korean War, and the United States* (1974) was a highly descriptive, theoretically unadorned, analysis of the ways in which policy-makers attempted to enhance the functions of the United Nations as a means of imposing limits on American power.

Political scientists have also dominated the analysis of contemporary history. The only sustained attempt by historians to interpret recent history, *Canada since 1945: Power, Politics, and Provincialism* (1981), by Robert Bothwell, Ian Drummond, and John English, set out to correct the bias of the contemporary media towards decline and division by fixing upon undramatic long-term tendencies (the best and most valuable chapters were on economic and population changes and fiscal policy) and on developments since the war that sustain the view of Canadian history as a success story, especially the growth of social policy, vigorous internationalism, and a richer cultural life. Refreshingly opinionated, if one agrees with them, or, if not, simply ventilating the bias of 'Toronto Whigs', the authors confess to a preference for the relatively centralized, outward-looking country of the forties and fifties and—iconoclastic even in this—do not present a sustained analysis of the growth in importance of provincial governments and regional and local identities.

The writing of the military history of the armed forces, engagements and campaigns (as distinct from diplomatic leadership in wartime), was vigorously promoted by the federal government through the Directorate of History, Department of National Defence. Though the twenty or so historians employed there published on such varied subjects as the Royal Canadian Medical Corps, the Commonwealth Air Training Plan, and the naval war in the Atlantic,[31] the Directorate's most impressive project was a history of the Royal Canadian Air Force. In the first of four projected volumes, *Canadian Airmen and the First World War: The Official History of the Royal Canadian Air Force* (1980), S.F. Wise and his staff solved a unique problem of presenting a coherent account of the many Canadians who were scattered throughout the British air services and were not directly subject to Canadian authority. The result was a dense history, not only on the development of military aviation and training procedures but also on the exploits of individuals.

The unification of the services in 1968 occasioned an acute sense of loss in the Royal Canadian Navy and most of the naval veterans, official historians, and maritime scholars who contributed to the excellent collection edited by James A. Boutilier, *The RCN in Retrospect, 1910–1968* (1982), papers both analytical and anecdotal on commanders, warships, and engagements, shared the feeling that Canadians were indifferent to their maritime tradition. Though Barry M. Gough came to the study of the British navy and the northwest coast from the angle of imperial history, his trilogy served to underscore the crucial role of seapower in Canada's colonial past in consolidating British claims to the Pacific coast as well as in enforcing European authority among the native peoples.[32]

The diversity of war studies was further magnified by two scholars with a long involvement in the field: George F.G. Stanley, who published *Canada Invaded, 1775–1776* (1977) and *The War of 1812: Land Operations*

(1983), and Richard Preston, who revealed the other side of a tenacious myth in *The Defence of the Undefended Border: Planning for War in North America, 1867-1939* (1977). Reginald H. Roy, the biographer of Major General George Pearkes, responded to the fortieth anniversary of the invasion of Europe with *1944: The Canadians in Normandy* (1984), as did J.L. Granatstein and Desmond Morton with *Bloody Victory* (1984). And Roy MacLaren, ex-diplomat, advertising executive, and publisher, compensated for the relative neglect of military subjects by 'amateur' historians (apart from Pierre Berton) with lively narratives on such tangential subjects as the Canadian Expeditionary Force in Russia just after the revolution and the Nile voyageurs.[33]

VII

The upsurge of publications in regional and provincial history represented the extension of a pre-existing tendency rather than an abrupt departure from the tradition of Canadian historical writing. Local studies had been assiduously cultivated since the Victorian period (even though they were often disparaged as parochial and lacking in rigorous standards) and in the fifties and early sixties such professional historians as William Morton, Margaret Ormsby, and W. Stewart MacNutt published important histories of, respectively, Manitoba, British Columbia, and New Brunswick before Confederation. In planning the Canadian Centenary Series in the early sixties Donald Creighton and Morton defined that series' 'main theme' as the development of those regional communities which had made up the Canadian nation. No less than eleven of the original projected seventeen volumes were given over to the separate histories of old Quebec, Upper and Lower Canada, the Maritimes, the northwest, and the north.[34]

Regional history subsequently forged to the forefront of attention because of the manifest prominence of provincial governments within the federal system and the depth of discontent and 'alienation', especially in Quebec and the prairies, in the seventies. Regional historians revived the accusations that certain parts of Canada—usually the Maritimes and the west—had paid and continued to pay a disproportionate price for national unity and that Confederation perpetuated a system of injustice.[35] Even when appeals for regional histories were not cast as indictments, they still emphasized that any adequate history of modern Canada as a whole had to keep in the foreground the interests, characters, and perspectives of the parts. This appreciation for the local and regional arose from a strong positive identification with, and admiration for, the integrity of localities and provincial cultures. This was, at bottom, a matter of sympathy, a feeling that history was not something that happened somewhere else—it happened in *this* place and was therefore worthy of attention and study. Localist studies also became more conspicuous as a byproduct of specialization and of ever larger numbers of researchers working on ever smaller subjects. Thus even where historians were primarily concerned with, say, the working classes in particular industrial centres, or ethnic relations within individual provinces, their findings provided information that was readily incorporated into regional studies.[36]

Influences from outside the historical profession reinforced this trend. Political scientists like S.J.R. Noel and David Smith traced the historical patterns that moulded distinct provincial political cultures; and such literary historians as Laurence Ricou, Dick Harrison, and Patrick O'Flaherty examined the interaction of people and landscapes in the literature of the prairies and Newfoundland.[37] This focus on region was also fundamental in the historical geography of Andrew Hill Clark, a Canadian who had taught at the University of Wisconsin and died in 1975. In his books on Prince Edward Island and Old Acadia, Clark was concerned with people and their physical environments, less from the once fashionable perspective of how climate and landforms influenced the course of events than with human beings as active forces who imprinted their perceptions and values upon the surroundings. Historical geography was empirical, descriptive, and resolutely regional in focus as was exemplified in the finest survey of early Canada, *Canada before Confederation: A Study in Historical Geography* (1974), by R. Cole Harris and John Warkentin. In this study the localism and diversity of the Maritimes, the seigneurial agriculture of Quebec, the towns and rural landscapes of Ontario, the Indian and fur trade societies of the plains, and the mining communities of the west coast were all depicted as separate entities, each with unique features. Graeme Wynn's finely crafted *Timber Colony: A Historical Geography of Early Nineteenth-Century New Brunswick* (1981) combined the older staples approach to economic development with the geographer's concern with man-land relations to explore not only the business and economic history of the industry but also the ways in which it created a particular landscape and way of life.[38] Regionalism in historical writing was thus sustained by the convergence of tendencies within several disciplines as well as self-conscious attempts by historians to characterize limited identities.

How far the search for a provincial character superseded the quest for a national identity was apparent in the rationale for one of the most ambitious projects launched in the seventies. The Ontario Historical Studies Series under the editorship of Goldwin French, with Peter Oliver as associate editor, was conceived in 1971 as a group of biographies of the premiers of the province along the lines of Oliver's study of

G. Howard Ferguson and Charles W. Humphries' life and times of Sir James P. Whitney. The series itself mirrored the changing fashions in historical writing and was eventually extended to encompass—in no less than thirty-five volumes—projected studies of the economy, social structure, labour, minority groups, education, literature, and the arts. Thus it was able to incorporate such thematic works conceived independently as Christopher Armstrong's *The Politics of Federalism: Ontario's Relations with the Federal Government, 1867–1942* (1981), which demonstrated how Ontario premiers extended provincial powers, territories, and control over resources, and also how private interests had successfully played off one level of government against the other. Even though the series changed, the justification for it remained the same: it was claimed that Ontario was imperfectly understood and that its values and convictions were vague, elusive, and baffling. Possessing no tradition of regional grievance, having confidently accepted its dominant role within Confederation, Ontario had simply been confused by historians with the country as a whole.[39]

Far better than these aspirations for Ontario history, the actual development of prairie and maritime studies illustrated the character of recent publications in regionalism. The prairie west possessed one of the richest and most mature traditions of historical writing, which was extended and perpetuated by a younger generation, most of whom taught in prairie universities and many of whom contributed to books of essays presented in appreciation to the three men—Lewis G. Thomas, William L. Morton, and Lewis H. Thomas—who had pioneered the field.[40] These scholars frequently published their first research papers in the proceedings of the interdisciplinary Western Canadian Studies Conferences and, to a lesser extent, in the biennial *Prairie Forum*, issued since 1973 by the Great Plains Research Centre at Regina. One of the volumes of papers that resulted from the Calgary conferences, *The Canadian West: Social Change and Economic Development* (1980), edited by Henry Klassen, typified the diversity of prairie studies: it included investigations of utopian ideals and community settlements, women on the Alberta ranching frontier, the Lake of the Woods Milling Company, and Frederick Philip Grove's attitudes to technology.

More than any other area the prairies were the creation of old Canada and the best prairie history has always highlighted the interplay of the nation and the region. Doug Owram centred upon a novel dimension of this relationship in *Promise of Eden: The Canadian Expansionist Movement and the Idea of the West, 1856–1900* (1980), which analysed the writings and assessed the influence of a relatively small Ontario group who advocated the acquisition of the territory and altered the popular image of the area from that of an undesirable wilderness fit only for the fur trade to that of a fertile garden, an agricultural paradise. In the subtlest part of his analysis he showed how out of the collision of utopian expectations and actual frustrating experience was born a feeling of regional grievance even among original expansionists. Rod C. Macleod, *The NWMP and Law Enforcement, 1873–1905* (1976), depicted the mounted police as carriers of the conservative social values of eastern Canada to the frontier and explained their success in preserving order in terms of the composition of the force and its organization, military tradition, and centralization of authority. The same implanting of British and Canadian cultures was illustrated by David Breen, *The Canadian Prairie West and the Ranching Frontier, 1874–1924* (1983). Though concentrating on the evolution of land policy, conflicts between farmers and ranchers, and the ranchers as a political lobby, he also underlined that the Canadian cattle ranching economy and society was different in origin and character from the cattle-kingdom south of the border because of the dominant role of the central government, which controlled and administered land policy, and because of the strong financial and personal ties of the ranchers to Montreal and Great Britain.

Expansion westwards was hardly an unblemished success story as the continuing fascination with Louis Riel attested. He was accorded scholarly attention extended to no other Canadian figure: in 1978 the University of Alberta launched the *Projet Riel Project*, under the direction of George F.G. Stanley, which in 1986 reprinted in five volumes every recoverable word that Riel had put on paper. Riel had been as much a symbol as a person and reactions to him were litmus tests of the historians' attitudes to more general aspects of Canadian history. He had been portrayed, successively, as a traitor, victim of Ontario prejudices against French Canadians, defender of the west, champion of native peoples, and an early casualty of the way Canada treated dissidents.[41] He was also, as Thomas Flanagan made clear in two books, much more complex in his beliefs and motives. In *Louis 'David' Riel: Prophet of the New World* (1979), Flanagan attempted to make sense of Riel's conviction that he had a divine mission to save his people and inaugurate a new stage of Christianity. This belief was explained as a compensation for his own feelings of frustration, as an extreme form of ultramontanism, and as a millenarian promise that had appealed to other marginalized people in history. While in this account the western rebellion appeared as much a religious as a political movement, in *Riel and the Rebellion of 1885 Reconsidered* (1983) Flanagan challenged directly the claim that the revolt was justified because of the total indifference of the federal government to the reasonable land claims of the Métis. Without exonerating the federal agents for their lack of imagination and will in designing and speedily applying a survey system that would have satisfied most of the Métis, he proved how extensive was Riel's definition of aboriginal rights and how relentlessly he pursued a private strategy of getting money for himself from the government.

Paralleling these reinterpretations of Riel's motives and his leadership of the Métis people have been closer and more sympathetic examinations of the Indians and their complex internal political divisions at the time of the rebellion. In *Crowfoot: Chief of the Blackfeet* (1972), Hugh Dempsey drew upon the Indians' oral traditions to provide an intimate picture of a leader who understood that the only alternatives to his people were annihilation or accommodation on white terms and therefore threw his influence against involvement in the Métis revolt. Dempsey's *Big Bear: The Loss of Freedom* (1984) was a moving biography of a shrewd and eloquent Cree chief and an altogether plausible presentation of how the events of the day appeared to a man who placed great faith in signs and supernatural forces and who understood the need to get behind the local officials and renegotiate the treaties with the man called 'Government'.

The restoration of native peoples to a more prominent place in the history of western Canada was carried much further by Gerald Friesen in *The Canadian Prairies* (1984), which allocated a third of the text to the three centuries before 1900 and dealt fully with aboriginal societies and the fur trade, the mixed bloods of the Red River settlement, and the traumatic crisis of the Plains tribes that followed the disappearance of the buffalo and the signing of the treaties. In this work of synthesis, which consolidated the specialized writing of the previous decade, Friesen highlighted many of the themes which preoccupied contemporary prairie historians—immigrant communities, capital and labour, cities and rural society, the Depression, and the 'new' west since 1945—and he was explicit in incorporating and evaluating (though not always reconciling) quite different interpretations. Significantly, the parties of agrarian protest that bulked so large in the history of the prairies written in the fifties were drastically diminished. John H. Thompson, in *Harvests of War: The Prairie West, 1914–1918* (1978), examined for a more limited period the impact of national events upon the region. While he found that the effects of the war experience were in some respects unique, notably upon the economy and treatment of ethnic minorities, his book also confirmed, at least by implication, that the people of the prairies shared much with those of Ontario in their perceptions of the issues in the war and the necessity for conscription.

The historians of the Maritime provinces defined their objectives at least partially in reaction to both the existing literature on the region and the once dominant national approach. They inherited a substantial body of writing on the golden age before 1867 at which point history seemed to have come to an abrupt halt: historians had been inhibited about examining the less happy period after Confederation which was associated with a loss of local control, coercion, and long-term relative decline. As Kenneth G. Pryke, *Nova Scotia and Confederation, 1864–74* (1979), pointed out, union was an inevitable necessity, rather than a desired destiny. Biographies of the defenders of local independence—Joseph Howe and Timothy Anglin—traced common patterns of opposition to Confederation, defeat, and reconcilation to the new state.[42] Historians trained in the late sixties and early seventies, who often wrote their first post-graduate theses on Maritime history at Maritime universities and whose articles made *Acadiensis* one of the most exciting historical periodicals in the country, have tended to concentrate upon social history, especially labour history, and have broken through the barrier that confined Maritime history to the pre-Confederation era. Some of them have vigorously protested against the relegation of the region to the margins of the historical imagination or—worse—the vague association of the Maritimes in general with an unchanging conservatism and the politics of patronage. And they have confronted, far more directly than their predecessors, the task of assessing the position of the seaboard provinces within Confederation.[43]

One of the central themes in their writings was the economic history of underdevelopment and regional disparity. The long-term decline of the economy was once easily explained—or explained away—as an inevitable consequence of the shift in technology from wooden ships and sail to steel and steam and the failure to adjust to an industrial, transcontinental economy. It was abundantly clear, however, from T.W. Acheson's now classic article, 'The National Policy and the Industrialization of the Maritimes, 1880–1910',[44] that Nova Scotia and New Brunswick responded positively to the national policy and that in the 1880s they diversified their economies and reduced their dependence on the exports of staples. In that decade the growth of manufacturing in Nova Scotia on a per capita basis was the highest in the country, and that of Saint John exceeded Hamilton's. This rate of development, however, was not maintained and by the Great War the Maritimes could no longer compete in the markets of central and western Canada. The economy stagnated, thousands left, and natural products became relatively more important for economic survival. Acheson explained this as the result of the vulnerability of the family entrepreneurial tradition, the persistence of a colonial attitude among businessmen who had always looked for leadership to outside metropolitan centres, and the absence of a strong regional metropolis, all of which facilitated the consolidation movement of the early twentieth century which transferred control of secondary industry and banks to central Canada. Both Acheson and

Ernest Forbes[45] underlined the significance of diminished political representation and thus regional influence over national policies. Forbes in particular argued that the rate increases on the Intercolonial Railway at the end of the First World War undermined the competitive position of Maritime industry. This 'rationalization' of freight rate structures was in effect a unilateral repudiation of the commitment made at the time of Confederation that the Intercolonial would be managed in the interests of both regional and national development.

This tendency to attribute the malaise of the Maritimes to policy rather than the shortcomings in resource endowment or economic inevitability was also at the very core of the work of David Alexander, a political economist whose essays were always more extended in scope and implication than their titles implied. Alexander was one of the founders of the Atlantic Canada Shipping Project at Memorial University of Newfoundland in 1976. This project assembled an immense body of information on vessel registrations from the files of the British Board of Trade in London and aimed at a comprehensive analysis of both shipbuilding and the shipping trade in five Maritime ports in the nineteenth century. Thus far the results of this inquiry have been published in six collections of articles which have detailed the rise and decline of the east coast shipping economy, recovered much detail on investment and profitability of shipbuilding and shipping, and contributed new perspectives on both business and labour history.[46]

Closely associated with these enquiries into economic history was the discovery of class conflict and a radical tradition that formed part of the region's political culture, all too often characterized as historically averse to change. Successive issues of *Acadiensis* reported on the conflicts in the Cape Breton coal mining communities, the 1919 general strike at Amherst, and the existence of a lively, if small, Maritime socialist movement in the early years of this century.

The most comprehensive and sustained analysis of protest, however, Ernest Forbes's *The Maritime Rights Movement, 1919-1927: A Study in Canadian Regionalism* (1979), emphasized that this progressive attempt to remedy grievances was supported by members of all classes and that it transcended internal divisions to address the problems of the region as a whole. Forbes' monograph effectively examined the roots of a tradition of regional injustice and also provided a mordant comment on two protest movements—the eastern advocates of Maritime rights and the western agrarian progressives—that operated at cross-purposes in national politics.

The chief virtue of these and other regional studies was that they reflected and enhanced a sense of the pluralism of experience and applied a multiplicity of viewpoints to the relations of parts of the country to other parts and to the national government. Yet they displayed no unanimity about the basic unit of analysis, the region: historians by and large have assumed that a region existed to the extent that people believed that they not only lived in a definite territory but that they possessed a set of common interests and attributes. Region was in some ways as much an abstraction as nation for, as *The Acadians of the Maritimes: Thematic Studies* (1982), edited by Jean Daigle, reminded us, there were always limited identities within limited identities. The concept was also vague in that historians, like other Canadians, equated some regions with individual provinces. Critics of the concept of region in historical studies have pointed out that provinces, not regions, were the basic functioning units of government with precise boundaries, constitutional powers, and unique political cultures.[47]

Historical writings in English on Quebec or French Canada formed a paradoxical commentary on the intellectual history of the seventies. Despite the prominence of separatism fewer books were written by English-Canadian historians on Quebec than on, say, the prairies before 1900, and those that were published were preoccupied with themes that had concerned French-Canadian historians in the sixties but no longer did so. Over the last two decades French-Canadian scholars shifted their attention away from nationalist themes to social history in general and to the transformation of a rural into an industrial society after the mid-nineteenth century.[48] This priority was fully reflected in a cogent synthesis, *Quebec: A History, 1867–1929* (1983; first published in French in 1979) by Paul-André Linteau, René Durocher, and Jean-Claude Robert, which gave most weight to the economic base, structure of classes, role of the state, living conditions, women, labour, and, almost as after-thoughts, political ideologies and cultural expression. In contrast, *The Dream of Nation: A Social and Intellectual History of Quebec* (1982) by Susan Mann Trofimenkoff accentuated the development of a national conscious-ness and the ideas of political leaders and intellectuals even though it also incorporated aspects of social history and feminism. Historians writing in English outside the province tended to concentrate upon accommodations made by political leaders, as did Jacques Monet in *The Last Cannon Shot: A Study of French-Canadian Nationalism, 1837–1850* (1969), which showed how British institutions and reform alliances were employed to protect French-Canadian nationality; or they have been preoccupied with episodes of cultural conflict and with the *nationaliste* tradition.

In a study of attitudes based on an intensive reading of the press, *The French-Canadian Idea of Confederation, 1864–1900* (1982), Arthur I. Silver pointed out that the politicians and editors who supported union believed that it would give French Canada a separate, semi-autonomous state only loosely associated with the other provinces. In the following decades, however, French Canadians grew conscious of the contrast between the extensive rights that had been granted to the English minority within Quebec and the attacks in other parts of the country upon the linguistic and religious rights of Acadians, Franco-Ontarians, and Métis. Out of their identification and involvement with these minorities emerged a rather different view of the meaning of Confederation for French Canada, one that still insisted upon provincial autonomy for Quebec but also upon Quebec's role as a guarantor of minority rights across the country. The idea of Canada as a bicultural community, at least as far as French Canada was concerned, did not originate with Confederation: it was a byproduct of the cultural conflicts of the subsequent generation. Two episodes in that pattern of division were investigated by James R. Miller, *Equal Rights: The Jesuits' Estates Act Controversy* (1979), and Paul Crunican, *Priests and Politicians: Manitoba Schools and the Election of 1896* (1974). Miller attributed the public outcry in Ontario in 1889 against Quebec's legislation compensating the Jesuits and the Pope's adjudication of competing claims within the Church not merely to traditional Protestant animosity but also to feelings of frustration with the unfulfilled hopes inspired by Confederation and an uneasiness about social changes and class tension. In his richly documented and subtle analysis, Crunican explored the divisions within the Church hierarchy and explained the acceptance of Laurier as a defender of French-Canadian interests.

Two phases in the long history of traditional nationalism were surveyed by Joseph Levitt, in *Henri Bourassa and the Golden Calf: The Social Program of the Nationalists of Quebec, 1900–1914* (1969), which contended that the intellectuals of the Nationalist League were utopian corporatists in their prescriptions for the problems of an industrial and urban society, and by Susan Mann Trofimenkoff, in *Action Française: French Canadian Nationalism in the Twenties* (1975). This latter group, guided by the priest-historian Abbé Lionel Groulx, emphasized the perils of modernity—the city, foreign economic domination, materialism, American movies, the Jew— and appealed for a national leader. *Le chef* soon arrived in an unexpected form and his career has been examined—vindicated would be a better word—in *Duplessis* (1977) by Conrad Black who seemed to admire him for all the faults and shortcomings historians have censured. Black's book was very long, ill-organized, and wallowed in trivia: but it also presented a highly entertaining impression of Duplessis' personality and the operation of his patronage system, and put in a more positive light his legislation achievements in social policy. For all its defects, it was a necessary antidote to the mythology that held Duplessis personally responsible for the whole political culture of the dark ages of Quebec.

The ideologies of his enemies have been dissected in Michael D. Behiels, *Prelude to Quebec's Quiet Revolution: Liberalism versus Neo-Nationalism, 1945–1960* (1985). Though the exponents of liberalism and neo-nationalism recognized that Quebec's society had already been drastically altered by industrialization and urbanization and agreed that institutions had to be modernized, they diverged in their attitudes to nationalism. The liberals looked forward to a social democratic ideal of effective equality of opportunity for all; the neo-nationalists sought to ensure increased Francophone control over Quebec and an activist state that would promote the interests of the ethnic majority.

This fixation with nationalist ideas and movements was to a degree offset by inquiries into economic history, but in this case too historians and social scientists took up a theme that came into prominence with the quiet revolution—the extent to which French Canadians had participated in the economic development of their own society and the reasons for the peculiar structure of economic power in the province. While William F. Ryan in *The Clergy and Economic Growth in Quebec, 1896–1914* (1966) argued that at least some clerics actively promoted industrial development, he concluded that religion, or the Church, was not a major factor in either encouraging or hampering French-Canadian aptitudes in business. Brian Young's *Promoters and Politicians: The North-Shore Railways in the History of Quebec, 1854–85* (1978) showed how the provincial government, municipal leaders, and clergymen extended substantial support to this rail network and that clerical leaders in particular did so because they expected the railway would open up lumbering and mining and thereby facilitate colonization. Paul-André Linteau, *The Promoters' City: Building the Industrial Town of Maisonneuve, 1883–1918* (published in French in 1981, and in English translation in 1985), discovered a group of French-Canadian businessmen who gained considerable financial power through real estate development, and Ronald Rudin in *Banking en Français: The French Banks of Quebec, 1835–1925* (1985) made quite clear that French-Canadian businessmen ran their financial institutions along much the same lines as did Anglo-Canadian managers of banks of the same size, but that they controlled much smaller reserves of investment capital. These monographs have confirmed that French Canadians were historically more conspicuous in the economy than was once thought, that they tended to specialize in certain lines of business, and that the Quebec state, and some clerics, were in some instances actively involved in promoting economic growth.

VII

Historians who wrote on aspects of cultural history explored many subjects, including religion, higher education, and science. They have, with a few exceptions, concentrated upon the beliefs and creations of articulate, educated individuals and groups and upon the institutions with which they were associated. Of all the subfields that accorded priority to ideas, convictions, and values, the history of religion experienced the most curious fate. While historians had acknowledged its pervasive presence in the past, they tended to treat it as subsidiary to other topics. Arthur Lower had explained the Catholic and Protestant origins of the French-English duality, and others wrote of conflicts of church and state in the nineteenth century, the parallels between the consolidation of the Canadian nation and the amalgamations of the Protestant denominations, and the fundamentalist sects and the rise of the Social Credit movement. The history of religion, however, existed on the margins of historical scholarship; as for a history that treated religion as a way of defining self, of feeling and faith, this was hardly developed at all.[49]

Historians after the sixties continued to subordinate religion to other presumably more important subjects even when they tried to demonstrate its impact on society at large. This was true even of such a provocative study as James Penton's *Jehovah's Witnesses in Canada: Champions of Freedom of Speech and Worship* (1976), which, as the subtitle accurately indicated, was more revealing of Canadian standards of civil liberties that were tested by these dissenters than of the inner history of the sect. Thanks in large part to Richard Allen's *The Social Passion: Religion and Social Reform in Canada, 1914–28* (1971), historians became more aware of the importance of the Protestant social gospel as the taproot of social activism. In *The Regenerators: Social Criticism in Late Victorian English Canada* (1985), Ramsay Cook portrayed an astonishing gallery of reformers—socialists, free-thinkers, spiritualists, and other idealists—who had discovered some semi-religious cure for society's ills (or some substitute for religion) and who unwittingly hastened secularization.

Biographers have rendered illuminating studies of religion as both a positive and negative force in the lives of individuals. Margaret Prang's *N.W. Rowell: Ontario Nationalist* (1975) revealed the religious impulse in the activity of a prominent Methodist, a liberal who supported missionary movements, prohibition, and church union; Claude Bissell, *The Young Vincent Massey* (1981), sensitively traced the redirection of religious earnestness into the arts; Elspeth Cameron, *Hugh MacLennan: A Writer's Life* (1981), had as one of its major themes the enduring and oppressive legacy of Calvinism upon an author who made it the subject of some of his best works; and David G. Pitt, *E.J. Pratt: The Truant Years, 1882–1927* (1984), was virtually organized around the story of the poet's rejection of Methodism.

The relative neglect of religion by historians might once have been explained away as the predictable reaction of people of an older generation who had partially extricated themselves from the constrictions of their own religious heritages and were hardly likely to re-enter and re-create them sympathetically. Many contemporary—and presumably more secular—historians have in addition gravitated towards various forms of social history which emphasized material conditions and class structure. Even when religion was not explicitly relegated to the status of epiphenomenon, however, those who wrote of submerged groups and classes were apt to identify religion and its upholders with social control, middle-class values, or European imperialism. New perspectives that emerged from the writings on Amerindian-European relations drastically altered the picture of missionaries who were now treated as unwitting, if not malevolent, destroyers of legitimate and admirable ways of life.[50]

John Webster Grant took on an exceptionally difficult topic in attempting to explain the motivations of Christian missionaries and, at the same time, keeping in mind the long-term fate of the native peoples. His synthesis of over four hundred years of interaction, *Moon of Wintertime: Missionaries and the Indians of Canada in Encounter since 1534* (1984), was also an extended reflection upon the ambiguities of the relationship. In his eyes the missionaries were ambivalent about the civilization they represented: of course the values of Christian Europe were central to their programmes of conversion, but Europe also represented corrupt and evil tendencies. Thus they endeavoured to Christianize and to isolate, to assimilate and to segregate. As for the native peoples, Grant believed that they were introduced to the new religion at the moment when ancestral spirits that had once offered consolation had fled, but that they did not so much abandon traditional beliefs as supplement them with elements of Christian practices.

George Rawlyk, who had co-operated with Gordon Stewart in a study of the revivals led by Henry Alline and the ways in which religion helped the Nova Scotia Yankees formulate a new loyalty at the time of the American revolution,[51] returned to the subject in four lectures in *Ravished by the Spirit: Religious Revivals, Baptists, and Henry Alline* (1984). Rawlyk sympathetically conveyed the meaning of Henry Alline's theological writings and hymns, the experience of conversion and the conviction of salvation, and isolated the mystical and pietistic elements that entered into the Baptist tradition in the Maritimes.

That institutional studies of denominations need not be divorced from social and intellectual history was convincingly demonstrated by John Moir in *Enduring Witness: A History of the Presbyterian Church in Canada* (1975), occasioned by the centennial of the union of four branches into a single General Assembly. Both an examination of internal divisions in the colonial period and a survey of the interaction of one church and the national community, it was most informative on the interplay of the faith and missions abroad and in the west, social activism, and on the church union of 1925. In *The Resistance to Church Union in Canada, 1904–1939* (1985), N. Keith Clifford put the Presbyterian opponents to union into a more positive light by arguing that they were defending the principle of religious pluralism.

Some of the most significant advances in the recovery and reinstatement of the religious dimension of the past have been made by historians of ideas. Brian McKillop began his excellent *A Disciplined Intelligence: Critical Inquiry and Canadian Thought in the Victorian Era* (1979) by reminding his readers that in the colonial colleges the main purpose of education was the promotion of Christian morality and a comprehension of the will of God. And he then proceeded to analyse the interplay between this moral purpose and a succession of intellectual currents— among them Scottish common sense philosophy, natural theology, evolution and evolutionary ethics, and idealism—and traced the gradual erosion of this combination of the moral imperative and critical enquiry. So strongly, however, had the two been fused that a strain of moralism persisted well beyond the Victorian period. In *The Search for an Ideal: Six Canadian Intellectuals and Their Convictions in an Age of Transition, 1890–1930* (1976), Sam E.D. Shortt discovered in the beliefs and pronouncements of certain university figures a pattern of tension between idealism, a faith in an intuitive comprehension of the spiritual order in the world, and an empiricism that depended on the methods of the social sciences. Though *The Faces of Reason: An Essay on Philosophy and Culture in English-Canada, 1850–1950* (1981) by Leslie Armour and Elizabeth Trott was a welcome attempt to relate philosophy to national culture, it was also a difficult book for the historian to read, for the authors—both teachers of philosophy—tended to interject their own reflections into the text in ways that were more distracting than helpful. Still, it was a storehouse of information about both familiar and little-known scholars and thinkers and an essential beginning for a more historically rooted intellectual history.

Historical writing on universities never quite managed to convey adequately the most essential elements in these institutions: the life of the mind, advances in knowledge, and changing perceptions of what was important to preserve and transmit. Though Robin Harris in *A History of Higher Education in Canada, 1663–1960* (1976) surveyed the teaching curriculum and support systems for research and scholarship, by and large histories of individual universities were chronicles of corporate bodies, based on official records, structured around successive administrations, and obsessed with the achievements of the statesmen of academe. Officially sponsored histories were initiated to commemorate anniversaries, as essays in public relations, and often assigned to either senior professors steeped in local lore or superannuated administrators who were masters at writing communiqués of bland judiciousness. The most that can be said of the generality of such works was that they traced the transition from church control to lay management and communicated aspects of distinct institutional personalities of, say, the Queen's tradition of state service or McGill's emphasis on medicine and engineering. There were indications in such recent works as Charles M. Johnston's study of McMaster of more determined efforts to escape the perspective of the presidential office and deal more adequately with the students.[52] Relations between the state and the universities have been critically judged in Paul Axelrod, *Scholars and Dollars: Politics, Economics, and the Universities of Ontario, 1945–1980* (1982), which explained the growth in the numbers of institutions from three to fifteen in the period mainly as a result of the belief, shared by businessmen and politicians, that universities contributed directly to economic growth. Not only did universities fail to fulfil this function, he argued, but they compromised themselves in the process, for the values that had brought the new ones into being perverted their true role in society as islands of contemplation and critical thought.

Literature on the history of science in Canada has concentrated on those features of it that were comprehensible to historians who lacked any formal training in the field. They have in general not written of the internal developments of the various sub-specialties but rather of the operation of government agencies, the activities of explorer-scientists, exponents of popular science, and nature writers. By far the most imposing study, *Reading the Rocks: The Story of the Geological Survey of Canada, 1842–1972* (1975), by Morris Zaslow, was a densely detailed narrative of the country's premier scientific organization that struggled to satisfy the competing demands for immediate practical results and the desire for disinterested theoretical knowledge. Into its complex history Zaslow skilfully interwove accounts of the advances in geology, reconnaissance surveys, and the tangled personal relationships both inside the agency and between geologists and politicians. Scientists employed by the federal government also figured prominently in an account of the early conservation movement by Janet Foster, *Working for Wildlife: The Beginning of Preservation in Canada* (1978), which traced the development of policies to protect animal and bird life in the generation after the 1880s through the creation of sanctuaries and the negotiation of the Migratory Bird Convention with the United States. Foster attributed the change in attitude to a small group of far-sighted Ottawa civil servants, like the ornithologist Percy Taverner and the entomologist Gordon Hewitt, who argued their case for conservation mainly on the grounds of economic benefits. Richard Diubaldo, *Stefansson and the Canadian Arctic* (1978), reduced the heroic stature of this advocate of northern destiny, ethnologist, and explorer, and traced the rise and fall of his reputation. He offered a lucid and convincing analysis of the origins of Stefansson's attitudes and ideas, and a superb account of the outfitting and financing of one segment of the Canadian Arctic Expedition of 1913–18 and the political infighting and public relations surrounding it.

In the Victorian period science, especially geology and natural history, was popular and accessible to the educated public. Carl Berger, *Science, God, and Nature in Victorian Canada: The Joanne Goodman Lectures for 1982* (1984), briefly surveyed some of the reasons for this vogue, the association of science and religion, and some Canadian responses to Darwin. The most satisfying study of the popular culture of science was *David Boyle: From Artisan to Archaeologist* (1983) by Gerald Killan, a biography of a self-taught blacksmith apprentice who became a teacher of natural science and one of Canada's outstanding recoverers and interpreters of the material culture of the Iroquoian peoples. This book was most impressive for capturing the astonishing range of Boyle's activities as a popularizer, bookseller, and museum builder, and as an exemplar of the working-class tradition of self-improvement. John Wadland's *Ernest Thompson Seton: Man in Nature and the Progressive Era, 1880–1915* (1978) closely identified with the artist-naturalist, pioneer of the animal story, and originator of the Woodcraft Indians whose programme became the basis for the Boy Scouts. Wadland was most persuasive in revealing the personal roots and intellectual origins of Seton's feeling for the sanctity of all life, the kinship of man and the animals, and his admiration for the North American Indians because of their intuitive understanding of the true relationship of man to the natural world. In *Captured Heritage: The Scramble for Northwest Coast Artifacts* (1985), Douglas Cole explained how major items of the material culture of the natives of the Pacific coast came to be housed in museums in the United States. He traced the competition among the major institutions and their collectors in British Columbia, laid out the rules and patterns of the trade in artifacts, and elucidated the connection between anthropological thought and the interpretation and display of these objects.

Professional historians attached to university departments have rarely ventured beyond these highly selective aspects of cultural history and have added little to our knowledge of painting or imaginative literature. The serious history of painting was sustained by art historians and especially by the increasing numbers of gallery curators who, in the process of arranging exhibitions, compiled many *catalogues raisonnés* containing information about paintings and artists. A few of these evolved into substantial monographs.[53] Similarly the study of Canadian literature derived its main impetus from within literature departments. On the whole the profusion of studies in literature and art history hardly impinged on the consciousness of most historians and were not assimilated into the mainstream of historical writing. Part of the reason for this neglect, or failure to communicate, was that for historians of art and literature history was important because it illuminated a picture or a text; a few historians, on the other hand, were more concerned with what these documents revealed about a period. The rise of social history, moreover, expressed a distrust if not disdain for the activities and achievements of elites and a preference for attempting to understand the mentalities and popular beliefs of large groups of people. As a result historians of Canada seemed to possess a limited view of cultural history.

IX

Most of the works mentioned thus far in cultural, political, and economic history represented strong continuities with earlier Canadian historical writing. They were extensions and elaborations of themes and problems that would have been at least recognizable, if not familiar, to those in the mainstream in the early and middle 1960s. Even the most original and imaginative of these books took as their points of departure bodies of information that were common possessions of a profession. This was less true of the various species of social history that emerged in the late sixties and that have since partially transformed Canadian historical literature.

The advocates of social history shared a strong determination to recover the life experiences of ordinary people and reduce the prominence of unrepresentative individuals and elites and past politics. Social history was presented as an all-inclusive approach to the past that would accord priority to transformations in the economic base, the character of institutions, and the interaction of classes and groups. Far more than their predecessors, social historians possessed a keen appreciation of the importance of class and class conflict, and of the subtle ways in which membership in an economic, ethnic, or sexual group shaped consciousness and behaviour. They were more aware, too, of patterns of hegemony maintained by such institutions as the public school, more sensitive to the persistence of ethnic feeling, and more sympathetic to groups that had been the victims of history.

Though social history promised a new synthesis that would supersede and not merely supplement existing historical literature, its initial impact was to magnify the diversity of Canadian history in both subject matter and, to a lesser extent, methods. The biannual journal *Social History* (1967), which did not confine itself to Canadian subjects only, carried in its early issues articles on such sundry topics as social profiles of the Montreal merchants at the time of the Conquest and of the Boer War contingents; attitudes to improvements in the common schools in Upper Canada and theories of Anglican missionaries regarding the most effective strategies for christianizing western Indians; trends in female school attendance; a strike at the Chaudière Falls in 1891; and Mennonites' responses to the Second World War. Even a collection of articles on one theme—*Medicine in Canadian Society: Historical Perspectives* (1981), edited by Sam E.D. Shortt—had the character of a miscellany: these included studies of birth control and abortion, lunatic asylums in the Maritime provinces, pre-Freudian attitudes to sex, and physicians' views of health insurance.

This diversity of subjects was paralleled by competing claims that history had to be reinterpreted in terms of class, gender, and ethnicity as basic units of analysis. The subfields within social history followed similar life-cycles: first came the manifestos repudiating old history and arguing for the legitimacy as well as the social utility of the new; then the formation of coteries of the like-minded, networks and conferences; followed by the publication of newsletters, bibliographical aids, and such specialized journals as *Canadian Ethnic Studies* (1968), *The Urban History Review* (1972), *Atlantis: A Women's Studies Journal* (1975), and *Labour* (1976). The proponents of each of these subfields came to share a self-conscious identity and each field was cultivated in increasing isolation from the others.

Historians of society were also more open to influences from the social sciences—a few would perhaps say the other social sciences. There was hardly a better example of the enormously fertile convergence and informal co-operation of several disciplines upon a single theme in social history than the growth of writing on Amerindian-European contact and relations. While the Indians had been accorded an important place in the historical literature on both the fur trade and New France, they were often treated as homogeneous groups and as passively reacting to European initiatives and economic dictates. Though this European-centred view had been qualified earlier by William Eccles, an informal alliance of historians, anthropologists, historical geographers, and economists began a more systematic effort to explore the natives' side of the exchange and their institutions and motivations. The most impressive contribution was made by Bruce Trigger, *The Children of Aataentsic: A History of the Huron People to 1660* (1976), a two-volume study that defied tidy classification in any discipline. The most original features of this comprehensive examination of the Hurons from pre-historic times to their dispersal was not so much the information, which was in the main drawn from previously published sources; it was rather the application to historical materials of a sensitivity and knowledge gained from the study of other non-literate peoples and the determination to differentiate the various groupings within Huron society just as historians had previously discriminated among French traders, officials, and missionaries. Trigger provided an interior view of this culture that made sense of seemingly inexplicable customs, showed how it had altered even before contact with Europeans, and illustrated how the Hurons adapted to the fur trade in terms of their customs, experiences, and inter-tribal relations. In the process he reinstated the Hurons into the mainstream of early Canadian history, so that we came to see it not from the ships and canoes moving westwards but through eyes looking at invading strangers.[54]

In a more limited but no less rewarding book, *Friend and Foe: Aspects of French-Amerindian Cultural Contact in the Sixteenth and Seventeenth Centuries* (1976), Cornelius J. Jaenen unravelled, with a fine sense of irony, the reactions of natives and Europeans to each other's social mores, religions, and styles of warfare. Using European accounts of things that they recorded but could not understand, Jaenen noted intriguing parallels such as the mystical elements present in Huron religion and seventeenth-century Catholicism, and the practices of the faithful believers in transubstantiation, literally eating the Lord, and those of the natives, who thought desirable qualities of enemies could be acquired by consuming parts of their bodies.

The fur trade was more than an economic link; it was a cultural interchange between groups that were in the beginning by no means unequal and to which they brought quite different expectations. In *'Give Us Good Measure': An Economic Analysis of Relations between the Indians and the Hudson's Bay Company before 1763* (1978), Arthur J. Ray and Donald B. Freeman investigated native and European trading conventions and economic motivations: basing their conclusions on the account books kept at six posts, they depicted the Indian as a sophisticated trader, with a critical eye for the quality of goods and a hard bargainer in situations where the British competed with the French. Still, the natives did not in all respects behave according to European conventional wisdom: when prices for furs rose, they sensibly brought in few pelts. An immensely stimulating—and highly questionable[55]—addition to this literature, Calvin Martin's *Keepers of the Game: Indian-Animal Relationships and the Fur Trade* (1978), argued that the Micmacs of the Atlantic coast and the Ojibwa of the Great Lakes were natural conservationists in pre-contact times: they hunted on a very limited basis for they believed that between men and animals there existed a compact of mutual respect and interdependence. With the fur trade, however, natives slaughtered game and fur-bearing animals ruthlessly to the point of extinction. They did so, Martin explained, not merely because of their growing dependence on trade goods, but also because devastating diseases and epidemics had preceded actual European penetration into the interior and the Indians believed that the animals had broken the compact and were making war on them.

That Indians in the fur trade period were able to control the scope of change was further amplified in Robin Fisher's *Contact and Conflict: Indian-European Relations in British Columbia, 1774-1890* (1977) and L.F.S. Upton's *Micmacs and Colonists: Indian-White Relations in the Maritimes, 1713-1867* (1979). The fur trade on the west coast was a balanced, mutually accommodating system: Europeans did not try to alter the Indian pattern of life because they were powerless to do so and because it was in their own economic interest to maintain it. With the gold rush in 1859 and subsequent settlement, however, this balance was drastically upset: the 'indolent savages' became obstacles to civilization, missionaries attacked their social practices and attempted to isolate them, and government administrators systematically took away lands that had been allocated to them. Upton told a similar story of the impact of British settlement in Nova Scotia, New Brunswick, and Prince Edward Island in which white settlers blocked the designation of reserves, squatters took up holdings, and colonial authorities encouraged the alienation of freehold lands. In both areas, settlement—in contrast to the fur trade— had traumatic consequences, for the Indians literally lost control over their lives.

How deeply the fur trade affected the personal lives and feelings of those it brought together was appraised from the perspective of women's and family history. Sylvia Van Kirk, in *'Many Tender Ties': Women in Fur-Trade Society in Western Canada, 1670-1870* (1980), explained how native women supported the trade as interpreters, guides, and labourers, and how they actively sought connections with the European traders in order to increase their own influence and status. One of the major themes of this sensitive study was the customs governing marriage between native women and white men, the formation of enduring and affectionate families, and the decline and degradation of these practices (and native women) after the 1820s with the arrival of white females. Where Van Kirk centred upon the relatively autonomous role of Indian women and marriage practices, Jennifer Brown, *Strangers in Blood: Fur Trade Company Families in Indian Country* (1980), examined the divergent domestic arrangements and family traditions of the traders that resulted from the different structures and personnel of the North West Company and the Hudson's Bay Company. The former, Highland Scots and Canadians, were highly mobile and independent and their alliances with native women were quite casual and impermanent; the latter, drawn mainly from Protestant Englishmen and Scotsmen who were isolated from Britain, entered into long-term marriages and family life. To put the matter rather simplistically, two trading institutions nurtured two different peoples—the independent Métis and the country-born who were assimilated into European culture. The examination of the encounters of Amerindians and Europeans merged into 'fur trade studies', another form of social history, which was less concerned with the trade as a business enterprise than with native societies, recruitment of company personnel, and even with maps that illustrated Indian conceptions of space, subjects which were developed in a representative collection of nineteen papers, *Old Trails and New Directions: Papers of the Third North American Fur Trade Conference* (1980), edited by Carol M. Judd and Arthur J. Ray.[56]

Social history in general represented a more intense involvement with anonymous social processes and structures that underpinned whole ways of life. According to some of its more radical exponents a history that concentrated upon conscious intentions and actions was quite insufficient; the historian must understand human behaviour in relation to the material framework and structural formations within which they occurred and of which people in the past were unaware even though their lives were affected by them. Most social historians were Marxists in the loose sense that they agreed that people made their own history but not in conditions of their own choosing. There was, however, no agreement on how these structures were to be isolated and examined.

Fernand Ouellet's two books, *Economic and Social History of Quebec, 1760–1850: Structures and Conjonctures* and *Lower Canada, 1791–1840: Social Change and Nationalism* (originally published in French in 1966 and 1976 respectively, and both available in English in 1980), applied to Canadian history the mode of analysis of the French *annales* school. Ouellet marshalled statistical evidence regarding prices, exports, agricultural production, population, and taxation in order to establish the nature of long-term economic changes and the character of social classes. His discussion of events—especially in the second work, which dealt more fully with the political crisis of the rebellion in 1837-8—was at all points related to this material basis and the conflicts of classes. Ouellet argued that French-Canadian nationalism was born out of the failure of that society to adjust to economic change, that its leaders deflected attention away from the need to reform or abolish obsolete institutions, and channelled discontent towards the British minority. Though this line of argument was challenged in some quarters, Ouellet's works constituted the most compelling demonstrations of how economics, social structures, and political ideologies were bound together, and how they could be analysed. In English Canada, however, almost no one followed his example except Allan Greer, who in *Peasant, Lord, and Merchant: Rural Society in Three Quebec Parishes, 1740-1840* (1985) examined the configuration of a self-sufficient peasant society, stressed the continuity of its character throughout a century, and contended that exactions in the form of rents and tithes collected by clerics and seigneurs constituted real, not symbolic, burdens.

Another approach to social structure, one that derived from American social science, was applied by Michael Katz, the director of one of the first large-scale collaborative research undertakings, the Canadian Social History Project, begun at the Ontario Institute for Studies in Education in 1967. This project grew out of the convergence in the sixties of the popularity among social scientists of measuring social mobility as a test of American pretensions to equality of opportunity; the discovery of the amazing richness of such sources as manuscript censuses, assessment rolls, marriage and church documents, for recovering the life experiences of people who left no literary remains; and the advent of the computer which made possible the assembly and manipulation of large quantities of statistical information. In his *The People of Hamilton, Canada West: Family and Class in a Mid-Nineteenth Century City* (1975), Katz presented a striking paradox. There had been an astonishingly high rate of transiency of the population with less than a third of those who lived in the city in 1851 still there a decade later. On the other hand, social inequality persisted: the structures which Katz identified according to the division of wealth, property ownership, and distances between people in stratified ranks remained the same. He examined, in addition, family composition and youth and adolescence, and made a commendable effort at humanizing a history of numbers, but he also seemed as preoccupied with the technical problems of research methods and computation as with the history uncovered. Katz's study was addressed both to American and British scholars, who had undertaken similar studies of urban populations to which he compared his own conclusions, and to historians of Canada, most of whom were not familiar with this type of analysis and responded cautiously or critically. They were struck by the profusion of comparisons of Hamilton to other distant places, and the sparsity of references to the Canadian historical context; wondered what became of all the transients; and questioned whether Hamilton was typical of all British North American cities. In another work in the same genre, *Hopeful Travellers: Families, Land, and Social Change in Mid-Victorian Peel County, Canada West* (1981), David Gagan analysed the circumstances of life of some ten thousand families in a predominantly rural county between 1850 and 1870. Like Katz, he found a high degree of transiency, but the most original aspect of his work was the explanation of how people adapted to the growing shortage and expense of land and the decline in wheat yields by devising a new inheritance system for transferring property, restraining family size, and lengthening the period of children's dependence. Unlike Katz, who had not explained the destinations of the transients, Gagan drew a direct connection between the land crisis in Peel County and the settlement of Manitoba.

These two studies were the most ambitious and original applications of quantitative techniques to social history and they told historians a great deal about how people lived and about the distribution of economic resources. It was not obvious, however, what this information explained or how it was to be related to the more conventional literature. Nor was this history altogether successful in making the inarticulate articulate; from these books we learn more about the conditions of life than about people's thoughts and feelings. Even historians who were sympathetic to social history found Katz's work deficient: Marxists quarrelled with his definitions of class, complained that his structures were static and frozen, and argued that more was to be learned about social organization in moments of conflict. Thus even within social history the influence of these works was quite limited.

The most exciting and ideologically turbulent department of social history was the study of labour,[57] a subfield which in the seventies diverged into two distinct strands. This subject was initially explored by both historians and social scientists who were primarily interested in labour as a component of left-wing political protest and who were in the main sympathetic to the social democratic tradition of the CCF and NDP. Labour as an organized force shared the vision of a more humane, co-operative society and its political affiliation with these parties seemed natural if not inevitable. From this perspective of 'labour and the left' many studies that did not focus directly upon trade unions or industrial relations were nonetheless important because they provided the context in which labour's struggles for protection and recognition could be better understood. Gad Horowitz prefaced his *Canadian Labour in Politics* (1968), a straightforward survey of the relations between the labour movement and the CCF that culminated in the formation of the NDP, with a brilliant speculative essay on why socialism had been a stronger force in Canadian political culture than in the United States. Another political scientist, Walter D. Young, in *The Anatomy of a Party: The National CCF, 1932–61* (1969), traced more analytically and comprehensively the evolution of the movement from its origins as an association of labour parties and agrarian protest movements to its formal alliance with the Canadian Labour Congress. And Michiel Horn dissected the eclectic ideology and reformist writings of academic radicals who promoted the CCF in *The League for Social Reconstruction: Intellectual Origins of the Democratic Left in Canada, 1930–1942* (1980).

Apart from histories of labour politics and socialism, studies of the labour movement as such concentrated upon the development of unions as the most important institutions controlled by working people, and on conflicts and strikes for union recognition and collective bargaining rights. Eugene Forsey carried forward this approach in *Trade Unions in Canada, 1812–1902* (1982), an encyclopedic archive of information, lovingly and unselectively culled, on the origins and functions of workers' associations and on their parades, regalia, and rituals. The terminal date of Forsey's study marked the climax in a process—examined by Robert Babcock, *Gompers in Canada: A Study in American Continentalism before the First World War* (1974)—by which the American Federation of Labour came to dominate organized labour in Canada and thereby destroyed not only the prospects of a national trade union centre but, equally important, forms of unionism other than that based upon the skilled crafts. The impact of American industrial unionism in Canada after the late thirties was traced out by Irving Abella in *Nationalism, Communism, and Canadian Labour: The CIO, the Communist Party, and the Canadian Congress of Labour, 1935–1956* (1973).

An understanding of labour in wartime, especially radicalism in western Canada, was considerably advanced by David J. Bercuson, *Confrontation at Winnipeg: Labour, Industrial Relations, and the General Strike* (1974), which explained the conflict of 1919 as the culmination of decades of class polarization and difficult industrial relations in the new prairie city and censured both the repressive intervention of the federal government and the strike leaders who confused the general strike, a weapon of political revolution, with a large-scale withdrawal of services, and led their followers into predictable defeat. Ross McCormack, *Reformers, Rebels, and Revolutionaries: The Western Canadian Radical Movement, 1899–1919* (1977), approached the same subject from another angle and provided both a lucid analysis of three main groups within the labour movement—moderate liberals who sought changes within capitalism, militant industrial unionists, and Marxist revolutionaries—as well as a balanced examination of the complex impact of the war on the labour movement. The state of labour relations in Canada during the Second World War was the setting for Laurel S. MacDowell, 'Remember Kirkland Lake': The History and Effects of the Kirkland Lake Gold Miners' Strike, 1941–42 (1983), which was both an investigation of the anatomy of an important but unsuccessful strike and an explanation of the Canadian and Ontario governments' legislation guaranteeing collective bargaining.

These books on confrontations and radical ideologies only incidentally touched upon conditions of work, standards of living, and institutions other than unions or parties that affected the everyday lives of workers. Some studies of the seventies, however, moved closer towards an understanding of the more general structures that shaped working-class existence. In a little gem, 'The Winter's Tale: The Seasonal Contours of Pre-industrial Poverty in British North America, 1815–1860,'[58] Judith Fingard traced out the effects of the seasonality of work on some labourers, and in Jack in Port: Sailortowns of Eastern Canada (1982) she isolated the dominant features of the world of the merchant seamen in the age of sail from 1850 to 1880—including the labour market, rights, contractual obligations and pay, and the activities of 'crimps', often boardinghouse keepers, who traded in sailors—and showed how the dockside environments of Quebec, Saint John, and Halifax varied. Two books—Terry Copp's An Anatomy of Poverty: The Condition of the Working Class in Montreal, 1897–1929 (1974) and Michael Piva's The Condition of the Working Class in Toronto, 1900–1921 (1979)—examined incomes and living standards of groups of workers in an age of industrial development and prosperity and concluded that at least these employees hardly shared its benefits. Both of these studies confronted a problem as old as the industrial revolution itself—of whether working people benefited from it—but neither provided comparative information about previous standards of living in order to answer this question conclusively. And, though both accounts revealed much about the conditions in which at least some workers lived, they rested on sources generated by official bodies and social surveys rather than on working-class witnesses to their own experience.

Labour history was projected beyond these topics by Marxist scholars who redefined the field as working-class history, enunciated a more comprehensive agenda of research, and at least partially fulfilled their own prescriptions. In the introduction to Essays in Canadian Working-class History (1976), the editors, Greg S. Kealey and Peter Warrian, drew their inspiration from British and American historians who had situated the history of workers in a social matrix and had traced the history of a class in Marxist terms. Working-class history comprised the experiences of all working people, not merely the small number that had engaged in trade union or political activity, and it was to treat class not as something fixed and isolated but as a changing dialectical relationship of groups in relation to the process of production, in terms of values, beliefs, and class-consciousness. With the possible exception of Kealey's own essay on the Orange Order in Toronto as a working-class organization, few papers in the collection met these new standards which were far better exemplified in two rather different community studies. Bryan Palmer, *A Culture in Conflict: Skilled Workers and Industrial Capitalism in Hamilton, Ontario, 1860–1914* (1979), centred upon the making of a working-class culture not only through efforts to preserve customary rights and control over conditions of work on the shop floor, as well as through unions and industrial conflict, but above all through such associations as fraternal orders and mechanics' institutes, baseball teams, and festivities, for these nurtured and conditioned a sense of solidarity. Against the background of an excellent analysis of industrialization, Kealey's *Toronto Workers Respond to Industrial Capitalism, 1867–1892* (1980) also paid considerable attention to the ways in which the conventions and traditions of independence of such skilled artisans as shoemakers, printers, and iron-moulders persisted into the industrial era and provided these workers with incentives to resist encroachments on their rights as well as a critical perspective on industrial capitalism. Thus back of the early unions and labour politics—to which Kealey, surprisingly, devoted two-thirds of his book—lay artisanal traditions that mediated labour's adjustment to the new order. Kealey and Palmer combined to write *Dreaming of What Might Be: The Knights of Labour in Ontario, 1880–1900* (1982) on an organization that was not quite a union but much more than the self-protective association that historians had previously dismissed as ineffectual. In a work of very thick description they analysed its structure, explained its appeal to both skilled and unskilled men and women, documented involvements in politics and strikes, and, above all, reconstructed its reformist ideology. The Knights became in their account a promising force for social change in the period, a training ground for later advocates of a more co-operative society, and an expression of a 'movement culture' that transcended at least for a moment the internal divisions of the working class. This period of intense activity of the Knights represented a turning point at which history failed to turn; or, to use Donald Creighton's analogy, a fork in the road to a better future that was not taken.

The publication of these works in the so-called new working-class history sparked a debate among historians that was captious, intemperate, and confusing. The flash point of controversy was the concept of working-class culture underlying Palmer's study of the Hamilton workers. Critics questioned the very existence of a free-standing and exclusive culture of labourers as wrong-headed on the grounds that they had always been divided by region, ethnicity, and degrees of skill. And they pointed to the large gap between the essays in methodology which defined the new field as aimed at the recovery of working-class experience in its totality and the omission in all these applications of any consideration of religion in the life of the Victorian worker, or of the kind of information about family history uncovered by Katz. The resulting quarrels in some ways perpetuated the warfare of the sixties between the old left and the new—between the upholders of the social democratic tradition and those who had embraced a humanistic Marxism. These disagreements tended to obscure the common features of both types of labour history—including an emphasis upon industrial struggle and politics and conventional historical methodology. These exchanges also obscured the very significant achievements of those who had penetrated beyond the political confines. They recovered copious and scarcely suspected details on social life in the Victorian period; they have helped move to the centre of attention the social conflict that accompanied the arrival of industrial society, and have accorded a place to ideas and attitudes in history that belied the commonplace image of Marxist scholarship as materialistic; and they have contributed far more to the ultimate clarification of class—and class in history—than the statisticians of social mobility.

Ethnic studies comprised investigations of immigration, the internal histories of distinct groups of people, usually, though not exclusively, those of origins other than Anglo-Celtic or French, the implanting, consolidation, and modification of their cultures and traditions, and the attitudes of Canadian society towards them. Before the sixties English-Canadian academic historians paid virtually no attention to these subjects partly because of their own ethnocentrism and partly because of the conviction, maintained tenaciously by A.R.M. Lower, that the persistence of ethnic identifications was an impediment to the formation of a British-Canadian sentiment and loyalty. Nor did they explore in any systematic fashion the cultural baggage brought by immigrants to the new world, except perhaps for political ideas. Thus almost by default ethnic history was usually written by either sociologists like Carl Dawson who were primarily interested in immigrant adjustment and assimilation or by individuals with strong attachments to particular groups. The exercises in ancestor worship written by the latter followed a predictable formula: the reasons for leaving, the shock on arrival, toil and suffering, and success illustrated by short biographical sketches of individuals who had done well. In the case of such highly politically conscious people as the Ukrainians much was made by, for example, Michael Evanchuk's *Spruce, Swamp and Stone: A History of the Pioneer*

Ukrainian Settlements in the Gimli Area (1977), of their determination to maintain their language and culture, sustain religious institutions, and control schools in the face of both informal and official prejudice and assimilationist drives. Such histories—literally hundreds of them— continued to be published in the seventies and early eighties.

Since the late sixties the major influences upon the writing of ethnic histories have come from outside the academic history establishment. In *The Doukhobors* (1968), George Woodcock, man of letters and liberal anarchist, and Ivan Avakumovic, a political scientist, drew uncomfortable parallels between the treatment of this group by Canada and by tsarist authorities in Russia. The American historian Robin Winks published the most comprehensive survey of another minority group, *The Blacks in Canada* (1971). Among Canadian social scientists and historians the growing popularity of ethnic studies was a direct reflection of drastic changes in attitudes towards ethnicity, a recognition of the persistence of ethnic identities, and a greater consciousness of, and praise for, the ethnic variety of Canadian society.[59] The federal government's policy of multiculturalism was both a consequence of these changes and a major fillip to writing ethnic history. The multicultural programme was designed to pacify certain ethnic leaders who had criticized the preoccupation with Canada as a bicultural partnership, a definition of the country that denied recognition to a quarter of the population of other origins and made them feel that they were outsiders. According to the multicultural idea, Canada was an officially bilingual country with no single official culture and no ethnic group took precedence over others. In practice this recognition of pluralism meant government financial support for cultural organizations and for the writing—and rewriting— of history, a history that would give certain groups a larger place in the country's past. History would expose and thereby expunge the tradition of racial prejudice of the dominant groups; and it would have another therapeutic value, if written so that members of minority groups would no longer hold their own pasts in contempt. The impulse to explore more appreciatively the histories of ethnic groups was additionally strengthened by a generation in search of its own roots. The journalist Myrna Kostash, in *All of Baba's Children* (1977), attempted to penetrate behind the Ukrainian-Canadian mythologies of her parents' generation in order to describe the realities of her grandparents'; and several historians, whose first publications were in other fields of history, turned to study their ancestors, as did Gerald Tulchinsky in a series of essays on the Jews.[60]

The support systems for research and publication in ethnic studies proliferated in the form of the multidisciplinary journal *Canadian Ethnic Studies* and such bodies as the Canadian Ethnic Studies Association, the Canadian Institute of Ukrainian Studies (established in 1976 at Edmonton), and the Multicultural History Society of Ontario, which promoted the retrieval and preservation of the records of that province's ethnic communities. The director of this latter society, Robert F. Harney, wrote extensively about the ambience of the Italian-Canadian community and injected into the field a realistic appreciation of immigration as a form of commerce.[61] The Department of the Secretary of State of the federal government supported a series, 'Generations: A History of Canada's Peoples', projected in twenty-five volumes. *A Heritage in Transition: Essays on the History of the Ukrainians in Canada* (1982), edited by Manoly Lupul, was characteristic of the genre in that it was a co-operative venture of writers who were rooted in that community and who represented several disciplines, and in that it was a tentative foray rather than a definitive statement. The authors paid more attention to the urban dimension than was customary in earlier immigration histories, and focused upon the inner history and organizational life of the group and its relations with the surrounding society. These latter themes were especially important in an equally rewarding volume in this series, *From China to Canada: A History of Chinese Communities in Canada* (1982), edited by Edgar Wickberg, which showed how restrictive, and then exclusionist, immigration policies shaped a unique bachelor community with distinctive cultural and organizational traits that lasted until a generation ago.[62]

The major books by historians in this field fell into two categories. The first was the study of individual groups, often ones with longer histories in Canada than those usually written about by social scientists. In *The People's Clearance: Highland Emigration to North America, 1770-1815* (1982), Jack M. Bumsted explored in detail the background and motivations of these immigrants who were not an impoverished peasantry but relatively well-off people. For the Highlander, North America offered escape from disadvantages rather than the opportunity to do something new; having evaded change at home they maintained as much of the old life as they possibly could. This conservatism was developed in *Beyond the Atlantic Roar: A Study of the Nova Scotia Scots* (1977) by sociologist Douglas Campbell and historian Ray A. Maclean, an impressionistic and discursive survey, informed by many interviews, of the people of four counties in eastern Nova Scotia, their folkways, religious traditions, and political and economic behaviour. Written with a respect for their subjects' integrity and a feeling for the intangibles, they did not gloss over such shortcomings as the indifferences to material progress and the transference of loyalties from clan chieftains to an almost unchangeable allegiance to political leaders.

In a vigorous and iconoclastic study, *The Irish in Ontario: A Study in*

Rural History (1984), Donald H. Akenson reconsidered and revised many erroneous generalizations about a group that had settled predominantly in rural districts and villages rather than cities, were remarkably adaptable and responsive to economic opportunities, and were more successful than the average Canadian-born farmers. The core of his work was a micro-study of land acquisition, settlement, agricultural production, and the development of a network of social and political institutions in the township of Leeds and Lansdowne in the early nineteenth century. Though self-styled as a 'contribution to ethnic studies', this book made it clear that the success of the Irish was due more to social processes than cultural traditions. One of the many institutions considered by Akenson was reinterpreted by Cecil J. Houston and William J. Smyth, *The Sash Canada Wore: A Historical Geography of the Orange Order in Canada* (1980), which mapped its territorial expansion, explained its appeal in terms of conviviality, ritual, and mutual aid as well as religion, and stressed that its large and varied membership among the native-born was due to the fact that the order embodied the loyalist, monarchist, and Protestant values of the community as a whole. This study was a nice supplement to the earlier survey by Hereward Senior, *Orangeism: The Canadian Phase* (1972), which concentrated on the political activities of the order.

One of the most valuable results of these and other histories of ethnic groups has been the destruction of simplified impressions of them as homogeneous and the revelation of their internal divisions and complexity. Frank H. Epp. *Mennonites in Canada, 1786–1920: The History of a Separate People* (1974) and *Mennonites in Canada, 1920–1940: A People's Struggle for Survival* (1982), illustrated this point in isolating the two separate streams of Anabaptists that entered Canada—the one from the United States after the Revolution, the other from Russia in the 1870s—revealing the consequences of the group's tendencies towards fragmentation, and successfully relating their histories to the larger Canadian setting. In a similar fashion, Stephan A. Speisman, *The Jews of Toronto: A History to 1937* (1979), played upon the differences between those who originated in Germany and Britain and those who came later from eastern Europe, between the upholders of reform and orthodox Judaism, and among occupational groups and classes. Ken Adachi, *The Enemy That Never Was: A History of the Japanese Canadians* (1976), delineated the strains within that group occasioned by the adoption by the second generation of mores and political involvements quite different from those of their parents, though his main theme was the catastrophic evacuation of the whole group from the west coast in 1942.

The second type of historical studies in this field was the examination of popular attitudes towards ethnic minorities. In general these tell us less about individual ethnic communities than about the opinions and feelings of elements of the native-born, British-Canadian majority who were able to pressure governments to bend to their wishes. For example, Donald Avery's 'Dangerous Foreigners': European Immigrant Workers and Labour Radicalism in Canada, 1896–1932 (1979) contained a novel account of the change in immigration policy that favoured unskilled workers over agricultural settlers, and examined the growth of the legend that equated certain ethnic groups with Bolshevism. It was less satisfactory, however, in dealing with the actual course of radicalism among the Ukrainians and Finns. Two superior examinations of attitudes towards minority ethnic groups dealt with whole provincial societies. Howard Palmer, Patterns of Prejudice: A History of Nativism in Alberta (1982), surveyed the permutations of anti-foreign sentiment and discrimination up to the Second World War against a background of that province's particular mix of peoples and its maverick political traditions. He explored the religious, anti-radical, and Anglo-Saxon roots of prejudice, carefully related expressions of it to such groups as farm leaders and clergymen, and found that there was no single connection between the undulations of nativism and economic conditions. In White Canada Forever: Popular Attitudes and Public Policy towards Orientals in British Columbia (1978), Peter Ward argued that so strong and pervasive was the desire among whites for an ethnically homogeneous society that anti-orientalism flourished independent of social and economic circumstances. Though other scholars were not convinced by this dismissal of the fears of economic competition as the origins of prejudice, Ward did much to explain the removal of Japanese Canadians during the Second World War as the culmination of a long-standing drive and not simply as a misguided response to wartime insecurities. This episode was investigated also by Ann Gomer Sunahara, The Politics of Racism: The Uprooting of Japanese Canadians during the Second World War (1981), a fine-grained analysis of the federal government's policy, of the pressures upon it, and of the varied reactions of the Japanese Canadians themselves. Less well known was the story told by Irving Abella and Harold Troper in None Is Too Many: Canada and the Jews of Europe, 1933–1948 (1982), which implicated Canada in the Holocaust. That the country accepted fewer refugees than almost any other nation in the western world was attributed to an anti-semitism that permeated society and was taken into account in Mackenzie King's political calculations and faithfully reflected by the bureaucrats in charge of immigration. These studies of prejudice, nativism, and group conflicts have done much to qualify, if not overthrow, the image of Canada as a relatively tolerant community in which a variety of people have intermingled harmoniously in the past. In this, the influence of ethnic history paralleled that of working-class studies which have highlighted class tensions and struggles.

Like ethnic history, women's history derived its momentum from the social changes of the later sixties and was one facet of a many-sided movement aimed at altering attitudes, instilling self-confidence in women, and obliterating obstacles to their treatment as equal human beings. Thus the determination to recover the distinctive historical experiences of woman was quite consciously fostered to redress the bias of a history that had been written by men, and to satisfy a demand for recognition of members of the female sex not only as a passive group but as important actors in their own right. Women's history, in addition, was not the same thing as the history of women; it was more ambitious and was intended to bring a feminist perspective to all historical writing. Since the experiences of women were different from those of men, women's history would place greater emphasis on such subjects as life cycles, family, kinship, and childhood, and make all historians more aware of the unsuspected dimensions of even familiar subjects. So successful in this regard were Sylvia Van Kirk's study of women in the fur trade and Jennifer Brown's examination of fur-trade families that it was impossible to assign them to any single, exclusive category of history.

Most of the some two hundred publications in women's history that appeared in the dozen years before 1982[63] were written or edited by women, and the vast majority were collections of documents, reprints of early texts, scholarly articles, and anthologies of essays, with very few interpretive monographs. These writings have developed two themes. The first, which built upon considerable existing work, was the 'woman question' in the late Victorian period, the emergence of middle-class women as a self-conscious group, their agitation for the suffrage, and support for a many-sided reform programme. Veronica Strong-Boag, in *The Parliament of Women: The National Council of Women of Canada* (1976), located the origins of this national federation of elite women in voluntary associations, cultural clubs, and church groups; set it into the context of the response to industrialism and the extension of a national communications network; and highlighted the ways in which promoting social regeneration and patriotism channelled both the anxieties of the middle class over social change and the desire of some women to escape the confines of the household. Many of the essays in *A Not Unreasonable Claim: Women and Reform in Canada, 1880s–1920s* (1979), edited by Linda Kealey, traced the links between emancipation and changes and challenges in society at large. They elaborated upon the distinct and class-bound nature of suffragette and reform leaders, their negative attitudes to certain immigrant groups, and their differences with working-class and farm women; displayed a keen appreciation of the restraints upon those few women who entered into such careers as medicine; and showed how organizations like the Women's Christian Temperance Union, for all its emphasis upon family life, promoted early feminism.

One of the effects of these and other examinations into the ideology of the first wave of Canadian feminists was to underscore the fundamental importance of maternal feminism, the belief that women's special nurturing qualities entitled them to political rights and to a greater and more active role in social reforms that would protect the family. This claim ultimately ensured the acceptance of their case for the franchise, but it also reinforced their separate sphere and continual subservience. The most severe appraisal of the early feminists was submitted in *Liberation Deferred? The Ideas of the English-Canadian Suffragists, 1877–1918* (1983) by Carol Bacchi, who explored the division between those founders of the earliest women's organizations who advocated female political equality as a principle and as a preliminary to broadening women's spheres of activity, and those who based their case on the late Victorian stereotype of women and subordinated women's interests to puritanical, moralistic reformism. This account drew too sharp a line between two tendencies, exaggerated the influence of the idea of sexual equality, and underestimated the extent to which the demand for the suffrage was a radical challenge to prevailing views about women in Victorian society.

The second theme in the history of women that has come in for considerable investigation has been patterns of their employment outside the home. Women's history merged into labour history in *Women at Work: Ontario, 1850–1930* (1974), edited by Janice Acton, Penny Goldsmith, and Bonnie Shepard, which contained illuminating studies of women in domestic service, nursing, and school teaching. Equally important were those essays in the two-volume *The Neglected Majority: Essays in Canadian Women's History* (1977 and 1986), edited by Susan M. Trofimenkoff and Alison Prentice, which revealed how substantial was the female work-force in the Montreal garment industry in the late nineteenth century, explained the feminization of the teaching profession in the same period, and surveyed Canadian working women in the twenties. When these studies were supplemented by Ruth R. Pierson's *'They're Still Women After All': The Second World War and Canadian Womanhood* (1986), patterns in female employment emerged with striking clarity. Not only were working women highly concentrated in certain socially approved and ill-paid sectors of the economy, but not even the entry of women into new fields of work during the world wars was sufficient to advance their equality with men or dislodge a tenacious view about their proper, that is, limited, role in society.

These investigations into the sexual bias in the world of work and of conservatism of the early suffragists were, in effect, encounters with the historical origins and persistence of practices and patterns that the second wave of feminists were bent on overthrowing. By showing these patterns to have been historically rooted and therefore relative and not preordained, they took the first step in escaping them. This tendency was no less evident in the study of demography, family, and childhood which some feminist historians associated with the history of women, though it was not, of course, solely confined to them. An awareness of the importance of these subjects derived from European and British scholarship on population changes, the lively controversy over the origins of the nuclear family, and a burgeoning literature on the ways in which anonymous economic and social forces impinged upon the most private and intimate aspects of human activity. In their inquiries into social mobility both Katz and Gagan paid considerable attention to the manner in which class and economic change determined family formation, the ages of the sexes at marriage, family size and household composition, and the shifting definitions and durations of childhood and adolescence. These and parallel topics were developed by others who did not share their enthusiasm for statistical methods but were no less devoted to demonstrating that such apparently biologically determined institutions as family and childhood actually varied enormously in historical experience. Joy Parr, who examined the fates of some eighty thousand boys and girls sent to Canada by philanthropic agencies in *Labouring Children: British Immigrant Apprentices to Canada, 1869–1924* (1980), also edited *Childhood and Family in Canadian History* (1982), which offered glimpses of children in New France, the treatment of juvenile delinquents in late Victorian Toronto, and family survival strategies among the working class in Montreal between 1860 and 1885.

The study of childhood and attitudes towards the young were developed in conjunction with the history of public education as well as with women's history, for an adequate explanation of the origins and evolution of the public school systems necessarily involved an understanding of perceptions of childhood. Up to the sixties the history of public education had been quite marginal to Canadian historical writing except for those episodes covered by political history in which schools figured in clashes of church and state or in the conflicts of cultures over language and religion. The institutional histories of educational systems and schooling tended to be written by educators as relentless chronicles of improvement. Mainly by way of the example of American writing in the sixties, the scope of educational history was enlarged to encompass the social, intellectual, and political environments in which these systems originated and developed, and historians turned to enquire more closely into the class and ethnic dimensions of education institutions.[64] For example, Jean Barman, in *Growing up British in British Columbia: Boys in Private School* (1984), examined the ideal of the old world model and the successful transplanting of an ethic summed up by one headmaster as Christianity, classics, cricket, cadet corps, cold baths, courtesy, and corporal punishment. Barman not only demonstrated that these institutions sustained a British allegiance but also claimed that schooling based on the separation of classes reinforced the social-economic structure of the province.

Even the apparently more open public school systems were censured by historians like Michael Katz for their excessive centralization, unresponsiveness to democratic needs, and heavy bureaucracy. Katz, in association with graduate students at the Ontario Institute for Studies in Education, inverted the conventional explanation for the origins of Ontario's school system in the mid-nineteenth century, a system that arose, he claimed, not from a commitment to promote individual opportunity or social advancement at large but rather from the response of a middle class threatened by the urban poor and certain ethnic groups, and was designed to ensure stability, order, and the continuing hegemony of that class. Like penitentiaries and insane asylums, schools were instruments of 'social control' intended to impose class values and discipline. Though some aspects of this interpretation were adumbrated in *Education and Social Change: Themes from Ontario's Past* (1975), edited by Paul H. Mattingly and Michael Katz, it was most fully explored in Alison Prentice's *The School Promoters: Education and Social Class in Mid-Nineteenth-Century Upper Canada* (1977). Prentice examined the ideas of Egerton Ryerson and other advocates of mass public schooling and argued that their primary aim was to prevent social unrest, criminal behaviour, and class conflicts and that the system they designed was inegalitarian and promoted middle-class values of respectability and achievement.

In *Children in English-Canadian Society: Framing the Twentieth-Century Consensus* (1976), Neil Sutherland offered a more sympathetic interpretation of the motives and accomplishments of reformers who focused upon the new needs of the young in an industrial, urban society. He traced their efforts to improve the health and welfare of children, better the treatment of juvenile delinquents, and extend the scope of school instruction to include vocational training, physical education, and, in the prairie provinces, the promotion of unilingualism. To the charge that reformers had created overly centralized and repressive institutions, he replied that the alternative at the time was not another strategy of change but simply doing nothing at all. Robert Stamp, in *The Schools of Ontario, 1876–1976* (1982), recognized that education reform movements were aimed at inculcating desirable behaviour and their thrusts were essentially conservative; but he also laid to rest the myth of a highly centralized system, controlled by an unaccountable bureaucracy, by showing how responsive it was to local needs and to pressures from many groups—turn-of-the-century imperialists, progressives, cultural nationalists—that sought to use the schools for their own purposes.

Of all the aspects of the study of society urban history was most lacking in coherence, possibly because it derived from two different traditions and had been influenced by several disciplines. The idea of metropolitanism, which was rooted in the economic history of the thirties and subsequently made explicit and clarified by Maurice Careless, focused upon the economic dimensions of urban growth and the relationship between cities, especially their business classes, and their hinterlands.[65] Ruben C. Bellan's *Winnipeg's First Century: An Economic History* (written in the late fifties and published in 1978) illustrated this approach to urban history in its preoccupation with explaining that city's rise to metropolitan status and its influence over the western wheat economy, and with such subjects as the favourable freight rate conceded to Winnipeg businessmen ensuring their dominance of the wholesale trade. The second approach to urban history, which dated from the late sixties, paid more attention to the internal social texture of urban places, the segregation of classes and ethnic groups into different districts, to social mobility, and to urban social problems and reform movements. Alan F.J. Artibise, in *Winnipeg: A Social History of Urban Growth, 1878–1914* (1975), downplayed the relations of the prairie centre to both the regional economy and eastern business and gave more emphasis to the urban environment, class and ethnic structures, and types of social services. He stressed that Winnipeg's growth was energetically promoted by a relatively homogeneous, commercial elite which employed their own considerable financial resources and undue influence in municipal government to attract railways, industry, and immigration regardless of the resulting deplorable social conditions. This emphasis upon the promotional activities of civic and business leaders devoted to 'boosterism' imparted a certain degree of unity to the fifteen local studies in *Town and City: Aspects of Western Canadian Urban Development* (1981) edited by Artibise, even though the collection also included considerations of child welfare in Calgary and Vancouver as the mecca of the unemployed.

While the city-building process provided some consistency to urban history, the expansion of social history in general made the subfield more diverse and eclectic. A collection of essays compiled by the chief exponents of the subject, Artibise and Gilbert A. Stelter, incorporated such a variety of approaches that it seemed that urban history was meant to include everything that happened in cities. *The Canadian City: Essays in Urban History* (1977) encompassed studies of the national tariff policy and the industrialization of the Maritimes, working women in Montreal, the Calgary school system, architectural styles in public buildings in Toronto and private dwellings in Vancouver, and urban reform movements. *Forging a Consensus: Historical Essays on Toronto* (1984), edited by Victor L. Russell, contained fine studies of the police force and office buildings, and a brilliant essay on the basis and ideology of civic populism by Christopher Armstrong and H.V. Nelles, who had dealt with a portion of this theme in their jocose *The Revenge of the Methodist Bicycle Company: Sunday Streetcars and Municipal Reform in Toronto, 1888–1897* (1977). This collection of essays on the queen city, however, was more impressive for its parts than as a coherent statement regarding the municipal consensus that was forged.

Urban history was evidently a capacious field with an almost unlimited ability to absorb, or assert control over, findings from the other varieties of social history. It was not at all clear what was regarded as generically urban, and urban history appeared to its more astringent critics as a field in search of a problem. This inclusiveness was only partly brought under control in the History of Canadian Cities Series. Its editor, Alan Artibise, attempted to strike a balance between treating individual cities as distinctive places while at the same time isolating such common elements as ethnic relations, regionalism, provincial-municipal interaction, social mobility, labour-management relations, urban planning, and economic development. The six volumes[66] published in this series were in general models of compression and synthesis; they did not, however, in themselves resolve the problem of diffuseness inherent in the formula to which they were written.

That it was in fact possible to write a more integrated and coherent history of an urban place was brilliantly demonstrated in *Saint John: The Making of a Colonial Urban Community* (1985) by T.W. Acheson. This was an exceptionally complex, but always lucid, analysis of the groups within the city—merchants and artisans, Irish immigrants, and 'Bluenoses'—and the material interests and ethnic and religious differences that separated them, and also the values they shared. Acheson skilfully interwove considerations of the evangelical movement, temperance and education, reform and police, to document thoroughly the fragmentation and reintegration of a community.

Social history as a general impulse exercised an influence upon historical writing far beyond the subfields of urban studies, women's history, and working-class history. Many important books that defied the tyranny of categories bore the imprint of the new awareness of society in different ways. In *A Victorian Authority: The Daily Press in Late Nineteenth-Century Canada* (1982), Paul Rutherford focused on the newspaper as an institution, analysed the structure, financing, and technology of the industry, surveyed the profession of journalism, and charted the emergence of the popular, mass daily and the reasons for its success. In a new look at an aspect of an old subject, *The Rising in Western Upper Canada, 1837-8: The Duncombe Revolt and After* (1982), Colin Read tested, and found wanting, the hypothesis that rebels and loyalists could be differentiated on the basis of land ownership and other social traits. Geoffrey Bilson, in *A Darkened House: Cholera in Nineteenth-Century Canada* (1980), traced the devastation of the periodic epidemics of this disease between 1832 and 1877, and investigated popular responses, the state of medical knowledge, and the impact of these outbreaks on the rudimentary health care facilities. And a succession of volumes of essays explored the history of the law in a social setting. Legal scholars examined not only the ideology and administration of the law and legal education, but also considered law in relation to economic development and social stability as well as how a society defined crime.[67]

In spite of the many-sidedness of social history it has been plagued by a reification of categories. These were no doubt originally devised to focus research; some of course were also designed to advance the political interests of certain groups and their historians. The very process by which these subfields sought out niches and established their legitimacy, moreover, exaggerated their separation from other forms of history. 'The alarming subdivision of social history into minuscule specialties,' warned Greg Kealey, 'has become a serious problem. Those of us who do work on education history, immigration history, urban history, labour history, women's history, family history or whatever must continue to see our work as interacting and forming part of a larger whole. Without this constant dialectic the new social history will not only fail to provide the desired synthesis but also runs the real danger of falsifying the past by fragmenting reality beyond experience.'[68] All histories, not merely the strands of social history, converge and intersect, but few historians have paused to consider the relationship of the findings of the new and old histories, between, say, population patterns and politics. Social historians have recovered the worlds of previously neglected groups and revealed the capacity of women, workers, and native peoples to shape their own ways of life; they have etched the details of a possible synthesis that accords priority to underlying economic structures and to the conflicts of classes and other groups. They have not, however (at least not yet), fulfilled their more ambitious aspirations of creating whole new formulations of Canadian history.

(Some of these historians did not in fact see their works in terms of Canadian history at all: they were primarily concerned with peasant society or social mobility as the basic units of historical analysis.) For all its revisionist spirit, English-Canadian social history seemed quite conservative in method.[69] Ouellet and Katz had presented historians with different ways of doing history but they have had few emulators. Contemporary Canadian historians have shown themselves to be no more receptive to quantitative methods than their predecessors had been to the historical sociology of S.D. Clark.

X

'The last ten years,' the editors of the Canadian Historical Review announced in 1977, 'have witnessed a revolution in historical writing in Canada.' It is obvious that historical study expanded in scale and subject matter and took on an unprecedented complexity and pluralism. These changes in the seventies were reminiscent of the shift away from constitutional history to economic history around 1930 and the abandonment of the economic interpretation of history in favour of political biography after 1950. Each generation writes the type of history it considers appropriate to its own time and answers to its own needs, but generations are not homogeneous and do not exist in isolation from each other. And historians, like other people, change their minds and see things differently from the way they once did. Thus the pattern of historical publication in the two decades after the mid-1960s exhibited two contrasting tendencies: the one elaborating upon the concerns that most historians shared in the early sixties, the other exploring quite unfamiliar topics, occasionally with radically different methods, invariably with a critical spirit coupled with appeals to relevance. Judged—quite impressionistically—by the crude measure of monographs published (and bearing in mind that in social history the article was the favoured vehicle), the elements of continuity—represented by the persistence of biography, political and military history, institutional studies in labour history, and most forms of regional history—were stronger than those making for an abrupt break with previous historical writing. Even those fields of history that seemed to be novel owed not a little to those who had gone before: back of urban history stood the writings of Gras, Lower, and Careless; the renewal of regional and provincial history rested on the precedents of Morton and others; and revisionists in political economy rejected their fathers and reached beyond them to another generation to rediscover part of the legacy of Harold Innis. Those who live through revolutions are apt to exaggerate change and underestimate continuities.

It is ironical in the light of historians' long-standing resistance to the social sciences that some of the most original studies in the Canadian past have come from the borderlands where history encountered political science, historical geography, and ethno-history. These disciplines expanded in the sixties and seventies at an even faster rate than the historical profession and some individuals within them perpetuated historicist traditions that ran back to the descriptive political science of R. MacGregor Dawson, the geography of Andrew Hill Clark, and the anthropology of Alfred G. Bailey. Canadian historical literature would be infinitely poorer without Bruce Trigger's ethno-history of the Huron people, James Eayrs' books on defence and external policy, or Graeme Wynn's historical geography of early New Brunswick. The ties between historical study and these other disciplines became far stronger than they had been in the two decades after the Second World War.

The diversification of historical writing and experimentation in many fields were greeted by some historians as a liberation from a stultifying formula, an exciting new beginning. Few of them regretted that the historian had been at last released from the burden of constantly performing as some kind of national sage. Others who stood closer to the centre of a tradition that stretched back from Creighton to George M. Wrong were apt to regret the excesses of revisionism and the fact that a substantial proportion of contemporary history was more likely to raise painful questions of guilt and grievance rather than provide positive perspectives on the major currents of national life.[70] Of only one thing we may be certain: in time the new history will experience the same fate as the old history, for Clio is still an inspiring muse but she has the alarming habit of devouring those who respond to her charms.

BIBLIOGRAPHICAL NOTE

A listing of articles, books, and journals used in the preparation of this study would be repetitious, since the main items have been discussed in the text and identified in the notes. There are, however, useful listings of the works of a number of the historians who have been considered that have been published as appendices to the following obituaries or books of essays written in honour of certain scholars: W.S. Wallace, 'The Life and Work of George Wrong', *CHR* XXIX (Sept. 1948), 229-37; R.F. Neil, 'Adam Shortt: A Bibliographical Comment', *Journal of Canadian Studies* II (Feb. 1967), 54-61; William A. Mackintosh, 'O.D. Skelton, 1878-1941', *CJEPS* VII (May 1941), 270-6; Norman Penlington, ed., *On Canada: Essays in Honour of Frank H. Underhill* (Toronto, 1971), Bibliography, 133-96; Jane Ward, 'The Published Works of H.A. Innis', *CJEPS* XIX (May 1953), 233-44, to which R.F. Neill has made additions and corrections in his *A New Theory of Value: The Canadian Economics of H.A. Innis* (Toronto, 1972), 126-45; W.H. Heick and Roger Graham, eds., *His Own Man: Essays in Honour of Arthur Reginald Marsden Lower* (Montreal, 1974), 'A Select List of Publications by A.R.M. Lower', 163-82, which is a selection from a more comprehensive inventory in the Lower Papers in the Douglas Library, Queen's University; Michael Cross and Robert Bothwell, eds., *Policy by Other Means: Essays in Honour of C.P. Stacey* (Toronto, 1972), 247-58; John S. Moir, ed., *Character and Circumstance: Essays in Honour of Donald Grant Creighton* (Toronto, 1970), 235-9. There is a good summary of Underhill's opinions in Robert Douglas Francis, *Frank H. Underhill: Canadian Intellectual* (York University, Ph.D. thesis, 1975), which I read after this manuscript was completed.

The manuscript sources available varied enormously in quality and quantity. By far the richest collections that illuminate not only the personalities of certain figures but the intellectual and social settings in which they worked are the Frank H. Underhill, Alfred L. Burt, Sir Arthur Doughty Papers, and certain volumes of the Public Archives Records, at the Public Archives of Canada; the Adam Shortt, Lorne Pierce, Arthur Lower, and Reginald G. Trotter Papers at the Douglas Library, Queen's University; the Harold A. Innis Papers and Innis Family Papers at the Archives and Rare Book Room in the University of Toronto Library; the Bartlet Brebner collection in the Butler Library, Columbia University; and the correspondence of Arthur S. Morton in the Murray Memorial Library, University of Saskatchewan, Saskatoon. Lewis H. Thomas, *The Renaissance of Canadian History: A Biography of A.L. Burt* (Toronto, 1975) contains a generous sampling of his correspondence.

Less substantial in bulk, and of more marginal interest for my purposes, were the following: at the Public Archives of Canada, the papers of Hume Wrong, Charles B. Sissons, William L. Grant, Joseph E. Roy, Ernest Cruikschank, Gustave Lanctôt, Douglas Brymner, David Parker, and Eugene Forsey; at Queen's, the William A. Mackintosh collection, which consists mainly of printed material relating to his work on agrarian co-operation and financial policy in the Second World War; at the University of Toronto Library, the papers of William S. Wallace, George Brown, George M. Wrong, and manuscripts of W.P.M. Kennedy; at the Public Archives of Nova Scotia, the Daniel C. Harvey papers; at the University of Saskatchewan, the papers of Vernon Fowke and George Britnell; and at the Huntington Library and Art Gallery, San Marino, California, the papers of William B. Munro.

In addition to the items mentioned in the notes to Chapter 11, the following substantial studies provide both additional information and some new perspectives on historical writing before 1970: on the Victorian tradition and predecessors, M. Brook Taylor, 'The Writing of English-Canadian History in the Nineteenth Century' (Ph.D. thesis, University of Toronto, 1984); on Adam Shortt, Sam E.D. Shortt, *The Search for an Ideal: Six Canadian Intellectuals and Their Convictions in an Age of Transition, 1890-1930* (Toronto, 1976), Chapter 6; on Underhill, R. Douglas Francis, *Frank H. Underhill: Intellectual Provocateur* (Toronto, 1986); and, on the social sciences, Marlene G. Shore, 'The Science of Society: Sociology at McGill University, 1918-1939' (Ph.D. thesis, University of Toronto, 1984), and 'Carl Dawson and the Research Ideal: The Evolution of a Canadian Sociologist', *CHAP*, 1985, 45-73. (The latter two studies are far more wide-ranging than their titles imply.) Harry H. Hiller, *Society and Change: S.D. Clark and the Development of Canadian Sociology* (Toronto, 1982), is a sociological analysis of sociology. Michael S. Cross has surveyed the major books published between 1960 and 1974 in 'Canadian History',

Literary History of Canada: Canadian Literature in English, Second Edition, vol. III, ed. Carl F. Klinck (Toronto, 1976), 63-83. Joseph Levitt, *A Vision Beyond Reach: A Century of Images of Canadian Destiny* (Ottawa, 1982), tells us much more about the political pronouncements of historians than about the history they wrote.

The backgrounds of regional and provincial historical writing are appraised in Allan Smith, 'The Writing of British Columbia History', *BC Studies* XLV (Spring 1980), 73-102, and in two contributions to *Eastern and Western Perspectives: Papers from the Joint Atlantic/Western Canadian Studies Conferences* (Toronto, 1981), edited by David J. Bercuson and Phillip A. Buckner, which took as their points of departure shortcomings in the original edition of this book: E.R. Forbes, 'In Search of a Post-Confederation Maritime Historiography, 1900-1967', 47-67, and Lewis G. Thomas, 'The Writing of History in Western Canada', 69-83. George Rawlyk considered Brebner's Maritime studies in 'J.B. Brebner and the Writing of Canadian History', *JCS* XIII (Fall 1978), 84-93. On French Canada, see Serge Gagnon, *Le Québec et ses Historiens de 1840 à 1920: La Nouvelle-France de Garneau à Groulx* (Quebec, 1978), *Quebec and Its Historians: 1840 to 1920* (Montreal, 1982), and *Quebec and Its Historians: The Twentieth Century* (Montreal, 1985). Fernand Ouellet has surveyed Canadian writing in both languages around a particular theme in 'L'émergence dans le Canada du xxe siècle de l'histoire comme science sociale', *TRSC*, Centenary volume (1982), 35-81, and 'La modernisation de l'historiographie et l'émergence de l'histoire sociale', *Recherches sociographiques* XXVI (1985), 10-83. Apart from the publications on Innis and political economy mentioned in note 24 to Chapter 11 there are two valuable studies of the Toronto department—Ian M. Drummond, *Political Economy at the University of Toronto: A History of the Department, 1882-1982* (Toronto, 1983), and Vincent Bladen, *Bladen on Bladen: Memoirs of a Political Economist* (Toronto, 1978). The Queen's tradition has been appraised in Barry Ferguson, 'The New Political Economy and Canadian Liberal Democratic Thought, 1890-1925' (Ph.D. thesis, York University, 1982), which contains an excellent analysis of the work of O.D. Skelton. Of the few autobiographies by historians, Arthur G. Dorland, *Along the Trail of Life: A Quaker Retrospect* (Belleville, 1979), recalls his teaching career at the University of Western Ontario; H.S. Ferns, *Reading from Left to Right: One Man's Political History* (Toronto, 1983), presents an acerbic recollection of his collaboration with B. Ostry on the King biography; and Charles Stacey, *A Date with History: Memoirs of a Canadian Historian* (Ottawa, 1982), contains a full account of his career as an official military historian. Some of Donald Creighton's essays on politics, literature, and historians have been republished in *The Passionate Observer: Selected Writings* (Toronto, 1980).

NOTES

All manuscript sources cited in the notes are held by the Public Archives of Canada, Ottawa, unless otherwise specified. The following abbreviations have been used throughout the notes:

CF	*Canadian Forum*
CHAP	Canadian Historical Association *Historical Papers*
CHAR	Canadian Historical Association *Annual Report*
CHR	*Canadian Historical Review*
CJEPS	*Canadian Journal of Economics and Political Science*
JCS	*Journal of Canadian Studies*
L	*Labour/Le Travailleur*
QQ	*Queen's Quarterly*
QUL	Douglas Library, Queen's University
TRSC	*Transactions of the Royal Society of Canada*, Section II
UTQ	*University of Toronto Quarterly*
UTL	Rare Book Room and Archives, University of Toronto Library

1. THE FOUNDERS OF CRITICAL HISTORY: GEORGE WRONG AND ADAM SHORTT

[1] D.C. Harvey, 'History and its Uses in Pre-Confederation Nova Scotia', *CHAR*, 1938, 8.

[2] For a comprehensive discussion of the work of the period, see Kenneth Windsor, 'Historical Writing in Canada (to 1920)', *Literary History of Canada. Canadian Literature in English*, ed., Carl Klinck *et. al.* (Toronto, 1965), 191-250.

[3] J.M. McConica, 'William Kingsford and Whiggery in Canadian History', *CHR*, XL (No. 2, 1959), 108-20.

[4] J.G. Bourinot, *Our Intellectual Strength and Weakness* (Montreal, 1893), 18.

[5] For typical assessments along these lines see James Douglas, 'The Intellectual Progress of Canada During the Last Fifty Years, and the Present State of its Literature', *Canadian Monthly and National Review* VII (June 1875), 465-76, and J.G. Bourinot, *The Intellectual Development of the Canadian People* (Toronto, 1881) and *Our Intellectual Strength and Weakness*.

[6] William H. Withrow, *A Canadian in Europe* (Toronto, 1881), 17.

[7] Bourinot, *The Intellectual Development of the Canadian People*, 126.

[8] Public Archives of Nova Scotia, Family Papers, J.G. Bourinot Scrapbook, Number 2, 291, Parkman to Bourinot, June 13, 1887.

[9] There is an extensive critical literature on Parkman. Among the more recent works are: Wilbur Jacobs, 'Some Social Ideas of Francis Parkman', *American Quarterly* IX (Winter 1957), 387-97; William R. Taylor, 'A Journey into the Human Mind: Motivation in Francis Parkman's La Salle', *William and Mary Quarterly*, Third Series, XIX (April 1962), 220-37; W.J. Eccles, 'The History of New France According to Francis Parkman', *ibid.*, XVIII (April 1961), 163-75; and Howard Doughty, *Francis Parkman* (New York, 1962).

10 Henry H. Miles, 'On "Canadian Archives"', *Transactions of the Literary and Historical Society of Quebec*, Session of 1870-1, New Series, Part 8 (Quebec, 1871), 53-71; W.J. Anderson, 'The Archives of Canada', *ibid.*, Part 9 (Quebec, 1872), 117-31; Public Archives of Canada, *Archives: Mirror of Canada Past* (Toronto, 1972). John H. Archer, *A Study of Archival Institutions in Canada* (Ph.D. thesis, Queen's University, 1969) deals with the history of the Public Archives of Canada as well as provincial institutions from their origins to the mid-twentieth century.

11 M.O. Scott, 'Douglas Brymner, Archivist', *The Canadian Magazine*, XVI (January 1901), 206-8.

12 Douglas Brymner Papers, vol. 4, 'Notebook', unpaginated; See also 'Report on Archives', *Report of the Minister of Agriculture of the Dominion of Canada for the Calendar Year 1873* (Ottawa, 1874), Appendix 24, 170.

13 Brymner Papers, Letterbook, vol. I, Brymner to Marmette, October 24, 1893.

14 David Parker Papers, Doughty to H.P. Biggar, January 25, 1921, copy; G. Lanctôt, 'Past Historians and Present History in Canada', *CHR* XXII (September 1941), 251.

15 Lawrence J. Burpee, 'Co-Operation in Historical Research', *University Magazine* VII (October 1908), 366; D.C. Harvey, 'Douglas Brymner, 1823-1902', *CHR* XXIV (September 1943), 249-52.

16 J. Langton, 'Opening Address', *Transactions of the Literary and Historical Society of Quebec*, Session of 1863-4, New Series, Part 2 (Quebec, 1864), 5; J.M. Buchan, 'The Scientific Treatment of History', *Canadian Monthly* XIII (April 1878), 366-74.

17 W.J. Ashley, *Nine Lectures on the Earlier Constitutional History of Canada, Delivered before the University of Toronto in Easter Term, 1889* (Toronto, 1889), 13-14.

18 Georg G. Iggers, 'The Image of Ranke in American and German Historical Thought', *History and Theory*, II (1962), 17-40.

19 UTL, G.M. Wrong Papers, H.P. Biggar to Wrong, October 13, 1895.

20 Gertrude Himmelfarb, *Lord Acton: A Study in Conscience and Politics* (Chicago, 1962), 223.

21 John Higham with Leonard Krieger and Felix Gilbert, *History: The Development of Historical Studies in the United States* (Englewood Cliffs, N.J., 1965), 97. Chapter I in Part Two is the best analysis of scientific history in the United States. W. Stull Holt, 'The Idea of Scientific History in America', *Journal of the History of Ideas*, I (June 1940), 352-62, is also useful. For an overview of British historical writing, see J.R. Hale, ed., *The Evolution of British Historiography from Bacon to Namier* (New York, 1964) 'Introduction'.

22 C. Berger, 'Race and Liberty: The Historical Ideas of Sir John George Bourinot', *CHAR*, 1965, 87-104.

23 W.S. Wallace, 'The Life and Work of George M. Wrong', *CHR*, XXIX (September 1948), 229-37; Stuart Calais, 'Canadian Celebrities: 70, Professor George M. Wrong', *Canadian Magazine* XXVII (July 1906), 208-10; Wrong, *The Chronicle of a Family* (Toronto, 1938); Chester Martin, 'Professor G.M. Wrong and History in Canada', in *Essays in Canadian History*, ed., R. Flenley (Toronto, 1939), 1-23; and Alan Bowker, *Truly Useful Men: Maurice Hutton, George Wrong, James Mavor and the University of Toronto, 1880-1927* (Ph.D. thesis, University of Toronto, 1975), chapter III.

24 Vincent Massey, *What's Past is Prologue* (Toronto, 1963), 21-2.

25 William Good Papers, Good to his mother, November 29, 1896.

26 F.H. Underhill Papers, Wrong to Underhill, March 14, 1912.

27 Sir George Parkin Papers, vol. 34, Wrong to Parkin, October 12, 1911.

28 Editorial, 'The Origins of the Teaching Staff', *The University Monthly* XII (November 1911), 4. For criticism of hiring abroad see Gordon Waldron, letter to the Editor, *ibid.*, XV (December 1913), 117-18, and, for a defence of the English academics, see R. Hodder-Williams, 'The Incomplete Angles', *The Arbor*, IV (April 1913), 289-99.

29 Underhill Papers, Wrong to Underhill, February 15, 1912.

30 Wrong, 'Fifty Years of Federation in Canada', *Addresses Delivered Before the Canadian Club of Ottawa, 1916-1917* (Ottawa, 1917), 139; 'Democracy in Canada', *CHR*, II (December 1921), 315-32.

31 Wrong, 'Canadian Nationalism and the Imperial Tie', *Proceedings of the American Political Science Association . . . 1909* (Baltimore, 1910), 107.

32 Wrong, 'The Attitude of Canada', *The Nineteenth Century* LXVI (October 1909), 706-7.

33 Wrong, 'The Growth of Nationalism in the British Empire', *American Historical Review* XXII (October 1916), 50.

34 Wrong, 'Fifty Years of Confederation', *TRSC*, Series III, 1917, 68.

35 Angus Gilbert, *The Political Influence of Imperialist Thought in Canada, 1899-1923* (Ph.D. thesis, University of Toronto, 1973), 362. John Kendle, *The Round Table Movement and Imperial Union* (Toronto, 1975) is a full scale study of the groups throughout the Empire.

36 Sir Robert Borden Papers, vol. 125, Wrong to Borden, July 8, 1912.

37 Cited in Margaret Prang, 'N.W. Rowell and Canada's External Policy, 1917-1921', *CHAR*, 1961, 91.

38 Wrong, 'The Beginnings of Historical Criticism in Canada: A Retrospect, 1896-1936', *CHR*, XVII (March 1936), 2-8.

39 Joseph Edmond Roy Papers, Wrong to Roy, October 31, 1906.

40 Bourinot, *Review of Historical Publications Relating to Canada*, I (1897), 90-1.

41 *Ibid.*, II (1898), 11-23.

42 The Champlain Society, *First Annual Report, May, 1906* (Toronto, 1907). A case for the creation of a Canadian Camden or Hakluyt society was made over twenty years before in George Bryce, 'A Plea for a Canadian Camden Society', *TRSC*, II, 1884, 45-53.

43 Wrong, *Historical Study in the University and the Place of Medieval History. An Inaugural Lecture Delivered on Saturday, January 12th, 1895* (Toronto, 1895).

44 Wrong, *A Canadian Manor and its Seigneurs* (Toronto, 1908), 241.

45 J.H. Plumb, *G.M. Trevelyan* (London, 1951), 8.

46 Wrong, 'Cecil Rhodes and His Work', *The Arbor* IV (January 1913), 137.

47 Wrong, 'The Historian and Society', *CHR* XIV (March 1933), 5-6; on Acton's convictions regarding the historian and moral judgement see Lionel Kochan, *Acton on History* (London, 1954).

48 Wrong, 'Fifty Years of Federation in Canada', 128-9.

49 Wrong, 'The Historian's Problem', *CHAR*, 1927, 6-7.

50 Review of J.J. Jusserand *et. al., The Writing of History* in *CHR* VIII (March 1927), 56-60.

51 Charles W. Colby, 'Patriotism and History', *Addresses Delivered Before the Canadian Club of Toronto, Season 1904-05* (Toronto, n.d.), 112.

52 J.L. Morrison, 'Some Recent Historical Literature', *QQ* XIX (January 1912), 269-73; W.S. Wallace, 'Some Vices of Clio', *CHR* VII (September 1926), 197-203.

53 Wrong, *A Canadian Manor*, 5.

54 Wrong, 'St. Augustin', *The University Magazine*, XII (February 1913), 65-76.

55 Mary Elizabeth Hallett, *The 4th Earl Grey as Governor General of Canada, 1904-1911* (University of London, Ph.D. thesis, 1974), Chapter 4.

56 Cited in B.R. Marshall, *Sir Edmund Walker, Servant of Canada* (Master's Thesis, University of British Columbia, 1971), 126.

57 Andrew Macphail, 'The Conservative', *University Magazine* XVIII (no. 4, 1919), 419-44; W.H. Blake, *In a Fishing Country* (Toronto, 1922), 62.

58 Hume Wrong Papers, Hume Wrong to John Dove, December 13, 1925, copy.

59 Wrong, *A Canadian Manor*, 186, 197-8.

60 *Ibid.*, 239-40.

61 Wrong, 'Francis Parkman', *CHR* IV (December 1923), 294, 302.

62 Wrong, *The Rise and Fall of New France* (Toronto, 1928) I, 367. See also Wrong, *The Fall of Canada* (Oxford, 1914), 257.

63 Wrong, 'The Two Races in Canada', *CHAR*, 1925, 21-7.

64 Wrong, 'The Bi-Lingual Question', *The New Era in Canada*, ed., J.O. Miller (Toronto, 1917), 229-59.

65 Wrong, 'Problems Issuing From Confederation', *Addresses Delivered Before the Canadian Club of Toronto, Season of 1927-28* (Toronto, 1928), 9.

66 QUL, Adam Shortt Papers, Watson, 'Copy of Report on Essay', n.d.

67 *Ibid.*, Shortt to Andrew Haydon, January 7, 1894, copy.

68 There is further biographical information about Shortt in Andrew Haydon, 'Adam Shortt', *QQ* XXXVIII (Autumn 1931), 609-23; W.A. Mackintosh, 'Adam Shortt', *CJEPS* IV (May 1938), 164-76; A.R.M. Lower, 'Adam Shortt, Founder', *Historic Kingston* #17 (1968) 3-15; and Samuel E.D. Shortt, *Conviction in an Age of Transition: A Study of Selected Canadian Intellectuals, 1890-1920* (Ph.D. thesis, Queen's University, 1973), Chapter VI, which contains a fine exposition of his empiricism.

69 Parkin Papers, Grant to Parkin, April 9, 1895.

70 Shortt Papers, F. Mahaffy to Shortt, September 16, no year.

71 For a succinct account of the German historical economists and their influence in the United States, see Sidney Fine, *Laissez Faire and the General-Welfare State: A Study of Conflict in American Thought, 1865-1901* (Ann Arbor, 1964), Chapter VII.

72 Ashley, *What is Political Science? An Inaugural Lecture . . .* (Toronto, 1888). On Ashley's career see Anne Ashley, *William James Ashley, A Life* (London, 1932), and, on his social reformist imperialism, Bernard Semmel, *Imperialism and Social Reform: English Social-Imperial Thought, 1895-1914* (London, 1960), Chapter XI.

73 W.J. Ashley, Introduction, J.M. McEvoy, *The Ontario Township* (University of Toronto Studies in Political Science, First Series, #1) (Toronto, 1889), 5-6.

74 Shortt, 'The Nature and Sphere of Political Science', *QQ* I (October 1893), 93-101.

75 Shortt Papers, Clipping from St. John *Standard*, December 13, 1909. On Mrs Shortt, see Charlotte Whitton, 'An Appreciation of Mrs. Adam Shortt', *Queen's Review* XXIII (February 1949), 39-41.

76 Shortt, 'Recent Phases of Socialism', *QQ* V (July 1897), 11-21, and 'Co-operation', *ibid.*, (October 1897), 124-34.

77 Shortt Papers, Shortt to Carl D. Thompson, September 23, 1919, copy.

78 Shortt, 'In Defence of Millionaires', *Canadian Magazine* XIII (October 1899), 493-8.

79 Shortt Papers, Clipping from Halifax *Chronicle*, December 9, 1909.

80 *Ibid.*, Clipping from *Manitoba Free Press*, June 26, 1912.

81 Shortt, 'Aims of the Political Science Association', *Papers and Proceedings of the Canadian Political Science Association* I (1913), 9-19.

82 Shortt Papers, O.D. Skelton to Shortt, December 9, 1913.

83 *Ibid.*, Bourassa to Shortt, February 9, 1905, and Grant to Shortt, February 15, 1904.

84 *Ibid.*, Clipping from Montreal *Gazette*, March 5, 1907.

85 *Ibid.*, Shortt to A. Haydon, December 31, 1895, copy; clipping from *Hamilton Herald*, March 19, 1927.

86 James Gibson Hume, *Political Economy and Ethics* (Toronto, 1892).

87 Public Archives Records, vol. 161, Doughty Correspondence, 1925-6, unidentified press clipping.

88 *Ibid.*, vol. 153, Lord Grey to Doughty, August 21, 1916.

89 *Ibid.*, vol. 143, J.C. Webster to Sir Robert Borden, July 6, 1926, copy.

90 *Ibid.*, Evelyn Devonshire to Doughty, February 22, 1927.

91 E.A. Cruikshank Papers, H.P. Biggar to Cruikshank, n.d.

92 Doughty, 'The Preservation of Historical Documents in Canada', *TRSC*, Third Series, XVIII, 1924, 73.

[93] Ian Wilson, 'Shortt and Doughty: The Cultural Role of the Public Archives of Canada, 1904-1935', *The Canadian Archivist*, II (#4, 1973), #4-25.

[94] Shortt Papers, Shortt to W.L. Grant, March 9, 1926, copy.

[95] *Ibid.*, Shortt to Sir Robert Borden, February 10, 1921, copy.

[96] Shortt, 'The Significance for Canadian History of the Work of the Board of Historical Publications', *TRSC*, Series III, XIII, 1919, 103-4.

[97] Shortt Papers, Shortt to A. Haydon, May 16, 1926.

[98] QUL, W.A. MacIntosh Papers, statement by Munro on Shortt, n.d., in file 'Shortt, Adam, Obit.', Carton #6.

[99] Shortt Papers, Innis to Shortt, May 29, 1923; Wrong to Shortt, November 29, 1922, and Shortt's reply, December 6, 1922, copy.

[100] A.L.Burt Papers, Burt to his wife, July 13, 1926. A most informative picture of the personalities and enthusiasms at the Archives emerges from Burt's letters to his wife, which have been reprinted in L.H. Thomas, *The Renaissance of Canadian History: A Biography of A.L. Burt*, (Toronto, 1975).

2. THE RISE OF LIBERTY

[1] [W.S. Wallace] 'Notes and Comments', *CHR* I (December 1920), 344.

[2] This was one of the reasons why the importance of his *Report* in British policy was vastly overestimated. See Ged Martin, *The Durham Report and British Policy: A Critical Essay* (Cambridge, 1972).

[3] D.G. Creighton, 'Chester Martin' *TRSC*, Series III, LII, 1958, 98; and *CHR* XXXIX (September 1958), 263-4.

[4] W.L. Grant, 'The Teaching of Colonial History', *QQ* XVIII (January 1911), 181-8.

[5] On the American 'imperial school', see Michael Kraus, *The Writing of American History* (Norman, Oklahoma, 1953), Chapter XI.

[6] Chester Martin, 'The United States and Canadian Nationality', *CHR* XVIII (March 1937), 5.

[7] Chester Martin, *Empire and Commonwealth: Studies in Governance and Self-Government in Canada* (Oxford, 1929), 149, 305, 341. Martin reaffirmed the central conclusion of an earlier study, Aileen Dunham, *Political Unrest in Upper Canada, 1815-1836* (London, 1926), which reduced the importance of the radicals and contended that the Rebellion was an anti-climax, and out of harmony with the real sentiments of Upper Canadians.

[8] Martin, *Empire and Commonwealth*, 314, 343, 349.

[9] Martin, 'Responsible Government and Its Corollaries in the Canadian Constitution', *TRSC*, Series III, XVII, 1923, 55-6.

[10] Martin, *What is Happening to Our Traditions? The Opening Address to the University of Manitoba, September 27, 1916* (n.p., n.d.), 6.

[11] Martin, 'Confederation and the West', *CHAR*, 1927, 20, 24; 'The Colonial Policy of the Dominion', *TRSC*, Series III, XVI, 1922, 35-47; 'The Completion of Confederation', *QQ* XXXVIII (Spring 1931), 197-210.

[12] Wrong, 'Canada and the Imperial War Cabinet', *CHR* I (March 1920), 9; 'The Evolution of the Foreign Relations of Canada', *ibid.*, VI (March 1925), 6.

[13] *CHR* IV (March 1923), 80.

[14] D.M. Page, *Canadians and the League of Nations before the Manchurian Crisis* (Ph.D. thesis, University of Toronto, 1972), 209.

[15] N.W. Rowell, *The British Empire and World Peace. Being the Burwash Memorial Lectures delivered in Convocation Hall, University of Toronto, November, 1921* (Toronto, 1922), 1.

[16] Sir Robert L. Borden, *Canada in the Commonwealth: From Conflict to Cooperation* (Oxford, 1929), 129, 130.

17 Martin, *Empire and Commonwealth*, 356.
18 W.P.M. Kennedy, 'Nationalism and Self-Determination', *CHR* II (March 1921), 14, 17. For a similar statement by another British-born historian see, J.L. Morrison, 'Nationality and Common Sense', *QQ* XXVIII (October 1920), 145-60.
19 Sir Robert Borden, *Canadian Constitutional Studies: The Marfleet Lectures, University of Toronto, October, 1921* (Toronto, 1922), 139-40.
20 Kennedy, *The Constitution of Canada: An Introduction to its Development and Law* (Oxford, 1922), 455-6.
21 W.P.M. Kennedy, 'Canada's National Status', *North American Review* CCXVI (August 1922) 299-311; John Ewart, ' "Canada's National Status": A Reply', *ibid.*, (December 1922), 773-80; and Kennedy, ' "Canada's National Status": A Last Word', *ibid.*, CCXVII (February 1923), 204-6.
22 David M.L. Farr, 'John S. Ewart', *Our Living Tradition. Second and Third Series*, ed., R.L. McDougall (Toronto, 1959), 185-214; D.L. Cole, 'John S. Ewart and Canadian Nationalism', CHA *Historical Papers*, 1969, 62-73.
23 W.S. Wallace, 'The Growth of Canadian National Feeling', *CHR* I (June 1920), 136-65. Wallace also claimed that Canadian history would rise in repute when seen as a model for the League; 'The Unpopularity of Canadian History', *Canadian Bookman*, II (January 1920), 14.
24 A.L. Burt, *The Old Province of Quebec* (Toronto, 1933), 56, 200; Lewis H. Thomas, *The Renaissance of Canadian History: A Biography of A.L. Burt* (Toronto, 1975).
25 Sir Robert L. Borden, *Canadian Constitutional Studies*, 35, 36, 22, 115-16.
26 C.P. Lucas, ' "Want of Vision" ', *CHR* III (December 1922), 343-50; Sir Robert Borden, ' "Want of Vision"—or What?', *ibid.*, (March 1923), 5-11.
27 UTL, George Brown Papers, Dafoe to Brown, September 16, 1943.
28 Wrong, 'Opinion in Canada', *New Statesman* XXV (July 4, 1925), 331.
29 Wrong, 'Canada's Problems of Equality with Great Britain', *Empire Club of Canada, Addresses Delivered before the Members During the Year, 1926* (Toronto, 1927), 307.
30 Wrong, 'Nationalism in Canada', *Journal of the Royal Institute of International Affairs*, V (July 1926), 182-3.
31 Wrong, *Canada and the American Revolution: The Disruption of the First British Empire* (Toronto, 1935), 475, 120, 131, 476, 14.
32 *CHR* IV (March 1923), 63.
33 QUL, Shortt Papers, Wrong to Shortt, April 16, 1923.
34 *Ibid.*, Skelton to Shortt, March 29, 1903. On Skelton's character and career, see [W.A. Mackintosh], 'O.D. Skelton, 1878-1941', *CJEPS* VII (May 1941), 270-6; W.C. Clark, 'Oscar Douglas Skelton (1878-1941)', *TRSC*, Third Series, XXXV, 1941, 141-7; N. Hillmer, 'O.D. Skelton: The Scholar Who Set a Future Pattern', *International Perspectives*, September-October 1973; and the entries in note #40, below.
35 Shortt Papers, Skelton to Shortt, July 27, 1907.
36 *CHR*, II (March 1921), 86.
37 C.B. Sissons Papers, Skelton to Sissons, February 6, 1923. Dafoe's extended reviews were published as *Laurier: A Study in Canadian Politics* (Toronto, 1922).
38 Shortt Papers, Wallace to Shortt, February 1, 1922; Wallace, 'The White Plume', *Canadian Bookman* IV (March 1922), 88.
39 Shortt Papers, Skelton to Shortt, March 1, 1902.
40 David M.L. Farr, 'Introduction', O.D. Skelton, *Life and Letters of Sir Wilfrid Laurier, vol. I, 1841-1896* (Carleton Library edition, Toronto, 1965) xvi-xvii; Grant Dexter, 'Oscar Douglas Skelton,' *QQ* XLVIII (Spring 1941), 1-6.
41 *New Republic*, XXI (Aug. 9, 1922), 313.
42 Skelton, *The Canadian Dominion* (New Haven, 1919), 129-30.

[43] *Ibid.*, 158.

[44] *Ibid.*, 212, 276.

[45] Skelton, 'Canada and Foreign Policy', *Addresses delivered before the Canadian Club of Toronto, Season of 1921-22* (Toronto, 1923), 142-54.

[46] C.P. Stacey, 'From Meighen to King: The Reversal of Canadian External Policies, 1921-1923', *TRSC*, Series IV, VII, 1969, 239.

[47] Skelton, 'The New Partnership in Industry', *Canadian Bookman*, I (April 1919), 62.

[48] Shortt Papers, Skelton to Shortt, March 4 (?), 1909.

3. FRANK UNDERHILL: HISTORY AS POLITICAL CRITICISM

[1] F.H. Underhill, 'Goldwin Smith', *In Search of Canadian Liberalism* (Toronto, 1960), 87.

[2] F.H. Underhill Papers, Interview with Duncan Meikle, September 1968, 28-9.

[3] *Torontonensis. The Annual Yearbook of the Students of the University of Toronto Published by the Undergraduates' Parliament*, XII (Toronto, 1911), 89.

[4] W.S. Milner, 'The Higher National Life', *Canada and Its Provinces*, eds., A. Shortt and A.G. Doughty (Toronto, 1914), XII, 403-31.

[5] Underhill, 'Commission Government of Cities', *The Arbor* II (April 1911), 284-94.

[6] UTA, G.M. Wrong Papers, Underhill to Wrong, February 2, 1912.

[7] Underhill Papers, Meikle interview, 22.

[8] W.S. Wallace, 'The Khaki University of Canada', *McMaster University Monthly* XXVIII (December 1918), 97-100.

[9] Sir Charles Lucas, ed., *The Empire at War* (London, 1923), II, 286.

[10] Underhill Papers, Underhill to Kenneth Bell, January 29, 1926, copy.

[11] *Ibid.*, Underhill to Carleton Stanley, July 24, 1925, copy.

[12] University of Saskatchewan Archives, Murray Memorial Library, Saskatoon, George Britnell Papers, Lecture notes, October 1, 1926. Thirteen of the periodicals he recommended were British, four American.

[13] *Ibid.*, April 14, 1927.

[14] Underhill Papers, Underhill to Lothian, March 1926, copy.

[15] University of Saskatchewan Archives, Murray Memorial Library, Saskatoon, A.S. Morton Papers, Underhill to Morton, April 2, 1926.

[16] Underhill Papers, Underhill to Lothian, March 26, 1926, copy.

[17] William B. Munro, *CHR* XI (December 1930), 339-40; J.B.B. [Brebner], *University of Toronto Monthly* XXXI (#2, 1930-1), 128.

[18] The best general appraisals are Richard Hofstadter, *The Progressive Historians* (New York, 1968); John Higham, *History: The Development of Historical Studies in the United States* (Princeton, 1965) Part III, Chapter 3; and Lee Benson, *Turner and Beard: American Historical Writing Reconsidered* (Glencoe, Ill., 1960).

[19] Underhill, 'The Revival of Conservatism in North America', *TRSC*, Series III, LII, 1958, 7.

[20] Stanley Elkins and Eric McKitrick, 'Progressive Scholars and the Founding Fathers', in Cushing Strout, ed., *Intellectual History in America: From Darwin to Neibuhr* (New York, 1968), 123-31; Richard Hofstadter, 'Beard and the Constitution: The History of an Idea', *American Quarterly*, II (Fall 1950), 195-213.

[21] Harry Elmer Barnes, 'Dynamic History and Social Reform', *CF* IV (August 1924) 331-3.

[22] Cushing Strout, *The Pragmatic Revolt in American History: Carl Becker and Charles Beard* (New Haven, 1958).

[23] Underhill, *CF* XII (June 1932), 345.

[24] Underhill, 'O Canada', *CF* X (January 1930), 117.

[25] Underhill, 'Canadian and American History—and Historians', *CF* VIII (June 1928), 686.

26 *CF* x (December 1929), 79.

27 'O Canada' *CF* xi (October 1930), 12.

28 *CF* ix (March 1929), 198.

29 Underhill Papers, Fred Landon to Underhill, June 15, 1928; W.L. Grant to Underhill, October 21, 1930.

30 The following six paragraphs are based on Underhill, 'Some Aspects of Upper Canadian Radical Opinion in the Decade before Confederation', 'The Development of National Political Parties in Canada', 'The Party System in Canada', and 'The Conception of National Interest', all of which are reprinted in his *In Search of Canadian Liberalism*. The last article omits several significant paragraphs from the original in *CJEPS* i (August 1935), 396-408. Underhill also wrote Chapter xx on parties in *Social Planning for Canada* by the Research Committee of the League for Social Reconstruction (Toronto, 1935).

31 Underhill, 'The Conception of National Interest', *In Search*, 179.

32 Robert A. Skotheim, *American Intellectual Histories and Historians* (Princeton, N.J., 1966), 169.

33 'Canadian Politics and Canadian National Feeling', *CF* viii (December 1927), 466.

34 Michiel Horn, 'The League for Social Reconstruction: Socialism and Nationalism in Canada, 1931-1945', (Ph.D. thesis, University of Toronto, 1969) is a thorough and detailed study.

35 Howe Martyn, 'Wanted—A Gospel', *Canadian Mercury* i (March 1929), 88-9.

36 Underhill Papers, Woodsworth to Underhill, March 22, 1929 and April 26, 1929.

37 F.R. Scott, 'The Nineteen Thirties in the United States and Canada', *The Great Depression*, ed., Victor Hoar (Toronto, 1969), 170.

38 Eugene Forsey, 'The Future of Canadian Politics', *Canadian Mercury* i (June 1929), 123-5.

39 Though the origins of lsr democratic socialism were British there are numerous striking parallels with American radical thought at this time as described by Richard Pells, *Radical Visions and American Dreams: Culture and Social Thought in the Depression Years* (New York, 1973), Chapter ii.

40 *Social Planning for Canada*, 225-6.

41 Felix Walter, 'The Universities and the Depression', *New Frontier* i (April 1936), 5.

42 Underhill, 'O Canada', *CF* x (April 1930), 235.

43 Underhill, 'Bentham and Benthamism', *QQ* xxxix (November 1932), 664.

44 Underhill, 'Democracy and Leadership in Canada', *CF* xiv (April 1934), 247-8.

45 *Ibid.*, 247.

46 Underhill, 'Revolt in Canadian Politics', *The Nation* 139 (December 12, 1934), 671.

47 Underhill, 'O Canada', *CF* x (December 1929), 80.

48 Arthur Mann, 'British Social Thought and American Reformers of the Progressive Era', *Mississippi Valley Historical Review* xlii (March 1956), 672-92.

49 Underhill Papers, Underhill to I.B. Howatt, January 19, 1926, copy.

50 Underhill, 'Mr. Good's Political Philosophy', *CF* xiii (August 1933), 411.

51 Underhill, 'Commerce Courses and the Arts Faculty', *University of Toronto Monthly*, xxxi (No. 1, 1930-1), 23-7, and 'O Canada', *CF* ix (January 1929), 303-4; *Honours Classics in the University of Toronto by a Group of Classical Graduates with a Foreword by Sir Robert Falconer* (Toronto, 1929).

52 Margaret Prang, 'F.H.U. of *The Canadian Forum*', *On Canada: Essays in Honour of Frank H. Underhill*, ed., Norman Penlington, (Toronto, 1971), 3-23.

53 Quoted in Ian Robertson, 'Sir Andrew Macphail as a Social Critic', (Ph.D. thesis, University of Toronto, 1974), 196.

54 Carleton Stanley, 'Spiritual Conditions in Canada', *The Hibbert Journal* xxi (January 1923), 281.

55 J.B. Brebner, *Scholarship for Canada: The Functions of Graduate Studies* (Ottawa, Canadian Social Science Research Council, 1945), 13-14.

[56] Underhill, 'The Political Ideas of John S. Ewart', *CHAR*, 1933, 23-32.

[57] Underhill, 'Edward Blake and Canadian Liberalism', in R. Flenley, ed., *Essays in Canadian History* (Toronto, 1939), 132-53; 'Laurier and Blake', *CHR* xx (December 1939), 392-408; 'Blake, the Liberal Party, and Unrestricted Reciprocity', *CHAR*, 1939, 133-41; 'Edward Blake, the Supreme Court Act, and the Appeal to the Privy Council, 1875-6', *CHR* xix (September 1938), 245-63.

[58] 'Canada's Relations with the Empire as seen by the Toronto *Globe*, 1857-1867', *CHR* x (June 1929), 128.

[59] Underhill, 'O Canada', *CF* x (October 1929), 11.

[60] Underhill, 'Canada and International Peace', *Canadian Journal of Religious Thought* ix (March-May 1932), 124.

[61] *Social Planning for Canada*, 518.

[62] *Ibid.*, 520.

[63] 'Spiritual Enlargement', *CF* xv (August 1935), 321.

[64] 'Canadian Policy in a War World', *CF* xvi (July 1936), 7.

[65] 'The Debate on Foreign Policy', *CF* xvi (March 1937), 10.

[66] 'Canada and War', *CF* xiii (May 1933), 286.

[67] Hugh MacLennan, 'What it was like to be in your Twenties in the Thirties', Hoar, ed., *The Great Depression*, 149-51.

[68] *The Pickersgill Letters: Written by Frank Pickersgill during the period 1934-1943 and edited with a memoir by George H. Ford* (Toronto, 1948), 32.

[69] Sir Robert Falconer, *Academic Freedom* (Toronto, 1922).

[70] Underhill Papers, Falconer to Underhill, September 28, 1931.

[71] *Ibid.*, Wrong to Underhill, December 7 and 11, 1933.

[72] *Ibid.*, Underhill to Cody, April 18, 1939, copy.

[73] *Toronto Daily Star*, April 14, 1939.

[74] Underhill, 'North American Front', *CF* xx (September 1940), 166-7, and 'A United American Front', typescript in Underhill Papers.

[75] Roger Graham, *Arthur Meighen: No Surrender* (Toronto, 1965), 123-4.

[76] Underhill Papers, Cody to Hugh Keenleyside, January 13, 1941, enclosed in Keenleyside to Underhill, January 16, 1941.

[77] Columbia University, Butler Library, J.B. Brebner Papers, Underhill to Brebner, September 18, 1940.

[78] *Ibid.*, Brebner to Innis, January 10, 1941, copy.

[79] *Ibid.*, Underhill to Brebner, September 18, 1940.

4. HAROLD INNIS: THE SEARCH FOR LIMITS

[1] UTA, Innis Family Papers, Notes on Innis by Mary Innis, n.d. The Innis Papers which were held by the combined Rare Book Room and University Archives of the University of Toronto Library when I examined them consisted of two distinct collections. The one contained his office correspondence mainly, and the other was composed of more personal material. These two collections are referred to respectively as the Innis Papers and the Innis Family Papers throughout the footnotes.

[2] D.G. Creighton, *Harold Adams Innis: Portrait of a Scholar* (Toronto, 1957), 19.

[3] QUL, W.D. Gregory Papers, MS Autobiography, 42-3.

[4] Innis Family Papers, Innis to Mother and all, n.d.

[5] *Ibid.*, Innis to his sister, April 4, 1916.

[6] *Ibid.*, Innis to his sister, April 7, 1916.

[7] *Ibid.*, Innis to family, December 1, 1916.

8 Innis, 'The Economic Problems of Army Life', *McMaster University Monthly* XXVIII (December 1918), 109.

9 Innis Family Papers, Innis to mother, December 2, 1917.

10 Innis Papers, MS Autobiography, 44, 109.

11 *Ibid.*, 83, 108.

12 Innis, 'The Work of Thorstein Veblen', *Essays in Canadian Economic History*, ed., Mary Q. Innis (Toronto, 1956), 17-26; originally published in *Southwestern Political and Social Science Quarterly* in 1929.

13 Innis, *A History of the Canadian Pacific Railway* (London, 1923), 287.

14 *Ibid.*, 290-4.

15 J.B. Brebner, 'Harold Adams Innis as Historian', *CHAR*, 1953, 15.

16 MS Autobiography, 108.

17 Innis, 'A Trip Through the Mackenzie River Basin', *University of Toronto Monthly* XXV (January 1925), 151-3.

18 Innis, ed., *The Diary of Alexander James McPhail* (Toronto, 1940).

19 Innis Family Papers, Innis to his mother, June 24, 1927.

20 *Ibid.*, Innis to Mary, July 31, 1932.

21 *Ibid.*, Innis to Mary, August 4, 1929.

22 *Ibid.*, Innis to Mary, June 26, 1928.

23 *Ibid.*, Innis to Mary, June 7, 1933.

24 Innis, 'The Teaching of Economic History in Canada', *Essays in Canadian Economic History*, 10, 11. The essay originally appeared in *Contributions to Canadian Economics*, II (University of Toronto Studies, History and Economics, 1930), 52-68.

25 W.A. Mackintosh, 'Economic Factors in Canadian History', *CHR* IV (March 1923), 12-25.

26 Mackintosh, *Agricultural Cooperation in Western Canada* (Kingston, 1924), 1.

27 Mackintosh, 'Innis on Canadian Economic Development', *Journal of Political Economy* LXI (June 1953), 187.

28 M. Newbigin, *Canada: The Great River, the Lands and the Men* (London, 1926), 284, 288.

29 *CHR* VIII (June 1927), 142.

30 *American Economic Review*, XVII (September 1927), 497-8.

31 George Brown wrote a number of articles in support of the project and dealt with the river in Canadian-American diplomatic relations in 'The Opening of the St Lawrence to American Shipping', *CHR* VII (March 1926), 4-12, and 'The St Lawrence Waterway in the Nineteenth Century', *QQ* XXXV (Autumn 1928), 628-42.

32 Innis, *The Fur Trade in Canada: An Introduction to Canadian Economic History* (Toronto, Revised Edition, 1956), 114.

33 *Ibid.*, 262, 393.

34 *Ibid.*, 385.

35 *Ibid.*, 401, 385.

36 Innis, 'The Canadian North', *University of Toronto Monthly* XXX (January 1930), 163.

37 Robin Neill, *A New Theory of Value: The Canadian Economics of H.A. Innis* (Toronto, 1972).

38 Innis, 'The Canadian North', 165.

39 Innis Papers, N.J. Donaldson to Innis, October 23, 1946.

40 Innis Family Papers, Scrapbook 1923-1935, clipping from Toronto *Star*, January 25, 1930.

41 Innis, 'Transportation as a Factor in Canadian Economic History', in *Essays*, 68. The paper originally appeared in *Proceedings of the Canadian Political Science Association*, 1931.

42 Innis, 'The Teaching of Economic History in Canada', *Essays*, 15.

43 Innis, 'Canada Needs Trade to Pay Debts', *Financial Post*, July 9, 1932, and 'Government Ownership and the Canadian Scene', *Essays*, 78-96.

44 Innis, 'Significant Factors in Canadian Economic Development', *CHR* XVIII (December 1937), 383.

[45] Innis, 'Economic Trends in Canadian-American Relations', *Essays*, 240. The essay was first published in 1938.

[46] Innis Papers, Innis to Carleton Stanley, January 18, 1938, copy.

[47] F.H. Underhill, 'The Conception of National Interest', *CJEPS* I (August 1935), 406-7.

[48] Mackintosh, 'Innis on Canadian Economic Development', 193-4.

[49] QUL, A.R.M. Lower Papers, Innis to Lower, n.d. [1937].

[50] Innis Papers, Innis to A.H. Cole, August 8, 1943, copy.

[51] Lower Papers, Innis to Lower, February 2, 1935.

[52] Innis, 'The Rowell-Sirois Report', *CJEPS* VI (November 1940), 568.

[53] Innis Papers, Innis to Angus Macdonald, January 17, 1946, copy.

[54] Innis, 'The Role of Intelligence: Some Further Notes', *CJEPS* I (May 1935), 280-7.

[55] Innis, *Political Economy in the Modern State* (Toronto, 1946), viii.

[56] Innis, 'For the People', *UTQ* V (January 1936), 287.

[57] Lower Papers, Innis to Lower, November 1, 1935.

[58] Innis, *Political Economy in the Modern State*, xvii.

[59] *CF* IX (May 1929), 284.

[60] Lower Papers, Brebner to Lower, October 22, 1937.

[61] Innis Papers, 'Idea File', 104.

[62] Marshall McLuhan, 'The Later Innis', *QQ* LX (Autumn 1953), 386.

[63] Innis Family Papers, Notes on Innis by Mary Innis, n.d.

[64] QUL, Lorne Pierce Papers, Innis to Pierce, September 9, 1939.

[65] Lower Papers, Innis to Lower, November 15, 193[9].

[66] Lorne Pierce Papers, Innis to Pierce, May 3, 1939, and 'Memorandum for Dr. Pierce' by Innis [1939].

[67] UTL, H.J. Cody Papers, Innis to Cody, June 16, 1944. Mr. Paul Bator drew this letter to my attention.

[68] Innis, *The Bias of Communications* (Toronto, 1951), 195.

[69] Innis, 'Some English-Canadian University Problems', *QQ* L (Spring 1943), 35-6.

[70] F.R. Scott, *Overture* (Toronto, 1945), 19.

[71] John Porter, *The Vertical Mosaic* (Toronto, 1965), 503.

5. ARTHUR LOWER AND A NATIONAL COMMUNITY

[1] Lower, *My First Seventy-Five Years* (Toronto, 1967), 4, 6, 39.

[2] *Ibid.*, 59.

[3] Lower, 'National Policy . . . . Revised Version', *The Manitoba Arts Review* III (Spring 1943), 9.

[4] QUL, A.R.M. Lower Papers, Box #28, 'The History of My Education', 1914.

[5] Lower, *Unconventional Voyages* (Toronto, 1953), 26.

[6] Lower, 'Paddling Your Own Canoe', *The New Outlook* VIII (May 18, 1932), 469.

[7] Lower, *Unconventional Voyages*, viii.

[8] *My First Seventy-five Years*, 125.

[9] A fourth study, based on the research of this early period, appeared as *Great Britain's Woodyard: British America and the Timber Trade, 1763-1867* (Montreal, 1973).

[10] Lower, 'The Trade in Square Timber', *Contributions to Canadian Economics*, Vol. 6, 1933, 40.

[11] Lower Papers, Lower to Innis, December 2, 1933, copy.

[12] Lower, *The North American Assault on the Canadian Forest: A History of the Lumber Industry Between Canada and the United States* (Toronto and New Haven, 1938), 1.

[13] Lower, *My First Seventy-five Years*, 152; Lower Papers, Box #9, MS 'Some Reflections on Writing History' (1966), 7.

14 This description of the frontier thesis is based on R.A. Billington, ed., *Selected Essays of Frederick Jackson Turner* (Englewood Cliffs, N.J., 1961); his *Frederick Jackson Turner: Historian, Scholar, Teacher* (New York, 1973); Richard Hofstadter, *The Progressive Historians* (New York, 1968), Chapters 2-4.

15 John L. McDougall, 'The Frontier School and Canadian History', *CHAR*, 1929, 121-5.

16 Walter N. Sage, 'Some Aspects of the Frontier in Canadian History' *CHAR*, 1928, 62-72.

17 Lower, 'Some Neglected Aspects of Canadian History' *CHAR*, 1929, 65-71.

18 Lower, 'The Origins of Democracy in Canada', *CHAR*, 1930, 65-70.

19 Lower, *Colony to Nation* (Toronto, 1957; 3rd edition), 48-9.

20 'Origins . . . . ', 69.

21 *Colony to Nation*, 196.

22 *Ibid.*, 109-10.

23 *Ibid.*, 256.

24 Lower, 'Our Shoddy Ideals', *Maclean's Magazine* 50 (November 1, 1937), 24.

25 Lower, *North American Assault*, 26. Lower tended to share the point of view of the early nineteenth century critics of lumbering who contrasted it unfavourably with agriculture. See Graham Wynn, *The Assault on the New Brunswick Forest* (University of Toronto, Ph.D. thesis, 1973), Ch. VIII, 'Lumbering, Farming and the Agrarian Myth'.

26 Lower Papers, J.B. Brebner to Lower, Box #11, June 16, 1936.

27 Lower, 'The Assault on the Laurentian Barrier, 1850-1870' *CHR* X (December 1929), 295, 303.

28 N.S.B. Gras, *An Introduction to Economic History* (New York, 1922).

29 *Colony to Nation*, 199.

30 Welf H. Heick, 'Historical Perspectives: An Interview with Arthur R.M. Lower', *QQ* LXXVIII (Winter 1971), 525-6; Heick, 'The Character and Spirit of an Age: A Study of the Thought of Arthur R.M. Lower', *His Own Man. Essays in Honour of Arthur Reginald Marsden Lower*, eds, W.H. Heick and Roger Graham (Montreal, 1974), 19-34.

31 Lower, 'Two Ways of Life: the Primary Antithesis of Canadian History', *CHAR*, 1943, 12, 14.

32 Lower, 'Calling Our Souls Our Own', 24.

33 Lower, *Settlement and the Forest Frontier*, 89, 93.

34 Lower, 'Two Ways of Life', 7.

35 *Ibid.*, 8.

36 Lower, *Colony to Nation*, 69.

37 Lower, review of Everett C. Hughes, *French Canada in Transition* (Chicago, 1943), *CJEPS* X (February 1944), 99-101.

38 Lower, 'Two Nations or Two Nationalities', *Culture* IV (1943), 470-81.

39 Public Archives of Ontario, J.P. Whitney Papers, Lower to Whitney, February 1, 1913, enclosure. I owe this reference to Professor Charles Humphries.

40 Lower, *Canada and the Far East* (New York, 1940), 135-6.

41 Bibliography for article 'New France in New England', in Lower Papers, Box #5, file 25. The article was published in *The New England Quarterly* II (No. 2, 1929), 278-95.

42 See for example James Gray, *The Winter Years* (Toronto, 1966), Chapter 13, on the experience of immigrants during the depression in Winnipeg.

43 Arthur Lismer, 'Art a Common Necessity', *Canadian Bookman* VII (October 1925), 159-60.

44 Lower, 'Canada—A Motherland', *Dalhousie Review* VI (January 1927), 448; 'Geographical Determinants in Canadian History', *Essays in Canadian History*, ed., R. Flenley (Toronto 1939), 252.

45 Lower, 'The Case Against Immigration', *QQ* XXXVII (Summer 1930), 557-74.

46 Lower, 'Can Canada Do Without the Immigrant?' *Maclean's Magazine* XLIII (June 1, 1930), 3-4, 70-1.

[47] Lower, 'Calling Our Souls Our Own', 24.

[48] Lower, 'External Policy and Internal Problems' *UTQ* VI (April 1937), 327.

[49] Lower, 'Two Ways of Life', 151.

[50] Lower, 'External Policy and Internal Problems', 331.

[51] Lower, *Canada and the Far East*, 63.

[52] Lower, review of Gwethalyn Graham, *Earth and High Heaven*, and Hugh MacLennan, *Two Solitudes* in *CHR* XXVI (September 1945), 328.

[53] Lower, 'Foreign Policy and Canadian Nationalism', *Dalhousie Review* XV (April 1935), 30.

[54] *Ibid.*, 33.

[55] Lower Papers, *The Native Sun* IV (December 1934), 1. The substance of Lower's case may be found in two essays, 'The Social and Economic Bases of Canadian Foreign Policy' and 'General and Specific Aspects of Canadian Foreign Policy', in *Canada: The Empire and the League. Lectures given at the Canadian Institute in Economics and Politics, July 31st to August 14th, 1936* (Toronto, 1936), 100-11, 145-54.

[56] Lower, 'Foreign Policy and the Empire', *Nineteenth Century and After* CXIV (September 1933), 6.

[57] Lower, 'Foreign Policy and Canadian Nationalism', 32.

[58] C.P. Stacey, *CHR* XXVIII (June 1947), 197.

[59] Underhill, *CHR* XXV (March 1944), 67.

[60] *Winnipeg Free Press*, December 10, 1932.

[61] Lower Papers, Lower to Innis, March 15, 1937, copy.

[62] *Ibid.*, Lower to Innis, April 18, 1937, copy.

[63] Lower, 'A Bright Future for a Dull Subject', *Manitoba Arts Review*, III (Fall 1943), 13.

[64] Alexander Brady, *UTQ* XVI (April 1947), 308.

6. A NORTH AMERICAN NATION

[1] A complete list of these books may be found at the back of J.B. Brebner, *North Atlantic Triangle: The Interplay of Canada, the United States and Great Britain* (Toronto and New Haven, 1945).

[2] Samuel E. Moffatt, *The Americanization of Canada* (n.p., 1907).

[3] Hugh L. Keenleyside, 'The American Economic Penetration of Canada', *CHR* VIII (March 1927), 31-40.

[4] Carl Goldenberg, ' "Americanization" of Canada', *Fortnightly Review* CXXXIX, New Series, (June 1936), 689.

[5] *Saturday Night*, January 8, 1927, 1.

[6] Archibald MacMechan, 'Canada as a Vassal State', *CHR* I (December 1920), 347-53.

[7] J.A. Stevenson, 'Canadian Sentiment Toward the United States', *Current History* XXXIII (October 1930), 61.

[8] W.A. Deacon, 'The Bogey of Annexation', *Poteen: A Pot-Pourri of Canadian Essays* (Ottawa, 1926), 22.

[9] John Weaver, *Imperilled Dreams: Canadian Opposition to the American Empire, 1918-1930* (Ph.D. thesis, Duke University, 1973).

[10] P.E. Corbett, 'Anti-Americanism', *Dalhousie Review* X (October 1930), 295-300.

[11] 'R'., 'Neighbours, A Canadian View', *Foreign Affairs* X (April 1932), 422.

[12] Chester Martin, 'The United States and Canadian Nationality', *CHR* XVIII (March 1937), 11.

[13] Sir Robert Falconer, 'The United States, Canada's Friend', *Current History* XXIV (May 1926), 181-8.

[14] Sir Robert Falconer, *The United States as a Neighbour from a Canadian Point of View* (Cambridge, 1925), 243.

[15] Lawrence J. Burpee, 'A Peace Pact that Works', *Canadian Comment* III (December 1934), 5-7.

[16] R.G. Trotter, 'Historical Research in Canada', *CHR* XX (September 1939), 252.

[17] *CHR* VIII (March 1927), 51-5, and XIV (September 1933), 296.

[18] Trotter, 'Canadian History in the Universities of the United States', *CHR* VIII (September 1927), 190-207.

[19] H.J. Morgan and L. Burpee, *Canadian Life in Town and Country* (London, 1905), 182; Falconer, *The United States as a Neighbour*, 206.

[20] QUL, Adam Shortt Papers, W. Swanson to Shortt, January 13, 1906.

[21] Douglas Bush, 'Pride and Prejudice', *Canadian Mercury* I (June 1929), 136-7.

[22] UTL, Innis Papers, Shotwell to H.A. Innis, August 23, 1946; James T. Shotwell, 'A Personal Note on the Theme of Canadian-American Relations', *CHR* XXVIII (March 1947), 42.

[23] J.B. Brebner, 'Oxford, Toronto, Columbia', *Columbia University Quarterly* XXIII (September 1931), 224-40.

[24] H.S. Patten, 'A Canadian at Harvard', *CF* I (December 1920), 75-6.

[25] Conference on Educational Problems in Canadian-American Relations Held at the University of Maine, Orono, Maine, June 21-3, 1938, *Proceedings*, ed., R.L. Morrow (Orono, 1939), 128.

[26] Brebner, *Scholarship for Canada* (Ottawa, 1945), 5, 7.

[27] Columbia University, Butler Library, J.B. Brebner Papers, Box 10, File 'McLaren-Generally', n.d.

[28] QUL, R.G. Trotter Papers, A. Gordon Dewey to Trotter, December 21, 1933.

[29] Ray Palmer Baker, *A History of English-Canadian Literature to the Confederation. Its Relation to the Literature of Great Britain and the United States* (Cambridge, Mass., 1920), 183-4.

[30] W.B. Munro, *American Influences on Canadian Government* (Toronto, 1929); Harvey Eagleson, *William Bennett Munro, 1875-1957* (Pasadena, California, 1959).

[31] Hugh Keenleyside, *Canada and the United States* (New York, 1929).

[32] Brebner, 'Canadian and North American History', *CHAR*, 1931, 37, 48.

[33] Trotter, 'The Canadian Back-Fence in Anglo-American Relations', *QQ* XL (August 1933), 383-97.

[34] J.W. Dafoe, *Canada: An American Nation* (New York, 1935). For a similar view see J.T. Shotwell, *The Heritage of Freedom: the United States and Canada in the Community of Nations* (New York, 1934).

[35] Herbert Bolton, *History of the Americas: A Syllabus with Maps* (Boston, 1928) and his 'Epic of Greater America', *American Historical Review* XXXVIII (April 1933), 448-74; Arthur P. Whitaker, *The Western Hemisphere Idea: Its Rise and Decline* (Ithaca, 1954).

[36] Trotter Papers, Trotter to Edith Ware, April 26, 1933, copy; Trotter to A.B. Corey, June 15, 1935, copy.

[37] Shotwell, 'The World War in History', *Addresses Delivered before the Canadian Club of Toronto, Season 1923-24* (Toronto, 1924), 110-17; J.T. Shotwell, *Autobiography* (New York, 1961).

[38] One of its most fulsome expressions was *The North American Idea* (Toronto, 1917) by Rev. James A. Macdonald, editor of the Toronto *Globe* and a director of the New York based World Peace Foundation. Mackenzie King frequently invoked it; see particularly his 'One Hundred Years of Peace', an address delivered at Harvard in 1909, in his *The Message of the Carillon and Other Addresses* (London, 1927), 163-78. Its uses in the isolationist armoury of the twenties is brilliantly traced by James Eayrs, *In Defence of Canada: From the Great War to the Great Depression* (Toronto, 1964), 'Introduction'.

[39] Shotwell, 'The International Significance of the Canadian-American Peace Tradition', Conference on Educational Problems in Canadian-American Relations *Proceedings*, 8.

[40] L.J. Burpee, 'Canada's Debt to the Carnegie Corporation', *QQ* XLV (Summer 1938), 232-7.

[41] *Conference on Canadian-American Affairs Held at the St Lawrence University, Canton, New York, June 19-22, 1939*, eds., A.B. Corey, R.G. Trotter and W.W. McLaren (Boston, 1939), 4.

[42] Trotter Papers, 'Outline of Plan. Survey of the Economic, Social, and Political Relations of Canada and the United States', May 12, 1934, 12.

[43] Herbert Marshall, Frank A. Southard Jr. and Kenneth W. Taylor, *Canadian American Industry: A Study in International Investment* (New Haven and Toronto, 1936), 295.

[44] W.C. Clark, 'Movement of Capital', Conference on Canadian-American Affairs Held at the St Lawrence University, Canton, New York, June 17-22, 1935, *Proceedings*, eds., W.W. McLaren, A.B.Corey, and R.G. Trotter (New York, 1936), 66.

[45] M.L. Hansen, 'A resume of Canadian-American Population Relations', Conference on Canadian-American Affairs Held at Queen's University, Kingston, Ontario, June 14-18, 1937, *Proceedings*, eds., R.G. Trotter, A.B. Corey, W.W. McLaren (New York, 1937), 106: M.L. Hansen and J.B. Brebner, *The Mingling of the Canadian and American Peoples* (New Haven and Toronto, 1940), x. This volume was supported by two statistical studies: L.E. Truesdell, *The Canadian Born in the United States* (Toronto and New Haven, 1943), and R.H. Coats and M.C. Maclean, *The American Born in Canada* (Toronto and New Haven, 1943).

[46] M. Savelle, *The Diplomatic History of the Canadian Boundary, 1749-63* (Toronto and New Haven, 1940); A.L. Burt, *The United States, Great Britain and British North America: From the Revolution to the Establishment of Peace After the War of 1812* (Toronto and New Haven, 1940); A.B. Corey, *The Crisis of 1830-1842 in Canadian-American Relations* (Toronto and New Haven, 1942); L.B. Shippee, *Canadian-American Relations, 1849-1874* (Toronto and New Haven, 1939); C. Tansill, *Canadian-American Relations, 1875-1911* (Toronto and New Haven, 1943).

[47] P.E. Corbett, *The Settlement of Canadian-American Disputes* (Toronto and New Haven, 1937).

[48] A.B. Corey and R.G. Trotter, Conference on Canadian-American Affairs held at the St Lawrence University, Canton, New York, June 17-22, 1935, *Proceedings*, eds., W.W. McLaren, A.B.Corey, R.G. Trotter, (New York, 1936), 139, 148.

[49] The other two studies were J.P. Pritchett, *The Red River Valley, 1811-1849: A Regional Study* (1942) and F.H. Howay, W.N. Sage and H.F. Angus, *British Columbia and the United States: The North Pacific Slope From Fur Trade to Aviation* (1942).

[50] R.M. MacIver, *A Tale that is Told* (Chicago, 1968).

[51] R.M. MacIver, 'Introduction', *Canada and Her Great Neighbor*, ed., H.F. Angus (Toronto and New Haven, 1938) xxv-xxvi.

[52] L.E. Ellis, *Reciprocity, 1911* (Toronto and New Haven, 1939).

[53] Shotwell, 'The International Significance of the Canadian-American Peace Tradition', *op. cit.*: and 'North America and the World Today', Conference on Canadian-American Affairs Held at Queen's University, Kingston, Ontario, June 23-6, 1941. *Proceedings*, ed., R.G. Trotter and A.B. Corey (New York, 1941), 5-7.

[54] *CHAR*, 1942, 65; 'The Appalachian Barrier in Canadian History', *CHAR*, 1939, 9. See also his 'Which Way Canada?', *QQ* 45 (Autumn 1938), 289-99.

[55] George Brown, 'A Canadian View', *CHR* XXIII (June 1942), 132-9.

[56] F.R. Scott, *Canada and the United States* (World Peace Foundation, Boston, 1941), 14-15.

[57] Brebner, 'The Survival of Canada', *Essays in Canadian History*, ed. R. Flenley (Toronto, 1939), 253-77, and 'Canadianism', *CHAR*, 1940, 5-15.

[58] Brebner Papers, Brebner to Herbert Heaton, September 17, 1945, copy.

⁵⁹ See, for example, Paul F. Sharp, *The Agrarian Revolt in Western Canada: A Survey Showing American Parallels* (Minneapolis, 1948); Gerald Craig, 'The American Impact on the Upper Canadian Reform Movement Before 1837', *CHR* XXIX (December 1948), 333-52.

⁶⁰ Brebner, 'History and Today: Forces of Change', in W.C. Graham, ed., *Education and the Modern World* (Toronto, 1947), 31.

7. REORIENTATION

1 George Brown and D.G. Creighton, 'Canadian History in Retrospect and Prospect', *CHR* XXV (December 1944), 362.

2 Innis, 'The Social Sciences: Brief Survey of Recent Literature', *Canadian Geographical Journal* XXV (September 1942), XI.

3 Jean-Charles Falardeau, 'Léon Gérin: His Life and Work', *Four O'Clock Lectures: French-Canadian Thinkers of the Nineteenth and Twentieth Centuries*, ed. Laurier La Pierre (Montreal, 1966), 59-75, and 'Problems and First Experiments of Social Research in Quebec', *CJEPS* X (August 1944), 365-71.

4 John Madge, *The Origins of Scientific Sociology* (Glencoe, Ill., 1962), 125; C.A. Dawson, 'Sociology as a Specialized Science', *Essays in Sociology*, ed., C.W.M. Hart (Toronto, 1940), 19-35.

5 Bowman's purposes were set out in *The Pioneer Fringe* (New York, 1931). His thought is discussed in Gladys M. Wrigley, 'Isaiah Bowman', *The Geographical Review*, XLI (January 1951), 7-65, which also contains a bibliography of his writings.

6 W.A. Mackintosh, *Prairie Settlement: The Geographical Setting* (1934) and *Economic Problems of the Prairie Provinces* (1935); A.S. Morton and C. Martin, *History of Prairie Settlement and 'Dominion Lands' Policy* (1938); R.W. Murchie, *Agricultural Progress on the Prairie Frontier* (1936); A.R.M. Lower and H.A. Innis, *Settlement and the Forest and Mining Frontiers* (1936). All were published in Toronto.

7 Clark, 'Sociology and Canadian History', *CJEPS* V (August 1939), 349-50; review of Dawson, *Pioneering in the Prairie Provinces*, *CHR* XXI (September 1940), 336-8.

8 University of Saskatchewan Archives, Murray Memorial Library, Saskatoon, A.S. Morton Papers, Clark to Morton, February 1, 1932.

9 Clark, 'Sociology and Canadian History', *CJEPS* V (August 1939), 351.

10 Clark, 'The United Farmers of Alberta', *CF* XIII (October 1932), 78.

11 Clark, *The Social Development of Canada: An Introductory Study With Select Documents* (Toronto, 1942), 1 n.; Clark, 'Economic Expansion and the Moral Order', *CJEPS* VI (May 1940), 203-25.

12 Clark, 'The Religious Sect in Canadian Politics', *The Developing Canadian Community* (Toronto, 1962), 131-46. This essay was first published in 1945.

13 W.L. Morton, *The Progressive Party* (1950); D.C. Masters, *The Winnipeg General Strike* (1950); L.G. Thomas, *The Liberal Party in Alberta: A History of Politics in the Province of Alberta, 1905-1921* (1959); V.C. Fowke, *The National Policy and the Wheat Economy* (1957); C.B. Macpherson, *Democracy in Alberta* (1953); J.R. Mallory, *Social Credit and the Federal Power in Canada* (1954); J. Irving, *The Social Credit Movement in Alberta* (1959); J. Burnet, *Next-Year Country* (1951); W.E. Mann, *Sect, Cult, and Church in Alberta* (1955). All were published in Toronto.

14 Clark, 'The Canadian Community and the American Continental System', and 'The Frontier in the Development of the Canadian Political Community'; in *The Developing Canadian Community*, 185-98 and 207-20. The articles originally appeared under different titles in 1950 and 1954 respectively.

15 Clark, *Movements of Political Protest in Canada, 1640-1840* (Toronto, 1959), 430-34.

[16] Clark, 'Foreword', W.L. Morton, *The Progressive Party* (Toronto, 1950), viii.

[17] Clark, *Movements of Political Protest*, 504.

[18] Brebner, review of *Church and Sect in Canada, CHR* xxx (March 1949), 75-7; David Spring, 'History and Sociology: A Plea for Humility', *ibid.*, (September 1949), 211-26; H.H. Walsh, 'Canada and the Church: A Job for Historians', *QQ* LXI (Spring 1954), 71-9.

[19] Morton, review of Clark, *The Developing Canadian Community, CHR* XLIV (September 1963), 235-6 and review of *Movements of Political Protest in Canada, ibid.*, XLI (September 1960), 243-5. Historians' subsequent treatments of the reformers in Upper Canada did little to confirm Clark's reading of the role of frontier radicalism, and, in the case of the Yukon during the Gold Rush era, laid greater emphasis on the successful imposition of Canadian controls. See Gerald M. Craig, *Upper Canada: The Formative Years, 1784-1841* (Toronto, 1963), Chapters 10-12, and Morris Zaslow, *The Opening of the Canadian North, 1870-1914* (Toronto, 1971), Chapter 5.

[20] A.E. Prince, 'The Need for a Wider Study of Military History', *CHR* xxv (March 1944), 20-8.

[21] *CHR* xxi (December 1940), 451.

[22] C.P. Stacey, 'The Myth of the Unguarded Frontier, 1815-1871', *American Historical Review*, LVI (October 1950), 1-18.

[23] C.P. Stacey, 'The Historical Programme of the Canadian Army Overseas', *CHR* xxvi (September 1945), 229-38.

[24] C.P. Stacey, 'Fenian Troubles and Canadian Military Development, 1865-1871', *CHAR*, 1935, 33.

[25] Stacey, 'The Nature of Official History', *CHAR* 1946, 76-7.

[26] *Ibid.*, 81-2.

[27] C.P. Stacey, 'The Life and Hard Times of an Official Historian', *CHR* LI (March 1970), 21-47.

[28] C.P. Stacey, *Six Years of War: The Army in Canada, Britain and the Pacific* (1955); *The Victory Campaign: The Operations in North-West Europe, 1944-1945* (1960); *Arms, Men and Governments: The War Policies of Canada, 1939-1945* (1970).

[29] G.N. Tucker, *The Naval Service of Canada: Its Official History* (Ottawa, 1952), Two volumes.

[30] See also his inaugural lecture as Rhodes Professor of Imperial History at the University of London, 'The Maritime Foundations of Imperial History', *CHR* xxi (June 1950), 113-24.

[31] *CHAR*, 1940, 116.

[32] Chester Martin, 'The British Commonwealth', *CHR* xxv (June 1944), 139.

[33] R.G. Trotter, 'Aims in the Study and Teaching of History in Canadian Universities Today', *CHAR*, 1943, 50-60; George Brown, 'Canada in the Making', *ibid*, 1944, 5-15; A.L. Burt, 'Broad Horizons', *ibid.*, 1950, 10.

[34] *CHR* xxxii (June 1951), 158.

[35] *Montreal Star*, May 22, 1952.

[36] Symposium on A.R.M. Lower's paper, 'The Social Scientist in the Modern World', *CHAR*, 1941, 83.

[37] H.N. Fieldhouse, 'The Failure of Historians', *CHAR*, 1942, 52-65.

[38] G.P. de T. Glazebrook, 'In Defence of Political History . . . . ', *CHR* xxxi (December 1950), 445.

[39] R.A. Mackay, 'The Political Ideas of William Lyon Mackenzie', *CJEPS* III (February 1937), 1-22; C.B. Sissons, 'Canadian Political Ideas in the Sixties and Seventies: Egerton Ryerson', *CHAR*, 1942, 94-103; John I. Cooper, 'The Political Ideas of Georges Etienne Cartier', *CHR* xxiii (September 1948), 286-94; G. Brown, 'The Early Methodist Church and the Canadian Point of View', (1938), reprinted in his *Canada in the Making* (Toronto, 1953), 40-65; D.C. Harvey, 'The Intellectual Awakening of Nova Scotia', *Dalhousie Review* xiii (April 1933), 1-22.

40 H.H. Walsh, 'Research in Canadian Church History', *CHR* xxxv (September 1954), 208-16; H.G.J. Aitken, 'The Family Compact and the Welland Canal Company', *CJEPS* xviii (February 1952), 63-76.

41 Morris Zaslow, 'The Frontier Hypothesis in Recent Historiography', *CHR* xxix (June 1948), 153-66.

42 A.L. Burt, 'The Frontier in the History of New France', *CHAR*, 1940, 93-9; Morden Long, *A History of the Canadian People: New France* (Toronto, 1942).

43 J.B. Brebner, *North Atlantic Triangle* (New York, 1945), Chapter 8; D.G. Creighton, 'Sir John A. Macdonald and Canadian Historians', *CHR* xxix (March 1948), 12.

44 G.F.G. Stanley, *The Birth of Western Canada* (Toronto, 1936), Preface.

45 G.F.G. Stanley, 'Western Canada and the Frontier Thesis', *CHAR* 1940, 105-14.

46 A.M. Schlesinger Sr, *The Rise of the City* (1933); D.R. Fox, ed., *Sources of Culture in the Middle West* (1934) and *Ideas in Motion* (1935).

47 J.M.S. Careless, 'The Toronto *Globe* and Agrarian Radicalism, 1850-1867', *CHR* xxix (March 1948), 14-39, and 'Mid-Victorian Liberalism in Central Canadian Newspapers, 1850-1867', *CHR* xxxi (September 1950), 221-36.

48 J.M.S. Careless, 'Frontierism, Metropolitanism, and Canadian History', *CHR* xxxv (March 1954), 1-21.

49 C.A. Dawson, *Pioneering in the Prairie Provinces: The Social Side of the Settlement Process* (Toronto, 1940), Chapter iv.

50 H.A. Innis, 'Industrialism and Settlement in Western Canada', *Report of the International Geographical Congress, Cambridge, July, 1928*, 369-76; 'The Rise and Decline of Toronto', *CF* xiii (April 1933), 251.

51 J.M.S. Careless, 'Canadian Nationalism—Immature or Obsolete?', *CHAR* 1954, 12-18.

52 As he himself later pointed out in 'Urban Development in Canada', *Urban History / Revue d'Histoire Urbaine*, no. 1 (Ottawa, 1974), 9-14.

53 Merrill Denison, '4,000 Miles of Irritation', *Saturday Review* xxxv (June 7, 1952), 25-56.

54 Royal Commission on National Development in the Arts, Letters and Sciences, *Report* (Ottawa, 1951), 4.

55 *Ibid.*, 18, 40-1.

56 Hilda Neatby, *So Little for the Mind: An Indictment of Canadian Education* (Toronto, 1953), 325-6. For earlier as well as contemporaneous American criticism of progressive education see Lawrence A. Cremin, *The Transformation of the School: Progressivism in American Education, 1876-1957* (New York, 1961), Chapter 9.

57 George Grant, 'The Minds of Men in the Atomic Age', *Texts of Addresses Delivered at the 24th Annual Couchiching Conference ... August 13th-20th, 1955* (n.p., n.d.), 39-43; and *Philosophy in the Mass Age* (Toronto, 1959).

58 E.R. Adair, 'The Canadian Contribution to Historical Science', *Culture* iv 1943, 68.

59 Hilda Neatby, 'National History', *Royal Commission Studies: A Selection of Essays Prepared for the Royal Commission on National Development in the Arts, Letters and Sciences* (Ottawa, 1951), 211.

60 Jean-Charles Bonenfant, 'Sir Thomas Chapais', *Culture* vii (September 1946), 265-76; Ramsay Cook, 'French Canadian Interpretations of Canadian History', *Journal of Canadian Studies*, ii (May 1967), 3-17.

61 Jean-Pierre Gaboury, *Le Nationalisme de Lionel Groulx: Aspects Idéologiques* (Ottawa, 1970); G.F.G. Stanley, 'Lionel-Adolphe Groulx: Historian and Prophet of French Canada', *Four O'Clock Lectures ...* ed., L. La Pierre, 97-114; Susan Mann Trofimenkoff, *Action Française: French-Canadian Nationalism in the Twenties* (Toronto, 1975).

62 E.R. Adair, 'Dollard des Ormeaux and the Fight at the Long Sault. A Re-interpretation of Dollard's Exploit', *CHR* xiii (June 1932), 121-38; Gustave Lanctôt, 'Was Dollard the Saviour of New France?', *ibid.*, 138-46 reasserted a modified traditional view.

[63] Underhill, *CHR*, XVI (December 1936), 438-9.
[64] Adair, 'The Canadian Contribution . . . . ', 69.
[65] H.B. Myers, 'Profile of a Patriot: Mrg. Arthur Maheux', *Culture* XXIX (1968), 323-7; Lucian Lortie, *Bibliographie Analytique de L'Abbé Maheux* (Quebec, 1942).
[66] Abbé Arthur Maheux, *French Canada & Britain: A New Interpretation* (Toronto, 1943), 16. Maheux's other wartime publications that were translated included *What Keeps Us Apart?* (Québec, 1944) and *Problems of Canadian Unity* (Québec, 1944).
[67] R.M. Saunders, 'History and French-Canadian Survival', *CHAR*, 1943, 31.
[68] Jean Blain, 'Maurice Séguin ou la Rationalisation de l'histoire Nationale', Preface, Maurice Séguin, *La Nation 'Canadienne' et l'agriculture (1760-1850)* (Trois Riviéres, 1970), 17-40.
[69] Collected in M. Brunet, *La Présence Anglaise et les Canadiens* (Montréal, 1964).
[70] M. Brunet, 'French Canadian Interpretations of Canadian History', *CF* XLIV (April 1964), 5-7.
[71] Fernand Ouellet, 'La recherche historique au Canada français', Louis Baudouin, ed., *La Recherche au Canada Français* (Montréal, 1968), 87-98; Pierre Savard, 'Un Quart de Siécle d'Historiographie Québécoise, 1947-1972', *Recherches Sociographiques* XV (Janvier—Avril 1974), 77-96.

8. REORIENTATION AND TRADITION

[1] W.T. Easterbrook, 'Innis and Economics', *CJEPS* XIX (August 1953), 298.
[2] Innis, *Empire and Communications* (Oxford, 1950), 6.
[3] Innis, 'Charles Norris Cochrane, 1889-1945', *CJEPS*, XII (February 1946), 96.
[4] Innis, *The Bias of Communications* (Toronto, 1951), 191.
[5] Innis, *Empire and Communications*, 11-12.
[6] *Ibid.*, 215.
[7] Innis, *Bias of Communications*, 85, 90.
[8] J.E. Hodgetts, 'Dives and Lazarus: Three Reports on the Teaching of Political Science', *CJEPS* XVIII (February 1952), 88-92.
[9] Herbert Heaton, 'Clio's New Overalls', *CJEPS* XX (November 1954), 475.
[10] Innis, 'The Problem of Mutual Understanding with Russia', *QQ* LIII (Spring 1946), 92-100.
[11] Innis, 'Great Britain, the United States and Canada', in *Essays in Canadian Economic History*, ed., M.Q. Innis (Toronto, 1956), 394-412.
[12] Innis, *The Strategy of Culture* (Toronto, 1952), 19-20.
[13] *Ibid.*, 20.
[14] Innis Papers, MS Autobiography, 75.
[15] Columbia University, Butler Library, J.B. Brebner Papers, Innis to Brebner, April 7, 1952.
[16] J.B. Brebner, 'In Search of a Canadian Accent', *Saturday Review of Literature*, XXXIV (September 1951), 6-8, 31; 'Our Mirror in Canadian Fears', *ibid.*, XXXV (June 7, 1952), 24-5; and review of Innis's *Changing Concepts of Time* (1952) in *CHR* XXXIV (June 1953), 171-3.
[17] Innis Papers, Brebner to Innis, March 19, 1949.
[18] Brebner Papers, Innis to Brebner, July 6, 1950.
[19] Innis Papers, Innis to Anne Bezanson, November 23, 1948, copy.
[20] *Ibid.*, Ferguson to Innis, May 20, 1950?
[21] Karl W. Deutsch, review of *Bias of Communications* in *CJEPS* XVIII (August 1952), 388-90 and B.S. Kierstead, review of *Political Economy in the Modern State* in *ibid.*, XIII (November 1947), 600-3.
[22] Innis Papers, McLuhan to Innis, March 14, 1951; McLuhan, 'The Later Innis', *QQ* LX (Autumn 1953), 385-94.

[23] James Carey, 'Harold Adams Innis and Marshall McLuhan', *Antioch Review* XXVII (Spring 1967), 5-39.

[24] Underhill, 'The Rowell-Sirois Commission as Historians', *CF* XX (November 1940), 233-5, and 'Some Reflections on the Liberal Tradition in Canada', *CHAR* 1946, 5-17.

[25] Underhill, 'Trends in American Foreign Policy', *UTQ* XIII (April 1944), 286.

[26] Underhill, 'The Canadian Party System in Transition', (1943) and the essays on King are in his *In Search of Canadian Liberalism* (Toronto, 1960), 192-202, and 114-40; K. McNaught, 'Frank Underhill: A Personal Interpretation', *QQ* LXXX (Summer 1972), 127-35.

[27] Underhill, 'A Canadian-Philosopher Historian', *CF* XXVII (July 1947), 83-4.

[28] Canadian Broadcasting Corporation, *The Radical Tradition: A Second View of Canadian History* (Toronto, 1960), 6.

[29] Underhill, 'The Politics of Freedom', *CF* XXIX (December 1949), 197-8.

[30] Underhill, 'The Revival of Conservatism in North America', *TRSC*, Series III, 1958.

[31] Underhill, 'Arnold Toynbee, Metahistorian', *CHR* XXXII (September 1951), 216.

[32] Underhill, 'Randon Remarks on Socialism and Freedom', *CF* XXVII (August 1947), 110-11; 'Canadian Socialism and World Politics', *CF* XXX (October 1950), 149-51; 'Korea' *CF* XXX (August 1950), 97-8, 102.

[33] Underhill, 'What's Left', *CF* XXXI (February 1952), 243-4; 'Power Politics in the Ontario C.C.F.', *CF* XXXII (April 1952), 7-8.

[34] Review of S.M. Lipset's *Agrarian Socialism*, *CF* XXX (February 1951), 256-7.

[35] *CF* XXXIV (February 1955), 253-4.

[36] Underhill, 'Democracy and Nationalism: The Canadian Conflict', in T.E.H. Reid, *Values in Conflict: 32nd Couchiching Conference, C.I.P.A.* (Toronto, 1963), 73.

[37] *The Radical Tradition*, 9.

[38] On the role of similar institutions in deflating intellectual radicalism in Britain see, Stuart Samuels, 'English Intellectuals and Politics in the 1930's', in Philip Rieff, *On Intellectuals* (New York, 1970), 213-68.

[39] Cyril Connolly, *The Enemies of Promise* (London, 1938), 121.

[40] Lower, *Canada: Nation and Neighbour* (Toronto, 1952), 40.

[41] Toronto *Globe and Mail*, October 20, 1962.

[42] Lower, *This Most Famous Stream* (Toronto, 1954), vii.

[43] G. Ramsay Cook, *Canadian Liberalism in Wartime: A Study of the Defence of Canada Regulations and Some Canadian Attitudes to Civil Liberties in Wartime, 1939-1945* (M.A. thesis, Queen's University, 1955).

[44] Lower, 'Essence of Liberalism', *Winnipeg Free Press Pamphlet No. 20, Convention Prelude (A Survey of Liberal Opinion)* (Winnipeg, 1948), 13.

[45] *This Most Famous Stream*, 21.

[46] *Ibid.*, 11, 75.

[47] *Ibid.*, 89, 90: on foreign ownership see *Canada: Nation and Neighbour*, 39-40.

[48] Lower, *Canadians in the Making: A Social History of Canada* (1958), 433-5.

[49] Lower, 'The Canadian University', *TRSC*, Series III, XLII, 1953, 15-16.

[50] *Canadians in the Making*, 442.

[51] Lower, 'Time, Myth and Fact. The Historian's Commodities', *QQ* LXIV (Summer 1957), 248-9.

9. DONALD CREIGHTON AND THE ARTISTRY OF HISTORY

[1] John Webster Grant, *George Pidgeon* (Toronto, 1962), 122; W.B. Creighton's attitude to the war is described in M. Bliss, 'The Methodist Church and World War I', *CHR* XLIX (September 1968), 213-33, and his affiliations with the social gospel in Richard Allen, *The Social Passion: Religion and Social Reform in Canada, 1914-28* (Toronto, 1971).

2 'Out of turmoil comes a new awareness of ourselves: Donald Creighton interviewed by Allan Anderson', University of Toronto *Graduate*, June 1968, 43.

3 Editorial, *Acta Victoriana*, 49 (November 1924), 20; *Torontonensis, The Year Book of the University of Toronto, 1925*, 75.

4 D.G.C., 'The Myth of the Universal Standard', *Acta Victoriana*, 50 (March 1926), 9-13.

5 F.H. Underhill Papers, Kenneth Bell to Underhill, May 7, 1927.

6 Creighton, 'The Struggle for Financial Control in Lower Canada, 1818-1831', *CHR* XII (June 1931), 120-44, and 'The Commercial Class in Canadian Politics, 1792-1840', *Papers and Proceedings of the Canadian Political Science Association*, V (1933), 43-58.

7 J.B. Brebner, review of Creighton, *British North America at Confederation, CJEPS*, VII (February 1941), 69.

8 QUL, Trotter Papers, *A Survey of Canadian American Relations. Carnegie Endowment for International Peace, Division of Economics and History, June, 1935*, 11-12.

9 *The New Outlook*, April 8, 1931, quoted in Ramsay Cook, *The Maple Leaf Forever: Essays on Nationalism and Politics in Canada* (Toronto, 1971), 232.

10 Heaton, review of *The Commercial Empire of the St Lawrence, 1760-1850* in *CJEPS* IV (November 1938), 565-70.

11 Creighton, *The Empire of the St Lawrence, 1760-1850* (Toronto, 1956, 2nd edition), 6-7.

12 *Ibid.*, 79.

13 *Ibid.*, 382.

14 *Ibid.*, 71.

15 Arthur Lower, review of *The Commercial Empire, CHR* XIX (June 1938), 207-10, and Alexander Brady, review in *UTQ* VII (April 1938), 380.

16 Creighton, 'Conservatism and National Unity', in R. Flenley, ed., *Essays in Canadian History* (Toronto, 1939), 161, 165.

17 Creighton, *British North America at Confederation. A Study Prepared for the Royal Commission on Dominion Provincial Relations* (Appendix 2) (Ottawa, 1939).

18 Creighton, *Empire of the St Lawrence*, 79.

19 Stanley Ryerson, ' "God Be Thanked for Those Rebels" ', *New Frontier* I (May 1936), 6-8. Creighton found Ryerson's case unconvincing; see his review of Ryerson, *1837—The Birth of Canadian Democracy* (1937), *CHR* XIX (March 1938), 73-4.

20 Creighton, 'The Crisis of 1837', *Canadian Banker* XLIV (April 1937), 383-91.

21 Creighton, *Dominion of the North* (New York, 1944), 368.

22 Creighton, 'Sir John A. Macdonald and Canadian Historians', *CHR* XXXIX (March 1948), 4.

23 John Garraty, *The Nature of Biography* (New York, 1964), 136; Lionel Gelber, 'History and the New Biography', *QQ* XXXVII (Winter 1930), 127-44.

24 E.R. Adair, 'The Military Reputation of Major-General James Wolfe', *CHAR*, 1936, 7-31.

25 J.A. Roy, *Joseph Howe: A Study in Achievement and Frustration* (Toronto, 1935).

26 A.L. Burt, 'Guy Carleton, Lord Dorchester. An Estimate', *CHAR*, 1935, 76.

27 T.W.L. MacDermot, 'John A. Macdonald—His Biographies and Biographers', *CHAR*, 1931, 77-84.

28 J.B. Brebner, 'Patronage and Parliamentary Government', *CHAR*, 1938, 22-30.

29 Creighton, *Founders' Day Address, University of New Brunswick*, Feb. 19, 1945 (n.p., n.d.), 16.

30 Garraty, *Nature of Biography*, 148-9.

31 William Kilbourn, *The Firebrand: William Lyon Mackenzie and the Rebellion in Upper Canada* (Toronto, 1956); K. McNaught, *A Prophet in Politics: A Biography of J.S. Woodsworth* (Toronto, 1959); John M. Gray, *Lord Selkirk of Red River* (Toronto, 1963); W.J. Eccles, *Frontenac, the Courtier Governor* (Toronto, 1959); J.M.S. Careless, *Brown of the Globe: vol. one: The Voice of Upper Canada 1818-1859* and *vol. two: Statesman of Confederation, 1860-1880* (Toronto, 1959, 1963); Bruce Hutchison, *The Incredible Canadian* (Toronto, 1952); H.S. Ferns and B. Ostry, *The Age of Mackenzie King: The Rise*

of the Leader (London, 1955); R. MacGregor Dawson, *William Lyon Mackenzie King, A Political Biography, 1874-1923* (Toronto, 1958); Roger Graham, *Arthur Meighen, vol. I. The Door of Opportunity; vol. II And Fortune Fled; vol. III No Surrender* (1960, 1963, 1965); George Stanley, *Louis Riel* (Toronto, 1963).

32 Robert Weaver, 'The Economics of Our Literature', *QQ* LX (Winter 1953-4), 483.

33 Paul Murray Kendall, *The Art of Biography* (London, 1965), 15.

34 John Gray, 'Biography as History', *CHAR*, 1965, 145.

35 J.H. Plumb, 'History and Biography', *Men and Places* (London, 1963), 220.

36 H.R. Trevor-Roper, *The Romantic Movement and the Study of History. The John Coffin Memorial Lecture delivered before the University of London on 17 February 1969* (London, 1969), and H.G. Schenk, *The Mind of the European Romantics* (New York, 1966), Chapter 5. For accounts of the procedures of the romantic historians, see David Levin, *History as Romantic Art* (New York, 1963) and George H. Callcot, *History in the United States, 1800-1860. Its Practice and Purpose* (Baltimore and London, 1970).

37 Creighton, 'Sir John Macdonald and Kingston', *CHAR*, 1950, 77.

38 Creighton, *John A. Macdonald: The Young Politician* (Toronto, 1951), 158-9.

39 Creighton, *John A. Macdonald: The Old Chieftain* (Toronto, 1955), 191.

40 *The Young Politician*, 398.

41 *The Old Chieftain*, 416.

42 Underhill, 'The Revival of Conservatism in North America', *TRSC*, Series III, LII, 1958, 17, and *CF* XXXIX (August 1959), 102. A rather different picture of Macdonald and his early business interests is suggested in J.K. Johnson, 'John A. Macdonald, The Young Non-Politician', CHA *Historical Papers*, 1971, 138-53.

43 Underhill Papers, Neatby to Underhill, August 25, 1957.

44 *Ibid.*, Creighton to Underhill, September 29, 1940.

45 Creighton, 'Canada in the English-Speaking World', *CHR* XXVI (June 1945), 119-27.

46 Creighton, 'Canada in the World', *Canada's Tomorrow: Papers and Discussions, Canada's Tomorrow-Conference, Quebec City, November, 1953*, ed., G.P. Gilmour (Toronto, 1954), 227-54.

47 Creighton, 'Sir John A. Macdonald', *Our Living Tradition, Seven Canadians*, ed., C.T. Bissell (Toronto, 1957), 61.

48 *Ibid.*, 52.

49 *Ibid.*, 61.

50 *Ibid.*, 50.

51 Creighton, 'Towards the Discovery of Canada', *UTQ* XXV (April 1956), 276.

52 Creighton, 'Presidential Address', *CHAR*, 1957, 1-12. See also his 'A Long View of Canadian History', *Script* (CBC Publication, Toronto, 1959).

53 Creighton, 'Sir John Macdonald and Kingston', 80.

54 E. Forsey Papers, Meighen to Forsey, October 28, 1941.

55 E. Forsey, 'Mr. King and Parliamentary Government', *CJEPS* XVII (November 1951), 464.

56 UTL, Innis Family Papers, Creighton to Innis, May 3, 1952. Creighton recalled his association with Forsey in an introduction to Eugene Forsey, *Freedom and Order: Collected Essays* (Toronto, 1974), 1-19.

57 Michael Barkway, 'Canada Rediscovers Its History', *Foreign Affairs* XXXVI (April 1958), 416.

58 Gad Horowitz, *Canadian Labour in Politics* (Toronto, 1968) Chapter I.

59 George Grant, *Lament for a Nation* (Toronto, 1965), 24.

60 Creighton, *The Young Politician*, 180.

61 Creighton, 'Education for Government', *QQ* XLI (Winter 1955), 431.

62 Creighton, 'American Pressures and Canadian Individuality', *The Centennial Review* I (Fall 1957), 356.

63 Creighton, *Canada's First Century, 1867-1967* (Toronto, 1970), 132.

[64] Creighton, 'The Myth of Biculturalism or the Great French-Canadian Sales Campaign', *Saturday Night* 81 (September 1966), 35-9. See also below, pages 255-6.
[65] Review of Morton, *Progressive Party*, CHR XXXII (March 1951), 71 and 'Macdonald and Kingston', 78.
[66] Creighton, 'Watching the Sun Quietly Set on Canada', *Maclean's* 84 (November 1971), 89.
[67] Creighton, 'A dangerous corner into which Canada was driven', *The Globe and Mail*, November 17, 1970.

10. WILLIAM MORTON: THE DELICATE BALANCE OF REGION AND NATION

[1] Morton, 'The Dualism of Culture and the Federalism of Power', Canadian Union of Students, VII Seminar, *A New Concept of Conderation?* (n.p. 1964), 123.
[2] Morton, 'Seeing an Unliterary Landscape', *Mosaic* III (Spring 1970), 2.
[3] G.M. Wrong, Chester Martin and W.N. Sage, *The Story of Canada* (Toronto, 1929), 225.
[4] University of Saskatchewan Archives, Murray Memorial Library, Saskatoon, A.S. Morton Papers, Morton to Leveson Gower, January 15, 1935, copy. There is a fine sketch of Morton's life and an estimation of his major work in Lewis G. Thomas 'Introduction', *A History of the Canadian West to 1870-71* (Second edition, Toronto, 1973).
[5] *Ibid.*, A.S. Morton to William Smith, October 15, 1931, copy.
[6] Morton, 'Clio in Canada: The Interpretation of Canadian History', *UTQ* XV (April 1946), 232.
[7] Morton, 'Marginal' *Manitoba Arts Review* V (Spring 1946), 26-31.
[8] Margaret Morton Fahrni and W.L. Morton, *Third Crossing: A History of the First Quarter Century of the Town and District of Gladstone in the Province of Manitoba* (Winnipeg, 1946), 55.
[9] Morton, 'Marginal', 27-8.
[10] Morton, 'The Significance of Site in the Settlement of the American and Canadian Wests', *Agricultural History* XXV (July 1951), 97-104.
[11] Morton, *The Progressive Party in Canada* (Toronto, 1950), 295.
[12] Morton, 'The Bias of Prairie Politics', *TRSC* Series III, XLIX, 1955, 66.
[13] Paul Sharp, *The Agrarian Revolt in Western Canada: A Survey Showing American Parallels* (New York, Octagon Reprint, 1971), vii.
[14] 'Significance of Site', 102.
[15] Morton, 'The Battle at the Grand Coteau, July 13-14, 1851', Historical and Scientific Society of Manitoba, *Transactions*, Third Series, #16, 1961, 49.
[16] Morton, 'Raw Country', *Red River Valley Historian*, Summer 1974, 3-8.
[17] G.F.G. Stanley, *The Birth of Western Canada* (Toronto, 1960), 61, 67, 49.
[18] Morton, 'Introduction', *Alexander Begg's Red River Journal and Other Papers Relative to the Red River Resistance of 1869-70* (Toronto, 1956), 3.
[19] Morton, 'The Red River Parish: Its Place in the Development of Manitoba', *Manitoba Essays*, ed., R.C. Lodge (Toronto, 1937), 105.
[20] Morton, 'Introduction', *Alexander Begg's Red River Journal*, 148.
[21] Morton, *Manitoba, A History* (Toronto, 1957), viii-ix.
[22] *Ibid.*, 410.
[23] *Ibid.*, 471, 472.
[24] Morton, 'The North in Canadian History', *Canada's Changing North*, ed., W.C. Wonders (Toronto, 1971), 86; *The Canadian Identity* (Toronto and Madison, 1961), 89-93; 'The "North" in Canadian Historiography', *TRSC* Series IV, VIII, 1970, 31-40.
[25] Morton, *Manitoba, A History* (Toronto, 1967, 2nd edition), 501, 495.
[26] Review of N.A. Benson, *None of it Came Easy: The Story of James Garfield Gardiner*, CHR XXXVII (December 1956), 367.

27 Review of H.B. Neatby, *William Lyon Mackenzie King. II. The Lonely Heights, 1924-1932*, *CHR* xLV (December 1964), 317-19.
28 Review of *Canadians in the Making*, *Winnipeg Free Press*, December 13, 1958.
29 Comment on R.G. Trotter, 'Aims in the Study and Teaching of History in Canadian Universities Today', *CHAR* 1943, 61.
30 Morton, 'Canadian Conservatism Now', *Conservative Concepts* I (Spring 1959), 7-18.
31 Morton, 'Winnipeg and Manitoba, 1874-1922: A Study in Representative Democracy', *Manitoba Arts Review* I (Winter 1939), 38-9.
32 Morton, 'The Extension of the Franchise in Canada: A Study in Democratic Nationalism', *CHAR*, 1943, 80.
33 Morton, 'The Meaning of Monarchy in Confederation', *TRSC*, Series IV I, 1963, 271-82.
34 *The Canadian Identity*, 85.
35 Toronto *Globe and Mail*, Globe Magazine, November 26, 1966.
36 Morton, 'The Dualism of Culture . . . ', 122.
37 Solange Chaput Rolland, *My Country, Canada or Quebec?* (Toronto, 1966), 87.
38 Morton, 'Dualism of Culture . . . ', 131-2.
39 Morton, 'Quebec-Federation or Association?', *The Centennial Review* x (Fall 1966), 471.
40 Morton, *The Kingdom of Canada* (Toronto, 1963), 319.
41 Morton, *The Critical Years: The Union of British North America, 1857-1873* (Toronto, 1964), 277.
42 Morton, 'Confederation: 1870-1896', *Journal of Canadian Studies* I (March 1966), 11-24, and 'The Conservative Principle in Confederation', *QQ* LXXI (Winter 1965), 528-46.
43 Morton, 'Manitoba's Historic Role', Historical and Scientific Society of Manitoba, *Transactions*, Series III, # 19, 1964, 50-6; *Winnipeg Free Press*, May 18, 1965.
44 Morton, 'The West and the Nation, 1870-1970', *Prairie Perspectives*, 2. eds., A.W. Rasporich and H.C. Klassen (Toronto and Montreal, 1973), 8-24. The issues of this controversy of course are more complicated than this summary statement implies and may be followed in D.G. Creighton, 'John A. Macdonald, Confederation, and the Canadian West' reprinted in D. Swainson, ed., *Essays on the Prairie Provinces* (Toronto, 1970), 60-70; R. Heintzman, 'The Spirit of Confederation: Professor Creighton, Biculturalism, and the Uses of History', *CHR* LII (September 1971), 245-75; and D.J. Hall, ' "The Spirit of Confederation": Ralph Heintzman, Professor Creighton, and the bicultural theory', *Journal of Canadian Studies* IX (November 1974), 24-43.
45 *Manitoba*, 2nd edition, 501.
46 Northrop Frye, *The Bush Garden: Essays on the Canadian Imagination* (Toronto, 1971), iii.
47 Morton, 'Some Thoughts on Understanding Canadian History', *Acadiensis* II (Spring 1973), 105.
48 J.E. Rea, 'Images of the West', *Western Perspectives* I, ed., David J. Bercuson (Toronto, 1974), 5-6.
49 H.C. Pentland, 'Foreword', Victor Peters, *All Things Common: The Hutterian Way of Life* (Minneapolis, 1963), viii.
50 Morton, 'Seeing an Unliterary Landscape . . . . ', 7.
51 Wallace Stegner, *Wolf Willow* (New York, Viking Paperback edition, 1971), 22-3.

11. TRADITION AND THE 'NEW' HISTORY

1 Bernard Bailyn, 'The Challenge of Modern Historiography', *American Historical Review* LXXXVII (February 1982), 2; Graeme Davidson, 'Slicing Australian History: Reflections on the Bicentennial History Project', *The New Zealand Journal of History* XVI (April 1982), 4; Michael Kammen, ed., *The Past before Us: Contemporary Historical Writing in the United*

States (Ithaca, 1980).

2 P.B. Waite, *The Life and Times of Confederation: Politics, Newspapers and the Union of British North America, 1864-1867* (Toronto, 1962); H. Blair Neatby, *Laurier and a Liberal Quebec: A Study in Political Management* (Toronto, 1973; completed as a thesis in 1956), and his *William Lyon Mackenzie King, Volume II, 1924-1932: The Lonely Heights* (Toronto, 1963); and Ramsay Cook, *The Politics of John W. Dafoe and the Free Press* (Toronto, 1963).

3 Ramsay Cook, *Canada and the French-Canadian Question* (Toronto, 1966).

4 Margaret E. Prang, 'Nationalism in Canada's First Century', *CHAP*, 1968, 114-25; John Porter, *The Vertical Mosaic: An Analysis of Social Class and Power in Canada* (Toronto, 1965), Chapter 16.

5 William J. Eccles, *The Canadian Frontier, 1534-1760* (New York, 1969); *Canadian Society during the French Regime: E.R. Adair Memorial Lectures* (Montreal, 1968); 'Forty Years Back', *The William and Mary Quarterly*, Third Series, XLI (July 1984), 410-21.

6 Morris Zaslow, *The Opening of the Canadian North, 1870-1914* (Toronto, 1971).

7 S.F. Wise, 'Sermon Literature and Canadian Intellectual History', *The Bulletin*, #18 (1965), 3-18; Carl Berger, *The Sense of Power: Studies in the Ideas of Canadian Imperialism, 1867-1914* (Toronto, 1970).

8 Ramsay Cook, 'Canadian Historical Writing', in R.H. Hubbard, ed., *Scholarship in Canada, 1967: Achievement and Outlook* (Toronto, 1968), 71-81; J.M.S. Careless, '"Limited Identities" in Canada', *CHR* L (March 1969), 1-10; S.R. Mealing, 'The Concept of Class and the Interpretation of Canadian History', *CHR* XLVI (September 1965), 201-18.

9 H. Blair Neatby, 'The Gospel of Research: The Transformation of English-Canadian Universities', *TRSC*, Centenary Volume (1982), 275-84.

10 On this phenomenon, see a memoir by Myrna Kostash, *Long Way from Home* (Toronto, 1980), and a sociological analysis by Cyril Levitt, *Children of Privilege: Student Revolt in the Sixties* (Toronto, 1984).

11 Northrop Frye, *Spiritus Mundi: Essays on Literature, Myth, and Society* (Toronto, 1976), 35.

12 Janice Acton et al., eds., *Women at Work: Ontario, 1850-1930* (Toronto, 1974), iii.

13 Howard Adams, *Prison of Grass: Canada from the Native Point of View* (Toronto, 1975), 43.

14 I owe this figure to Professor Ian Robertson. According to one estimate almost a thousand local histories on prairie communities have appeared since the mid-sixties. Paul Voisey, 'Rural Local History and the Prairie West', *Prairie Forum* X (Fall 1985), 327.

15 See, for example, Broadfoot's *Ten Lost Years, 1929-1939: Memoirs of Canadians Who Survived the Depression* (Toronto, 1973).

16 Ruth McKendry, *Quilts and Other Bedcoverings in the Canadian Tradition* (Toronto, 1979); Eric Arthur and Thomas Ritchie, *Iron: Cast and Wrought Iron in Canada from the Seventeenth Century to the Present* (Toronto, 1982); Elizabeth Collard, *The Potters' View of Canada: Canadian Scenes on Nineteenth-Century Earthenware* (Kingston and Montreal, 1985).

17 Pierre Berton, *The National Dream* (Toronto, 1970); *The Last Spike* (Toronto, 1971); *The Invasion of Canada: 1812-1813* (Toronto, 1980); *Flames across the Border, 1813-1814* (Toronto, 1981).

18 Viv Nelles, 'Rewriting History', *Saturday Night* (February 1981), 16.

19 R. Craig Brown, 'Biography in Canadian History', *CHAP*, 1980, 2.

20 'Jailbirds in Mid-Victorian Halifax', in P.B. Waite, Sandra Oxner, and Thomas Barnes, eds., *Law in Colonial Society: The Nova Scotia Experience* (Halifax, 1984), 81-102; 'Joe Beef of Montreal: Working Class Culture and the Tavern, 1869-1889', *L* VIII/IX (Autumn-Spring 1981/2), 9-40.

21 H.B. Neatby, 'Mackenzie King and Psychobiography', *Social Sciences in Canada* III (1975), 15-16.

22 Donald Swainson, 'Neurosis and Causality in Canadian History', *QQ* LXXXIX (Autumn 1982), 611-16. For a more positive response to the use of psychological insight in biography, see P.A. Buckner, 'Canadian Biography and the Search for Joseph Howe', *Acadiensis* XIV (Autumn 1984), 113-15.

23 David McNally, 'Staple Theory as Commodity Fetishism: Marx, Innis and Canadian Political Economy', *Studies in Political Economy: A Socialist Review* VI (Autumn 1981), 35-63.

24 Robin Neill, *A New Theory of Value: The Canadian Economics of H.A. Innis* (Toronto, 1977); Innis Issue, *JCS* XII (Winter 1977); *The Idea File of Harold Adams Innis* (Toronto, 1980), introduced and edited by William Christian; Mel Watkins, 'The Innis Tradition in Canadian Political Economy', *Canadian Journal of Political and Social Theory* VI (Winter/Spring 1982), 12-34; Daniel Drache, 'Rediscovering Canadian Political Economy', *JCS* XI (August 1975), 3-18; William Christian, 'Harold Innis as Political Theorist', *Canadian Journal of Political Science* X (March 1977), 21-42; Graeme Patterson, 'Harold Innis and the Writing of History', *Canadian Literature* LXXXIII (Winter 1979), 118-30; W.J. Eccles, 'A Belated Review of Harold Adams Innis, *The Fur Trade in Canada*', *CHR* LX (December 1979), 419-41; Hugh M. Grant, 'One Step Forward, Two Steps Back: Innis, Eccles, and the Fur Trade', *CHR* LXII (September 1981), 304-22; W.J. Eccles, 'A Response to Hugh M. Grant on Innis', *ibid.*, 323-9. Marshall McLuhan paid his respects to Innis by saying that Innis taught him most of what he knew, and adding: 'Harold Innis is the real freak. How did that hick Baptist ever come up with this amazing method of studying the effects of technology?' *Maclean's*, March 7, 1977.

25 Doug McCalla, 'Tom Naylor's A History of Canadian Business, 1867-1914: A Comment', and Naylor, 'Trends in the Business History of Canada 1867-1914', *CHAP*, 1976, 249-54, 255-67; G. Tulchinsky, 'Recent Controversies in Canadian Business History', *Acadiensis* VIII (Autumn 1978), 133-9.

26 Albert Tucker, *Steam into Wilderness: Ontario Northland Railway, 1902-1962* (Toronto, 1978), Tom Traves, *The State and Enterprise: Canadian Manufacturers and the Federal Government, 1917-1931* (Toronto, 1979).

27 Dale Miquelon, *Dugard of Rouen: French Trade to Canada and the West Indies, 1729-1770* (Montreal, 1975); Bruce G. Wilson, *The Enterprises of Robert Hamilton: A Study of Wealth and Influence in Early Upper Canada, 1776-1812* (Ottawa, 1983); Douglas McCalla, *The Upper Canada Trade, 1834-1872: A Study of the Buchanans' Business* (Toronto, 1979).

28 Desmond Morton, *Ministers and Generals: Politics and the Canadian Militia, 1868-1904* (Toronto, 1970); *The Last War Drum: The North West Rebellion of 1885* (Toronto, 1972); *The Canadian General: Sir William Otter* (Toronto, 1974), *Canada and War: A Military and Political History* (Toronto, 1981).

29 Escott Reid, *Time of Fear and Hope: The Making of the North Atlantic Treaty, 1947-1949* (Toronto, 1979); A.F. Wynne Plumptre, *Three Decades of Decision: Canada and the World Monetary System, 1944-75* (1977).

30 The titles are listed in the most recent volume with the subtitle *Indo-China: Roots of Complicity* (Toronto, 1983).

31 George W.L. Nicholson, *Seventy Years of Service: A History of the Royal Canadian Medical Corps* (Ottawa, 1977); F.J. Hatch, *The Aerodrome of Democracy: Canada and the British Commonwealth Air Training Plan, 1939-1945* (Ottawa, 1983); Marc Milner, *North Atlantic Run: The Royal Canadian Navy and the Battle for the Convoys* (Toronto, 1985); W.A.B. Douglas, 'Filling Gaps in the Military Past: Recent Developments in Canadian Official History', *JCS* XIX (Fall 1984), 112-24; A.M.J. Hyatt, 'Military Studies in Canada: An Overview', *Review Internationale d'Histoire Militaire*, No. 51 (1982), 328-49; C.P. Stacey, *A Date with History: Memoirs of a Canadian Historian* (Ottawa, 1982).

32 Barry M. Gough, *The Royal Navy and the Northwest Coast of North America, 1810-1914:*

A Study of British Maritime Ascendancy (Vancouver, 1971); *Distant Dominion: Britain and the Northwest Coast of North America, 1579-1809* (Vancouver, 1980); *Gunboat Frontier: British Maritime Authority and Northwest Coast Indians, 1846-1890* (Vancouver, 1984).

33 Roy MacLaren, *The Canadians in Russia, 1918-1919* (Toronto, 1976); *Canadians on the Nile, 1882-1898: Being the Adventures of the Voyageurs on the Khartoum Relief Expedition and Other Exploits* (Toronto, 1978); and *Canadians behind Enemy Lines, 1939-1945* (Toronto, 1981).

34 Margaret Ormsby, *British Columbia: A History* (Toronto, 1958); W. Stewart MacNutt, *New Brunswick: A History, 1784-1867* (Toronto, 1963). On Ormsby, see John Norris' essay in *Personality and History in British Columbia: Esssays in Honour of Margaret Ormsby*, an issue of *BC Studies*, XXXII (Winter 1976-7), 11-27, and Allan Smith, 'The Writing of British Columbia History', *BC Studies* XLV (Spring 1980), 73-102. The efforts of one provincial historical society are chronicled in Gerald Killan, *Preserving Ontario's Heritage: A History of the Ontario Historical Society* (Ottawa, 1976). The titles published in the Centenary Series are listed in the front of J.L. Granatstein, *Canada, 1957-1967: The Years of Uncertainty and Innovation* (Toronto, 1986).

35 David J. Bercuson, ed., *Canada and the Burden of Unity* (Toronto, 1977).

36 Thus *British Columbia: Historical Readings* (Toronto, 1981), edited by W. Peter Ward and Robert A.J. McDonald, brought together some original recent writing on Indian-European relations, racial tensions, labour militancy and radicalism, and economic development. Few of the authors of these papers, however, had begun with the explicit intention of illuminating the character of the province.

37 S.J.R. Noel, *Politics in Newfoundland* (Toronto, 1971); David Smith, *Prairie Liberalism: The Liberal Party in Saskatchewan, 1905-1971* (Toronto, 1975); Laurence Ricou, *Vertical Man/ Horizontal World: Man and Landscape in Canadian Prairie Fiction* (Vancouver, 1973); Patrick O'Flaherty, *The Rock Observed: Studies in the Literature of Newfoundland* (Toronto, 1979); Dick Harrison, *Unnamed Country: The Struggle for a Canadian Prairie Fiction* (Edmonton, 1977).

38 For an assessment of Clark's work and examples of the writing of his students, see James R. Gibson, ed., *European Settlement and Development in North America: Essays on Geographical Change in Honour and Memory of Andrew Hill Clark* (Toronto, 1978). A more general survey of the field is given in Michael P. Conzen, 'Historical Geography: North American Progress during the 1970s', *Progress in Human Geography* IV (December 1980), 549-59.

39 Peter Oliver, *G. Howard Ferguson: Ontario Tory* (Toronto, 1977); Charles W. Humphries, *'Honest Enough to Be Bold': The Life and Times of Sir James Pliny Whitney* (Toronto, 1985); Maurice Careless, ed., *The Pre-Confederation Premiers: Ontario Government Leaders, 1841-1867* (1980), a group of biographical portraits, including a superb appraisal of Sir John A. Macdonald by J. Keith Johnson.

40 Lewis H. Thomas, ed., *Essays in Western History in Honour of Lewis Gwynne Thomas* (Edmonton, 1976); Carl Berger and Ramsay Cook, eds., *The West and the Nation: Essays in Honour of W.L. Morton* (Toronto, 1976); John J. Foster, *The Developing West: Essays in Canadian History in Honor of Lewis H. Thomas* (Edmonton, 1983).

41 Doug Owram, 'The Myth of Louis Riel', *CHR* LXIII (September 1982), 315-36.

42 J. Murray Beck, *Joseph Howe, Volume I: Conservative Reformer, 1804-1848* (Montreal, 1982), and *Joseph Howe, Volume II: The Briton Becomes Canadian, 1848-1873* (Montreal, 1983); William M. Baker, *Timothy Warren Anglin, 1822-96: Irish Catholic Canadian* (Toronto, 1977).

43 William G. Godfrey, '"A New Golden Age": Recent Historical Writing on the Maritimes', *QQ* XCI (Summer 1984), 350-82. Some of the most important article literature has been made more accessible by Philip A. Buckner and David Frank, eds., *The Acadiensis Reader, Volume I: Atlantic Canada before Confederation*, and *Volume II: Atlantic Canada after Confederation* (Fredericton, 1985).

44 *Acadiensis* I (1971), 3-28.

45 'Misguided Symmetry: The Destruction of the Regional Transportation Policy for the Maritimes', in Bercuson, *Burden*, 60-81.

46 Alexander's essays have been collected by Eric W. Sager, Lewis R. Fischer, and Stuart O. Pierson, *Atlantic Canada and Confederation: Essays in Canadian Political Economy* (Toronto, 1983). The reports of the Atlantic Canada Shipping Project are discussed in Eric W. Sager and Lewis R. Fischer, 'Atlantic Canada and the Age of Sail Revisited', *CHR* LXIII (June 1982), 125-50.

47 R. Cole Harris, 'Regionalism and the Canadian Archipelago', in L.D. McCann, ed., *Heartland and Hinterland: A Geography of Canada* (Scarborough, Ont., 1982), 471-2; Ramsay Cook, 'Regionalism Unmasked', *Acadiensis* XIII (Autumn 1983), 137-42; Roger Gibbins, *Prairie Politics and Society: Regionalism in Decline* (Toronto, 1980).

48 Ronald Rudin, 'Recent Trends in Quebec Historiography', *QQ* XCII (Spring 1985), 80-93; Jean-Paul Coupal, 'Les dix dernières années de la *Revue d'histoire de l'Amérique française, 1972-1982'*, *Revue d'histoire de l'Amérique française* XXXVI (March 1983), 553-67.

49 John Moir, 'Coming of Age, But Slowly: Aspects of Canadian Religious Historiography since Confederation', *The Canadian Catholic Historical Association Study Sessions* L (1983), 89-98; Terrance Murphy, 'The Religious History of Atlantic Canada: The State of the Art', *Acadiensis* XV (Autumn 1985), 152-74; N.K. Clifford, 'Religion and the Development of Canadian Society: An Historiographical Analysis', *Church History* IV (December 1969), 1-18.

50 Jean Usher, *William Duncan of Metlakatla: A Victorian Missionary in British Columbia* (Ottawa, 1974).

51 Gordon Stewart and George Rawlyk, *A People Highly Favoured of God: The Nova Scotia Yankees and the American Revolution* (Toronto, 1972); J.M. Bumsted, *Henry Alline, 1748-1784* (Toronto, 1971).

52 Hilda Neatby, *Queen's University, Volume I, 1841-1917: And Not to Yield* (Montreal, 1978), edited by Frederick W. Gibson and Roger Graham; Frederick W. Gibson, *Queen's University, Volume II, 1917-1961: To Serve and Yet Be Free* (Montreal, 1983); Charles M. Johnston, *McMaster University, Volume I: The Toronto Years* (Toronto, 1981), *Volume II: The Early Years in Hamilton, 1930-1957* (1981); Stanley B. Frost, *McGill University: For the Advancement of Learning, Volume I, 1801-1895* (Montreal, 1980), and *Volume II, 1895-1971* (Montreal, 1984); John G. Reid, *Mount Allison University, Volume I, 1843-1914*, and *Volume II, 1914-1963* (Toronto, 1984). For a critical survey, see Paul Axelrod, 'Historical Writing and Canadian Universities: The State of the Art', *QQ* LXXXIX (Spring 1982).

53 Douglas Cole, 'The History of Art in Canada', *Acadiensis* X (Autumn 1980), 171-7.

54 Bruce Trigger, *Natives and Newcomers: Canada's 'Heroic Age' Reconsidered* (Montreal, 1985).

55 Shepard Krech, III, ed., *Indians, Animals and the Fur Trade: A Critique of Keepers of the Game* (Athens, Georgia, 1981).

56 Adrian Tanner, 'The End of Fur Trade History', *QQ* XC (Spring 1983), 176-91.

57 Gregory S. Kealey, 'Labour and Working-Class History in Canada: Perspectives in the 1980s', *L* VII (Spring 1981), 67-94; Kenneth McNaught, 'E.P. Thompson vs. Harold Logan: Writing about Labour and the Left in the 1970s', *CHR* LXII (June 1981), 141-68; Desmond Morton, 'E.P. Thompson dans des arpents de neige: Les historiens canadiens-anglais et la classe ouvrière', *Revue d'histoire de l'Amérique française*, XXXVII (September 1983), 165-84.

58 *CHAP*, 1974, 65-94.

59 Allan Smith, 'National Images and National Maintenance: The Ascendancy of the Ethnic Idea in North America', *Canadian Journal of Political Science* XIV (June 1981), 227-57; Howard Palmer, 'History and Present State of Ethnic Studies in Canada', in W. Isajiw, ed., *Identities: The Impact of Ethnicity on Canadian Society* (Toronto, 1977), 167-79.

[60] Gerald Tulchinsky, 'The Third Solitude: A.M. Klein's Montreal, 1910-1950', *JCS* XIX (Summer 1984), 96-112, and 'The Contours of Canadian Jewish History', *JCS* XVII (Winter 1982-3), 46-57.

[61] 'Montreal's King of Italian Labour: A Case Study of Padronism', *L* IV (1979), 57-84, and 'Toronto's Little Italy, 1885-1945', in Robert F. Harney and J. Vincenza Scarpaci, eds., *Little Italies in North America* (Toronto, 1981), 41-62.

[62] The other volumes that have appeared are discussed in conjunction with recent article literature in Roberto Perin, 'Clio as an Ethnic: The Third Force in Canadian Historiography', *CHR* LXIV (December 1983), 441-67.

[63] The figure is from Elaine L. Silverman, 'Writing Women's History, 1970-82: An Historiographical Analysis', *CHR* LXIII (December 1982), 513; see also Margaret Conrad, 'The Re-Birth of Canada's Past: A Decade of Women's History', *Acadiensis* XII (Spring 1983), 140-62.

[64] J. Donald Wilson, 'Some Observations on Recent Trends in Canadian Educational History', in Wilson, ed., *An Imperfect Past: Education and Society in Canadian History* (Vancouver, 1984).

[65] For an appraisal of the varied meanings of this concept, see Donald F. Davis, 'The "Metropolitan Thesis" and the Writing of Canadian Urban History', *Urban History Review* XIV (October 1985), 95-113.

[66] Artibise, *Winnipeg* (1977); Max Foran, *Calgary* (1978); Patricia Roy, *Vancouver* (1980); John Weaver, *Hamilton* (1982); Maurice Careless, *Toronto to 1918* (1984); and James Lemon, *Toronto since 1918* (1985), all published in Toronto.

[67] David H. Flaherty, ed., *Essays in the History of Canadian Law* (Toronto, 1982 and 1983); Louis A. Knafla, ed., *Law and Justice in a New Land: Essays in Western Canadian Legal History* (Toronto, 1986).

[68] *CHR* LVIII (September 1977), 317.

[69] David Gagan and H.E. Turner, 'Social History in Canada: A Report on the State of the Art', *Archivaria* XIV (Summer 1982), 27-52.

[70] Maurice Careless, 'Limited Identities—Ten Years Later', *Manitoba History* I (Spring 1976), 3-9; Desmond Morton, 'History and Nationality in Canada: Variations on an Old Theme', *CHAP*, 1979, 1-13.

INDEX

Abella, Irving 304, 311
Academic freedom: Sir Robert Falconer's
definition of 80; Underhill's understand-
ing of 80-1; crisis over at University of
Toronto in 1940-1 81-4
Acadiensis 263, 287, 288
Acheson, T.W. 287-8, 317
Acton, Lord 7, 256; on history as moral
teacher 15; Shortt on 28; on nationalism
40; and Cook 261
Adachi, Ken 310
Adair, E.R.: on cleavage between French-
and English-Canadian historical scholar-
ship 180, 184; on Dollard 183, 219; on
Wolfe 219
Adams, Herbert Baxter 7
Adams, Howard 265
Akenson, Donald H. 309-10
Alexander, David 288
Alexander, W.H. 79
Allen, Richard 292
American Revolution: colonial school of US
historians on 35; Martin on 35-6; Wrong
on significance of 46-7
Ames, Herbert 161
Andrews, Charles M. 35
Anti-Americanism 139-40, 155, 200
Archives: *see* Brymner, Doughty, Public
Archives of Canada
Armour, Leslie 294
Armstrong, Christopher 284, 317
Armstrong, Elizabeth 184
Artibise, Alan F.J. 316, 317
Ashley, William 24; on evolution and his-
torical change 6-7; on German historical
school 22-3
Atlantic Canada Shipping Project 288
Avery, Donald 311
Axelrod, Paul 295

Babcock, Robert 304
Bacchi, Carol 313
Bailey, Alfred G. 100
Bain, Dr James 35
Baker, Ray Palmer 143

Barman, Jean 315
Beard, Charles A. 55, 61, 62; on Skelton's
biography of Laurier 50
Becker, Carl 62
Beer, George Louis 35
Behiels, Michael D. 291
Bellan, Ruben C. 316
Bercuson, David J. 304
Berger, Carl 261, 296
Berton, Pierre 266, 267, 268
Biggar, H.P. 7, 26
Bilson, Geoffrey 318
Biography: in late-Victorian period 218; in
twenties and thirties 218-19; and eco-
nomic interpretation of history 219-20;
renewed popularity of in forties and fif-
ties 220, 221; Creighton and 218, 220;
character of 221-2; in sixties and seven-
ties 269-72, 275, 292-3, 296
Bissell, Claude 292
Black, Conrad 290-1
Blake, Edward: Underhill on 75; Creighton
on 224
Blake, William Hume: on Quebec 18
Bliss, Michael 268, 275
Board of Historical Publications 28
Bolton, Herbert: on hemispheric history
148
Bonne entente tradition 17-18, 184-5
Borden, Sir Robert L. 39, 41; on League of
Nations and Commonwealth 40; on lack
of vision of British 44-5
Bothwell, Robert 270, 276, 281
Bourassa, Henri 25
Bourinot, John George 3, 8, 13
Boutilier, James A. 281
Bovey, Wilfrid 109
Bowman, Isaiah: and concept of pioneer
fringe 162
Brebner, John Bartlet 30, 31, 142, 149, 153,
168, 209, 219-20; on Underhill academic
freedom case 84; on Innis 89, 107; on
Lower's study of timber trade 122; on
continental interpretation of Canadian
history 144; historical interests of 144-5;

North Atlantic Triangle (1945) 157-8; on fate of Carnegie series 158; on Canadian scholarship 178; on Innis's communications studies 193
Breen, David 285
Britnell, George: *The Wheat Economy* (1939) 103
Broadfoot, Barry 266
Brode, Patrick 269
Brown, George: Underhill on 65; Carless on 176, 221; Creighton on 224
Brown, George W. 141, 184, 276 (n31); on Canadian-American relations 157; on Atlantic world 172-3
Brown, Jennifer 301
Brown, Robert Craig 270-1, 276
Brunet, Michel 185
Brymner, Douglas: work as Archivist 5-6
Bumsted, Jack M. 309
Burgess, John 7
Burnet, Jean 166
Burt, A.L. 39, 151, 153, 175, 183; on Public Archives in twenties 30; *The Old Province of Quebec* (1933) 43; on sociology 168; on Guy Carleton 219
Bush, Douglas 209; on Canadian image of US 142
Business history 275-6

Callender, G.S. 91-2
Cambridge History of the British Empire 61
Cameron, Elspeth 293
Campbell, Douglas 309
Canada and Its Provinces (1913-17) 28
Canada Council 179, 200, 263
Canada First 2
Canadian-American relations: in twenties and thirties 138-40; Canadian uneasiness over in fifties 178-80; Innis on 191-2; Creighton's views of 226-7; scholarly study of, *see* American Revolution, Carnegie series
Canadian Authors' Association 54
Canadian Centenary series 251, 282
Canadian Forum 54; Underhill and 60, 61
Canadian Frontiers of Settlement series 162-3
Canadian Historical Association 54, 100, 181, 268
Canadian Historical Review 14, 141, 181, 266
Canadian History Society 27

Canadian Institute of International Affairs 76
Canadian Pacific Railway: Innis's history of 88-9
Canadian Political Science Association 24, 54, 100
Canadian Radio League 139
Canadian Social History Project 302
Careless, J.M.S. 172, 181, 316; on frontier thesis 175-6; on metropolitanism 176-8; on George Brown 176, 221; criticism of nation-building approach to Canadian history 261-2
Carnegie Corporation: financial support for Canadian educational institutions 151
Carnegie series on Canadian-American relations: origins of 140-9; J.T. Shotwell and 149-52, 155-6; main themes examined in 152-5; challenges to underlying point of view of 156-8; Brebner on significance of 158-9
Cartier, George E.: Underhill on 64-5
Cassidy, Harry 68, 79; Innis disagrees with appointment of 109-10
Champlain Society 14
Chapais, Sir Thomas 181
Childhood: study of history of 314-15
Chronicles of Canada series 14
Civil liberties 203, 204
Clark, Andrew Hill 283
Clark, J.M. 87
Clark, Samuel Delbert 100; background and education of 163-4; criticism of social-ecology approach to sociology 163; on Canadian social development as series of social breakdowns 164-5; *Church and Sect in Canada* (1948) 165; and Social Credit series 166-7; *Movements of Political Protest in Canada* (1959) 167-8; historians' responses to historical sociology of 168-9
Clark, W.C. 153
Clear Grits: Underhill on 65
Clifford, N. Keith 294
Coats, Robert 74
Cochrane, Charles 189
Cody, H.J. 81, 82, 83
Colby, Charles 8, 14, 28, 140; on provisional nature of written history 17
Cold war: heightens historians' awareness of liberal values and freedoms 173, 174;

Innis on Canada's position in 192-2; Underhill and 198; Lower and challenges of 203-4; Creighton on Canada's role in 226-7
Cole, Douglas 296-7
Collingwood, R.G.: see Creighton
Colville, Alex 170
Comfort, Charles 170
Commonwealth: see Imperialism, Responsible government
Communications: Innis on biases of various media 188-9; criticism of Innis's studies of 193-4; McLuhan and 194
Conacher, J.B. 172
Confederation: Underhill's view of 65; Innis's understanding of 88, 98; Creighton's interpretation of 214-15, 215-16, 234; Morton on 241-2, 253-5
Connolly, Cyril 201
Conquest of New France: Parkman on 4; Wrong on 20; Lower on meaning of 126-7; Maheux on mildness of 185; in French-Canadian historiography 185-6
Conservatism: intellectuals attracted to in fifties 229-33; Morton on principles of 252-3; see also Creighton, Party system
Constitutional history: see Responsible government
Contributions to Canadian Economics 89
Cook, Ramsay 260, 261, 276, 292
Cooper, J.I. 174
Co-operative Commonwealth Federation: see League for Social Reconstruction, Underhill
Copp, Terry 305
Corey, Albert 145, 153
Coupland, Reginald 35
Craig, Gerald M. 260
Craven, Paul 278
Creighton, Donald G. 31, 79, 100, 158, 160,188, 260, 282; family background and education 208-10; early interest in French Revolution 210; turns to Lord Dalhousie 210; on conflict between agriculture and commerce in Lower Canada 210-11; The Commercial Empire of the St. Lawrence (1937) 127, 211-14; and Innis 212, 215, 217; on Canada as successor state to St Lawrence commercial system 214-15; aloofness from politics in thirties and forties 215, 225; implications of early

work for constitution 215-16; on role of commercial class 216-17; treatment of reformers 217; Dominion of the North (1944) 217; interest in Macdonald 217; on R.G. Collingwood's The Idea of History 220; on nature of biography 220-1; on contemporaneity of history 220-1; on history as literary art 222-3, 234, 237; on Macdonald 221, 222-5, 232; on Canada in English-speaking world in 1945 225-6; on Canada in cold war 226-7; criticism of Liberal historical writing 228-9; affinities with Conservative tradition 232-3; on humanistic education 233; recognition of 234; The Road to Confederation (1964) 234; growing pessimism of 234; Canada's First Century (1970) 235-7; on regionalism 235-6; on French-Canadian nationalism 235; in dispraise of material progress 236; Morton on 241; on biculturalism in the West 255; last work 263-4
Creighton, William Black 209
Crerar, Gen. H.D.G. 170
Croly, Herbert 70
Cruikshank, Ernest 30, 169
Crunican, Paul 290
Cuff, Robert 280
Cultural nationalism: in twenties 54-5; in late forties and early fifties 178-9; Lower on 205-6; in sixties and seventies 265 ff.
Curtis, Lionel 12, 57, 58

Dafoe, John 28, 39; on Borden 45; Skelton on 49; on Canadian-American relations 147-8
Daigle, Jean 289
Darwinism and history 6-8
Dawson, Carl A.: interest in sociology 162; and Canadian Frontiers of Settlement series 162-3, 307
Dawson, R. MacGregor 221
Deacon, William Arthur 139
DeLottinville, Peter 271
Dempsey, Hugh 286
Denison, Merrill 122
Dent, John Charles 72
Dictionary of Canadian Biography 221, 269-70
Diefenbaker, John 227, 231-2, 234; Underhill on 199
Diubaldo, Richard 296

Dollard des Ormeaux 182, 183
Donald, William 87
Doughty, Sir Arthur: background of 26; as Dominion Archivist 27-8
Drummond, Ian 281
Duguid, Col. A. Fortescue 169
Duncan, C.S. 88
Dunham, Aileen 271 (n7)
Durham, Lord: significance attached to report of 33
Durocher, René 289

Eayrs, James 280
Eccles, William 299; on Frontenac 221; on New France 261
Economic history: see Innis, Shortt, Staples thesis; in sixties and seventies 273-6; of Maritimes 287-8, of Quebec 291
Economic interpretation of history; see Creighton, Innis, Underhill
Education; history of 314-16; university histories 294-5
Egerton, Hugh 35
Ely, Richard T. 22
England, Robert 129
English, John 276, 281
Epp, Frank H. 310
Esberey, Joy; on King 272
Ethnic studies 307-12
Evanchuk, Michael 307-8
Ewart, John S. 12, 34, 42

Fairley, Barker 60, 79
Falconer, Sir Robert: on academic freedom 80
Farthing, John 229
Fay, C.R. 90, 92
Fellowship for a Christian Social Order 69
Ferguson, The Rev. George D. 8
Ferguson, George V. 193
Fernow, B.E. 28
Ferns, H.S. 221
Fingard, Judith 271, 305
First World War: and constitutional status of Canada 33; and moral unity of Commonwealth 39; and internationalism 39 ff.; Skelton on Military Service Act in 49; Underhill on Canadian Corps in 58-9, and on automatic Canadian involvement in 77; revisionist interpretations of causes of 78; Innis in 86-7; Lower in 116; memory of in isolationism 134; official history of 169; see also Second World War, Military history
Fisher, Robin 300
Flanagan, Tom 285-6
Forbes, Ernest 288
Forrest, The Rev. John 8
Forsey, Eugene 68, 69, 209, 229; Royal Power of Dissolution of Parliament in the British Commonwealth (1943) 230; and Meighen 230; criticism of Mackenzie King and his successors 230-1, 304
Foster, Janet 296
Fowke, Vernon 166
Freeman, Donald B. 299
Freeman, Edward 7
Frégault, Guy 185
French Canada: Wrong on society of 17-21; Wallace on nationality of 42-3; Burt on treatment of in post-conquest period 43; Underhill on political interests of 64; Lower on social philosophy of 125-6; Creighton on nationalism of 235; recent literature on in English 289-92; see also New France, Conquest of New France, Quiet Revolution
French-Canadian historical writing 181-6, 289, 291, 301-2
French, Goldwin 283
Friesen, Gerald 286
Frontier: Turner on role of in American history 118; Canadian historians' reservations about 119; Innis on 96; Lower on 119-22; Clark's definition of as area of new economic enterprise 164; Clark on separatist spirit of 167-8; reaction against frontier thesis after Second World War 168, 174-5; Stanley on 175; Careless on 175-6; Creighton's dismissal of 229; Morton on 242-3; Stegner on intellectual schizophrenia produced by 258
Frye, Northrop: on New Left 264
Fur trade: Innis on 94-6; social history of 298-301

Gagan, David 303
Galbraith, John S. 270
Galt, Alexander: Innis on tariff of 99
Garneaux, François-Xavier 2
Geography: see Bowman, Creighton, Innis,

Newbigin, St Lawrence River, Historical geography
Gérin, Léon 161
German historical school of economists 22
Glasgow, Robert 14
Glazebrook, George 30
Gordon, Charles W. 28
Gordon, King 68, 79
Gosselin, Abbé August 17, 28
Gough, Barry M. 281
Graham, Gerald 172
Graham, Roger 221, 229; portrait of Meighen 231
Granatstein, J.L. 277, 278, 279, 280, 282
Grant, G.M. 73; on Shortt 21
Grant, G.P. 180, 229, 232; *Lament for a Nation* (1965) 234-5
Grant, John Webster 293
Grant, W.L. 25, 35
Gras, N.S.B. 123; on four stages of metropolitan status 177
Gray, James 269
Gray, John 221
Greer, Allan 302
Grey, Lord: on Doughty 27
Groulx, Abbé 43, 180, 181-2, 185, 206
Group of Seven 55
Grube, George 81
Gwyn, Sandra 267

Haliburton, Thomas Chandler 4
Halpenny, Francess 269
Hamelin, Jean 269
Hamilton, Louis 90
Hansen, Marcus 153
Harney, Robert F. 309
Harris, R. Cole 283
Harris, Robin 295
Harrison, Eric 172
Harvey, Daniel C. 30, 174
Havelock, Eric 68
Hémon, Louis 18
Herring, Pendleton 196
Hildebrand, Bruno 22
Historical Club 11
Historical geography 283
Historical Manuscripts Commission 28
Historical profession, after mid-sixties 262-3
Historical sociology: Clark and 161-9
Hitsman, J. Mackay 277

Holmes, John 279
Hopkins, Castell 218
Horn, Michiel 304
Horowitz, Gad 303-4
Houston, Cecil J. 310
Howe, Joseph: Creighton on 224
Hughes, Everett C. 163
Humphries, Charles W. 284
Hutchison, Bruce 221, 222
Hutton, Maurice 9, 31, 56

Immigration: Lower's criticism of 128-31; studies of 307-12
Imperialism: Wrong's commitment to 11-13; Shortt's rejection of preferential trade 25; and internationalism 38-40; Skelton on 49; Underhill on 77-9
Indian culture 100
Ingram, J.K. 22
Innis, Harold A. 30, 79, 82, 114, 151, 166, 169; background and character 85-6; war service and nationalism of 86-7; at Chicago 87-8; *History of the Canadian Pacific Railway* (1923) 88-9; travels in Canada and Europe 89-91; on economic history of new countries 91; debt to Mackintosh 91-2; and geography of Newbigin 92-3; *The Fur Trade in Canada* (1930) 94-7; significance of for historians 97-8; *The Cod Fisheries* (1940) 98-9, 102; on geographical unity of Canada 97-8; on effects of shift from fur staple to timber and wheat 99-100; determinism of 101-3; hostility to centralization and bureaucracy of 103-5; liberalism of 104; conception of social sciences of 105-7; style of writing of 107-8; personal influence of 108-9; resignations of 109-110; on role of scholarship 106-7, 110-11; on Canadian-American relations 142; turns to study of communications 187-8; continuity between work and staples and media communications 188; on biases of forms of communications 188-9; desire for balance and perspective of 189-90; attack on Canada's position in cold war 191-2; on preserving Canadian culture 192-3; historians' reactions to his communications studies 193-4; and McLuhan 194; reputation of 195; and Creighton 212, 215, 217, 228; Morton on 241; new rele-

vance of in late sixties and seventies
272-3; McLuhan on 349 (n24)
Innis, Mary Quayle 107
Institut d'Histoire de l'Amérique Française
185
Institute for Imperial Studies 35
Intellectual history 261, 294-7
International Joint Commission 140
Internationalism: and imperialism 38-40;
and the study of Canadian-American
relations 146-7
Irvine, William 63
Irving, John 166
Island Magazine, The 265-6
Isolationism: Underhill advocacy of 77-9;
Lower support for 131-4

Jackson, A.Y. 54
Jaenen, Cornelius J. 299
Johnston, Alexander 90
Johnston, A.B. 267
Johnston, Charles M. 295

Katz, Michael 302-3, 315
Kealey, Greg S. 305, 306, 318
Keenleyside, Hugh 84, 144
Kendle, John 270
Kennedy, William P.M. 31, 32, 210; criti-
cism of extreme doctrines of national
self-determination 40-1; The Constitution
of Canada (1922) 41-2
Kerr, Donald 172
Khaki College 58
Kilbourn, William 221, 270
Killan, Gerald 296
King, Carlyle 79
King, W.L.M.: and Skelton 49, 52; Under-
hill's estimation of 70, 196-7; condemna-
tion of legacy of in fifties 229-31; Morton
on 251-2; Stacey on 271-2; Esberey on
272; Neatby on 277-8; studies of as
industrial relations expert and reformer
278-9
Kingsford, William 2-3, 13-14
Kirby, William 3-4
Kirkconnell, Watson 129
Klassen, Henry 284
Knies, Karl 22
Knight, Frank 87
Kostash, Myrna 308

Labour history 303-7
Lamb, Kaye 200
Lanctôt, Gustave 184
Landon, Fred 64, 154
Langton, H.H. 14
Langton, John 6
'Laurentian' interpretation of Canadian
history: Morton on 241-2
Laurier, Sir Wilfrid: Skelton biography of
49-50; Underhill on 70, 197
Leacock, Stephen 31, 73, 140; Innis on 107
League for Social Reconstruction 73; orig-
ins and members 68-9; manifesto and
program of 69
League of Nations: Underhill on 78; and
analogy with Commonwealth 39-42
League of Nations Society 39
LePan, Douglas 279
LePlay, Frédéric 161
Leslie, Cliff 22
LeSueur, William 218
Leung, Felicity L. 267
Lévesque, Georges-Henri 179
Levitt, Joseph 290
Lewis, John 28
Liberalism: and early academic political
economy 25-6; of deocratic socialism
and League for Social Reconstruction
69-70; Underhill on Canadian variety of
70-1; and defence of in cold war period
197-9; of Innis 104; Careless on mid-
Victorian 176; Lower's definition of 203-
4; G.P. Grant rejection of 234-5;
Creighton on historical outlook of 228-9
Linteau, Paul-André 289, 291
Lippmann, Walter: Underhill and ideas of
60, 72
Lismer, Arthur 129
Literary and Historical Society of Quebec
4
Local history 265-6; see also Regional history
Longley, R.S. 218
Louisbourg, Fortress 267
Lower, Arthur R.M. 31, 59, 89, 90, 160, family background and education 113;
methodism of 114; love for nature of
114-15; Colony to Nation (1946) 112, 121,
135, 136, 197, 202; on nation as family
113-14; war service of 116; and Shortt
116; studies of timber trade 116-18, 278

(n25); contrasted with Innis 117; and
frontier thesis 117, 118-21; on New
France 120-1; on frontier and social
democracy 121; on exploitative values of
frontier 121-2; definition of metropolitanism 123; on puritanism and capitalist
spirit 123-4; on French-English relations
124-8; critique of immigration and desire
for ethnic homogeneity 128-31, 307; on
puritanism and race suicide 131; isolationist foreign policy of 131-4; and principle of national cohesion 135-6; later
publications 202-3; *This Most Famous
Stream* (1954) 202, 203-4; *Canadians in the
Making* (1958) 202, 205; on liberalism
203-4; on mass culture 204-6; on antithesis of two cultures 206; on historian's
vocation 206; Morton on 252
Lucas, Sir C.P. 35, 45
Lupul, Manoly 309

McArthur, Duncan 30
McCallum, John 274
McCormack, Ross 304
McCullagh, George 81
Macdonald, D. Bruce 83
Macdonald, Sir John A.: Underhill on party
of 64-5; Creighton on 217, 221, 222-5,
227, 232
Macdonnell, J.M. 83
McDougall, D.J. 173
McDowall, Duncan 275-6
MacDowell, Laurel S. 305
MacFarlane, R.O. 242
MacGibbon, Duncan 74
McInnis, Edgar 160
MacIver, Robert M. 154-5
MacKay, Donald 268
MacKay, R.A. 174
Mackenzie, Alexander 218
Mackenzie, Norman 179
McKillop, Brian 294
Macintosh, William A. 104, 163, 188; on sig-
nificance of staple commodities 91-2
MacLaren, Roy 282
Mclean, J.S. 83
Maclean, Ray A. 309
MacLennan, Hugh 128, 246
Macleod, Rod C. 285
McLuhan, Marshall 180, 194
MacMechan, Archibald 139, 140

McMullen, John Mercier: *History of Canada*
(1855) 1-2
McNaught, Kenneth 221
MacNutt, W. Stewart 282
Macphail, Sir Andrew 28, 31, 90; on
Quebec 18; on intellectuals 73
Macpherson, C.B. 166
Maheux, Abbé Arthur: and *bonne entente*
tradition 184-5
Mair, Charles 4
Makers of Canada series 28, 218
Mallory, J.R. 166
Manitoba: Morton on distinctive history of
245-50
Manitoba Historical and Scientific Society
248
Mann, William 166
Maritimes: recent histories of 283, 286-8
Martin, Calvin 300
Martin, Chester 28, 31, 32, 40, 79, 82, 140,
146, 147, 163, 173, 240; background and
career 34; view of history 34; debt to U.S.
colonial historians 34-5; *Empire and Com-
monwealth* (1929) 34, 35-7; on constitu-
tional evolution of western Canada 38;
on natural resources claims 38
Marx, Karl: Innis on 106
Marxism: and economic history 273; and
working class studies 305-7
Mass culture: concern with in fifties 180;
Underhill on 199-200; Lower on threat of
204-6; *see also* Massey Commission
Report
Massey, Vincent 9, 57, 170, 179
Massey Commission Report 161, 179-80;
Innis on 192; Underhill on 200
Masters, D.C. 123, 166, 243
Material culture 266-7
Mathiez, Albert 210
Mavor, James 25, 90
Merriam, Charles 48
Metropolitanism: Lower on 123; origins of
176-7; Gras on 177; Innis on 177; Care-
less's exposition of 177-8; Morton on
243, 316
Military history 169-72, 276-7, 281-2
Miller, James R. 290
Milner, W.S. 56-7
Miner, Horace 163
Minto, Lord 26
Moffett, Samuel 138

Moir, John 294
Monet, Jacques 289
Moore, Christopher 267, 271
Morality and history: Wrong on 15
Morley, Percival F. 18
Morrison, J.L. 17, 30; *British Supremacy and Canadian Self-Government* (1919) 44
Morton, Arthur S. 30, 163, 240-1
Morton, Desmond 277, 282
Morton, William L. 166, 229, 260, 282; background, education, and career 238-9, 251; and civil liberties 240; critique of Laurentian approach to Canadian history of 241-2; on frontier thesis 242-3; on metropolitan-hinterland relationship 243; *The Progressive Party in Canada* (1950) 243-5; on the bias of prairie politics 244-5; on separate histories of u.s. and Canadian wests 245; *Manitoba, A History* (1957) 245-50; desire of for authentic regional history 246; on Red River society and resistance of 1869-70 246-7; on ethnic pluralism of Manitoba 248; continuities between western and national histories of 250-1; on northern character of Canada 250; on Winnipeg establishment 251; on legacy of King 251-2; on Lower 252; on Underhill 252; definition of conservative principles 252-3; on majoritarian democracy 253; on monarchical institutions and pluralism 253-4; on Quiet Revolution in Quebec 254; on biculturalism in West 255-6; belief of in pluralism of Canadian experience 256-7; view of ethnic relations 257; preference for land and agricultural life 257-8
Multiculturalism, and ethnic studies 308
Munro, William B.: on Shortt's character 29; on Canadian-American history 143-4
Murchie, R.W. 163
Myers, Gustavus 63

National history: criticism of 261-2, 265
National self-determination: *see* Kennedy
Native history 265, 286, 293; studies of cultural contacts with Europeans 298-301
Naylor, Tom 273
Neatby, H. Blair 260; on King 271-2, 277-8
Neatby, Hilda 179, 183; criticism of mass education 180; on Creighton's Mac-
donald 225
Nelles, H. Viv 274, 317
New France: Parkman on 4; Newbigin on geographical factors in history of 92-3; Innis on fur trade in 94-5, 98; Lower on influence of frontier upon 120-1; Eccles on 261
New Left 264
Newbigin, Marion 212; *Canada: The Great River, the Lands and the Men* (1926) 92-3; Innis on 93
Newton, A.P. 35
Nicholson, Byron 17
Nicholson, G.W.L. 172
Niebuhr, Reinhold 198
Noel, S.J.R. 283

Ogdensburg agreement: Underhill on significance of 82; Creighton on 226
Ogilvie, Will 170
Oliver, Peter 283
Ontario Historical Studies Series 283-4
Ormsby, Margaret 282
Osgood, Herbert L. 35
Ostry, B. 221
Ouellet, Fernand 301-2
Owram, Doug 284-5

Palmer, Bryan 306-7
Palmer, Howard 311
Park, Robert 123; and social ecology 162
Parkinson, J.F. 68
Parkman, Francis: character of books on New France 4; anti-clerical bias of 4; Wrong's debt to and disagreement with 20
Parks Canada 267
Parr, Joy 314
Parrington, Vernon 61
Partridge, E.A. 63
Party system: Underhill on development of 64-5, 196-7; *see also* Co-operative Commonwealth Federation, Progressive Party, Social Credit
Patton, M.J. 28
Pearson, Lester 30, 199, 200
Peden, Murray 269
Pentland, Clare 264
Penton, James 292
Pickersgill, J. 200
Pierson, Ruth R. 313

Pioneer fringe 162
Pitt, David G. 293
Piva, Michael 305
Plaunt, Alan 139
Plumptre, A.F. Wynne 279
Political economy tradition 261-2, 272-3
Political ideas: early study of 174
Popular history 267-8, 269
Prairie Forum 284
Prang, Margaret 261, 292
Pratt, Larry 274
Prentice, Alison 315
Preston, Richard 282
Progressive history: origins in U.S. and general features of 61-2
Progressive Party 62-3; Underhill on antecedents of 60, and weaknesses of 72; Morton on 243-5
Projet Riel Project 285
Pryke, Kenneth G. 287
Psychobiography 272
Public Archives of Canada: establishment of 5; Brymner at 5-6; Doughty at 26-8
Puritanism: Lower on 123-4, 131, 203-4

Quiet Revolution: Morton on 254

Ralegh Club 58
Rawlyk, George 293-4
Ray, Arthur J. 299
Read, Colin 318
Rebellions of 1837: Martin's neglect of 36; Lower on significance of 121; and conflict of underlying philosophies in 126-7; Clark on nature of Upper Canadian frontier 167; Creighton on tensions in Lower Canada 210-11; Ouellet on Lower Canada 301-2
Red River Resistance of 1869-70: Stanley on 247; Morton on 247
Regehr, Ted D. 275
Regional history 282-92
Reid, Escott 279
Relativism of historical knowledge: Underhill on 62
Religion: history of 292-4
Responsible government 2; concentration upon in twenties 32-4; Martin on 34-8; assumptions about sovereignty and nationality in historiography of 39-44; Skelton on commercial background of

50-1; Clark on 167; Stacey on military corollaries of 170; Brebner on 219-20; *see also* Borden, Wrong
Review of Historical Publications Relating to Canada 13-14
Richards, John 274
Ridout, Godfrey 266
Riel, Louis: Stanley on 221; Creighton on 224; Flanagan on 285-6
Ritchie, Charles 280
Robert, Jean-Claude 289
Roberts, Sir Charles G.D. 4
Robertson, Heather 266
Robinson, James Harvey 61
Robinson, Judith 229
Rocher, Wilhelm 22
Romantic history 4, 223
Rothney, Gordon 184
Round Table 12
Rowell, Newton W. 39
Rowell-Sirois Commission 101, 188, 195; Innis's criticism of report of 104; Morton on 245
Roy, J.A.: on Howe 219
Roy, J. Edmond 17, 28
Roy, Reginald H. 282
Royal Commission on National Development in the Arts, Literature and Sciences: *see* Massey Commission
Royal Society of Canada 2, 109, 181
Rudin, Ronald 291
Rutherford, Paul 318
Ryan, William F. 291
Ryerson, Stanley 183, 217, 264

St Lawrence River: Newbigin on 92-3; as inspiration to transcontinental dominion in Creighton's work 211-14, 223-4; and defeat of 237
St Lawrence Waterway 93
Sapir, Edward 28
Saunders, Richard 184; on French-Canadian historiography 185
Savelle, Max 153
Schmoller, Gustav 22
Science: history of 295-6
Scientific history 6-8
Scott, F.R. 54, 68, 69, 78, 111; on Canadian-American relations in 1941 157
Second World War: Innis and threat to universities in 110; impact of on Canadian-

American relations 156-7; Stacey's official history of 170-2, 276; heightens awareness of Atlantic civilization and liberal values 172-5, 220; effects on Underhill 197-8

Séguin, Maurice 185

Senior, Hereward 310

Seton, Ernest Thompson 114

Sharp, Paul 225

Shippee, L.B. 153

Shortt, Adam 1, 91, 149; background and career 21-2; empirical outlook of 21; government service of 22; personality of 26; influence of historical economists on 22; conception of political economy of 23-6; scepticism regarding social reform 23-5, 29; on role of experts 24, 74; criticism of imperialism 25; co-operation with Doughty 28; biography of Sydenham by 28; archival work of 28-9; Munro on 29; Lower's reaction to 116

Shortt, Sam E.D. 294, 298

Shotwell, James T. 142, 151, 158; and origins of Carnegie series 145; internationalism of 149-50; on lessons for international peace of Canadian-American relations 155-6

Siegfried, André 90

Silver, Arthur I. 289-90

Sissons, C.B. 18, 174, 220

Skelton, O.D. 18, 25, 34, 140, 161, 218; background, education and career 47-8; critique of socialism 48-9; liberalism of 49; Life and Letters of Sir Wilfrid Laurier (1921) 49-50; anti-imperialism of 49; democratic instincts of 50; The Canadian Dominion (1919) 50-1; on commercial factors behind development of responsible government 50-1; prescription for Canadian foreign policy in 1922 51-2; and King 49, 52

Small, Albion 48

Smith, David 283

Smith, George 210

Smith, Goldwin 55, 138

Smyth, William 310

Social Credit: Underhill on 199

Social Credit series: Clark and 166-8; Creighton on 236

Social history: and biography 271; character of 297-8, 301, 318-19; social mobility studies 302-3; see also Ethnic studies, Fur trade, Native history, Urban history, Women's history, Working class history

Social History 298

Socialism: Shortt on 23-4; Skelton criticism of 48-9; and League for Social Reconstruction 68-70

Sociology: early academic teaching of 161; Dawson's contributions to 162; see also Clark

Soward, F.H. 39

Speisman, Stephen A. 310

Spengler, Oswald 237

Spring, David 172

Spry, Graham 68, 139

Stacey, Charles P. 169, 269; Canada and the British Army, 1846-1871 (1936) 170; on myth of undefended boundary 170; official history of Second World War of 170-2, 276; on King 271-2, 278

Stairs, Denis 280

Stamp, Robert 316

Stanley, George F.G. 238, 240, 242, 281-2, 285; and military history 169, 172; on frontier in prairie West 175; on Riel 221; on Red River resistance 247

Staples thesis 272-3; anticipations of by Mackintosh 91-2; exposition of by Innis 94-6; and concept of cyclonic growth 96-7; implications of for historians 97-100; Lower on 116-18

Stegner, Wallace 258

Stelter, Gilbert A. 317

Stewart, Gordon 293

Strachey, Lytton 219

Strong-Boag, Veronica 312

Struthers, James 279

Stubbs, Bishop William 7

Sunahara, Ann Gomer 34

Surveyer, Arthur 179

Sutherland, Neil 315

Sydenham, Lord: Shortt's biography of 28

Tansill, Charles C. 153

Tawney, R.H. 69

The Pas: Innis at 90

Thomas, Lewis G. 166, 284

Thomas, Lewis H. 284

Thompson, John H. 286

Timber trade: Lower on 116-18, 122-3

Tippett, Maria 270

Todd, Alpheus 3
Tory, Henry M. 58
Toynbee, Arnold: Underhill on 198
Traves, Tom 274
Trevelyan, G.M.: on poetic appeal of history 15
Trigger, Bruce 299
Trofimenkoff, Susan 289, 290
Troper, Harold 311
Trott, Elizabeth 294
Trotter, Reginald 145, 147, 156
Tucker, Albert 274
Tucker, G.N. 172
Tulchinsky, Gerald 273-4, 308
Turner, Frederick Jackson 55, 61; on frontier in American history 118

Undefended boundary, myth of 150, 171, 280 (n38)
Underhill, Frank H. 31, 173-4, 217, 220; family background and education 56-7; at Oxford 57-8; iconoclastic spirit of 55, 84; on need for educated élite 57, 71-5, 199, 200; on Canada and First World War 58-9; at Saskatchewan 58, 59-60; criticism of constitutional history 61-4; economic interpretation of party system 64-7; on relativism of historical knowledge 62; on interests and ideas in political tradition 67; on business 67; and League for Social Reconstruction 67-71; on failures of Canadian liberalism 70-1; on Blake 75; views of foreign relations in twenties 76-7; isolationism of in thirties 77-9, 133-4; and 'academic freedom' crisis at Toronto in 1940-1 80-4; on Lower 135; reaction of against economic history 195-6; on Canada's intellectual weaknesses 196; re-evaluation of party system and King 196-7; on French Canada 197; effects of Second World War on views of 197-8; support of for U.S. in cold war 198; criticism of CCF 198-9; on mass culture 199-200; ambiguous position of as historian 200-1; Lower on 201; on Creighton's Macdonald 224-5; Morton on 252
United States and Canada: see Canadian-American relations
Unity League of Ontario 18
Upton, L.F.S. 300

Urban history 316-17

Van Kirk, Sylvia 300-1
Veatch, Richard 280
Veblen, Thorstein: Skelton on 48; Innis and teachings of 88, 106
Viner, Jacob 145
von Ranke, Leopold 7

Wade, Mason 184
Wadland, John 296
Waite, P.B. 260, 270
Walker, Sir Edmund: on bonne entente 18
Wallace, Malcolm 82
Wallace, William S. 14, 17, 28, 32, 49, 80, 219; on Canada's supranationalism 42-3
Ward, Peter 311
Warkentin, John 283
Watson, John: on Shortt 21
Waugh, William 219
Webb, Walter Prescott 242
Webster, J.C., on Doughty 27
West, the: Martin on constitutional growth of 38; on resource claims of 38; Underhill on 59, 60, 62-3; Innis on sacrifices of 88-9; Lower and immigrants in 129; Canadian Frontiers of Settlement series volumes on 162-3; Clark's association with 163; and Social Credit series on 166; on separatist spirit of frontier in 167-8; Stanley on frontier in 175; recent regional history of 284-6; see also A.S. Morton, W.L. Morton, Progressive Party
Western Canadian Studies Conferences 263, 284
Western Producer Prairie Books 266
Wheat economy: see Britnell, Innis, MacGibbon, Mackintosh
Whitaker, Reginald 279
Wickberg, Edgar 309
Wilson, Sir Daniel 8
Wilson, George 218
Winks, Robin 308
Wise, S.F. 261, 281
Withrow, William 3
Wittke, Carl 141
Women's history 265, 300-1, 312-14
Wood, William 169
Woodcock, George 308
Woodsworth, J.S. 68, 129, 161
Working class history 303-7

Wright, Chester 88
Wrong, George M. 1, 13, 28, 30, 32, 39; background, training and character of 8-9; social convictions of 9-10; attitude of to public role of educated élite 10-11; and Toronto History Department 10; educational ideals of 9-10; imperialist outlook of 11-13; on nature of Canadian society 11-12; contributions to historical study 13-14; on nature of history 14-16, 28-9; *A Canadian Manor and Its Seigneurs* (1908) 15; on French Canada 17-21; atti-tude of to Canada's status in twenties 45-6; *Canada and the American Revolution* (1935) 46-7; on academic freedom 80; *Canada and the United States* (1920) 146
Wrong, Hume 18, 209
Wrong, Murray 57
Wynn, Graeme 283

Young, Brian 271, 291
Young, Walter D. 304

Zaslow, Morris 261, 295